Behavioural Economics and Policy for Pandemics

Behavioural economics and behavioural public policy have been fundamental parts of governmental responses to the COVID-19 pandemic. This was the case not only at the beginning of the pandemic as governments pondered how to get people to follow restrictions but also during delivery of the vaccination programme. *Behavioural Economics and Policy for Pandemics* brings together a world-class line-up of experts to examine the successes and failures of behavioural economics and policy in relation to the COVID-19 pandemic. It documents how people changed their behaviours and use of healthcare and discusses what we can learn in terms of addressing future pandemics. Featuring high-profile behavioural economists such as George Loewenstein, this book uniquely uncovers behavioural regularities that emerged in the different waves of COVID-19 and documents how pandemics change our lives.

JOAN COSTA-FONT is Professor of Health Economics in the Department of Health Policy at the London School of Economics and Political Science (LSE), where he leads the Ageing and Health Incentives Lab, Directs the MSc International Health Policy, and the International Inequality Institute where he co-directs the program on "perceptions of inequality". The bulk of his teaching is on behavioural health economics, health econometrics and political economy of health. He was a Harkness Fellow at Harvard University and a policy evaluation scholar at Sciences Po and has held visiting research positions at the University of Oxford, Boston College, and University College London.

MATTEO M. GALIZZI is Associate Professor of Behavioural Science in the Department of Psychological and Behavioural Science at the LSE. He is also Co-director of the LSE Behavioural Lab and Director of LSE Executive MSc in Behavioural Science. He is a behavioural and experimental economist working on randomised controlled trials and behavioural experiments in health and public policy.

Behavioural Economics and Policy for Pandemics

Insights from Responses to COVID-19

Edited by

JOAN COSTA-FONT
London School of Economics and Political Science

MATTEO M. GALIZZI
London School of Economics and Political Science

CAMBRIDGE
UNIVERSITY PRESS

Shaftesbury Road, Cambridge CB2 8EA, United Kingdom

One Liberty Plaza, 20th Floor, New York, NY 10006, USA

477 Williamstown Road, Port Melbourne, VIC 3207, Australia

314–321, 3rd Floor, Plot 3, Splendor Forum, Jasola District Centre, New Delhi – 110025, India

103 Penang Road, #05–06/07, Visioncrest Commercial, Singapore 238467

Cambridge University Press is part of Cambridge University Press & Assessment, a department of the University of Cambridge.

We share the University's mission to contribute to society through the pursuit of education, learning and research at the highest international levels of excellence.

www.cambridge.org
Information on this title: www.cambridge.org/9781009438414

DOI: 10.1017/9781009438438

First published 2024

A catalogue record for this publication is available from the British Library

Library of Congress Cataloging-in-Publication Data
Names: Costa-Font, Joan, editor. | Galizzi, Matteo M., editor.
Title: Behavioural economics and policy for pandemics : insights from responses to COVID-19 / edited by Joan Costa-Font, London School of Economics and Political Science, Matteo M. Galizzi, London School of Economics and Political Science.
Description: Cambridge, United Kingdom ; New York, NY : Cambridge University Press, 2024. | Includes bibliographical references and index.
Identifiers: LCCN 2023041848 (print) | LCCN 2023041849 (ebook) | ISBN 9781009438414 (hardback) | ISBN 9781009438438 (ebook)
Subjects: LCSH: Economics – Psychological aspects. | Finance – Psychological aspects. | COVID-19 Pandemic, 2020 – Influence.
Classification: LCC HB74.P8 B34 2024 (print) | LCC HB74.P8 (ebook) | DDC 330.01/9–dc23/eng/20230927
LC record available at https://lccn.loc.gov/2023041848
LC ebook record available at https://lccn.loc.gov/2023041849

ISBN 978-1-009-43841-4 Hardback
ISBN 978-1-009-43846-9 Paperback

To Elisabetta 'Etta' Ferrari, who, among many other things, taught me the most important lessons about science, behaviour, and caring for others. I deeply miss you and will always remember you, mum.

MMG

Contents

Contributors

Faical Achaiki is an applied economist specialising in behavioural economics, food marketing, and econometrics. His research aims to further the understanding of individuals' behaviour, its determining factors, and how policy can best make use of this understanding to promote more sustainable and healthier food production and consumption.

Jupiter Adams-Phipps has been a member of the 1Day Sooner research team since 2021, where he has done extensive work on a systematic review of past human challenge trials.

Natasha Aldulaimi is a medical student at the University of Southampton. She holds a master's degree from the London School of Economics and Political Science (LSE) and the London School of Hygiene and Tropical Medicine. Her interests include behavioural economics and health policy.

Miqdad Asaria is an assistant professor in the Department of Health Policy at the LSE. His research interests include health inequalities and health financing, with a particular focus on the health systems in India and the United Kingdom. He holds a fellowship from the Health Foundation to investigate the contribution of austerity policies to racial and socio-economic health inequalities, a grant from the Medical Research Council (MRC) to investigate the impacts of early interventions on inequalities in health and well-being over the life-course, and a grant from the National Institute of Health Research (NIHR) to develop methods for accounting for unmet needs in healthcare funding formulas.

Sanchayan Banerjee is Assistant Professor of Environmental and Behavioural Economics in the Institute of Environmental Studies at the Free University Amsterdam. He is also a visiting fellow of the LSE and a fellow of the UK Higher Education Academy. His research focuses on developing and testing citizen-oriented behavioural public policies and he has co-developed the Nudge+ framework with Peter John. Banerjee is also an associate editor of *Humanities and Social Sciences Communications* and *Behavioural Public Policy (New Voices)*.

Daniel Banko-Ferran is a PhD student in the Department of Economics at the University of Pittsburgh. His research primarily focuses on the causal identification of non-monetary factors that negatively impact individual decision-making, productivity, and well-being. He is researching the influence of social comparisons on effort, changes to sleep on mental health, and the unintended behavioural effects of policy changes.

Ilana Brody is a doctoral student of behavioural decision-making at the UCLA Anderson School of Management. She holds a bachelor's degree in psychology and economics from the University of Virginia. Brody has published insights from behavioural science to inform key policy challenges through *Scientific American* and the Decision Lab and presented her original research through the annual conferences of the Association for Psychological Science, the Society for Judgment and Decision Making, and the Society for Personality and Social Psychology. Prior to pursuing PhD, she evaluated and designed behaviourally informed policies to improve access and equity among the most vulnerable populations in the United States.

Tim Büthe is Professor of Politics and Public Policy and Chair for International Relations in the Munich School of Politics and Public Policy at the Technical University of Munich (TUM) and the TUM

School of Management. A former Robert Wood Johnson Foundation Scholar in health policy research at the University of California, Berkeley, and the University of California, San Francisco, he is also a technology policy scholar at the Sanford School of Public Policy, Duke University.

Nicola Cerutti is a behavioural and environmental economist and a post-doctoral researcher at the Mercator Research Institute on Global Commons and Climate Change in Berlin. His work focuses on the behavioural aspects of public health, of natural resource use, and of greenhouse gas emissions in the food chain. He received a PhD in economics from the Jacobs University of Bremen, Germany, in 2017. He previously worked at the Joint Research Centre of the European Commission, at the University of Verona, and at the Berlin School of Economics and Law.

Georgina Connolly recently completed an MSc in health policy, planning, and financing at the LSE and the London School of Hygiene and Tropical Medicine. She holds a bachelor's degree in applied health from the University of Leeds.

Joan Costa-Font is Professor of Health Economics in the Department of Health Policy at the LSE. He was a Harkness Fellow at Harvard University and a visiting fellow at Boston College, the University of Oxford, and University College London and has taught at Paris Dauphine University, the University of Barcelona, and the Catholic University of the Sacred Heart. His research interests focus on examining the economic and healthcare effects of ageing and long-term care programmes and behavioural incentives for, and constraints on, health, healthcare, and household behaviour.

Hengchen Dai is Associate Professor of Organization Behavior and Behavioral Decision Making at the UCLA Anderson School of Management. She holds a bachelor's degree from Peking University and a PhD from the University of Pennsylvania. She conducts field studies with organisations across industries to understand what drives motivation, how to steer people towards far-sighted decision-making, and when behaviour change interventions fail to scale and even backfire.

Liam Delaney is Professor of Behavioural Science and the head of the Department of Psychological and Behavioural Science at the LSE. He was a member of a behavioural change subgroup of the Irish National Public Health Emergency Team set up in response to COVID-19.

Barbara Fasolo is Associate Professor of Behavioural Science in the Department of Management at the LSE. She co-founded and co-directs the LSE Behavioural Lab. Her research is on improving judgements and decision processes in the presence of risks and trade-offs, with a specific focus on strategic decisions, de-biasing, and choice architecture. She served as Expert-in-Secondment for the European Medicines Agency during 2009–2012, and during the COVID-19 pandemic she worked on behavioural reactions to COVID-19 as part of PERISCOPE (a large pan-European project funded by the European Commission and involving the LSE Behavioural Lab with thirty other European institutions.)

Virginia Fedrigo is a behavioural scientist with an interest in understanding how time influences the expression of our personality and cognitive traits, with special interest in healthcare applications. She employs a wide range of methodologies, including secondary data analyses, behavioural studies, and physiological measurements. She is a PhD candidate in psychological and behavioural science at the LSE. She holds degrees in molecular biology and cognitive science from the University of California, San Diego, and in neuroeconomics from Maastricht University.

Matteo M. Galizzi is Associate Professor of Behavioural Science in the Department of Psychological and Behavioural Science at the LSE. He is also Director of the LSE Executive MSc in Behavioural Science and Co-director of the LSE Behavioural Lab. He is on the steering groups of the LSE Global Health Initiative and of the LSE Behavioural Science Hub. He is a behavioural and experimental economist working on randomised controlled trials and behavioural experiments in health and public policy. He graduated from the University of Pavia (Italy) and holds an MSc in econometrics and a PhD in economics from the University of York. He has taken research and teaching positions at the universities of Pavia, York, Varese, Brescia, and Durham and at the Autonomous University of Barcelona, Queen Mary University of London, and the Paris School of Economics. He founded and coordinates the Behavioural Experiments in Health Network.

Rania Gihleb is Assistant Professor of Economics in the Department of Economics at the University of Pittsburgh and a research affiliate at IZA – Institute of Labor Economics. She is a labour economist working on family economics, economic demography, and the economics of education.

Osea Giuntella is Assistant Professor of Economics in the Department of Economics at the University of Pittsburgh and a research fellow at IZA – Institute of Labor Economics and the National Bureau of Economic Research. His research focuses on health economics, labour economics, and economic demography.

Benno Guenther is a specialist in financial markets, behavioural economics, and international voluntary carbon markets. Amongst others, he applies behavioural insights in the context of financial markets, the environment, and the aviation industry. He has more than a decade of practical experience as a trading executive with leading international investment banks such as J. P. Morgan and

BNP Paribas. Guenther is also a PhD candidate in psychological and behavioural science at the LSE, where he researches risk-taking in high stakes contexts. He holds an MSc in behavioural science from the LSE as well as a master's degree in mathematical finance from the University of Konstanz, Germany.

Sayward Harrison is an assistant professor in the Department of Psychology at the University of South Carolina. She has a PhD in health psychology and a specialisation in the field of paediatric school psychology. Her research focuses on improving the health and well-being of youth who are impacted by acute and chronic health conditions. Harrison's primary research interests include psychosocial and behavioural aspects of the human immunodeficiency virus.

Juliet Hodges is a PhD candidate at the LSE. She holds a BSc in psychology from the University of York and an MSc in behavioural and economic science from the University of Warwick. She is Head of Experimental Design at Cowry Consulting, leading on the development of data science propositions and the design of rigorous trials, and has worked for ten years in applied behavioural science, both in consulting and in-house at a health insurer.

Steffen Kamenicek is an independent writer and researcher with extensive experience as an analyst in the healthcare sector. He works as a generalist researcher for 1Day Sooner. In this role, he is involved in different research projects in the field of human challenge trials, as well as in the dissemination of information relating to human challenge trials to the general public.

Archie Kinnane is a climate analytics consultant at International Shareholder Services ESG. He graduated from Yale University in 2018 with a bachelor of science in astrophysics.

Ploutarchos Kourtidis is a post-doctoral researcher in the Department of Psychological and Behavioural Science at the LSE. He obtained a PhD in medical decision-making from Imperial College London. His background is in cognitive psychology and decision science. His research interests lie broadly in behavioural science, experimental psychology, and judgement and decision-making, with a particular interest in the flaws of intuitive thinking and in debiasing techniques to improve reasoning. During the COVID-19 pandemic, Kourtidis worked on the effects of communication strategies on health-related behaviours.

George Loewenstein is Professor of Economics and Psychology in the Social and Decision Sciences Department at Carnegie Mellon University and the Director of the Center for Behavioral Decision Research. His research focuses on applications of psychology to economics and, more recently, applications of economics to psychology.

Veronika Luptakova is a behavioural scientist and a PhD candidate in the Department of Psychological and Behavioural Science at the LSE. Her PhD research lies at the intersection of experimental moral philosophy and cognitive psychology. She explores how people deal with incoherence in their moral judgements and how this might impact public policymaking and communication, including in healthcare.

Mario Macis is a professor of economics at the Johns Hopkins Carey Business School. He is also core faculty at the Hopkins Business of Health Initiative, affiliate faculty at the Johns Hopkins Berman Institute of Bioethics, and faculty research fellow at the National Bureau of Economic Research and IZA – Institute of Labor Economics.

Elias Mossialos is Brian Abel-Smith Professor of Health Policy in the Department of Social Policy at the LSE, Deputy Head of

Department of Health Policy, and Director of LSE Health. He has advised the World Health Organization, the European Parliament, the European Commission, the World Bank, the UK Office of Fair Trading, ministries of health and social affairs in Belgium, Brazil, China, Cyprus, Finland, Greece, Ireland, Kazakhstan, Russia, Slovenia, South Africa, Spain, and Sweden, and health insurance funds in Austria, Croatia, France, Hungary, and South Korea. His research focus is comparative health systems and policy, addressing questions related to health reforms, financing healthcare, pharmaceutical policies, the impact of EU law on healthcare systems, cancer care, and policy and antibiotics.

Adam Oliver is Professor of Behavioural Public Policy in the Department of Social Policy at the LSE. His principal expertise lies in the field of behavioural public policy, on which he has published widely. He is Editor of the journal *Behavioural Public Policy* and the author of *The Origins of Behavioural Public Policy* and *Reciprocity and the Art of Behavioural Public Policy*. His new book is titled *A Political Economy of Behavioural Public Policy*.

Lydia Prieto is a master's student at the University of Barcelona and graduated with a degree in economics from Pompeu Fabra University. Her interests lie in gender, health, inequality, and public policy.

Caroline Rudisill is an associate professor in the Arnold School of Public Health at the University of South Carolina. She examines individual decision-making regarding health-related behaviours, in particular treatment choices and preventative behaviours in the face of risk such as using financial incentives with patients in primary care and prevention settings, seeing how risk perceptions impact vaccination uptake, and understanding how people behave in the face of health-related risks such as avian flu.

Silvia Saccardo is Associate Professor of Behavioral Economics in the Department of Social and Decision Sciences at Carnegie Mellon University. She holds bachelor's and master's degrees in psychology from the University of Padua, Italy, and a PhD in management from the University of California, San Diego. Her research integrates insights from economics and psychology to uncover the drivers of behaviours that are beneficial to individuals, organisations, and society. Her work ranges from studying the impediments to ethical and pro-social behaviour, to promoting the uptake of life-saving vaccines, to understanding when behavioural interventions fail to scale.

Luca Salmasi is an associate professor in the Department of Economics and Finance at the Catholic University of the Sacred Heart. He received a PhD in economics and finance from the University of Verona in 2012. He was a researcher in political economy at the Department of Political Sciences of the University of Perugia, where he previously spent a period as a research fellow at the Department of Experimental Medicine and Public Health.

Jet Sanders is a behavioural scientist. She finds patterns that can be used to change behaviour for social good, with a particular interest in time, risk, and health. She holds a PhD in cognitive and experimental psychology, worked as a principal behavioural insights advisor with Public Health England and at the Center for Advanced Hindsight at Duke University and Kyoto University, and is now an assistant professor in the Psychological and Behavioural Science Department at the LSE. Since the start of the pandemic, Sanders has also been seconded for part of her time to the Corona Behavioural Unit of the National Institute of Public Health and the Environment of the Netherlands.

Manu Savani is Lecturer in Public Policy in the Department of Social and Political Sciences at Brunel University London. Her research examines how behavioural biases affect health and political behaviours, as well as the interplay between policy instruments and public support in the context of COVID-19 policymaking.

Virginia Schmit is the director of research for 1Day Sooner and has been working with the 1Day Sooner research team to answer questions that are salient for potential volunteers for human challenge trials and clinical trials since autumn 2020. Her background is as an infectious disease molecular biologist and she has worked in academia, in government, including at the Centers for Disease Control and Prevention, and as a US Public Health Service Officer as Deputy Director of Laboratory Operations and Scientist for a large programme through the Department of Homeland Security.

Ganga Shreedhar is an assistant professor in the Department of Psychological and Behavioural Science, LSE. Her research examines what motivates people to take collective and personal actions to address planetary challenges such as climate change and mass extinction, including the intersecting roles of environmental, health, and economic policy.

Divya Srivastava is a health economist and a guest lecturer at the LSE. The focus of her work is international comparative health policy, health financing, and pharmaceutical policy. She earlier worked at the LSE as a researcher, seminar leader, and lecturer. She has worked for international organisations, including the World Health Organization – Europe, in Brussels, and the Organisation for Economic Cooperation and Development, in Paris, in national authorities (Health Canada, NHS England, and the Office of Fair Trading), and as a consultant providing pharmaceutical policy advice to clients.

Janina Steinert is an assistant professor at the TUM School of Social Sciences and Technology and a research associate at the Department of Social Policy and Intervention, the University of Oxford, from where she has also obtained a PhD. Her research interest lies primarily in the fields of global health and development economics and research topics including gender-based violence, poverty alleviation, and research ethics. In recent projects, she has conducted randomised controlled trials, behavioural games, survey experiments, and mixed methods studies on how to alleviate gender inequality and poverty and on how to shape health behaviour.

Henrike Sternberg is a research associate and PhD candidate at the TUM School of Social Sciences and Technology. Her background and research interests lie in the intersection between development and behavioural economics, with her primary research topics being spousal cooperation and gender norms in intra-household decision-making. More generally, her research employs behavioural games, surveys, and field experiments to examine social preferences in the intra-household and individual contexts as drivers of public policies and interventions, which, recently, she has also investigated in the case of individual-level responses to COVID-19 policies.

Daniele Sudsataya has an MSc in international health policy from the LSE. Prior to this, he graduated from King's College London with a BSc in global health and social medicine with pharmacology. Originally from both New York City, USA, and Turin, Italy, Sudsataya has a keen interest in public health, infectious diseases, and disease control strategies. He conducts research on a broad range of topics within this space, including vaccination, behavioural incentives for healthcare, and ageing.

Sorin Thode holds a BSc in psychology from McGill University and a MSc in behavioural science from LSE. Her research interests include mental health, digital healthcare, and information disorders.

Judit Vall Castelló is an associate professor in the Department of Economics, University of Barcelona, and a research fellow at IZA – Institute of Labor Economics and at the Centre for Research in Health and Economics, Pompeu Fabra University. She is an applied economist specialising in policy evaluation, particularly in the areas of health economics and labour economics. She has been involved in international projects at the National Bureau of Economic Research, the United Nations Children's Fund, and the University of Cambridge.

Giuseppe A. Veltri is Full Professor of Computational Social Science and Cognitive Sociology at the Department of Sociology and Social Research, University of Trento. He is the academic coordinator of the doctoral programme in sociology. He was a senior lecturer at the University of Leicester, a lecturer at the University of East Anglia, and a scientific fellow at the European Commission JRC Institute for Prospective Technological Studies (IPTS). Before joining IPTS, he was a research associate at the Institut Jean Nicod (Ecole Normale Supérieure) in Paris.

Cristina Vilaplana-Prieto is an associate professor at the Department of Economic Analysis of the Faculty of Economics, University of Murcia. She has a degree in economics from the University of Murcia and received a pre-doctoral grant from the Ministry of Science and Education in Spain to complete a PhD in economics at the University Carlos III of Madrid. Her research specialises in health economics and the economics of ageing.

Emma Watson holds a BA in psychology and English from Trinity College Dublin and an MSc in behaviour change from University College London. She worked as a research assistant to Professor Liam Delaney for several years, during which time she completed a diploma in coaching from the University of Cambridge.

Preface

COVID-19 has been a shock that has affected almost every individual in the world either directly by suffering the consequence of the virus in their own health, or by being impacted by the policy restrictions that resulted from COVID-19, such as lockdowns, or by health or economic losses due to the pandemic. How has COVID-19 modified behaviour around the world? What insights have been learned from COVID-19 and the related policy responses from experiments and behavioural interventions? What are the underlying behavioural mechanisms in place? What is the evidence on changes in behaviours and attitudes in a pandemic? This book is the product of recent insights and contributions at the time of a global pandemic by several scholars in behavioural economics and health policy, most of which are, in one way or another, associated with the LSE. The COVID-19 pandemic has brought several behavioural challenges to global public attention and has highlighted the role played in health outcomes and public health by the complexities and unpredictability of human behaviour. The aim of this book is to bring together the perspectives and contributions of behavioural economics and health policy in learning lessons from the COVID-19 pandemic and in understanding the preparedness and response to future pandemics.

Acknowledgements

This research has been supported by the European Union's Horizon 2020 research and innovation programme PERISCOPE: Pan European Response to the Impacts of COVID-19 and Future Pandemics and Epidemics, under grant agreement no. 101016233.

1 Behavioural Economics and Policy for Pandemics

Pandemics as Tipping Points

Joan Costa-Font and Matteo M. Galizzi

1.1 PANDEMICS AND BEHAVIOUR

Pandemics are uncommon occurrences in human history. Most individuals do not anticipate pandemics in their life and do not include them in their daily planning. Indeed, while several epidemics have erupted into formal pandemics in recent decades – such as the swine flu or the N1H1 – COVID-19 is the first pandemic in a century to have systematically impacted the entire world, killing millions of human lives (8 million, at the time of writing) and upending global health and well-being, societies, economies, and labour markets all over the world.

Pandemics are 'one-off' events that can have enduring effects on the way people perceive the world and their health and how the political, economic, and health systems are organised. It is at the time of a pandemic, when the interests at stake are the largest, that individuals and institutions have a natural opportunity to cooperate. Pandemics can be seen as *tipping points* (Schelling, 2006; Scheffer, 2010) because they can radically affect the whole host of human behaviours, from physical and mental health to individual and societal well-being, from working conditions to leisure and organisation of time, from interpersonal and family relations to economic and social activities, from beliefs and perceptions to attitudes and preferences. Given that pandemics give rise to sudden changes in those behaviours, social scientists can also see them as unfortunate natural experiments, an opportunity to learn more about how individual behaviours adjust to sudden and radical changes in needs and contexts.

The COVID-19 pandemic has indeed brought several behavioural challenges to global public attention and has highlighted the key role played in health outcomes, public health, and public policy in general by the complexities of human behaviour. In accord with the notion that individuals tend to underestimate probabilities, at the beginning of the pandemic, before the World Health Organization had acknowledged it as such, COVID-19 was often compared to a flu epidemic, or even the seasonal flu. This likely affected how individuals interpreted risk information, often failing to understand the exponential risk that pandemics have, let alone the fatal consequences of the risk especially among older population. It is now time to start asking some questions. How has COVID-19 modified behaviours around the world so far? What insights have been learned from COVID-19 and the related policy responses? What are the underlying behavioural mechanisms in place? What is the evidence on changes in behaviours and attitudes in a pandemic?

This book examines from a behavioural economics and policy perspective what we can learn on health-related behaviours in a pandemic and the extent to which human behaviours have been at the core of individuals' reactions to the COVID-19 pandemic. Most chapters touch upon important policy responses.

One of the main lessons from the COVID-19 experience is that pandemics may act not only as tipping points but also as *magnifying glasses*: they amplify existing behavioural phenomena in nature, trends, and patterns and make differences sharper and more salient. For example, the health, economic, and social consequences of COVID-19 have hit the hardest the most disadvantaged segments of the populations, which already had poorer health outcomes and access to healthcare, worse socio-economic conditions, and more precarious jobs. Similarly, policy responses to COVID-19 have often made clearer which goal was the ultimate priority of many policymakers, experts, decision-makers, and stakeholders, for example by explicitly pitting the reasons of opening the economic and business activities against the objective to protect human lives and public health.

I.2 AIMS AND ORGANISATION OF THIS BOOK

This book is the product of recent insights and contributions on the COVID-19 pandemic by several scholars in behavioural economics and health policy most of which are, in one way or another, associated with the London School of Economics and Political Science. The book also benefits from many years of working together with a variety of collaborators in leading academic universities, policy-making bodies, public health authorities, and international institutions. The aim of this book is to bring closer the perspectives and contributions of behavioural economists specialising in health, health economists focused on behaviours, and scholars in behavioural public policy to distil lessons from the COVID-19 pandemic and to be able to better understand the preparedness and response to future pandemics.

The book is proposed to fill an existing double gap. It will crystalise, for the first time, the main insights and lessons learned from the COVID-19 crisis from both a behavioural economics and a health policy perspective. At the same time, it will facilitate the conversation and the cross-fertilisation of these two disciplines, which are still quite disconnected, in informing and shaping the policy responses to future pandemics.

The book is organised in two main parts in addition to this introduction. Part I (Chapters 2–13, edited by Matteo M. Galizzi) report an overview of the main insights and contributions from the field of behavioural economics focusing on health applications. Part II (Chapters 14–22, edited by Joan Costa-Font) reports an overview of the contributions of behavioural health economics and policy, focusing on behavioural incentives and interventions. The two parts integrate and complement each other both substantially and methodologically, as the chapters in Part I tend to be informed mainly by online, lab, and field experiments and by direct behavioural observation, whereas the chapters in Part II tend to leverage more theoretical and empirical analyses, often using large secondary datasets and surveys.

I.3   MAIN CONTRIBUTIONS AND INSIGHTS

In this section we provide a brief overview and summary of the main insights from each chapter.

In opening Part I of the book, Galizzi, Luptakova, Macis, and Thode put forward in Chapter 2 the argument that the main lesson that we have learned from behavioural economics research to inform policy responses to future pandemics is that we should fully account for *human heterogeneity*. Not only are people highly heterogeneous in their preferences, attitudes, beliefs, perceptions, circumstances, and constraints, but they also make very heterogeneous decisions and respond very differently to behavioural interventions. As a result, behavioural economists and policymakers need to both use the broadest and most comprehensive toolset of behavioural interventions and systematically engage with experiments and randomised controlled trials to learn what works for whom.

In keeping with this tipping points idea, Loewenstein and Kinnane discuss in Chapter 3 the connections between the COVID-19 pandemic and another major contemporary emergency: the climate change crisis. They highlight the similarities but also differences between the two global crises, discuss the key role played by human adaptation in the two crises, and offer some original lessons that can be learned from the COVID-19 pandemic about the climate change emergency.

Chapters 4 and 5 delve deeper into some specific sources of heterogeneity in human behaviour in the domain of risk. In Chapter 4 Guenther, Fedrigo, and Sanders summarise the experimental evidence on the impact of the COVID-19 pandemic on risk preferences, alongside the evolution of risk-taking and risk perception during the pandemic, and on the role of heterogeneity in risk tolerance in health behaviours during COVID-19, including the so-called 'risk compensation' hypothesis.

Given that individual risky behaviour is highly dependent on the institutional and social environment individuals face, in Chapter 5 Cerutti focuses specifically on the possible risk compensatory effects and unintended consequences related to wearing masks and face coverings, and reviews all the experimental studies conducted on mask-wearing before and after the COVID-19 pandemic.

The following two chapters focus on heterogeneity in decision-making and planning in a setting of increased risk of death. Indeed, in Chapter 6 Hodges assesses the heterogeneity of end-of-life preferences, their evolution during the COVID-19 pandemic, and specifically the lessons learned from behavioural economics experiments on advance care planning. Adams-Phipps, Kamenicek, and Schmit examine in Chapter 7 the experience of 1DaySooner during the pandemic and illustrate the key role of altruism and heterogeneous preferences in the context of volunteering for 'human challenge' trials.

The next three chapters focus on the role of heterogeneity in the design of, and responses to, behavioural interventions. More specifically Banerjee, Savani, and Shreedhar discuss in Chapter 8 the empirical and experimental evidence on the evolution during the COVID-19 pandemic of public preferences in support of 'hard' behavioural interventions (e.g., mandates, bans) as opposed to 'soft' behavioural interventions, such as 'nudges'. Next, in Chapter 9 Brody, Saccardo, and Dai summarise the experimental evidence on the different behavioural interventions to promote COVID-19 vaccination, with a particular emphasis on the nudging interventions and on the heterogeneity in the individual responses to such interventions. In Chapter 10 Kourtidis, Sternberg, Steinert, Büthe, Veltri, Fasolo, and Galizzi first distil evidence from a review of the systematic reviews on the behavioural aspects of the COVID-19 pandemic and then overview the experimental evidence available, with a focus on heterogeneity of COVID-19 vaccine hesitancy across different countries, and 'behavioural spillovers' and unintended consequences of behavioural interventions.[1]

Three further chapters focus on direct behavioural observations, rather than experimental evidence: Delaney and Watson (Chapter 11) discuss the role of behavioural science in the COVID-19 response in Ireland; Oliver (Chapter 12) critically discusses the more general use of behavioural science during the pandemic; and Galizzi (Chapter 13) describes the main biases by 'expert' decision-makers that emerged during the COVID-19 pandemic responses.[2]

Opening Part II of the book are three chapters on the mental health effects of the pandemic. Chapter 14 by Prieto and Castelló touches upon health behaviours and mental health. Drawing upon data from Spain, the chapter examines evidence of the first months of the pandemic on mental health and health behaviours. It documents important gender effects on mental health alongside critical changes in the use of medical resources, use of drugs, and daily consumption that were the result of COVID-19 risk exposure. Such trends in behaviours suggest that the pandemic and related lockdowns disrupted individual habits in a significant manner.

A complementary contribution by Banko-Ferran, Gihleb, and Giuntella, in Chapter 15, reviews the evidence of the effects of the COVID-19 pandemic on health behaviours and explores the trends in observational evidence of the effect of the pandemic on mental health, anxiety medications, and time use in the United States. More specifically, they document relevant changes in behaviours among vulnerable populations and the necessary public health measures implemented to mitigate its spread. Also, they show that the mental impact of COVID-19 is likely to outlast its physical impact, which is consistent with the evidence of other comparable disasters.

[1] The chapter is gathered as part of the behavioural economics work package WP5 of the European Union's Horizon 2020 research and innovation programme Pan European Response to the Impacts of COVID-19 and Future Pandemics and Epidemics (PERISCOPE), grant agreement no. 101016233.

[2] The chapter is a shorter, revised, version of the original article: Galizzi, M. M. (2022). Behavioural public health? Experts' biases and responses to pandemics. *Sistemi Intelligenti*, 34(2), 371–401, https://doi.org/10.1422/105045, www.rivisteweb.it/doi/10.1422/105045.

In Chapter 16 Costa-Font and Vilaplana-Prieto examine the mental health effects of lockdowns and document that whilst a 'preventive' lockdown in a low/moderate mortality environment increases symptoms of depression and anxiety, in a high mortality setting lockdowns actually can mitigate such negative effects, particularly on anxiety, which they coin as 'welcomed lockdown'.

Turning to examining the effects on some specific demographic groups, Costa-Font examines in Chapter 17 how the COVID-19 pandemic has modified attitudes with respect to old age, as well as the behaviours of older age individuals such as the probability of retirement and access to care for older age seniors. The chapter reveals the importance of trusted providers and specifically the role of age-specific stereotypes in influencing individuals' decision-making with regard to old age.

Next, Chapter 18 by Sudsataya, Asaria, Costa-Font, and Achaiki focus on minority ethnic groups. It provides an assessment of the state of the art of the evidence of vaccine hesitancy, and explaining the presence of an ethnic minority vector driving vaccine hesitancy, as well as a list of potential behavioural policy interventions to curb vaccination differences.

Another set of chapters look at questions related to healthcare use that result from the COVID-19 pandemic. Specifically, Chapter 19 by Connolly and Srivastava documents the effect of the pandemic shock and subsequent COVID-19 policies on the rise of digital health solutions and technologies, with a focus on healthcare settings, and discusses the role of behavioural insights and policy proposals.

In Chapter 20 Costa-Font, Asaria, and Mossialos examine the effect of the so-called 'erring on the side of rare events' bias in explaining vaccine authorisation in Europe, and superficially discussed how it related to precautionary principles and what doe the media play is making rare event associated with new vaccines more salient.

The final chapters in the book address the role of some behavioural mechanisms explaining decision-making during a pandemic and more specifically the role of trust and risk perceptions. In Chapter 21 Rudisill and Harrison discuss the role of trust in impacting decision-making in a pandemic such as COVID-19. Drawing on a multi-country study examining trust in a variety of key pandemic-related stakeholders (e.g., government, public health institutions), they show how the variation in trust has potential implications for risk perceptions and key health behaviours.

Finally, in Chapter 22, Aldulaimi, Costa-Font, and Salmasi examine, using data from a large multi-county survey, how individuals perceive risks in a pandemic, compared to similar risks such as food poisoning and influenza.

REFERENCES

Scheffer, M. (2010). Foreseeing tipping points. *Nature*, 467(7314), 411–412.

Schelling, T. C. (2006). *Micromotives and Macrobehavior*. WW Norton & Company.

PART I Evidence from Experiments and Behavioural Insights

Edited by Matteo M. Galizzi

2 What Have We Learned from Behavioural Economics for the COVID-19 Response?

Matteo M. Galizzi, Veronika Luptakova,
Mario Macis, and Sorin Thode

2.1 AIM AND STRUCTURE

What have we learned from research in behavioural economics that can inform the policy response to pandemics? In this chapter, we try to distil and summarise the key lessons we have learned during the COVID-19 pandemic and the subsequent policy responses from *behavioural economics*, that is, the interdisciplinary field that combines and cross-fertilises insights from economics and psychology.

There are three main take-home lessons, we believe, that could help advance our understanding of human behaviour in a time of a pandemic and enhance the preparedness of international institutions and governments for future pandemics and epidemics: (i) people are heterogeneous, and we should therefore fully account for human heterogeneity; (ii) our behavioural interventions must be heterogeneous as well – we need to use a full and diverse spectrum of behavioural interventions – going beyond 'nudges' when needed – and we should acknowledge heterogeneity in individual responses to such interventions; and (iii) as it is not clear upfront what will work for whom, we should engage more systematically with randomised controlled experiments for future pandemic responses.

In what follows, we elaborate in greater detail on each of these three aspects. In doing so, we also try to outline a conceptual framework for the chapters that will follow in this part of the book.

This opening chapter of Part I is followed by a chapter by George *Loewenstein and Archie Kinnane* (Chapter 3) that highlights how the COVID-19 pandemic is not only one of the main health emergencies in contemporary history but also a complex and truly global crisis. The chapter examines the connections between the COVID-19 pandemic and another major crisis we are living through: climate change. It highlights similarities but also differences between the two crises, for example, related to human adaptation, and discusses lessons that can be learned from the COVID-19 pandemic about climate change.

The other chapters in this part focus on different behavioural economics aspects of the COVID-19 global health crisis, which can be framed within the three critical lessons listed earlier.

2.2   ACCOUNTING FOR HETEROGENEITY

First, we should fully acknowledge and account for the broad *heterogeneity* of human motives, drivers, constraints, and choices. By and large, economists have stopped postulating the existence of a single-type ('representative') fully rational decision-maker with a given, stable, and consistent set of preferences, who can fully access and perfectly process information and who is capable of making perfectly consistent and optimal decisions by weighting all the relative costs and benefits of different courses of actions and by maximising personal utility.

Also with a critical impulse from behavioural economics, economists today acknowledge that *people are different* and that there is no 'one-size-fits-all' or 'standard' decision-maker. Further, research in behavioural economics has shown that people are often prone to biases, have prior beliefs that affect their judgements, and often think intuitively and act in emotional states. A vivid example is how people can change health judgements and behaviours when they experience *'visceral states'* such as hunger, pain, or sexual arousal (Loewenstein, 1996). Thus, fully rational and bias-free agents are just a special case of decision-makers within a widely diverse spectrum of human decision-makers. In fact, humans are inherently heterogeneous in at least three dimensions: (i) they have *heterogeneous preferences and attitudes*; (ii) they have *heterogeneous beliefs and perceptions*; and

(iii) they *face different sets of circumstances and constraints.* As a result (iv) they make *heterogeneous decisions.*

2.2.1   Heterogeneous Preferences and Attitudes

Human decision-makers may have clear, stable, and consistent sets of preferences, as traditionally postulated by neoclassical economics and rational choice theory. In particular, some decision-makers may have sets of *risk, time, and social preferences* –for example, they are consistently risk-neutral, risk-averse, or risk-seeking; they are consistently patient over time (time consistent); and they are purely self-interested in the sense that their only objective is to maximise their own utility. However, many human decision-makers have less stable or less consistent sets of preferences. They are even unsure or unaware of their preferences and have more complex and nuanced objectives. For the sake of space, in what follows we illustrate this point mainly for *risk preferences* in the context of the COVID-19 pandemic, but similar considerations could be articulated for *other types of preferences* as well.

A number of empirical studies in behavioural economics have documented that many people have preferences that deviate from consistently risk-neutral or consistently risk-averse preferences, as postulated by standard theories such as expected utility theory. For example, according to the *magnitude effect,* people may become increasingly risk-averse as the monetary stakes get larger: that is, people may be risk-seeking for small monetary gains but turn progressively more risk-averse as the magnitude of the monetary gains increases (Prelec & Loewenstein, 1991; Weber & Chapman, 2005b). Prospect theory and rank-dependent utility theory – which form the conceptual backbone of what is known as *cumulative prospect theory* – document three further deviations from standard expected utility theory models of risk preferences: *probability weighting, reference dependence,* and *loss aversion.* According to *probability weighting,* not only are the possible risky outcomes subjectively 'transformed' by the individual decision-maker but also the objective probabilities of the outcomes are. As a result, individuals may perceive objective probabilities through a distorted subjective lens that makes changes in probabilities perceived non-linearly. For example, the change from a 5 per cent to a 10 per cent probability is not treated subjectively the same as the change from a 90 per cent to a 95 per cent probability. Some individuals may typically place more weight on small probabilities, thus *overweighting small probabilities*. Others may place less weight on high probabilities, thus *underweighting high probabilities*. Moreover, according to the *certainty effect*, we may give a special status to certainty because we disproportionately value outcomes that are certain: that is, we may sacrifice a lot to get from a probability of 99 per cent to 100 per cent but not so much to get from a probability of 98 per cent to 99 per cent. Subjective probability weighting and risk preferences more generally have been documented to affect risk perception in a variety of health contexts, including the degenerative neurological Huntington's disease (Oster et al., 2013) and COVID-19 vaccination (Trueblood et al., 2022). For example, some people could have chosen not to get vaccinated against COVID-19 because they overweighted the small probability of experiencing side effects.

Besides cognitive aspects, there are also emotional aspects related to risk perception and risk preferences. Risks are often evoked by *emotional appeals* such as fear and by involving vivid, concrete images and cues (Slovic et al., 2004, 2007). Many people are more likely to react to and remember ṽivid narratives or case examples than bland statistics about risks (Haase et al., 2015; Janssen et al., 2013). Therefore, emotional appeals are more likely than logical appeals to prompt people to seek health information (Betsch et al., 2011).

Additionally, there is an open question about how individual heterogeneity in risk preferences interacts within the specific context of a pandemic such as COVID-19. Whereas there have been other epidemics in the past and pandemics from which we can potentially learn lessons about such an interaction, there is, unfortunately, no reliable data for studying the impact, for example, of the Spanish flu on individual risk-taking. Research in behavioural economics distinguishes two types of uncertainty: *'foreground' risk*, over which we have a degree of active choice in 'normal' situations, such as selecting one lottery over another or choosing financial products, and *'background' risk*, which is a source of risk that is out of our immediate control ('exogenous' risk), cannot be avoided, and cannot be insured against or diversified away (Eeckhoudt et al., 1996; Gollier & Pratt, 1996; Quiggin, 2003). The COVID-19 pandemic is arguably an example where such background risk plays a significant role.

Conceptually, however, it is unclear how individual risk-taking in 'normal' activities can interact with background risk. One hypothesis is that the major background uncertainty represented by the COVID-19 pandemic can induce *compensatory behaviour*, leading to a reduction in non-essential risk-taking activities, such as smoking or climbing, in an increased effort to protect ourselves. This hypothesis is in line with the *'risk compensation'* or *'risk homeostasis'* idea and also with the *'countercyclical risk aversion'* hypothesis, according to which risk exposure is reduced in a situation of high uncertainty. Reduced risk-taking in lottery gambles was indeed observed following natural disasters, such as after the 2004 tsunami in Thailand or after an earthquake or flood in Indonesia between 2005 and 2008 (Cameron & Shah, 2015; Cassar et al., 2017).

On the other hand, an alternative hypothesis is that the background uncertainty represented by the COVID-19 pandemic can induce *an increase* in non-essential risk-taking activities. This has been documented after natural disasters as well: for example, evacuees from hurricane Katrina, below-poverty-line households in Peru exposed to a volcanic threat, and flooded households in Pakistan and Australia all appeared to seek more risks in lottery gambles (Bchir & Willinger, 2013; Eckel et al., 2009; Page et al., 2014; Said et al., 2015). The possible behavioural mechanisms underlying such paradoxical reactions are unclear. Still, it may be that the presence of major background uncertainty such as the pandemic or natural disasters 'trumps' seemingly smaller, more familiar, sources of risk (the lottery gamble), which are perceived as less salient and less risky, thus leading to more risk-taking. We can call this the *large uncertainty trumps small risks'* hypothesis (Galizzi et al., 2020).

Chapter 4 by *Guenther, Fedrigo, and Sanders* summarises the recent studies that have investigated risk tolerance and heterogeneity in risk-taking, risk perception, and risk compensation since the start of the COVID-19 pandemic. Chapter 5 by *Cerutti* analyses the recent studies that have looked at possible compensatory effects related to mask-wearing during the COVID-19 pandemic.

As mentioned earlier, similar considerations could be articulated for *other types of preferences* as well. For example, *social preferences* and pro-social identity have indeed been found to *predict* vaccination intentions both in general and for COVID-19 (Bohm & Betsch, 2022; Bohm et al., 2016, 2019; Cucciniello et al., 2022; Heinrich-Morrison et al., 2015; Korn et al., 2020; Vietri et al., 2012). Moreover, social preferences, trust, social norms, and collectivism have also been found to predict various COVID-19 preventive behaviours (Bicchieri et al., 2021; Campos-Mercade et al., 2021b; Hensel et al., 2022; Lu et al., 2021; Rabb et al., 2022a). Chapter 7 by *Adams-Phipps, Kamenicek, and Schmit* summarises the recent discussion about using human challenge trials in the COVID-19 pandemic, including pro-social motivations of volunteers and ethical considerations. Chapter 6 by *Hodges* examines the discussion about *end-of-life preferences*, the role of behavioural economics in advance care planning, and the related evidence from the COVID-19 pandemic.

There are multiple sources of heterogeneity and individual differences in our *attitudes* as well. For example, people may have very different attitudes towards the sense of personal vulnerability to infectious diseases, in terms of both *perceived infectability* and *germ aversion*. In a past epidemic, for example, *perceived vulnerability to disease* predicted fears of contracting Avian flu (Green et al., 2010). We may also have very different levels of *disgust sensitivity*, that is, the degree of emotional distress and revulsion we tend to experience when confronted with disgust-evoking stimuli. Disgust sensitivity has been found to associate not only with contamination-related *obsessive-compulsive disorder*, manifested, for instance, through excessive hand-washing, but also with phobias such as *infection phobia*, a major psychological barrier to vaccine acceptance, or with *blood or injury phobias* (Ludvik et al., 2015; Olatunji et al., 2010).

Other attitudes that are naturally heterogeneous in a population are personality traits such as *trait anxiety* (i.e., proneness to experience anxiety); *harm avoidance* (i.e., the tendency to avoid potential risk); *bodily hypervigilance* (i.e., the tendency to be frightened of arousal or bodily sensations); *neuroticism* (or negative emotionality, i.e., the general tendency to become distressed by aversive stimuli); or *monitoring versus blunting attitudes* (i.e., the tendency to seek or avoid information about potential threats: Miller, 1987), which is conceptually related to *information avoidance* preferences (Golman et al., 2017; Ho et al., 2020). Some of these personality traits have been found to associate not only with more 'doctor shopping' and digital hypochondria ('cyberchondria') and with higher distress among healthcare workers or the general population in the past severe acute respiratory syndrome or 'avian flu' epidemics (Lu et al., 2006), but also with several perceptions, evaluations, and behaviours during the COVID-19 pandemic (Kaufmann et al., 2022; Zettler et al., 2022).

2.2.2 *Heterogeneous Beliefs and Perceptions*

Some human decision-makers may be able to fully access and perfectly process all the available information, as often postulated by conventional economics and rational choice theory. Most typically, however, human decision-makers have partial access to information. Moreover, they may have access to biased information or perceive distorted information due to cognitive biases. Some people may selectively ignore information, especially when this information does not fit in with their prior beliefs.

A number of possible sources of distorted perceptions and biased beliefs have been documented in behavioural economics. We have already mentioned one such source – the *perception of probabilities*. People often estimate the probability of an event based on simple *heuristic* rules, that is, judgement shortcuts or rules of thumb, that often deviate from reflective thinking and rational choice (Kahneman, 2011). For instance, people can judge the probability of two events occurring simultaneously as higher than the probability of one single event. This type of cognitive bias, called *conjunction fallacy*, occurs because people may rely on *representativeness* rather than on *likelihood* and can potentially permeate many possible judgements and decisions related to pathogens and epidemics. For instance, public health messages that present different statistical facts related to risks of infection, serious illness, or death are often expressed as *conditional to* some individual characteristics (age, gender, comorbidities).

People can also be affected by *projection bias*, the tendency to project our current state onto our future selves, creating an *empathy gap* between our present and our future selves, which leads us to underestimate the extent to which our preferences will change when we move from one state to another (Loewenstein, 2005a, b; Loewenstein et al., 2003). This can go in both directions. When in a 'hot' state – for example, we are hungry, aroused, or in pain – some of us can fall prey to a *'hot-to-cold' empathy gap* as we cannot divorce ourselves from our current hunger, arousal, or pain when thinking about our future. For example, cancer patients' willingness to live can dramatically fluctuate over the same day based on their temporary feelings of nausea generated by the treatments they receive (Chochinov et al., 1999). Similarly, this may lead some of us to retrospectively blame our choice to get vaccinated against COVID-19 when we experience some mild pain or discomfort after the jab, because we temporarily forget or dismiss the fact that suffering would be much worse by getting COVID-19 while unvaccinated. On the other hand, when we are in a 'cold' state, people may underestimate the impact that a future hot state (e.g., pain) will have on us.

A further source of distorted perceptions and biased beliefs is related to the *anchoring* effect (Kahneman & Tversky, 1974). Anchoring refers to the overreliance on an initial piece of information, a prior belief, or a first impression. First impressions are formed quickly, as a product of intuitive thinking, and are potentially fallible. Initial impressions often serve as anchors that drive human reasoning and determine human judgements. In the context of the COVID-19 pandemic, such anchors (e.g., beliefs about vaccination, initial guidance about the disease) may prevent people from updating their opinion in light of newly available information (e.g., new guidance, newly developed vaccines).

Briscese et al. (2020) showed that individual expectations about the duration of social distancing restrictions can act as an anchor and affect people's intention to comply with the measures. In particular, respondents in a panel representative of the Italian population reported being more likely to reduce their self-isolation effort if negatively surprised by a given hypothetical extension of the social distancing measures, whereas positive surprises had no impact. The authors interpret these results as being consistent with reference-dependent preferences and loss aversion.

Again, related to anchoring, in principle people should be able to correctly imagine and mentally visualise the rate of spread of an infectious disease such as COVID-19 as an exponential growth rate (depending on the so-called R_0, that is, the value that represents, on average, the number of people that a single infected person is expected to transmit an infectious disease to). In practice, however, individuals are likely to, consciously or unconsciously, base their estimate of today's new cases on the number of positive cases we saw yesterday or the day before, which would thus work as 'anchors' in our estimates. The *exponential growth bias*, that is, the pervasive tendency to perceive a growth process as linear when, in fact, it is exponential, has indeed been documented in a variety of contexts, including estimating the COVID-19 infections (Banerjee et al., 2021; Levy & Tasoff, 2017; Stango & Zinman, 2009; Wagenaar & Timmers, 1979).

Other possible sources of biased perceptions and beliefs are *planning fallacy* or *optimism bias*, that is, the tendency to overestimate our ability to perform future tasks; the related *unrealistic optimism bias*, that is, the tendency to believe that positive events are more likely to happen to ourselves than to others; and the also-related *invulnerability bias*, that is, the tendency to feel we are unlikely to be affected by threats such as serious infectious diseases. Some of these biases have been documented as associated with a lower likelihood of engaging in protective behaviours in previous epidemics: for example, *unrealistic optimism bias* was associated with lower hand-washing during the 'swine flu' (Kim & Niederdeppe, 2013), whereas people with high feeling of invulnerability were not only more likely to smoke and drink and drive (Morrell et al., 2016) but also less likely to vaccinate during the 'swine flu' epidemics (Taha et al., 2013).

2.2.3   *Heterogeneous Circumstances and Constraints*

Although this is not the focus of this chapter, heterogeneity of a variety of *individual circumstances, characteristics, and constraints* is an essential factor that can explain variation in people's behaviour and response to policies in the context of the COVID-19 pandemic. Papageorge et al. (2021) illustrate this point with survey data on US residents collected in April 2020. They find that low-income people are less likely to adopt self-protective behaviours, partly because they face circumstances that make adopting those behaviours more costly. For example, low-income individuals are less likely to be able to work from home. The results from Papageorge et al. (2021) highlight the importance for policymakers to recognise that people's circumstances and constraints affect compliance with social distancing measures and other preventive behaviours.

2.2.4   *Heterogeneous Decisions*

As discussed earlier, some human decision-makers may be capable of making perfectly consistent and optimal decisions by weighting all the costs and benefits of different courses of actions. However, other human decision-makers may not be capable of rationally weighting all the costs and benefits, or, in that assessment, they may be affected by contextual cues and effects that, in principle, should be completely irrelevant in informing a decision.

Research in behavioural economics has documented that contextual cues (sometimes even small and seemingly irrelevant ones) can have large effects on decisions. One such cue is the *messenger* effect. Individuals often base their decisions on not only the substance of a message, its factual content, but also whom that message is communicated from. For example, messages conveyed by messengers who are considered more trustworthy are more likely to reach, be listened to, and ultimately influence behaviour, such as in the cases of vaccination or other health-related messages conveyed by medical doctors in countries where trust in doctors is high (Bartoš et al., 2021), by respected public intellectual figures (Banerjee et al., 2020), by celebrities or by one's peers (Alatas et al., 2019). However, messaging campaigns that are successful at reaching their intended target population do not always produce behaviour change, as reported by Bahety et al. (2021) and Burlando et al. (2022) in the context of COVID-19 in India and Zambia, respectively. Also, messages conveyed by a doctor who is similar to the patient in one salient identity characteristic, such as ethnicity for example, have been documented as being effective in increasing demand for preventive care and in improving health outcomes (Allison et al., 1998; Alsan et al., 2019, 2021; Atanasov et al., 2013; Greenwood et al., 2020). However – and in line with the above call to account for heterogeneity – such an effect has not been universally documented (e.g., Alsan & Eichmeyer, 2021; Torres et al., 2021). Similar mixed impacts of messages due to the *concordance of messengers* and target audience along some relevant characteristics have been documented for political or religious beliefs in the case of messages about COVID-19 vaccination (Abu-Akel et al., 2021; Chu et al., 2021; Pink et al., 2021).

2.3   ACKNOWLEDGING DIVERSITY OF BEHAVIOURAL INTERVENTIONS AND HETEROGENEITY IN RESPONSES TO INTERVENTIONS

A second lesson learned from the COVID-19 pandemic relates to acknowledging that the behavioural interventions available to health policymakers are very broad and diverse. In fact, interventions inspired by behavioural economics are much broader and richer than just 'nudges', the popular term often used to refer to behavioural interventions. Nudges are behavioural interventions specifically aiming at re-designing the so-called 'choice architecture', that is, the environment where choices are made (Thaler & Sunstein, 2008). Nudges, therefore, do not restrict the number of options available to the decision-maker and neither introduce any financial incentive or any new piece of information nor alter the relative prices of the different options. They rather make certain choices more salient, more attractive, or easier to process, thus causing people to lean towards a specific target choice (e.g., placing vegetables at eye level in a supermarket can increase consumption of healthy food).

Besides (i) nudges, behavioural interventions also include (ii) preference-based policies, aimed at offering more choices to the decision-maker; (iii) information-based policies, aimed at providing more information to the decision-maker, including educational interventions in the spirit of cognitive 'boosts'; (iv) financial and non-financial incentives, aimed at offering conditional rewards to the decision-maker, including conditional cash transfers; and finally (v) regulatory policies, aimed at structurally correcting externalities, including mandates, taxes, and subsidies (Galizzi, 2014; Jarke et al., 2022). Chapter 8 *by Banerjee, Savani, and Shreedhar* summarises the discussion about the public support in favour of 'hard' or 'soft' behavioural interventions during the COVID-19 pandemic.

More and more evidence explicitly acknowledges that individual responses to different behavioural interventions can be highly heterogeneous (Bryan et al., 2021; Ijzerman et al., 2020). Although this seems to be a pretty general and pervasive phenomenon, it also applies specifically to the reactions to the COVID-19 policy measures (Ruggeri et al., 2024). In what follows, we will briefly discuss the evidence acknowledging the heterogeneity in responses to different COVID-19 interventions.

2.3.1 Heterogeneous Responses to Nudges

Some studies during the COVID-19 pandemic illustrate the high heterogeneity in the individual responses to nudges. Galizzi et al. (2022) noticed that 'nudge'-based social norms messages conveying high population vaccination coverage levels can encourage vaccination due to *bandwagoning effects* (i.e., imitating others' behaviours), but they can also discourage vaccination due to *free-riding effects* on low risk of infection (i.e., benefiting from others' behaviours without changing your own behaviour), making their impact on vaccination uptake ambiguous. Their study is novel in experimentally measuring the effects of different coverage rates of messages on vaccination intentions, to better capture the interplay between these free-riding and bandwagoning effects. This interplay is studied in the context of influenza vaccination, but the analysis and discussion are naturally extended to COVID-19 vaccines as well.

Galizzi et al. (2022) evaluated the causal effects of different messages about vaccination coverage rates on different self-reported and behavioural vaccination intention measures and examined how individual perceptions moderate intentions. Perceived coverage rates and perceived risks of infection can reflect imperfect information and heterogeneous beliefs across individuals and can influence how individuals experience different treatment messages.

UK adults were randomly assigned to one of seven treatment groups with messages about their social environment's coverage rate (between 10 per cent and 95 per cent) or a control group with no message. Galizzi et al. (2022) found that treated groups have significantly greater vaccination intention than the control. Treatment effects increased with the coverage rate up to a 75 per cent level, consistent with a *bandwagoning* effect. For coverage rates above 75 per cent, the treatment effects, albeit still positive, stopped increasing and remained flat. Their results suggest that, at higher coverage rates, *free-riding* behaviour may *partially crowd out bandwagoning* effects of coverage rates messages.

They also found that individual perceptions moderated the effect of coverage rates treatments on behavioural measures for vaccination intention. Individuals who had higher perceived risks of infection or higher perceived coverage rates than their treatment had greater vaccination intention than those untreated or than those whose treatment equalled their perceived risks of infection or perceived coverage rates. Conversely, those whose perceived risks of infection or whose perceived coverage rates were lower than their treatment had lower vaccination intention. Additionally, the further their perceptions lied above or below their treatment, the stronger was the increase or decrease in their vaccination intention.

Chapter 9 by *Brody, Saccardo, and Dai* summarises other recent behavioural interventions to promote COVID-19 vaccination and discusses in detail the nudging interventions by Dai et al. (2021), and Rabb et al. (2021, 2022a), and the heterogeneity in their findings.

2.3.2   *Heterogeneous Responses to Information-Based Policies*

Chapter 10 by *Kourtidis, Sternberg, Steinert, Büthe, Veltri, Fasolo, and Galizzi*, from the EU-funded H2020 PERISCOPE project, summarises several studies looking at heterogeneous responses to information-based policies.

Steinert et al. (2022), in particular, implemented a randomised controlled experiment across eight European countries by randomly assigning participants to a control group or a group with one of three messages: (i) *COVID-19 risk reduction:* information about the efficacy of different COVID-19 vaccines, specifically highlighting the effectiveness of vaccines to prevent COVID-19-related deaths and severe disease progressions among vaccinated individuals, relative to unvaccinated individuals; (ii) *vaccination certificate:* information about exclusive benefits for the vaccinated, including access to travel and leisure activities contingent on providing proof of vaccination in the form of a COVID-19 vaccination certificate; (iii) *hedonistic benefits:* information about the prospects of a full restoration of public life and a return to normality, including a wide range of leisure activities (restaurants, theatres, bars, etc.).

Steinert et al. (2022) found that there was vast heterogeneity across countries with regard to the impact of the three experimental messages on respondents' willingness to get vaccinated. In Germany, the odds of accepting the COVID-19 vaccine were 1.5 times higher for participants who were presented with the COVID-19 risk reduction message relative to participants in the control group. Messages highlighting hedonistic benefits and the benefits of owning a vaccination certificate were also associated with significantly higher odds of COVID-19 vaccination willingness: 1.43 and 1.44, respectively. In the United Kingdom, the vaccination certificate message significantly increased the odds of intending to get vaccinated by 1.51 compared to the control group. In Bulgaria, Poland, France, Italy, and Sweden, none of the messages significantly improved participants' reported vaccination intentions. In fact, treatment effects even pointed in the opposite direction in some countries, though these effects were significant only in Spain and Italy. Heterogeneity in treatment effects both across and within countries was further assessed using a machine learning approach (model-based recursive partitioning) which included (i) individual socio-economic characteristics: age, gender, education, and employment, and (ii) country-level characteristics: the level of misinformation and conspiracy beliefs held by the population, public trust in the government, the level of overall health literacy, and whether a lockdown was in place at the time of the survey.

Heterogeneity in responses to different messages was also found by Saaksvuori et al. (2022) in a cluster-randomised experiment in Finland. The interventions in this case aimed at increasing influenza vaccination, and the primary outcome variable was a record of influenza vaccination in the Finnish National Vaccination Register. The older adult population in two distinct regions in Finland was randomly allocated to a control group with no reminder or to one of two groups receiving different reminding messages, either of the individual benefits from vaccination or of its individual and social benefits. Saaksvuori et al. (2022) found that both reminders were effective in increasing vaccination rates compared to the control group but that the effects were particularly large among the individuals with no prior influenza vaccination. Furthermore, there was no significant difference in influenza vaccination rates between the two types of reminders, suggesting that introducing the description of the social benefits of vaccination into a message about individual benefits may not bring in any additional value to communications aimed at fostering vaccination uptakes.

2.3.3 Heterogeneous Responses to Incentives

Several studies have looked at financial incentives for COVID-19 vaccination and have documented heterogeneous responses to incentives. Campos-Mercade et al. (2021a) conducted an online randomised controlled trial (RCT) in Sweden where they randomly allocated participants either to receiving a monetary incentive of SEK 200 (around $24) or to being exposed to one of three nudges such as a reminder of the social impact of getting vaccinated, writing down an argument that could convince another person to get vaccinated, or answering a series of questions about the safety and effectiveness of the COVID-19 vaccines or to a control group. Besides measuring vaccination intentions, responses to the online experiment were linked to vaccination records within the Public Health Agency of Sweden. They found that while none of the three nudges significantly affected vaccination rates compared to the control group, the monetary incentive increased COVID-19 vaccine rates by 4 percentage points. Incentives also increased the intention to get vaccinated by 5 percentage points.

Chang et al. (2021) randomly allocated participants in the United States to either financial incentives for COVID-19 vaccination of a similar magnitude (around $10–$50), to different public health messages, to a simple appointment scheduler, or to a control group. They found that while public health messages increased vaccination intentions, none of the interventions, including the incentives, led to any significant increase in vaccination rates.

Several considerations could explain such a stark difference in the results between the two studies using incentives for COVID-19 vaccination. First, the setting was different (Sweden vs the United States), as well as the participants were different (a representative online panel in Sweden vs patients within the Contra Costa Health Plan). Second, the timing was different as well: while Campos-Mercade et al. (2021a) approached unvaccinated participants a month after the COVID-19 vaccines became available in Sweden, Chang et al. (2021) approached unvaccinated participants two or three months after they became eligible for a vaccine. Third, and relatedly, the vaccination rates in the control group of the two studies, which can be considered as a proxy for the baseline vaccination intention in the population, were also substantially different: 71.6 per cent of the participants in the control group of Campos-Mercade et al. (2021a) got vaccinated, while only 8 per cent of the participants in the control group in Chang et al. (2021) did. In other words, Chang et al. (2021) tested the effectiveness of incentives in a population that was substantially more vaccine hesitant than in Campos-Mercade et al. (2021a).

These substantially mixed results are confirmed by a city-wide field experiment in Philadelphia (Milkman et al., 2022) and by an empirical analysis of twenty-four state-wide financial incentive programmes for COVID-19 vaccination in the United States (Thirumurthy et al., 2022), both of which found that incentives were associated with non-significant differences in COVID-19 vaccination rates. Mixed results and heterogeneous responses to financial incentives were also found by Sprengholz et al. (2021) for vaccination and by Serra-Garcia and Szech (2022) for COVID-19 vaccination and testing.

2.4   SYSTEMATICALLY ENGAGING WITH EXPERIMENTS

Experiments, or RCTs, have been increasingly used to rigorously test the effectiveness of behavioural interventions in a variety of contexts, from education to public health, from development to social policies (Banerjee & Duflo, 2017; Harrison & List, 2004; List & Metcalfe, 2014).

Surprisingly, the use of experiments and RCTs has been remarkably limited in the policy responses to the COVID-19 pandemic, especially in real-world consequential settings (Ruggeri et al., 2024). This point was first highlighted by Haushofer and Metcalf (2020) at the beginning of the pandemic, who noticed that non-pharmaceutical interventions (NPIs) in response to COVID-19 'are often used without rigorous empirical evidence' and that 'RCTs … surprisingly have received little attention in the current pandemic, despite a long history in epidemiology and social science' (Haushofer & Metcalf, 2020: 1063).

Possible reasons explaining the limited use of experiments by policymakers in their responses to COVID-19 could be related to ethics or fairness issues associated with randomly assigning different groups of citizens, areas, or regions to different policies or to logistics considerations or feasibility concerns associated with the time and the resources required to implement an RCT, especially if multiple stakeholders are involved (Ruggeri et al., 2024). Some of these issues could have led policymakers to favour other scientific approaches to inform their decisions and policy responses to the pandemic, such as data-driven cross-country modelling, sometimes in combination with quasi-experimental methods (Cheng et al., 2020; Chernozhukhov et al., 2021; Singh et al., 2021).

However, as also argued by Haushofer and Metcalf (2020), policymakers could use a 'phase-in' or 'stepped-wedge' experimental design where some protective measures can begin earlier in some areas and slightly later in other areas, so that a rigorous evaluation of the effectiveness of the measure would be possible. Similarly, when policymakers believe that some of the measures can be loosened, the restrictions can be lifted gradually and in some areas first, and then later in other areas, so that, again, a rigorous evaluation would be possible. The use of phase-in experiments would thus allow policymakers to rigorously test different NPIs without compromising scientific and ethical standards: Haushofer and Metcalf (2020), in fact, argue that this phase-in approach would be ethically justifiable because areas in both the treatment and the control groups will eventually be exposed to the NPIs at some point in time, and policymakers will be neither 'knowingly withholding a beneficial intervention from constituents nor knowingly imposing a harmful one' (Haushofer & Metcalf, 2020: 1064).

To contribute more effectively to the collection of rigorous evidence to inform policymaking in future pandemic responses, scholars (and citizens) should advocate more convincingly for the systematic use of randomised controlled experiments starting from the early phases of the policy responses. When involved or consulted in a pandemic response as consultants or experts, for example, they should argue in favour of the use of experimentation even if the policymakers or the other experts in the panels are less familiar and less engaged with it. In order to do so, they should be able to anticipate and overcome the most commonly encountered hurdles in getting experiments to be taken seriously by policymakers, to respond to some common misconceptions about the ethics and logistics of experiments, and to propose a hands-on set of pragmatic solutions to implement experiments in practice (Al-Ubaydli et al., 2021; Dolan & Galizzi, 2014; John, 2021). Chapters 11–13 by *Delaney and Watson*, *Oliver*, and *Galizzi*, respectively, discuss some of the insights and challenges related to informing policymaking during the COVID-19 pandemic.

2.5 CONCLUSION

Insights from behavioural economics research have already proved to effectively inform public policy and decision-making (Thaler & Sunstein, 2008). One of its main attractions is that it gives policymakers a direction where to look for interventions most likely – though by no means certain – to be effective in changing behaviour. The COVID-19 pandemic provides an opportunity for behavioural economics to make a difference in global public health and for future pandemic responses. To effectively do so, behavioural economists should take stock of three main lessons learned during the COVID-19 pandemic: (i) we should fully account for the heterogeneity in preferences and attitudes, beliefs and perceptions, and constraints and decisions; (ii) we should acknowledge and employ a full and diverse spectrum of interventions – going beyond 'nudges' when needed – and we should acknowledge that individual responses to such behavioural interventions are inherently heterogeneous; and (iii) as it is not clear upfront what will work for whom, when informing future pandemic responses, we should advocate more strongly for, and engage more systematically with, randomised controlled experiments.

REFERENCES

Abu-Akel, A., Spitz, A., & West, R. (2021). The effect of spokesperson attribution on public health message sharing during the COVID-19 pandemic. *PLoS ONE*, 16, e0245100.

Alatas, V., Chandrasekhar, A., Mobius, M., Olken, B., & Paladines, C. (2019). When celebrities speak: A nationwide Twitter experiment promoting vaccination in Indonesia. Working Paper 25589. *National Bureau of Economic Research*. https://doi.org/10.3386/w25589

Allison, J. J., Kiefe, C. I., Cook, E. F., Gerrity, M. S., Orav, E. J., & Centor, R. (1998). The association of physician attitudes about uncertainty and risk taking with resource use in a Medicare HMO. *Medical Decision Making*, 18, 320–329.

Alsan, M., & Eichmeyer, S. (2021). Experimental evidence on the effectiveness of non-experts for improving vaccine demand. Working Paper 28593. National Bureau of Economic Research. https://doi.org/10.3386/w28593

Alsan, M., Garrick, O., & Graziani, G. C. (2019). Does diversity matter for health? Experimental evidence from Oakland. *American Economic Review*, 109(12), 4071–4111. https://doi.org/10.1257/aer.20181446.

Alsan, M., Stanford, F. C., Banerjee, A., Breza, E., Chandrasekhar, A. G., Eichmeyer, S., et al. (2021). Comparison of knowledge and information-seeking behavior after general COVID-19 public health messages and messages tailored for Black and Latinx communities: A randomized controlled trial. *Annals of Internal Medicine*, 174(4), 484–492. https://doi.org/10.7326/M20-6141

Al-Ubaydli, O., Lee, M. S., List, J. A., Mackevicius, C. L., & Suskind, D. (2021). How can experiments play a greater role in public policy? Twelve proposals from an economic model of scaling. *Behavioural Public Policy*, 5(1), 2–49.

Atanasov, P., Anderson, B. L., Cain, J., Schulkin, J., & Dana, J. (2013). Comparing physicians personal prevention practices and their recommendations to patients. *Journal for Healthcare Quality*, 37(3), 189–198. https://doi.org/10.1111/jhq.12042.

Bahety, G., Bauhoff, S., Patel, D., & Potter, J. (2021). Texts don't nudge: An adaptive trial to prevent the spread of COVID-19 in India. *Journal of Development Economics*, 153, 102747.

Banerjee, A., Alsan, M., Breza, E., Chandrasekhar, A., Chowdhury, A., Duflo, E., et al. (2020). Messages on COVID-19 prevention in India increased symptoms reporting and adherence to preventive behaviors among 25 million recipients with similar effects on non-recipient members of their communities. Working Paper 27496. National Bureau of Economic Research. https://doi.org/10.3386/w27496

Banerjee, A., & Duflo, E. (2017). *Handbook of Field Experiments*. Amsterdam: North Holland-Elsevier.

Banerjee, R., Bhattacharya, J., & Majumdar, P. (2021). Exponential-growth prediction bias and compliance with safety measures related to COVID-19. *Social Science & Medicine*, 268, 113473.

Bartoš, V., Bauer, M., Cahlíková, J., & Chytilová, J. (2021). Spreading consensus: Correcting misperceptions about the views of the medical community has lasting impacts on Covid-19 vaccine take-up. Working Paper 9617. CESifo. www.cesifo.org/en/publications/2022/working-paper/spreading-consensus-correcting-misperceptions-about-views-medical

Bavel, J. J. V., Baicker, K., Boggio, P. S., Capraro, V., Cichocka, A., Cikara, M., et al. (2020). Using social and behavioural science to support COVID-19 pandemic response. *Nature Human Behaviour*, 4(5), 460–471.

Bchir, M. A., & Willinger, M. (2013). Does the exposure to natural hazards affect risk and time preferences? Some insights from a field experiment in Perú. Working Paper 13-04, LAMETA, University of Montpellier.

Betsch,C., Ulshöfer, C., Renkewitz, F., Betsch, T. (2011). The influence of narrative v. statistical information on perceiving vaccination risks. *Medical Decision Making*, 31(5), 742–753. https://doi.org/10.1177/0272989X11400419

Betsch, C., Böhm, R., & Chapman, G. B. (2015). Using behavioral insights to increase vaccination policy effectiveness. *Policy Insights from the Behavioral and Brain Sciences*, 2(1), 61–73. https://doi.org/10.1177/2372732215600716

Betsch, C., & Sachse, K. (2013). Debunking vaccination myths: Strong risk negations can increase perceived vaccination risks. *Health Psychology*, 32(2), 146–
155. https://doi.org/10.1037/a0027387

Bicchieri, C., Fatas, E., Aldana, A., Casas, A., Deshpande, I., Lauro, M. G., et al.
(2021). In science we (should) trust: Expectations and compliance across nine
countries during the COVID-19 pandemic. *PLoS ONE*, 16, e0252892.

Böhm, R., & Betsch, C. (2022). Prosocial vaccination. *Current Opinion in
Psychology*, 43, 307–311. https://doi.org/10.1016/j.copsyc.2021.08.010

Böhm, R., Betsch, C., & Korn, L. (2016). Selfish-rational non-vaccination:
Experimental evidence from an interactive vaccination game. *Journal of
Economic Behavior and Organization*, 131, 183–195.

Böhm, R., Meier, N. W., Gross, M., Korn, L., & Betsch, C. (2019). The willingness
to vaccinate increases when vaccination protects others who have low responsibility for not being vaccinated. *Journal of Behavioral Medicine*, 42, 381–391.

Böhm, R., Meier, N., Korn, L., & Betsch, C. (2017). Behavioural consequences of
vaccination recommendations: An experimental analysis. *Health Economics*,
26(S3), 66–75.

Brewer, N. T., Chapman, G. B., Schwartz, J., & Bergus, G. R. (2007). Assimilation
and contrast effects in physician and patient treatment choices. *Medical
Decision Making*, 27, 203–211.

Briscese, G., Lacetera, N., Macis, M., & Tonin, M. (2020). Expectations, reference
points, and compliance with COVID-19 social distancing measures. Working
Paper 26916. National Bureau of Economic Research.

Brody, I., Dai, H., Saccardo, S., Milkman, K., Patel, M., Gromet, D., & Duckworth, A.
(2022a). Provide information or encourage follow-through? Effects of behavioral
interventions depend on baseline motivation. *Unpublished* Working Paper.

Brody, I., Hershfield, H., Milkman, K., Patel, M., Gromet, D., & Duckworth, A.
(2022b). Leveraging past adversity to increase preventative behavior.
Unpublished Working Paper.

Bryan, C. J., Tipton, E., & Yeager, D. S. (2021). Behavioural science is unlikely
to change the world without a heterogeneity revolution. *Nature Human
Behaviour*, 5, 980–989. https://doi.org/10.1038/s41562-021-01143-3

Burlando, A., Chintagunta, P., Goldberg, J., Graboyes, M., Hangoma, P., Karlan, D.,
et al. (2022). Replication and adaptation of incentivized peer outreach: From
tuberculosis in India to COVID-19 in Zambia. Working Paper 26916. National
Bureau of Economic Research.

Cameron, L., & Shah, M. (2015). Risk-taking behavior in the wake of natural disasters. *Journal of Human Resources*, 50(2), 484–515. https://doi.org/10.3368/
jhr.50.2.484

Campos-Mercade, P., Meier, A. N., Schneider, F. H., Meier, S., Pope, D., & Wengström, E. (2021a). Monetary incentives increase COVID-19 vaccinations. *Science*, 374(6569), 879–882. https://doi.org/10.1126/science.abm0475

Campos-Mercade, P., Meier, A. N., Schneider, F. H., & Wengström, E. (2021b). Prosociality predicts health behaviors during the COVID-19 pandemic. *Journal of Public Economics*, 195, 104367. https://doi.org/10.1016/j.jpubeco.2021.104367

Cassar, A., Healy, A., & von Kessler, C. (2017). Trust, risk, and time preferences after a natural disaster: Experimental evidence from Thailand. *World Development*, 94(June), 90–105. https://doi.org/10.1016/j.worlddev.2016.12.042

Chang, T., Jacobson, M., Shah, M., Pramanik, R., & Shah, S. (2021). Financial incentives and other nudges do not increase COVID-19 vaccinations among the vaccine hesitant. Working Paper 29403. National Bureau of Economic Research. https://doi.org/10.3386/w29403

Chapman, G. B., & Coups, E. J. (1999). Predictors of influenza vaccine acceptance among healthy adults. *Preventive Medicine*, 29(4), 249–262. https://doi.org/10.1006/pmed.1999.0535

Chapman, G. B., Li, M., Colby, H., & Yoon, H. (2010). Opting in vs opting out of influenza vaccination. *JAMA*, 304(1), 43. https://doi.org/10.1001/jama.2010.892

Cheng, C., Barcelo', J., Hartnett, A. S., Kubinec, R., & Messerschmidt, L. (2020). COVID-19 government response event dataset (Coronanet v.1.0). *Nature Human Behaviour*, 4(7), 756–768.

Chernozhukhov, V., Kasahara, H., & Schrimpf, P. (2021). Causal impact of masks, policies, behavior on early COVID-19 pandemic in the US. *Journal of Econometrics*, 220(1), 23–62.

Chochinov, H. M., Tataryn, D., Clinch, J. J., & Dudgeon, D. (1999). Will to live in the terminally ill. *The Lancet*, 354(9181), 816–819. https://doi.org/10.1016/S0140-6736(99)80011-7

Chu, J., Pink, S. L., & Willer, R. (2021). Religious identity cues increase vaccination intentions and trust in medical experts among American Christians. *Proceedings of the National Academy of Sciences*, 118(49), e2106481118.

Cucciniello, M., Pin, P., Imre, B., Porumbescu, G. A., & Melegaro, A. (2022). Altruism and vaccination intentions: Evidence from behavioral experiments. *Social Science & Medicine*, 292(January), 114195.

Dai, H., Saccardo, S., Han, M. A., Roh, L., Raja, N., Vangala, S., et al. (2021). Behavioral nudges increase COVID-19 vaccinations. *Nature*, 597, 404–409. https://doi.org/10.1038/s41586-021-03843-2

Dolan, P., & Galizzi, M. M. (2014). Getting policy-makers to listen to field experiments. *Oxford Review of Economic Policy*, 30(4), 725–752.

Dolan, P., & Galizzi, M. M. (2015). Like ripples on a pond: Behavioral spillovers and their implications for research and policy. *Journal of Economic Psychology*, 47, 1–16. https://doi.org/10.1016/j.joep.2014.12.003

Eckel, C. C., El-Gamal, M. A., & Wilson, R. K. (2009). Risk loving after the storm: A Bayesian-Network study of Hurricane Katrina evacuees. *Journal of Economic Behavior and Organization*, 69(2), 110–124. https://doi.org/10.1016/j.jebo.2007.08.012

Eeckhoudt, L. C., Gollier, C., & Schlesinger, H. (1996). Changes in background risk and risk-taking behavior. *Econometrica*, 64, 683–689.

Eyles, E., Moran, P., Okolie, C., Dekel, D., Macleod-Hall, C., Webb, R. T., et al. (2021). Systematic review of the impact of the COVID-19 pandemic on suicidal behaviour amongst health and social care workers across the world. *Journal of Affective Disorders Reports*, 6(100271), 1–4. https://doi.org/10.1016/j.jadr.2021.100271

Fetzer, T. R., Witte, M., Hensel, L., Jachimowicz, J., Haushofer, J., Ivchenko, A., et al. (2020). Global behaviors and perceptions at the onset of the COVID-19 pandemic. Discussion Paper *27082*. National Bureau of Economic Research.

Finucane, M. L., Alhakami, A., Slovic, P., & Johnson, S. M. (2000). The affect heuristic in judgements of risks and benefits. *Journal of Behavioral Decision Making*, 13(1), 1–17.

Galizzi, M. M. (2014). What is really behavioural in behavioural health policy? And, does it work? *Applied Economic Perspectives and Policy*, 36(1), 25–60.

Galizzi, M. M., Guenther, B., Quinlan, M., & Sanders, J. (2020). Risk in the time of Covid-19: What do we know and not know? *Economics Observatory*. www.coronavirusandtheeconomy.com/question/risk-time-covid-19-what-do-we-know-and-not-kno

Galizzi, M. M., Lau, K., Miraldo, M., & Hauck, K. (2022). Bandwagoning, free-riding and heterogeneity in influenza vaccine decisions: An online experiment. *Health Economics*, 31(4), 614–646. https://doi.org/10.1002/hec.4467

Goldberg, J., Macis, M., & Chintagunta, P. (2022). Incentivized peer referrals for tuberculosis screening: Evidence from India. *American Economic Journal: Applied Economics*, 15(1), 259–291.

Gollier, C., & Pratt, J. W. (1996). Risk vulnerability and the tempering effects of background risk. *Econometrica*, 64, 683–689.

Golman, R., Hagmann, D., & Loewenstein, G. (2017). Information avoidance. *Journal of Economic Literature*, 55(1), 96–135.

Green, E. G., Krings, F., Staerkle, C., Bangerter, A., Clemence, A., Wagner-Egger, P., & Bornand, T. (2010). Keeping the vermin out: Perceived disease threat and ideological orientation as predictors of exclusionary immigration attitudes. *Journal of Community and Applied Social Psychology*, 20, 299–316.

Greenhalgh, T., Schmid, M. B., Czypionka, T., Bassler, D., & Gruer, L. (2020). Face masks for the public during the COVID-19 crisis. *British Medical Journal, 369*(m1435), 1–4. https://doi.org/10.1136/bmj.m1435

Greenwood, B. N., Hardeman, R. R., Huang, L., & Sojourner, A. (2020). Physician-patient racial concordance and disparities in birthing mortality for newborns. *Proceedings of the National Academy of Sciences, 117*(35), 21194–21200. https://doi.org/10.1073/pnas.1913405117

Haase, N., Betsch, C., & Renkewitz, F. (2015). Source credibility and the biasing effect of narrative information on the perception of vaccination risks. *Journal of Health Communication, 20,* 920–929.

Harrison, G. W., Hofmeyr, A., Kincaid, H., Monroe, B., Ross, D., Schneider, M., & Swarthout, J. T. (2022). Subjective beliefs and economic preferences during the COVID-19 pandemic. *Experimental Economics, 25,* 795–823. https://doi.org/10.1007/s10683-021-09738-3

Harrison, G. W., & List, J. A. (2004). Field experiments. *Journal of Economic Literature, 42*(4), 1009–1055.

Hauck, K. (2018). The economics of infectious diseases. Oxford Research Encyclopedias: Economics and Finance. Oxford University Press. https://doi.org/10.1093/acrefore/9780190625979.013.251

Haushofer, J., & Metcalf. (2020). Which interventions work best in a pandemic? *Science, 368*(6495), 1063–1065. https://doi.org/10.1126/science.abb6144.

Heinrich-Morrison, K., McLellan, S., McGinnes, U., Carroll, B., Watson, K., Bass, P., et al. (2015). An effective strategy for influenza vaccination of healthcare workers in Australia: Experience at a large health service without a mandatory policy. *BMC Infectious Diseases, 15*(1), 42. https://doi.org/10.1186/s12879-015-0765-7

Hensel, L., Witte, M., Caria, A. S., Fetzer, T., Fiorin, S., Gotz, F. M., et al. (2022). Global behaviors, perceptions, and the emergence of social norms at the onset of the COVID-19 pandemic. *Journal of Economic Behavior & Organization, 193,* 473–496.

Ho, E. H., Hagmann, D., & Loewenstein, G. (2020). Measuring information preferences. Management Science. *67*(1), 126–145. https://doi.org/10.1287/mnsc.2019.3543

Ijzerman, H., Lewis, N. A. Jr., Przybylski, A. K., Weinstein, N., DeBruine, K., Ritchie, S. J., et al. (2020). Use caution when applying behavioural science to policy. *Nature Human Behaviour, 4,* 1092–1094.

Janssen, E., van Osch, L., de Vries, H., & Lechner, L. (2013). The influence of narrative risk communication on feelings of cancer risk. *British Journal of Health Psychology, 18,* 407–419.

Jarke, H., Ruggeri, K., Graeber, J., Tünte, M. R., Ojinaga-Alfageme, O., Verra, S., et al. (2022). Health behavior and decision-making in healthcare. In K. Ruggeri (ed.), *Psychology and Behavioral Economics: Applications for Public Policy* (pp. 71–98). Oxon: Routledge.

John, P. (2021). Let's walk before we can run: The uncertain demand from policymakers for trials. *Behavioural Public Policy*, 5(1), 112–116.

Kahneman, D. (2003). A perspective on judgement and choice: Mapping bounded rationality. *American Psychologist*, 58(9), 697–720. https://doi .org/10.1037/0003-066X.58.9.697

Kahneman, D. (2011). *Thinking, Fast and Slow*. London: Penguin.

Kahneman, D., & Tversky, A. (1974). Judgement under uncertainty: Heuristics and biases. *Science*, 185(4157), 1124–1131. https://doi.org/10.1017/CBO9780 511809477.002

Kaufmann, T. H., Lilleholt, L., Bohm, R., Zettler, I., & Heck, D. W. (2022). Sensitive attitudes and adherence to recommendations during the COVID-19 pandemic: Comparing direct and indirect questioning techniques. *Personality and Individual Differences*, 190, 111–525.

Kim, H. K., & Niederdeppe, J. (2013). Exploring optimistic bias and the integrative model of behavioral prediction in the context of a campus influenza outbreak. *Journal of Health Communication*, 18(2), 206–222. https://doi.org/10.1080/10 810730.2012.688247

Korn, L., Böhm, R., Meier, N. W., & Betsch, C. (2020). Vaccination as a social contract. *Proceedings of the National Academy of Sciences*, 117(26), 14890–14899.

Levy, M., & Tasoff, J. (2017). Exponential-growth bias and overconfidence. *Journal of Economic Psychology*, 58, 1–14.

List, J. A., & Metcalfe, R. (2014). Field experiments in the developed world: An introduction. *Oxford Review of Economic Policy*, 30(4), 585–596.

Loewenstein, G. (1996). Out of control: Visceral influences on behaviour. *Organizational Behavior and Human Decision Processes*, 65(3), 272–292.

Loewenstein, G. (2005a). Hot-cold empathy gaps and medical decision making. *Health Psychology*, 24(4S), S49–S56.

Loewenstein, G. (2005b). Projection bias in medical decision making. *Medical Decision Making*, 25(1), 96–105.

Loewenstein, G., Hsee, C., Weber, E., & Welch, R. (2001). Risk as feelings. *Psychological Bulletin*, 127(2), 267–286.

Loewenstein, G., O'Donoghue, T., & Rabin, M. (2003). Projection bias in predicting future utility. *Quarterly Journal of Economics*, 118(4), 1209–1248.

Lu, J. G., Jin, P., & English, A. S. (2021). Collectivism predicts mask use during COVID-19. *Proceedings of the National Academy of Sciences*, 118, e2021793118.

Lu, Y.-C., Shu, B.-C., Chang, Y.-Y., & Lung, F.-W. (2006). The mental health of hospital workers dealing with severe acute respiratory syndrome. *Psychotherapy and Psychosomatics*, 75, 370–375.

Ludvik, N., Boschen, M. J., & Neumann, D. L. (2015). Effective behavioural strategies for reducing disgust in contamination related OCD. *Clinical Psychology Review*, 42, 116–129.

Lunn, P. D., Belton, C. A., Lavin, C., McGowan, F. P., Timmons, S., & Robertson, D. A. (2020). Using behavioral science to help fight the coronavirus. *Journal of Behavioral Public Administration*, 3(1), 1–15. https://doi.org/10.30636/jbpa.31.147.

McLamore, Q., Syropoulos, S., Leidner, B., Hirschberger, G., Young, K., Zein, R. A., et al. (2022). Trust in scientific information mediates associations between conservatism and coronavirus responses in the U.S., but few other nations. *Scientific Reports*, 12(1), 3724. https://doi.org/10.1038/s41598-022-07508-6

Milkman, K. L., Beshears, J., Choi, J. J., Laibson, D., & Madrian, B. C. (2011). Using implementation intentions prompts to enhance influenza vaccination rates. *Proceedings of the National Academy of Sciences*, 108, 10415–10420.

Milkman, K. L., Beshears, J., Choi, J. J., Laibson, D., & Madrian, B. C. (2013). Planning prompts as a means of increasing preventive screening rates. *Preventive Medicine*, 56, 92–93.

Milkman, K. L., Gandhi, L., Ellis, S. F., Graci, H. N., Gromet, D. M., Mobarak, R. S., et al. (2022). A citywide experiment testing the impact of geographically targeted, high-payoff vaccine lotteries. *Nature Human Behaviour*, 6, 1515–1524.

Miller, S. M. (1987). Monitoring and blunting: Validation of a questionnaire to assess styles of information seeking under threat. *Journal of Personality and Social Psychology*, 52, 345–353.

Morrell, H. E. R., Lapsley, D. K., & Halpern-Felsher, B. L. (2016). Subjective invulnerability and perceptions of tobacco-related benefits predict adolescent smoking behavior. *Journal of Early Adolescence*, 36(5), 679–703. https://doi.org/10.1177/0272431615578274

Olatunji, B. O., Cisler, J., McKay, D., & Phillips, M. L. (2010). Is disgust associated with psychopathology? Emerging research in the anxiety disorders. *Psychiatry Research*, 175, 1–10.

Oster, E., Shoulson, I., & Dorsey, E. R. (2013). Optimal expectations and limited medical testing: Evidence from Huntingdon disease. *American Economic Review*, 103(2), 804–830.

Page, L., Savage, D. A., & Torgler, B. (2014). Variation in risk seeking behaviour following large losses: A natural experiment. *European Economic Review*. https://doi.org/10.1016/j.euroecorev.2014.04.009

Papageorge, N. W., Zahn, M. V., Belot, M., van den Broek-Altenburg, E., Choi, S., Jamison, J. C., & Tripodi, E. (2021). Socio-demographic factors associated with self-protecting behavior during the Covid-19 pandemic. *Journal of Population Economics*, 34(2), 691–738.

Pink, S., Chu, J., Druckman, J., Rand, D., & Willer, R. (2021). Elite party cues increase vaccination intentions among Republicans. *Proceedings of National Academy of Sciences*, 118(32), e2106559118. https://doi.org/10.1073/pnas.2106559118.

Prelec, D., & Loewenstein, G. (1991). Decision-making over time and under uncertainty: A common approach. *Management Science*, 37, 770–786.

Quiggin, J. (2003). Background risk in generalized expected utility. *Economic Theory*, 22, 607–611.

Rabb, N., Bowers, J., Glick, D., Wilson, K. H., & Yokum, D. (2022a). The influence of social norms varies with 'others' groups: Evidence from COVID-19 vaccination intentions. *Proceedings of the National Academy of Sciences*, 119, e2118770119.

Rabb, N., Glick, D., Houston, A., Bowers, J., & Yokum, D. (2021). No evidence that collective-good appeals best promote COVID-related health behaviors. *Proceedings of the National Academy of Sciences*, 118(14), e2100662118. https://doi.org/10.1073/pnas.2100662118

Rabb, N., Swindal, M., Glick, D., Bowers, J., Tomasulo, A., Oyelami, Z., et al. (2022b). Evidence from a statewide vaccination RCT shows the limits of nudges. *Nature*, 604, E1–E7.

Ruggeri, K., Stock, F., Haslam, S. A., Capraro, V., Boggio, P., Ellemers, N., et al. (2024). A synthesis of evidence for policy from behavioural science during COVID-19. *Nature*, 625, 134–147.

Saaksvuori, L., Betsch, C., Nohynek, H., Salo, H., Sivela, J., & Bohm, R. (2022). Information nudges for influenza vaccination: Evidence from a large-scale cluster-randomized controlled trial in Finland. *PLoS Medicine*, 19, e1003919.

Saccardo, S., Dai, H., Han, M., Roh, L., Raja, N., Vangala, S., et al. (2022). The impact and limits of nudges: Evidence from large-scale RCTs. *SSRN Electronic Journal*. https://doi.org/10.2139/ssrn.3971192

Saha, S., Komaromy, M., Koepsell, T. D., & Bindman, A. B. (1999). Patient-physician racial concordance and the perceived quality and use of health care. *Archives of Internal Medicine*, 159(9), 997–1004.

Said, F., Afzal, U., & Turner, G. (2015). Risk taking and risk learning after a rare event: Evidence from a field experiment in Pakistan. *Journal of Economic Behavior & Organization*, 118, 167–183.

Santos, H. C., Goren, A., Chabris, C. F., & Meyer, M. N. (2021). Effect of targeted behavioral science messages on COVID-19 vaccination registration among employees of a large health system: A randomized trial. *JAMA Network Open*, 4(7), e2118702.

Seres, G., Balleyer, A. H., Cerutti, N., Danilov, A., Friedrichsen, J., Liu, Y., & Süer, M. (2021a). Face masks increase compliance with physical distancing recommendations during the COVID-19 pandemic. *Journal of the Economic Science Association*, 7(2), 139–158.

Seres, G., Balleyer, A., Cerutti, N., Friedrichsen, J., & Süer, M. (2021b). Face mask use and physical distancing before and after mandatory masking: No evidence on risk compensation in public waiting lines. *Journal of Economic Behavior and Organization*, 192(December), 765–781. https://doi.org/10.1016/j.jebo.2021.10.032

Serra-Garcia, M., & Szech, N. (2022). Incentives and defaults can increase COVID-19 vaccine intensions and test demand. *Management Science*, 69(2), 1037–1049. https://doi.org/10.1287/mnsc.2022.4405.

Singh, S., Shaikh, M., Hauck, K., & Miraldo, M. (2021). Impacts of introducing and lifting nonpharmaceutical interventions on COVID-19 daily growth rate and compliance in the United States. *Proceedings of the National Academy of Sciences of the United States of America*, 118(12), 1–9.

Slovic, P., Finucane, M. L., Peters, E., & MacGregor, D. G. (2004). Risk as analysis and risk as feelings: Some thoughts about affect, reason, risk, and rationality. *Risk Analysis*, 24, 311–322.

Slovic, P., Finucane, M. L., Peters, E., & MacGregor, D. G. (2007). The affect heuristic. *European Journal of Operational Research*, 177, 1333–1352.

Smith, L. E., Amlôt, R., Weinman, J., Yiend, J., & Rubin, G. J. (2017). A systematic review of factors affecting vaccine uptake in young children. *Vaccine*, 35(45), 6059–6069.

Sprengholz, P., Eitze, S., Felgendreff, L., Korn, L., & Betsch, C. (2021). Money is not everything: Experimental evidence that payments do not increase willingness to be vaccinated against COVID-19. *Journal of Medical Ethics*, 47(8), 547–548. https://doi.org/10.1136/medethics-2020-107122

Stango, V., & Zinman, J. (2009). Exponential growth bias and household finance. *Journal of Finance*, 64(6), 2807–2849.

Steinert, J., Sternberg, H., Prince, H., Fasolo, B., Galizzi, M. M., Büthe, T., & Veltri, G. A. (2022). COVID-19 vaccine hesitancy in eight European countries: Prevalence, determinants and heterogeneity. *Science Advances*, 8(17). https://doi.org/10.1126/sciadv.abm9825

Taha, S. A., Matheson, K., & Anisman, H. (2013). The 2009 H1N1 influenza pandemic: The role of threat, coping, and media trust on vaccination intentions in Canada. *Journal of Health Communication*, 18(3), 278–290. https://doi.org/10.1080/10810730.2012.727960

Thaler, R. H. (1985). Mental accounting and consumer choice. *Marketing Science*, 4(3), 199–214. https://doi.org/10.1287/mksc.4.3.199

Thaler, R. H., & Sunstein, C. R. (2008). *Nudge: Improving Decisions about Health, Wealth, and Happiness*. Princeton, NJ: Princeton University Press.

Thirumurthy, H., Milkman, K. L., Volpp, K. G., Buttenheim, A. M., & Pope, D. G. (2022). Association between statewide financial incentive programs and COVID-19 vaccination rates. *PLoS ONE*, 17, e0263425.

Torres, C., Ogbu-Nwobodo, L., Alsan, M., Stanford, F. C., Banerjee, A., Breza, E., et al. (2021). Effect of physician-delivered COVID-19 public health messages and messages acknowledging racial inequity on black and white adults' knowledge, beliefs, and practices related to COVID-19: A randomized clinical trial. *JAMA Network Open*, 4(7), e2117115. https://doi.org/10.1001/jamanetworkopen.2021.17115

Trueblood, J. S., Sussman, A. B., & O'Leary, D. (2022). The role of risk preferences in responses to messaging about COVID-19 vaccine take-up. *Social Psychological and Personality Science*, 13(1), 311–319. https://doi.org/10.1177/1948550621999622

Tversky, A., & Kahneman, D. (1981). The framing of decisions and the psychology of choice. *Science*, 211, 173–178. https://doi.org/10.1007/978-1-4613-2391-4_2

Vietri, J. T., Li, M., Galvani, A. P., & Chapman, G. B. (2012). Vaccinating to help ourselves and others. *Medical Decision Making*, 32, 447–458.

Volpp, K. G., & Cannuscio, C. C. (2021). Incentives for immunity: Strategies for increasing Covid-19 vaccine uptake. *New England Journal of Medicine*, 385(1), e1.

Wagenaar, W. A., & Timmers, H. (1979). The pond-and-duckweed problem: Three experiments on the misperception of exponential growth. *Acta Psychologica*, 43, 239–251.

Weber, B. J., & Chapman, G. B. (2005a). The combined effects of risk and time on choices: Does uncertainty eliminate the immediacy effect? Does delay eliminate the certainty effect? *Organizational Behavior and Human Decision Processes*, 96, 104–118.

Weber, B. J., & Chapman, G. B. (2005b). Playing for peanuts: Why is risk seeking more common for low-stakes gambles? *Organizational Behavior and Human Decision Processes*, 97, 31–46.

Weisman, C. S., & Teitelbaum, M. A. (1985). Physician gender and the physician-patient relationship: Recent evidence and relevant questions. *Social Science and Medicine*, 20(11), 1119–1127.

Zettler, I., Schild, C., Lilleholt, L., Kroencke, L., Utesch, T., Moshagen, M., et al. (2022). The role of personality in COVID-19 related perceptions, evaluations, and behaviours: Findings across five samples, nine traits, and 17 criteria. *Social Psychological and Personality Science*, 13, 299–310.

3   Adaptation, COVID-19, and Climate Change

George Loewenstein and Archie Kinnane

3.1   INTRODUCTION

In this chapter, we examine connections between COVID-19 and climate, the two major crises we have been living through over the past few years. How has the former affected the world's collective response to the latter? What lessons have people learned about climate change from COVID-19, and what lessons should we (and policymakers) learn?

Clearly, COVID-19 and climate change are different in important ways that have implications for the answers to these questions. One important difference is that COVID-19, in a sense, came out of nowhere. There had been previous outbreaks of disease (e.g., H1N1, severe acute respiratory syndrome, Ebola), which could be viewed as 'wake-up calls', but each of these was successfully contained. And there were some voices warning about the potential for a pandemic, for example, Bill Gates and movies such as *Contagion*, but looking back one can always find Cassandras. As Paul Krugman expressed it in a recent opinion piece dealing with economics,[1] 'Essentially nobody saw the 2008 financial meltdown coming (other than people who predicted many other crises that didn't happen).'

Climate change is, in this respect, very different. It was identified as a threat decades ago, and since then it has unfolded very much as, or even more cataclysmically than, scientists predicted, becoming increasingly destructive and difficult to combat as time passes and no concerted remedial action is taken.

Although the extended warning might seem to make climate change easier to deal with than COVID-19, in fact the opposite is

---

[1] www.nytimes.com/2022/02/08/opinion/economic-theory-monetary-policy.html

probably the case. For reasons related to our powers of adaptation – ultimately the central theme of this chapter – humans seem to be far better at mobilising against a sudden threat, such as a military invasion, than against one that emerges slowly by fits and starts (Loewenstein, 2009; Loewenstein & Schwartz, 2010).

There are other important differences between the two problems. The biggest success in fighting the pandemic has been the development of vaccines. These cost billions to develop, and their success was by no means assured. However, the cost of developing and producing them was well within the budget of affluent countries or even pharmaceutical companies with deep pockets. When it comes to climate change, many likewise turn to new technology to provide hope for a solution. Technological development certainly has a role to play; the remarkable decline in cost for renewable energy and battery technologies over the past decade has opened many more possibilities for governments, businesses, or individuals aiming to reduce their emissions. Unfortunately, it is unlikely (or at the very least cannot be relied upon) that any 'breakthrough' technology – gigaton scale carbon capture, nuclear fission, and so on – that is not in deployment today will become widespread in time to stave off the worst impacts. The uncertainty is greater, the physical limitations are more restrictive, and the speed of deployment likely much slower (Bel & Joseph, 2018).[2]

Perhaps the most important difference between the two crises is that the pandemic can be, and has to some extent been, dealt with at a national level. Different countries have responded differently, with some (like New Zealand and China) aiming for zero rates, while, at the opposite extreme, countries such as Brazil have done little to mitigate spread and instead downplayed the pandemic's severity. These

---

[2] www.repository.cam.ac.uk/bitstream/handle/1810/299414/REP_Absolute_Zero_V3_20200505.pdf?sequence=9&isAllowed=y; This is not to say that research and development into new technology should not continue, as it absolutely should; this is simply to say that 2050 – many countries' target date for zero emissions – is twenty-six years away, while technological transitions typically take much longer than that.

differences are helpful in providing information about the costs and benefits of different policy approaches.[3]

Climate change is almost infinitely more difficult on this dimension. Carbon gases released anywhere in the world are rapidly assimilated into the world's atmosphere, so that any individual or even nation that substantially cut its emissions would incur the full costs of doing so but capture at most only a tiny fraction of the world-wide benefits. Of course, there are substantial co-benefits to climate action that are experienced locally, perhaps most notably in reduced air pollution. But it cannot be denied that climate change, unlike COVID-19, is a classic case of the pernicious tragedy of the commons (Hardin, 1968; Ostrom, 1990).

One lamentable parallel between COVID-19 and climate change is that they have both become highly politicised and hence subject to the forces of polarisation that are upending US democracy and also manifesting in many other countries, including the United Kingdom to some degree. In the United States, for example, 78 per cent of those leaning Democrat but only 21 per cent of those leaning Republican said that climate change should be a priority for the president and Congress.[4] Likewise, though not as extreme, Democrats and Republicans have substantially different views on what measures should be taken in response to COVID-19, and these differences have increased over the course of the pandemic.[5] For both problems, the existence of large sectors of the population with diametrically opposite scientific beliefs and linked opposing views on policy makes it exceptionally difficult to enact, and even more difficult to implement and garner compliance with, any kind of coherent policy.

---

[3] Despite the local orientation of most countries' policies, the pandemic is inherently a transnational phenomenon. For example, when affluent nations attempted to protect their own populations by first vaccinating locally, the proliferation of the virus in less developed countries enabled mutations.

[4] www.pewresearch.org/fact-tank/2020/02/28/more-americans-see-climate-change-as-a-priority-but-democrats-are-much-more-concerned-than-republicans/

[5] www.pewresearch.org/fact-tank/2021/03/24/despite-wide-partisan-gaps-in-views-of-many-aspects-of-the-pandemic-some-common-ground-exists/

How has the emergence of COVID-19 affected the worldwide response to climate change? Beyond the direct effects of COVID-19 on individual activities that affect carbon emissions (e.g., driving, flying), one can imagine various possible linkages. One possible linkage has to do with limitations on human time and attention; fear of COVID-19 and the need to deal with it very likely occupied attention that might have, in the absence of such an all-consuming disaster, been allocated to other problems, including climate change. It is natural that people have a limited capacity to worry about different problems (though we are not aware of empirical work directly addressing this issue), so increasing anxiety about one problem will tend to displace anxiety about others. Hints of such a connection can be seen both in Google searches for, and news coverage of climate-related and COVID-19-related terms. Both searches for and media coverage of climate change declined when COVID-19 first came to the fore, in February of 2020.

This could be related to the psychological concept of a 'prominence effect' (Tversky et al., 1988). Prominence can be thought of as an 'attentional spotlight' and has been shown to drive our decision-making. In a series of experiments illustrating this effect, subjects were allowed to construct two 'prizes', with the instruction that both options should be equally appealing to them, individually. One iteration featured subjects choosing between two bundles, both comprised of a different combination of cash and gift cards to a store they liked. One bundle had more cash than the other, but the value of the gift cards in the lower-cash bundle was set by the subject such that they felt both packages were exactly equal in value. When they were then asked to pick, however, 88 per cent of subjects picked the bundle with more cash. In theory, the options were exactly equal – the subjects stipulated that themselves. And yet, when push came to shove, the most prominent dimension (amount of hard cash) won out. Slovic argues that the most prominent dimension drives decision-making even when it is theoretically offset by secondary features because it is easier to defend to ourselves: 'I went for the option with the most cash, of course.' Concerns over COVID-19 have, with good reason, featured prominently for many of us during the past several years, which could have elbowed climate change out of our attentional spotlight. Perhaps relatedly, despite lots of talk about the opportunity for a 'green recovery' from the economic impacts of the pandemic, President Biden's most significant climate legislation has been stalled for months, while the Organisation for Economic Co-operation and Development found that just 4 per cent of the roughly USD 17 trillion devoted to COVID-19 recovery measures has positive environmental impacts.[6]

Another possible linkage working in the opposite direction could be that, after living through COVID-19, people might take the potential for disaster more seriously, enhancing the public's appreciation of the threat of climate change. We see no evidence of such a linkage.

Many of us who are desperately worried about climate change have had the hope that some cataclysmic event might act as a 'wake-up call', but loud alarms have been ringing – for example, the fires in Australia, California, and Siberia, the flood in Germany, the heat dome in the Pacific Northwest – and there is no evidence that any of these events have had much impact. To some extent, this chapter's theme of adaptation suggests that waiting for such a 'wake-up' moment may be akin to watching the proverbial frog in gradually heating water, hoping it will jump out before the boil.

What should policymakers learn from COVID-19 when it comes to climate change? This is the focus of the remainder of our chapter. Returning to a psychological phenomenon – adaptation – touched upon briefly, the gist of our argument is as follows:

- Research on adaptation shows that people are able to adapt rapidly and dramatically to changing circumstances.
- However, people underestimate their own rate of adaptation and how quickly they will learn to cope with a new situation. As a result, people will often resist change that they would end up being comfortable with.

---

[6] www.oecd.org/coronavirus/en/themes/green-recovery

- Unfortunately, policymakers are subject to the same bias. This under-appreciation of adaptation discourages policymakers from taking the types of bold initiatives that are required to deal with problems like climate change.

3.2 THE POWER OF ADAPTATION AND LEARNING

People can adapt remarkably well to a very wide range of adverse situations, including disabilities as dramatic as paraplegia, and even quadriplegia, and to horrible conditions such as solitary confinement (Frederick & Loewenstein, 1999). Adaptation involves a range of mechanisms, including, often, changes in the use of time, bodily changes (e.g., changes in musculature), and changes in preferences and even in personality and identity.

Adaptation is closely related to and frequently causally connected to learning, in part because adapting to circumstances such as paraplegia often involves the mastery of new technologies (e.g., special means of transportation). Many studies in both psychology and economics document the speed and functional form of learning both for individuals – for example, mirror tracing (Wilson, 1928) and cigar making (Crossman, 1959) – and for organisations – for example, Liberty ships in the Second World War (Thompson, 2001; Thornton & Thompson, 2001). Most research shows that learning follows a 'power law' – rapid to begin with but slowing down over time.

Both COVID-19 and climate change require massive adaptation as well as learning, both at the individual and organisational level. As Chater (2020: 5) writes, 'COVID-19 and the lockdowns and other restrictions imposed by governments around the world, in response to the virus, has required a huge amount of behaviour change. Individuals, businesses and governments have, despite great hardship, and disruption, responded remarkably rapidly.'

Likewise, the only possible rapid and effective response to climate change would require dramatic changes in lifestyles. This is not a moral argument; it is a practical one. The defining attributes of lifestyle change to reduce global emissions are that (1) it can happen nearly immediately and (2) to have the most impact, it would be concentrated among those with the means to make these sorts of changes. In fact, if the top 10 per cent of global emitters – a group to which nearly every middle- and upper-class person in the United States belongs – reduced their carbon emissions to the EU average (a group that enjoys a very high standard of living), then global emissions would drop a stunning 35 per cent.[7] There is no physical reason that this cannot happen this year. On the opposite end of the spectrum, many utility-scale infrastructure projects currently in the development pipeline will not even be completed by the time we exceed the Paris Agreement's carbon budget (if emissions remain near today's levels and deployment timelines are not dramatically shortened). To be effective, we cannot expect individuals to change their lifestyles unilaterally, of course; we need policies to lead people to these changes and policymakers who have learned to acknowledge and resist this same bias.

Perhaps the most important factor that determines the speed and extent of adaptation is certainty. When someone knows that a change is certain, and permanent, they will initiate the psychic and behavioural changes required to adapt. Uncertainty, perhaps more than any factor, impedes adaptation, by discouraging individuals from putting in the time and effort required for learning.

There is a lot of both non-fiction and fiction that talks about this phenomenon. In his book *The Desert and the Sea: 977 Days Captive on the Somali Pirate Coast*, for example, Michael Moore (2018: 274) discusses one of his captors named Bashko, who 'kept my hope alive with rumours of negotiations. He made it sound as if I would go free in a matter of days. Of course, I was happy to believe him. But then hope is like heroin for a hostage, and it can be just as destructive.' Likewise, in a novel about a woman's obsession with a mediocre artist, Lena Andersson (2015: 142) writes:

> Everything in existence wants to live, and hope is no exception. It is a parasite that lives and thrives on the most innocent of tissue. Its

[7] www.c40.org/news//making-our-collective-response-to-climate-change-more-equitable

survival lies in a well-developed ability to ignore everything that is not favourable to its growth while pouncing on anything that will feed it and help it to live on. Then it ruminates on these crumbs until every trace of nourishment has been extracted from them.

Several pages later she continues: 'Hope has to be starved to death if it is not to beguile and bedazzle its host. Hope can only be killed by the brutality of clarity' (2015: 195).

One of the few (indeed, possibly the only) work to rigorously examine the consequences of uncertainty for adaptation is an article by Dylan Smith et al. (2009). Titled 'Happily hopeless: Adaptation to a permanent but not to a temporary disability', the article surveyed patients who received either a permanent or potentially reversible colostomy or ileostomy (a surgery in which either the large or small intestine is connected to a tube emptying into a pouch). Each patient was interviewed at three points in time – a week, a month, and six months after they were released from the hospital – and indicated their well-being using two different scales. One week after the operation, as one might expect, people with the potentially reversible ostomies reported marginally higher happiness and life satisfaction than those with the permanent colostomies. But tracking them over time reveals an interesting pattern: people with potentially reversible colostomies got more and more miserable over time, but people with the permanent colostomies improved in happiness and life satisfaction until they were virtually indistinguishable from healthy people. When people know that something is irreversible they generally adapt to it.

What does this have to do with public policy? In our view, it says that policies if implemented decisively, with no perceived chance of reversal, will be adapted to rapidly; people will take the time and trouble to learn how to accommodate to the change. In many countries, COVID-19 policy has not followed this prescription but instead presented case studies in ambiguity and vacillation. For example, in the United States, instead of just mandating vaccination and masking for the wide range of activities exposing individuals to other people (and vice versa), different states, workplaces, and even public establishments such as restaurants each made their own policy. To encourage vaccination, states employed a wide range of different strategies, such as entering vaccinated individuals into lotteries, or strange inducements such as donuts, a chance to have dinner with New Jersey's governor, or even a free lap dance at Larry Flynt's Hustler Club.[8] These tactics send a variety of perverse signals, such as 'we are paying you to get vaccinated because it is in the public interest but not your personal interest' or 'vaccination is a matter of personal preference'. Given these wishy-washy policies and mixed messages, it should be no surprise that vaccination and even mask-wearing became politicised.

When it comes to climate change, adaptation is a double-edged sword: reducing our likelihood to respond to the destructive changes in the biosphere we will witness every year but increasing the policy ceiling for how rapidly we can make, and become happy with, large individual and societal changes.

On the downside, adaptation weakens our response to severe problems, if they are ongoing. With climate change, we may keep adjusting our baselines so quickly that we do not notice that what we are experiencing in the present may have once seemed inconceivable: days or weeks where you cannot go outside, longer and longer periods without power, fewer and fewer options at the supermarket. In his 1965 book, *Man Adapting*, René Dubos (1965: 278) made a prophetic observation: 'This very adaptability enables us to become adjusted to conditions and habits, which will eventually destroy the values most characteristic of human life.'

On the upside, however, adaptation can enable the kinds of substantive policy responses that are so desperately needed. Rather than adapting to an objectively crueller and more dangerous world, policymakers could instead ask people to utilise their surprising capacity for

---

[8] https://nymag.com/intelligencer/2021/05/lotteries-doughnuts-joints-weird-vaccine-incentives.html

adaptation to accept the changes we need to reduce, and then end, net carbon emissions. Research suggests that, freed from the horrifying spectre of mass annihilation, people would quickly become as happy as they were back in the days when they were pumping thirty-five billion tons of CO_2 into the atmosphere each year.

3.3 UNDERESTIMATION OF ADAPTATION AND LEARNING

Beyond the ubiquity of adaptation and learning, and the importance of certainty as a moderating factor, another regularity revealed by empirical literature on these topics is that people tend to *underestimate* their own rate and degree of both adaptation and learning. Diverse research shows that healthy people believe they would be more miserable with serious health conditions than those who have them report that they are: people think they would be miserable if they were disabled, but disabled people say that they are not all that bad off. In one study (Riis et al., 2005) patients who were on hemodialysis were given 'experience sampling' devices that beeped at random points in time and asked them various questions, including about their momentary mood. Dialysis patients experienced positive moods the majority of their waking hours (and, indeed, were almost indistinguishable from a healthy comparison group), but the sample of healthy individuals predicted that dialysis patients would experience unpleasant moods the majority of the time. Another study (Ubel et al., 2005) tested two major explanations for this misprediction and obtained strong evidence that it is caused by an under-appreciation of adaptation. When people were asked to simply predict how they would fare if they were paraplegic, they made the same mistake – that is, underestimating their well-being – as in earlier studies. However, when they were first instructed to remember a life experience that was emotionally difficult for them, then to think about whether their emotions changed over time and whether they ended up feeling worse than, about the same as, or better than they would have predicted right after the experience, they subsequently predicted that they would not be so unhappy if they were paraplegic – that is, they appreciated that they would similarly adapt to paraplegia.

Other studies have documented people's under-prediction of their own speed and extent of learning (Kornell & Bjork, 2009; Le Yaouanq & Schwardmann, 2019). In one series of studies (Billeter et al., 2011) experimental participants worked at a task (mirror-tracing, knot-tying, or playing a computer game called 'guitar hero') repeatedly. They were asked to predict their own performance, before they had any experience on the task, right after they had initial experience, and after each round of learning for future rounds. Before they did any mirror-tracing, they anticipated that they would be much better at each task than they turned out to be. However, the moment they had a little bit of experience with a task they became much more, and in fact overly, pessimistic – an effect previously documented and labelled the 'underconfidence with practice effect' (Koriat et al., 2002). Moreover, and consistent with another body of literature (Kornell & Hausman, 2017), they continued to underestimate their learning over time, even after substantial experience with the task.

What are the consequences for policy of under-appreciation of adaptation and learning? When policy changes are introduced, the people who are affected are likely to be especially upset because they fail to predict how quickly they will adapt and learn how to deal with a new environment. This initial, though often short-lasting, hesitation comes from an underestimation of both their rapid capacity for adaptation and, relatedly, of the speed with which they would be able to master the new situation. Moreover, policymakers make the same errors, underestimating the speed at which the public would adapt, which makes them reluctant to enact the types of far-reaching policies required to combat serious problems.

3.4   THE ROLE OF BEHAVIOURAL POLICY

A lot of academics who are focused on behavioural policy have been working on different types of interventions to encourage people to wear masks, get vaccinated, and other health behaviours. Economists have been very focused on relatively subtle interventions such as information campaigns to increase trust – the thought being that if we only we can get people to trust in the vaccine or in those administering it, they will get vaccinated. Our view, however, is that far more heavy-handed approaches are called for. Some of these approaches are articulated in a recent piece (Volpp et al., 2021) advocating firm policies to encourage vaccination, such as restricting access to public venues and workplaces by people who refuse to be vaccinated.

What about climate change? As for COVID-19, our view is that behavioural policy has not played an especially constructive role when it comes to climate change. Behavioural policy has tended to focus on proposing and testing individualistic interventions – for example, green energy nudges (see, e.g., Loewenstein & Chater, 2017). Not only do such interventions have little hope of 'moving the needle' on climate change but, as shown in an experimental article titled 'Nudging out support for a carbon tax' (Hagmann et al., 2019), the common belief that they *can* move the needle makes people support them at the expense of the more substantive interventions that are so sorely needed. We all know that a hefty carbon tax (or possibly cap and trade) is one of the most effective responses to climate change (Cramton et al., 2017: 268). A carbon tax would cut down on the extraction and use of fossil fuels and would accelerate the development of alternative sources of energy, transmission, and storage.

Behavioural economics, and specifically a consideration of adaptation and learning, suggests that a carbon tax would be much more rapidly and broadly accepted than policymakers might fear. As Chater (2020) writes in yet another passage (page 10) in his article with which we will end:

> The main lesson of COVID is that adaptation can occur surprisingly quickly – and much more quickly than we typically anticipate... Changes to ways of operating which are initially slow, costly and inefficient, may become highly effective over time. This is an important motivation for enhanced short- and

medium-term government policy support, where opportunities to move to better ways of living and working that may be socially and economically, highly cost-effective in the long term.

Our conclusions are generally pessimistic: on many dimensions, COVID-19 poses a less severe challenge than climate change, yet our collective response to COVID-19 leaves much to be desired. Adaptation has much to do with the reason. However, adaptation is a two-edged sword that could also be exploited to enact the kinds of substantive policies that are so sorely needed to deal with climate change. An appreciation of the power of adaptation could give policymakers confidence that the public would, in relatively short order, adapt both behaviourally and hedonically to the types of policies that are so desperately needed.

REFERENCES

Andersson, L. (2015). *Willful Disregard: A Novel about Love*. Picador.

Bel, G., & Joseph, S. (2018). Climate change mitigation and the role of technological change: Impact on selected headline targets of Europe's 2020 climate and energy package. *Renewable and Sustainable Energy Reviews*, 82, 3798–3807.

Billeter, D., Kalra, A., & Loewenstein, G. (2011). Underpredicting learning after initial experience with a product. *Journal of Consumer Research*, 37, 723–736.

Chater, N. (2020). Net zero after Covid: Behavioural principles for building back better. Policy Paper, UK Committee on Climate Change. www.h2knowledgecentre.com/content/policypaper1407

Cramton, P., MacKay, D. J., Ockenfels, A., & Stoft, S. (2017). *Global Carbon Pricing: The Path to Climate Cooperation*. The MIT Press.

Crossman, E. R. (1959). A theory of the acquisition of speed-skill. *Ergonomics*, 2(2), 153–166.

Dubos, R. (1965). *Man Adapting*. Yale University Press.

Frederick, S., & Loewenstein, G. (1999). Hedonic adaptation. In D. Kahneman, E. Diener, and N. Schwarz (eds.), *Wellbeing: The Foundations of Hedonic Psychology* (pp. 302–329).

Hagmann, D., Ho, E., & Loewenstein, G. (2019). Nudging out support for a carbon tax. *Nature: Climate Change*, (6), 484–489.

Hardin, G. (1968). The tragedy of the commons: The population problem has no technical solution; it requires a fundamental extension in morality. *Science*, 162(3859), 1243–1248.

Horn, S., & Loewenstein, G. (2021). Underestimating learning by doing. Social Science Research Network. https://ssrn.com/abstract=3941441 or http://dx.doi.org/10.2139/ssrn.3941441

Koriat, A., Sheffer, L., & Ma'ayan, H. (2002). Comparing objective and subjective learning curves: Judgments of learning exhibit increased underconfidence with practice. *Journal of Experimental Psychology: General*, 131(2), 147–162.

Kornell, N., & Bjork, R. A. (2009). A stability bias in human memory: Overestimating remembering and underestimating learning. *Journal of Experimental Psychology: General*, 138(4), 449–468.

Kornell, N., & Hausman, H. (2017). Performance bias: Why judgments of learning are not affected by learning. *Memory & Cognition*, 45(8), 1270–1280.

Le Yaouanq, Y., & Schwardmann, P. (2019). Learning about one's self. Working Paper 7455. CESifo. Social Science Research Network. https://ssrn.com/abstract=3338809 or http://dx.doi.org/10.2139/ssrn.3338809

Loewenstein, G. (2009). Psychological impediments to taking action on global warming (and implications for what must happen in order for action to occur). In A. Monsarrat and K. Skinner (eds.), *Renewing Globalization and Economic Growth in a Post-crisis World: The Future of the G-20 Agenda* (pp. 124–127). Carnegie Mellon University Press.

Loewenstein, G., & Chater, N. (2017). Putting nudges in perspective. *Behavioural Public Policy*, 1(1), 26–53.

Loewenstein, G., & Schwartz, D. (2010). Nothing to fear but a lack of fear: Climate change and the fear deficit. G8 Magazine, G8/G20 Summit 2010, 60–62.

Moore, M. S. (2018). *The Desert and the Sea: 977 Days Captive on the Somali Pirate Coast*. Harper Collins.

Ostrom, E. (1990). *Governing the Commons: The Evolution of Institutions for Collective Action*. Cambridge University Press.

Riis, J., Loewenstein, G., Baron, J., Jepson, C., Fagerlin, A., & Ubel, P. A. (2005). Ignorance of hedonic adaptation to hemodialysis: A study using ecological momentary assessment. *Journal of Experimental Psychology: General*, 134(1), 3.

Smith, D. M., Loewenstein, G., Jankovich, A. & Ubel, P. A. (2009). Happily hopeless: Adaptation to a permanent, but not to a temporary, disability. *Health Psychology*, 28(6), 787.

Thompson, P. (2001). How much did the liberty shipbuilders learn? New evidence for an old case study. *Journal of Political Economy*, 109(1), 103–137.

Thornton, R. A., & Thompson, P. (2001). Learning from experience and learning from others: An exploration of learning and spillovers in wartime shipbuilding. *American Economic Review*, 91(5), 1350–1368.

Tversky, A., Sattath, S., & Slovic, P. (1988). Contingent weighting in judgment and choice. *Psychological Review*, 95(3), 371–384. https://doi.org/10.1037/0033-295X.95.3.371

Ubel, P. A., Loewenstein, G., & Jepson, C. (2005). Disability and sunshine: Can hedonic predictions be improved by drawing attention to focusing illusions or emotional adaptation? *Journal of Experimental Psychology: Applied*, 11(2), 111.

Volpp, K. G., Loewenstein, G., & Buttenheim, A. M. (2021). Behaviorally informed strategies for a national COVID-19 vaccine promotion program. *JAMA*, 325(2), 125–126.

Wilson, F. T. (1928). Learning curves of boys of IQ's 76–148. *Journal of Educational Psychology*, 19(1), 50.

4 Risk-Taking, Risk Perception, and Risk Compensation in Times of COVID-19

Benno Guenther, Virginia Fedrigo, and Jet Sanders

4.1 INTRODUCTION

The onset of COVID-19 and its rapid global spread have had significant consequences on psychological state and behaviour (Eger et al., 2021; Mutz & Gerke, 2021; Serafini et al., 2020; Tee et al., 2020). An important feature of human experience and behaviour is decision-making, one key aspect of which is risk-taking (Kahneman & Tversky, 1979). Risk-taking is thought to be a trade-off between perceived risk in a situation and a tendency to act in light of risk. This is also called risk tolerance. Estimates of perceived risk have been particularly important during the COVID-19 pandemic, where behaviours that were previously deemed everyday activities, such as grocery shopping or taking public transport, harbour increased risk of contracting COVID-19. If contracting the disease is deemed a serious concern for one's health, these behaviours by extension are too. Some of the changes in behaviour and perception may be lasting even when an endemic phase is reached, such as continued increases in remote working, hand-washing, or elected social distancing as they have demonstrated to have benefits beyond reducing the spread of COVID-19. Thus, experiences over the three years of the COVID-19 pandemic may be an important predictor for experiences in post-pandemic times. In addition, they could offer insight for pandemic preparedness. In this chapter we summarise key insights on risk-taking prior to the pandemic and some of the most recent findings in relation to risk-taking in times of COVID-19.

4.2   RISK-TAKING PRIOR TO COVID-19

4.2.1   (Heterogeneity in) Risk Perception and Tolerance

Understanding risk-taking has been shown to be crucial in predicting behaviour across domains, including health and safety, finance, and ethical behaviours (Lejuez, 2002). Herein we make a distinction between the outcome behaviour (risk-taking), the tendency towards this behaviour (risk tolerance), and the perceived psychological costs of the behaviour (risk perception). Willingness to take risks can fluctuate between individuals and contexts and is not always predictable. Perceptions of risk are often emotional (also termed 'risk as feeling'; e.g., Slovic & Peters, 2006) and can be fuelled by public discourse. Similarly, studies have shown that risk-taking is heterogeneous across demographics and contexts. For example, men tend to take more risks than women (Byrnes et al., 1999; Croson & Gneezy, 2009; Vieider et al., 2015). It has also been shown that risk tolerance tends to decrease with age across different elicitation methods (Falk et al., 2018; Rolison et al., 2012). In one study conducted with 80,000 participants across 76 countries Falk et al. (2018) found men and younger participants to display higher risk tolerance. Other examples of heterogeneity in risk-taking include differences for behaviours such as gambling and financial risk-taking (Powell & Ansic, 1997) as well as risk-taking in situations such as car driving (Chen et al., 2000).

Many risk measures have been developed to measure heterogeneity in different contexts. Some of the common measures for risk tolerance include self-reported measures such as the Domain-Specific Risk-Taking (DOSPERT) scale (Weber et al., 2002) and the German Socioeconomic Panel (SOEP) survey questions (Dohmen et al., 2005) as well as incentive-compatible tasks or lotteries such as the Balloon Analog Risk Task (BART; Lejuez et al., 2002) and the Binswanger-Eckel and Grossman multiple lotteries task (BEG; Binswanger, 1980; Eckel & Grossman, 2002). Performance on these measures has been shown to predict some real-world risk-taking behaviour. For example,

Lejuez et al. (2003) found that BART could predict smoking behaviour. Similarly, the DOSPERT gambling subscale has been found to predict excessive stock trading (Markiewicz & Weber, 2013).

The impact of the COVID-19 pandemic on our daily lives is unprecedented, and we do not know what impact the drastic situational change has on individual risk perception and risk-taking. However, there is reason to believe that risk tolerance, and therefore risk-taking, may be affected by the changes in perceived risk of a global pandemic (as it is an almost omnipresent source of risk in the background of our daily lives). While the current pandemic is unprecedented, similar exogenous sources of risk, often called 'background risk', have been studied in the past and may offer some initial insights.

4.2.2 Background Risk

Background risk is a form of risk that cannot be avoided (or insured) (Fagereng et al., 2016) and thus differs from the risk in a typical risk-taking situation, where there is an element of volition and (active) choice involved about an outcome with (perceived) uncertainty (Trimpop, 1994). There is extensive literature around background risk in the financial domain. For example, Kimball (1990) suggests that such a risk, for example in the form of risky earnings, may result in a reduction of risky assets to reduce the overall risk exposure. This proposition is confirmed in a more recent study using Bank of Italy survey data (Guiso & Paiella, 2008).

Other forms of background risk or exogenous shocks of non-direct financial nature include natural disasters, war, and terrorism. There is some literature in these domains that investigates their impact on risk-taking. Some of the evidence suggests an increase in risk-seeking after a natural disaster or while exposed to a threat: for example, among evacuees of Hurricane Katrina (Eckel et al., 2009), poor households in Peru that were exposed to volcanic threat (Bchir & Willinger, 2013), and flooded households in Pakistan and Australia (Page et al., 2014; Said et al., 2015). Other studies, however, reach contrasting conclusions. They find more risk-averse behaviours following a disaster: for example, after a tsunami in Thailand (Cassar et al., 2017) and an earthquake or flood in Indonesia (Cameron & Shah, 2015).

4.2.3 Risk Compensation

Finally, a frequent point of discussion in the context of risk tolerance and risk-taking is the notion of risk compensation. The risk compensation hypothesis stipulates that individuals tend to adjust their behaviour in response to perceived levels of risk, becoming more risk-seeking when there is a lower sense of risk and vice versa (Wilde, 1998). A typical example is the idea that wearing a seat belt as the driver of a car may lead to increased risky driving such as speeding (Houston & Richardson, 2007). Studies that investigated the risk compensation hypothesis prior to the pandemic provide a mixed picture (Levym & Miller, 2000). For example, the concept of risk compensation has been studied in health contexts, separate from the pandemic. Marcus et al. (2013) looked at the usage of pre-exposure prophylaxis (PrEP), a daily drug designed to decrease the chance of contracting human immunodeficiency virus, and whether there is evidence for risk compensation among those who take PrEP and the riskiness of sexual behaviour. Participants (n=2,499) were randomised into two groups, the PrEP group and a placebo group. The authors found no evidence for increased rates of intercourse without a condom among those who believed they were receiving PrEP. Kasting et al. (2016) sought to understand whether vaccination with the human papilloma virus (HPV) vaccine increased risky sexual behaviours through a mechanism of risk compensation (a popular media narrative). A meta-analysis of twenty studies revealed no evidence for riskier sexual behaviours or increased rates of other sexually transmitted infections after HPV vaccination. Brewer et al. (2007), on the other hand, did find evidence that vaccination could lead to an increase in carelessness in the context of HPV vaccination.

4.3 RISK-TAKING IN TIMES OF COVID-19

4.3.1 Pre- and Post-pandemic Comparisons on Risk Perception and Risk Tolerance

While previous findings on background risk may offer a starting point for understanding the impact of COVID-19 on risk tolerance and decision-making, there is a growing body of literature that directly investigates risk tolerance during the pandemic and how – if at all – it may have changed relative to pre-pandemic times. Most of these studies used either self-reported questionnaires of perceived risk, risk tolerance, or risk-taking or incentive-compatible tasks, with an aim of understanding potential changes in risk-taking since the start of the pandemic.

Heo et al. (2021), for example, investigated the effect of the COVID-19 pandemic on financial risk tolerance based on a cross-sectional internet survey with a broad sample of $n=18,913$ household-level financial decision-makers in the United States. They found financial risk tolerance, as measured by a thirteen-item scale developed by Grable and Lytton (1999), to decrease after the COVID-19 pandemic emergency declaration. In an online experiment with 598 undergraduate students from Georgia State University, Harrison et al. (2022) measured atemporal risk preferences using binary lottery choices (Hey & Orme, 1994). They found a significant decrease in atemporal risk premia during the pandemic compared to pre-pandemic times, which is consistent with the effect of increased background risk on foreground risk attitudes as found by some studies. Similarly, Bu et al. (2020) found a decrease in risk tolerance after the onset of the pandemic compared to pre-pandemic levels. In their study with 225 graduate students from Wuhan, China, they measured risk tolerance using two risk-related survey questions motivated by Falk et al. (2018).

In contrast, Shachat et al. (2021) found an increase in risk tolerance amongst 396 Wuhan University students based on two incentivised lottery games. Using a sample of 1,000 Amazon Mechanical

Turk (MTurk) participants, Aksoy et al. (2021) elicited risk preferences at the end of 2020 based on two incentivised measures (the Gneezy and Potters (1997) method and a multiple price list method) as well as a self-reported measure (SOEP). Compared to the MTurk participants of a study by Snowberg and Yariv (2021) prior to the pandemic, Aksoy et al. (2021) found their participants to be more risk tolerant as measured by the Gneezy and Potters (1997) method as well as the SOEP but less risk tolerant as measured by the multiple price list method. Their findings were also controlled for demographic variables, demonstrating that the effects were robust to differences in the two MTurk samples.

Lastly, there are a number of studies that did not find any changes at all in risk tolerance (between pre-pandemic and during-pandemic measurements) in their respective samples. Angrisani et al. (2020) conducted a study with sixty undergraduate students and forty-eight professional traders in London using the Bomb Risk Elicitation Task (BRET; Crosetto & Filippin, 2013) and found no statistically significant changes in the risk preferences in their samples. Given the relatively small sample size, the authors noted that their study was sufficiently powered to detect a BRET score change of 4.5 per cent (based on a 5 per cent significance level and a power of 80 per cent). Drichoutis and Nayga (2022) assessed risk preferences among 1,008 undergraduate students in Athens before and after the first wave of the pandemic in Greece: comparing risk preferences based on the general SOEP question, the Holt and Laury (2002) multiple price list, and a fifteen-item version of DOSPERT (Drichoutis & Vassilopoulos, 2016) they also found no evidence for changes in risk preferences. Lohmann et al. (2023) elicited risk preferences from 539 students from Beijing University based on incentive-compatible lotteries and hypothetical tasks but did not find changes in risk tolerance. One noteworthy observation is that although many hypothesise, few of these studies measured direct effects on health-related behaviours, which would arguably be expected to have been impacted most significantly during these times.

4.3.2 Inter-individual Heterogeneity in Risk Tolerance

Another approach to assessing how risk tolerance and risk perception may have changed in times of COVID-19 is by looking at heterogeneity in the population. Understanding how risk tolerance differs across certain parts of the population can be helpful in identifying those groups that are more prone to risk-taking behaviour and thus more likely to contract and spread the virus. While we would ideally like to have direct information about COVID-19-related risk behaviours such as not wearing a mask or not practising social distancing, it can be difficult at best to obtain this information in an objective manner. Therefore, researchers and policymakers often rely on studies of risk (predictive of such behaviours) in tasks or questionnaires or at best self-reports on the behaviours.

One such study (Alsharawy et al., 2021) found women to take more preventative measures than men in response to COVID-19. Alsharawy et al. (2021) noted that the gender difference reduced when controlling for fear. They conclude that this highlights the role of emotion in perceived risk and risk tolerance. Ferrín (2022) also found women to be more risk-averse in self-reported risk behaviour but noted that the difference depended on the level of seriousness that participants ascribed to COVID-19. Fan et al. (2020) studied the data of a weekly panel in the United States with $n=5,500$ participants and found female participants to exhibit lower risk tolerance based on the SOEP as well as to be significantly more likely to engage in precautionary activities such as handwashing. Similarly, both Chuang and Liu (2020) and Drichoutis and Nayga (2022) found female participants to display lower risk tolerance compared to their male counterparts. While Iorfa et al. (2020) did not find gender differences in risk-taking in their online study with 1,554 participants in Nigeria, they found older participants to be more likely to engage in cautious COVID-19 behaviour. In contrast, Angrisani et al. (2020) did not find any significant differences based on the gender or age of their participants.

Largely in line with these results, Guenther et al. (2021) conducted two online studies with a total of 1,254 UK residents at the beginning of 2020. Unlike others, this study measured risk tolerance with four widely used measures: BART, BEG, DOSPERT, and self-reported SOEP questions. Participants also self-reported on a variety of questions regarding their COVID-19-related risk behaviour. The study also found risk tolerance to be higher in male participants and in younger participants. Of particular interest is that the authors observed lower risk tolerance amongst participants with poorer health status. Notably, they did not find any evidence of a similar pattern for self-reported risk behaviour (see Table 4.1). In fact, they did not find any robust patterns of association between the scores in their four elicitation tasks and self-reported real-world COVID-19-related risk behaviour, thus casting doubt on the appropriateness of these measures to approximate real-world behaviour in the context of COVID-19.

Across these studies it seems that gender and age differences in risk tolerance are robust and replicate in times of COVID-19. Interestingly, Guenther et al. (2021) find evidence that a third predictor of risk aversion may be health status and that this seems unique to this particular COVID-19 context. Finally, between the four common risk measures and real-world risk behaviour, an inconsistent picture emerges of their ability to predict COVID-19-related risk behaviour, despite evidence for the effectiveness of these measures in predicting behaviour in pre-COVID-19 times.

4.3.3   Intra-individual Heterogeneity in Risk Tolerance

Next to measures of inter-individual adaptations in post-COVID-19 times, another interesting approach has arisen by reviewing reported intra-individual fluctuations in risk tolerance (Roszkowski et al., 2009; Sahm, 2012). A recently noted pattern prior to the pandemic is that risk tolerance can fluctuate in predictable and cyclical ways over time (Sanders & Jenkins, 2016). Why fluctuations in risk tolerance occur is still unclear, but these fluctuations seem to be linked

Table 4.1 *Relationship between four common risk measures (BART, BEG, DOSPERT, and SOEP) and risk behaviour specific to COVID-19 (such as mask-wearing and proxies for social distancing) and risk behaviours that are more generalisable (drinking or smoking)*

	Drinker	Smoker	Left house	Mask ratio	Precautions	Contact outside	Contact inside	Isolation status
BART	0.104	0.007	-0.004	0.045	-0.087	0.007	0.029	0.024
BEG	0.043	0.045	0.136*	-0.054	-0.109	0.038	0.005	0.187**
DOSPERT	0.167**	0.172**	0.068	0.057	-0.149**	0.075	0.036	0.106
SOEP	0.125*	0.105	0.105	0.120*	0.003	0.054	-0.018	0.138*

*** p <0.001, ** p < 0.01, * p < 0.05.
Source: Guenther et al. (2021).

to experience of time (Ellis et al., 2015). As lockdown (and furlough for many; Allmand, 2020) substantially alters experiences of time (a 'groundhog day' effect; Loose et al., 2022: 112; Ogden, 2021), one may expect that lockdown could alter risk tolerance as well. With this in mind, Fedrigo et al. (2023) investigated whether these same fluctuations in risk tolerance occurred during the two UK government-imposed lockdowns in May and November 2020. The first study (n=865), during the first lockdown of May 2020, showed that those who did not report a strong sense of weekday indeed showed no fluctuations in risk tolerance, whilst those who did showed fluctuations in risk tolerance in the expected direction. In the second study (n=829), during lockdown of November 2020 (when a resemblance of temporally anchored activity as prior to COVID-19 may have evaporated entirely for many), participants no longer demonstrated the expected cyclical fluctuations.

Taken together, the evidence in Fedrigo et al. (2023) points to the differential effects of COVID-19 lockdown on individual risk tolerance fluctuations. Depending on the extent to which one's perception of the day of the week was altered, risk fluctuations veered away from previously found patterns. This suggests that intra-individual fluctuations in risk tolerance may be also shaped by COVID-19 and the associated changes in societal structure.

4.3.4   Risk Compensation

In the context of the COVID-19 pandemic, we can easily think of important examples where the risk compensation hypothesis may have a significant impact; for example, mask-wearing can reduce hand-washing hygiene, or vaccinated individuals may be less likely to follow advice around COVID-19 safety behaviour such as social distancing. Over the first two years of the COVID-19 pandemic, a number of studies have investigated the risk compensation hypothesis and provide a mixed picture about its existence.

For example, Liebst et al. (2022) analysed the data of 806 members of the public, combining video-observational records of public mask-wearing in two Dutch cities with a natural experimental approach. They found no evidence of an association between mask-wearing and social distancing. Similarly, Seres et al. (2021) found no evidence for risk compensation in their randomised field experiment in Berlin where they measured the impact of mask-wearing on social distancing behaviour in shop waiting lines with 480 participants. Similarly, in a natural experiment (n=639) conducted at an art fair, Blanken et al. (2021) did not find evidence that mask-wearing reduced physical distancing. Guenther et al. (2021) also find no evidence that supports the risk compensation hypothesis. In fact, one of their studies suggests that participants (n=299) taking more risk in real-life COVID-19-relevant behaviours (e.g., isolating or taking precautions) also exhibited higher risk tolerance in experimental and self-reported risk-taking measures. Similarly, an online study by Sun et al. (2022) of 592 healthcare workers in Taizhou, China, found no evidence for a decrease in self-reported COVID-19 precautious behaviour in a hospital setting after vaccination against COVID-19.

On the other hand, Wadud et al. (2022) found some evidence for risk compensation in the context of mask-wearing in Bangladesh. The authors analysed mobility data from Google Community Mobility Reports for six different types of locations such as retail and recreation, grocery and pharmacy, parks, transit stations, workplaces, and residences. In particular, they measured changes in mobility and activity after the introduction of the mask-wearing mandate. They found mobility to have increased in all the non-residential locations and the time spent at home locations to have decreased after the introduction of the mask-wearing mandate. In line with this account, another study using location data of smartphone users (Yan et al., 2021) found that after the introduction of face mask mandates in several US states, people were less at home and visited more commercial locations, supporting risk compensation. Another study by Luckman et al. (2021) conducted with 801 UK residents across two online experiments also suggested that mask-wearing reduces physical distancing, which was in line with the findings by Cartaud et al. (2020) amongst 457 French participants. These findings were also confirmed by Aranguren (2021), who observed distancing behaviour in front of traffic lights in Paris across two waves (June 2020: $n=1,396$, and September 2020: $n=1,326$) and found that in particular men were less likely to observe social distancing when approached by an experimenter wearing a face mask. We note an interesting contrast.

This concludes that, similar to pre-COVID-19 times, the risk compensation hypothesis cannot be confirmed consistently. Arguably though, recent evidence may provide stronger support against the hypothesis, as the opportunity to study risk compensation during this time is overwhelmingly present and it is relatively easy to compare effects across samples.

4.4   NEW TIMES CALL FOR NEW MEASURES

In this chapter, we summarise several facets by which risk perception and risk tolerance in times prior to the pandemic can be compared to COVID-19 times, by reviewing laboratory measures in relation to reported behaviour, inter- or intra-individual heterogeneity in risk tolerance, and by assessing evidence for commonly discussed features of risk such as the risk compensation hypothesis.

Similar to other previously studied forms of background risk, we conclude that there does not seem to be clear evidence of the impact of COVID-19 on risk tolerance. While some studies find an increase in risk tolerance, others find a decrease or no significant change with respect to the onset of the pandemic. Looking at the recent literature on heterogeneity in risk-taking, we find patterns similar to those that existed prior to the pandemic. In particular, a number of studies find men to be more risk tolerant than women as well as risk tolerance to decrease with age. When it comes to the risk compensation theory, the findings from the pandemic seem to paint a similar unconvincing picture about its existence with very mixed literature and findings. Also, we do not find consistent evidence for the predictive value of risk-taking measures for real-world risk behaviours relevant to COVID-19 behaviours.

We offer a possible explanation for this. One possibility is that the current (mostly self-reported) measures from times prior to COVID-19 may not translate into the pandemic times. For example, a number of the questions on the DOSPERT scale are about risk-taking behaviour that is incompatible with lockdown or social distancing measures. In an attempt to supplement measures in predicting real-world COVID-19- (or, more generally, pandemic-) related risk behaviour, Guenther et al. (in prep.) designed an amended version of the widely used DOSPERT (Blais & Weber, 2006) risk-taking questionnaire (the Pandemic-DOSPERT or P-DOSPERT). While the scale includes thirty self-reported questions about the likelihood of engaging in risky activities across five domains (financial, health/safety, recreational, ethical, and social), the original DOSPERT activities were replaced with activities compatible to life during a pandemic with lockdown and social distancing measures in place. In a study with a UK representative sample (n=299), the authors found their scale to be a more reliable predictor of a number of COVID-19-related risk behaviours; this was particularly the case for the most relevant health and safety subscale. The scale may offer a significant contribution to the original DOSPERT, in measuring and predicting behaviour during this and future pandemics.

4.5 CONCLUSION

For now we conclude that despite the distinctive nature of the post-COVID-19 world and a possible need to adapt the way we measure it, risk-taking in times of the COVID-19 pandemic, on average and in its heterogeneity does not display consistently distinctive patterns. This suggests that humans are remarkably adaptable. As we grow accustomed to the new normal, decision-making – albeit in context where new behaviours are perceived risky – is likely to settle over time. As the perceived background risk settles, this will normalise these new risk-taking behaviours too.

REFERENCES

Aksoy, B., Chadd, I., Osun, E. B., & Ozbay, E. Y. (2021). Behavioral changes of Mturkers during the COVID-19 pandemic. Social Science Research Network. https://ssrn.com/abstract=3920502 or http://dx.doi.org/10.2139/ssrn.3920502

Allmand, G. (2020). Comparison of furloughed jobs data: May to July 2020. Comparison of furloughed jobs data – Office for National Statistics. www.ons.gov.uk/businessindustryandtrade/business/businessservices/articles/comparisonoffurloughedjobsdata/maytojuly2020

Alsharawy, A., Spoon, R., Smith, A., & Ball, S. B. (2021). Gender differences in fear and risk perception during the COVID-19 pandemic. Social Science Research Network. https://ssrn.com/abstract=3817792 or http://dx.doi.org/10.2139/ssrn.3817792

Angrisani, M., Cipriani, M., Guarino, A., Kendall, R., & Ortiz de Zarate, J. (2020). Risk preferences at the time of COVID-19: An experiment with professional traders and students. Social Science Research Network. https://doi.org/10.2139/ssrn.3609586

Aranguren, M. (2021). Face mask use conditionally decreases compliance with physical distancing rules against COVID-19: Gender differences in risk compensation pattern. Annals of Behavioral Medicine, 56(4), 332–346. https://doi.org/10.1093/abm/kaab072

Bchir, M. A., & Willinger, M. (2013). Does the exposure to natural hazards affect risk and time preferences? Some insights from a field experiment in Perú. Economic Affairs. https://doi.org/10.1111/ecaf.12027

Binswanger, H. P. (1980). Attitudes toward risk: Experimental measurement in rural India. American Journal of Agricultural Economics. https://doi.org/10.2307/1240194

Blais, A.-R., & Weber, E. U. (2006). A Domain-Specific Risk-Taking (DOSPERT) scale for adult populations. Judgment and Decision Making, 1(1), 33–47. https://doi.org/10.1017/S1930297500000334

Blanken, T. F., Tanis, C. C., Nauta, F. H., Dablander, F., Zijlstra, B. J. H., Bouten, et al. (2021). Promoting physical distancing during COVID-19: A systematic approach to compare behavioral interventions. Scientific Reports, 11(1), 19463. https://doi.org/10.1038/s41598-021-98964-z

Brewer, N. T., Cuite, C. L., Herrington, J. E., & Weinstein, N. D. (2007). Risk compensation and vaccination: Can getting vaccinated cause people to engage in risky behaviors? Annals of Behavioral Medicine. https://doi.org/10.1007/BF02879925

Bu, D., Hanspal, T., Liao, Y., & Liu, Y. (2020). Risk taking, preferences, and beliefs: evidence from Wuhan (December 2020). *SAFE Working Paper No. 301*. Social Science Research Network. https://ssrn.com/abstract=3559870 or http://dx.doi.org/10.2139/ssrn.3559870

Byrnes, J. P., Miller, D. C., & Schafer, W. D. (1999). Gender differences in risk taking: A meta-analysis. *Psychological Bulletin*. https://doi.org/10.1037/0033-2909.125.3.367

Cameron, L., & Shah, M. (2015). Risk-taking behavior in the wake of natural disasters. *Journal of Human Resources*. https://doi.org/10.3368/jhr.50.2.484

Cartaud, A., Quesque, F., & Coello, Y. (2020). Wearing a face mask against COVID-19 results in a reduction of social distancing. *PloS One*, 15(12), e0243023.

Cassar, A., Healy, A., & von Kessler, C. (2017). Trust, risk, and time preferences after a natural disaster: Experimental evidence from Thailand. *World Development*. https://doi.org/10.1016/j.worlddev.2016.12.042

Chen, L. H., Baker, S. P., Braver, E. R., & Li, G. (2000). Carrying passengers as a risk factor for crashes fatal to 16- and 17-year-old drivers. *JAMA*, 283(12). https://doi.org/10.1001/jama.283.12.1578

Chuang, Y., & Liu, J. C. (2020). Who wears a mask? Gender differences in risk behaviors in the COVID-19 early days in Taiwan. *Economics Bulletin*, 40, 2619–2627.

Crosetto, P., & Filippin, A. (2013). The 'bomb' risk elicitation task. *Journal of Risk and Uncertainty*. https://doi.org/10.1007/s11166-013-9170-z

Croson, R., & Gneezy, U. (2009). Gender differences in preferences. *Journal of Economic Literature*. https://doi.org/10.1257/jel.47.2.448

Dohmen, T., Falk, A., Huffman, D., Sunde, U., Schupp, J., & Wagner, G. G. (2005). Individual risk attitudes: New evidence from a large, representative, experimentally-validated survey. Discussion Papers No. 511, DIW Berlin.

Drichoutis, A. C., & Nayga, R. M. (2022). On the stability of risk and time preferences amid the COVID-19 pandemic. *Experimental Economics*, 25, 759–794. https://doi.org/10.1007/s10683-021-09727-6

Drichoutis, A., & Vassilopoulos, A. (2016). Intertemporal stability of survey-based measures of risk and time preferences over a three-year course. Working Paper No. 2016-3. Agricultural University of Athens, Department of Agricultural Economics. https://EconPapers.repec.org/RePEc:aua:wpaper:2016-3

Eckel, C. C., El-Gamal, M. A., & Wilson, R. K. (2009). Risk loving after the storm: A Bayesian-Network study of Hurricane Katrina evacuees. *Journal of Economic Behavior and Organization*. https://doi.org/10.1016/j.jebo.2007.08.012

Eckel, C. C., & Grossman, P. J. (2002). Sex differences and statistical stereotyping in attitudes toward financial risk. *Evolution and Human Behavior*. https://doi.org/10.1016/S1090-5138(02)00097-1

Eger, L., Komárková, L., Egerová, D., & Mičík, M. (2021). The effect of COVID-19 on consumer shopping behaviour: Generational cohort perspective. *Journal of Retailing and Consumer Services*, 61. https://doi.org/10.1016/j.jretconser.2021.102542

Ellis, D. A., Wiseman, R., & Jenkins, R. (2015). Mental representations of weekdays. *PloS ONE*, 10(8). https://doi.org/10.1371/journal.pone.0134555

Fagereng, A., Guiso, L., & Pistaferri, L. (2016). Back to background risk? Discussion Papers no. 834. www.ssb.no/en/forskning/discussion-papers/back-to-background-risk

Falk, A., Becker, A., Dohmen, T., Enke, B., Huffman, D., & Sunde, U. (2018). Global evidence on economic preferences. *Quarterly Journal of Economics*. https://doi.org/10.1093/qje/qjy013

Fan, Y., Orhun, A. Y., & Turjeman, D. (2020). Heterogeneous actions, beliefs, constraints and risk tolerance during the COVID-19 pandemic. Working Paper 27211, NBER Working Paper Series. https://doi.org/10.3386/w27211

Fedrigo, V., Galizzi, M. M., Guenther, B., Jenkins, R., & Sanders, J. (2023). Weakened weekdays: Lockdown disrupts the weekly cycle of risk tolerance. *Scientific Reports*, 13, 21147.

Ferrín, M. (2022). Reassessing gender differences in COVID-19 risk perception and behavior. *Social Science Quarterly*. https://doi.org/https://doi.org/10.1111/ssqu.13116

Gneezy, U., & Potters, J. (1997). An experiment on risk taking and evaluation periods. *The Quarterly Journal of Economics*, 112(2), 631–645. www.jstor.org/stable/2951248

Grable, J., & Lytton, R. H. (1999). Financial risk tolerance revisited: The development of a risk assessment instrument. *Financial Services Review*, 8, 163–181.

Guenther, B., Galizzi, M. M., & Sanders, J. G. (in prep). P-DOSPERT: A new scale to assessing risk behaviours in times of a pandemic.

Guenther, B., Galizzi, M. M., & Sanders, J. G. (2021). Heterogeneity in risk-taking during the COVID-19 Pandemic: Evidence from the UK Lockdown. *Frontiers in Psychology*, 12. https://doi.org/10.3389/fpsyg.2021.643653

Guiso, L., & Paiella, M. (2008). Risk aversion, wealth, and background risk. *Journal of the European Economic Association*. https://doi.org/10.1162/JEEA.2008.6.6.1109

Harrison, G., Hofmeyr, A., Kincaid, H., Monroe, B., Ross, D., Schneider, M., & Swarthout, J. (2022). Subjective beliefs and economic preferences during the COVID-19 pandemic. *Experimental Economics*. https://doi.org/10.1007/s10683-021-09738-3

Heo, W., Rabbani, A., & Grable, J. E. (2021). An evaluation of the effect of the COVID-19 pandemic on the risk tolerance of financial decision makers. *Finance Research Letters.* https://doi.org/10.1016/j.frl.2020.101842

Hey, J. D., & Orme, C. (1994). Investigating generalizations of expected utility theory using experimental data. *Econometrica, 62*(6), 1291–1326. https://doi.org/10.2307/2951750

Holt, C. A., & Laury, S. K. (2002). Risk aversion and incentive effects. *American Economic Review.* https://doi.org/10.1257/000282802762024700

Houston, D. J., & Richardson, L. E. (2007). Risk compensation or risk reduction? Seatbelts, state laws, and traffic fatalities. *Social Science Quarterly.* https://doi.org/10.1111/j.1540-6237.2007.00510.x

Iorfa, S. K., Ottu, I. F. A., Oguntayo, R., Ayandele, O., Kolawole, S. O., Gandi, J. C., et al. (2020). COVID-19 knowledge, risk perception, and precautionary behavior among Nigerians: A moderated mediation approach. *Frontiers In Psychology, 11*, 566773. https://doi.org/10.3389/fpsyg.2020.566773

Kahneman, D., & Tversky, A. (1979). Prospect theory: An analysis of decision under risk. *Econometrica, 47*, 263–292. https://doi.org/10.2307/1914185

Kasting, M. L., Shapiro, G. K., Rosberger, Z., Kahn, J. A., & Zimet, G. D. (2016). Tempest in a teapot: A systematic review of HPV vaccination and risk compensation research. *Human Vaccines and Immunotherapeutics.* https://doi.org/10.1080/21645515.2016.1141158

Kimball, M. S. (1990). Precautionary saving in the small and in the large. *Econometrica.* https://doi.org/10.2307/2938334

Lejuez, C. W., Aklin, W. M., Jones, H. A., Strong, D. R., Richards, J. B., Kahler, C. W., & Read, J. P. (2003). The balloon analogue risk task (BART) differentiates smokers and nonsmokers. *Experimental and Clinical Psychopharmacology.* https://doi.org/10.1037/1064-1297.11.1.26

Lejuez, C. W., Read, J. P., Kahler, C. W., Richards, J. B., Ramsey, S. E., Stuart, G. L., et al. Evaluation of a behavioral measure of risk taking: the Balloon Analogue Risk Task (BART). *Journal of Experimental Psychology: Applied, 8*(2), 75–84. DOI: 10.1037//1076-898x.8.2.75.

Lejuez, C. W., Richards, J. B., Read, J. P., Kahler, C. W., Ramsey, S. E., Stuart, G. L., et al. (2002). Evaluation of a behavioral measure of risk taking: The balloon analogue risk task (BART). *Journal of Experimental Psychology: Applied.* https://doi.org/10.1037/1076-898X.8.2.75

Levym, D. T., & Miller, T. (2000). Review: Risk compensation literature – The theory and evidence. *Journal of Crash Prevention and Injury Control, 2*(1). https://doi.org/10.1080/10286580008902554

Liebst, L. S., Ejbye-Ernst, P., de Bruin, M., Thomas, J., & Lindegaard, M. R. (2022). No evidence that mask-wearing in public places elicits risk compensation behavior during the COVID-19 pandemic. *Scientific Reports, 12*(1), 1511. https://doi.org/10.1038/s41598-022-05270-3

Lohmann, P., Gsottbauer, E., You, J., & Kontoleon, A. (2023). Anti-social behaviour and economic decision-making: Panel experimental evidence in the wake of COVID-19. *Journal of Economic Behavior and Organization, 206*, 136–171. https://doi.org/10.1016/j.jebo.2022.12.007

Loose, T., Wittmann, M., & Vásquez-Echeverría, A. (2022). Disrupting times in the wake of the pandemic: Dispositional time attitudes, time perception and temporal focus. *Time & Society, 31*(1), 110–131.

Luckman, A., Zeitoun, H., Isoni, A., Loomes, G., Vlaev, I., Powdthavee, N., & Read, D. (2021). Risk compensation during COVID-19: The impact of face mask usage on social distancing. *Journal of Experimental Psychology: Applied, 27*(4), 722.

Marcus, J. L., Glidden, D. V., Mayer, K. H., Liu, A. Y., Buchbinder, S. P., Amico, K. R., et al. (2013). No evidence of sexual risk compensation in the iPrEx trial of daily oral HIV preexposure prophylaxis. *PloS One, 8*(12), e81997.

Markiewicz, Ł., & Weber, E. U. (2013). DOSPERT's gambling risk-taking propensity scale predicts excessive stock trading. *Journal of Behavioral Finance, 14*(1), 65–78. https://doi.org/10.1080/15427560.2013.762000

Mutz, M., & Gerke, M. (2021). Sport and exercise in times of self-quarantine: How Germans changed their behaviour at the beginning of the Covid-19 pandemic. *International Review for the Sociology of Sport, 56*(3), 305–316. https://doi.org/10.1177/1012690220934335

Ogden, R. S. (2021). The passage of time during the UK Covid-19 lockdown. *PLoS ONE, 15*(7), e0235871. https://doi.org/10.1371/journal.pone.0235871

Page, L., Savage, D. A., & Torgler, B. (2014). Variation in risk seeking behaviour following large losses: A natural experiment. *European Economic Review.* https://doi.org/10.1016/j.euroecorev.2014.04.009

Powell, M., & Ansic, D. (1997). Gender differences in risk behaviour in financial decision-making: An experimental analysis. *Journal of Economic Psychology, 18*(6), 605–628. https://doi.org/10.1016/S0167-4870(97)00026-3

Rolison, J. J., Hanoch, Y., & Wood, S. (2012). Risky decision making in younger and older adults: The role of learning. *Psychology and Aging, 27*(1), 129–140. https://doi.org/10.1037/a0024689

Roszkowski, M. J., Delaney, M. M., & Cordell, D. M. (2009). Intraperson consistency in financial risk tolerance assessment: Temporal stability, relationship to total score, and effect on criterion-related validity. *Journal of Business and Psychology, 24*(4), 455–467. https://doi.org/10.1007/s10869-009-9115-3

Sahm, C. R. (2012). How much does risk tolerance change? *The Quarterly Journal of Finance*, 2(4), 1250020. https://doi.org/10.1142/S2010139212500206

Said, F., Afzal, U., & Turner, G. (2015). Risk taking and risk learning after a rare event: Evidence from a field experiment in Pakistan, *Journal of Economic Behavior & Organization*, 118, 167–183. https://doi.org/10.1016/j.jebo.2015.03.001

Sanders, J. G., & Jenkins, R. (2016). Weekly fluctuations in risk tolerance and voting behaviour. *PLoS ONE*, 11(7), e0159017. https://doi.org/10.1371/journal.pone.0159017

Shachat, J., Walker, M., & Wei, L. (2021). How the onset of the Covid-19 pandemic impacted pro-social behaviour and individual preferences: Experimental evidence from China. Journal of Economic Behavior and Organization, 190, 480–494. https://doi.org/10.1016/j.jebo.2021.08.001190.

Serafini, G., Parmigiani, B., Amerio, A., Aguglia, A., Sher, L., & Amore, M. (2020). The psychological impact of COVID-19 on the mental health in the general population. *QJM*, 113(8), 531–537. https://doi.org/10.1093/qjmed/hcaa201

Seres, G., Balleyer, A., Cerutti, N., Friedrichsen, J., & Süer, M. (2021). Face mask use and physical distancing before and after mandatory masking: No evidence on risk compensation in public waiting lines. *Journal of Economic Behavior and Organization*, 192, 765–781. https://doi.org/10.1016/j.jebo.2021.10.032

Slovic, P., & Peters, E. (2006). Risk perception and affect. *Current Directions in Psychological Science*, 15(6), 322–325. https://doi.org/10.1111/j.1467-8721.2006.00461.x

Snowberg, E., & Yariv, L. (2021). Testing the waters: Behavior across participant pools. *American Economic Review*, 111(2), 687–719. https://doi.org/10.1257/aer.20181065

Sun, L.-X., Chen, L.-L., Chen, W.-Y., Zhang, M.-X., Yang, M.-G., Mo, L.-C., et al. (2022). Association between health behaviours and the COVID-19 vaccination: Risk compensation among healthcare workers in Taizhou, China. *Human Vaccines & Immunotherapeutics*, 18(1), 2029257. https://doi.org/10.1080/21645515.2022.2029257

Tee, M. L., Tee, C. A., Anlacan, J. P., Aligam, K. J. G., Reyes, P. W. C., Kuruchittham, V., & Ho, R. C. (2020). Psychological impact of COVID-19 pandemic in the Philippines. *Journal of Affective Disorders*, 277, 379–391. https://doi.org/10.1016/j.jad.2020.08.043

Trimpop, R. M. (1994). What is risk taking behavior. In *The Psychology of Risk Taking Behavior* (vol. 107, pp. 1–14). North-Holland. https://doi.org/10.1016/S0166-4115(08)61295-9

Vieider, F. M., Lefebvre, M., Bouchouicha, R., Chmura, T., Hakimov, R., Krawczyk, M., & Martinsson, P. (2015). Common components of risk and uncertainty attitudes across contexts and domains: Evidence from 30 countries. *Journal of the European Economic Association, 13*(3), 421–452. https://doi.org/10.1111/jeea.12102

Wadud, Z., Rahman, S. M., & Enam, A (2022). Face mask mandates and risk compensation: An analysis of mobility data during the COVID-19 pandemic in Bangladesh. *BMJ Global Health, 7*(1), e006803. https://doi.org/10.1136/bmjgh-2021-006803

Weber, E. U., Blais, A. R., & Betz, N. E. (2002). A domain-specific risk-attitude scale: Measuring risk perceptions and risk behaviors. *Journal of Behavioral Decision Making, 15*(4), 263–290. https://doi.org/10.1002/bdm.414

Wilde, G. J. S. (1998). Risk homeostasis theory: An overview. *Injury Prevention, 4*(2), 89–91. https://doi.org/10.1136/ip.4.2.89

Yan, Y., Malik, A. A., Bayham, J., Fenichel, E. P., Couzens, C., & Omer, S. B. (2021). Measuring voluntary and policy-induced social distancing behavior during the COVID-19 pandemic. *Proceedings of the National Academy of Sciences of the United States of America, 118*(16), e2008814118. https://doi.org/10.1073/pnas.2008814118

5   A False Sense of Security?

Face Masking and Social Distancing

Nicola Cerutti

5.1   BACKGROUND

After the identification of the first COVID-19 cases in China in December 2019 and throughout the month of February 2020, most countries implemented, at first, travel restrictions in the hope of avoiding the spread of the virus inside their borders. By the end of February 2020, as the world quickly started facing the prospect of the COVID-19 epidemic reaching beyond the areas of initial outbreak and transforming into a pandemic, governments across the world started planning and implementing restrictive policies to contain the spread of the virus. In the absence of any timeline for a vaccine and with much uncertainty regarding the efficacy of treatments, the importance of non-pharmaceutical interventions (NPI) and of their timely implementation was paramount. The major concern was avoiding oversaturation of the healthcare systems: had emergency rooms and intensive care units surpassed their capacity, mortality would have suddenly risen, as the examples of Wuhan, first, and Lombardy, later, had shown.

The adoption of a series of measures targeted at reducing the basic reproductive rate of the virus, or R_t (Haug et al., 2020), was commonly called flattening the curve. Although measures like curfews and lockdowns proved to be effective (see, e.g., Auger et al., 2020; Dehning et al., 2020; Gatto et al., 2020; Haug et al., 2020), the consequences on the economy and society at large suggested that they could be used to curb the infections in the initial stages of the emergency but could not otherwise be used for extended periods of time (Alvarez et al., 2021; Orben et al., 2020; Thunström et al., 2020; Tull et al., 2020). The governments soon started developing guidelines and regulations to implement a wider set of NPIs, in an attempt to reduce the R_t index while avoiding excessive restrictions on the society.

Previous research showed that face mask-wearing, a relatively inexpensive intervention, played an important role in reducing infection rates for other viral diseases (Rengasamy et al., 2010; Suess et al., 2012; Van der Sande et al., 2008), and more recent literature highlights similar effects on COVID-19 (Mitze et al., 2020). However, health authorities and governments showed hesitation in mandating universal face mask use, referring to potential negative effects on other measures due to a face mask-induced false sense of security (WHO, 2020), leading to a variety of uncoordinated measures regulating the use of face masks (Feng et al., 2020).

5.2 THE RISK COMPENSATION HYPOTHESIS

The idea of risk compensation is related, among other things, to the alleged claim that if mandated mask use may backfire. The idea is based on the assumption that people might react to a perceived increase in safety by acting less safely: in the COVID-19 case, people would react to the sudden presence of masks by lowering their engagement in other safety measures (e.g., washing their hands less often, spending more time indoors with other people, not respecting a safe distance from each other). The risk compensation hypothesis was first introduced in the context of traffic deaths in a seminal article by Peltzman (1975). He found that the effect of improvements in safety regulations on car accident deaths was almost completely offset by changes in the behaviour of drivers. The hypothesis was subsequently tested in various other contexts, such as seat-belt regulations (Evans & Graham, 1991; Houston & Richardson, 2007), bicycle helmets (Adams & Hillman, 2001), HIV prevention (Eaton & Kalichman, 2007; Marcus et al., 2013) and others (Cohen & Einav, 2003; Noland, 1995), with contrasting evidence. The discussion on risk compensation is, to date, ongoing, with no clear answer on the general applicability of the theory, on one hand, and of the robustness of the findings in this area even in specific contexts (Kasting et al., 2016; Mantzari et al., 2020; Pless, 2016; Radun et al., 2018), on the other. It was therefore uncertain if risk compensation could jeopardise the effort in flattening the curve as a result of mandated or recommended use of face masks. This led to hesitation, among governments and public health institution, in the implementation of policies concerning the use of masks.

Would risk-compensating behaviour emerge as a consequence of extended mask-wearing across the population? Would mandatory or recommended mask-wearing in public spaces exacerbate this effect? And would it be strong enough to completely offset the reduced risk of infection caused by the filtering properties of face masks? To answer these questions, several behavioural studies have been conducted to identify risk-compensating behaviour among the population and, more specifically, to study the effect of face masks and personal protective equipment (PPE) on social distancing. The rest of this chapter describes work focusing on this latter issue, while studies on other aspects of risk compensation (e.g., number of interactions, sneezing and coughing etiquette, and hand hygiene) are intentionally not covered here. The chapter covers mostly field and natural experiments but also reports a summary of the main findings from behavioural studies adopting other approaches.

5.3 FIELD AND NATURAL EXPERIMENTS

The first experimental study specifically aimed at testing the presence of risk-compensating behaviour in the context of the pandemic was conducted by Seres et al. (2021a) in April 2020. Acknowledging the little evidence available on the effect of face masks on distancing and, most importantly, the impossibility of extrapolating viable information from existing studies, the authors designed and ran a novel field experiment in Berlin, Germany. The confederates joined lines forming at the entrance of businesses around the city,[1]

---

[1] These lines were common around the city at the time, as access to shops and offices was limited to few people at a time, depending on the size of the establishment.

randomly wearing or not wearing a face mask. They then measured the distance kept by people joining the line behind them using an augmented reality application on their mobile phones.[2] Their findings suggest that face masks did not contribute to reducing compliance in maintaining a safe distance between individuals. On the contrary, subjects maintained on average a significantly larger distance from a masked experimenter, pointing towards an opposite effect (n = 300). To better understand the underlying mechanisms that may drive this result, the study also included an additional survey experiment, conducted at the same time, that closely mimicked the structure of the field experiment. It presented the participants with a picture of either a masked or an unmasked individual. The participants were then asked to imagine how this masked/unmasked individual would behave when joining a line, how this individual would prefer others to behave when joining a line, and how likely were they sick or infectious. The results suggest that mask wearers were not expected to differ significantly from the rest in terms of potential sickness or infectiousness. However, the presence of a mask appeared to be informative of the distancing preferences of the individual wearing it. The respondents, on average, expected mask wearers to prefer significantly larger distances. This suggests that wearing a face mask serves as a social signal and is indicative of a preference for a greater distance. This first study, hence, brings evidence that contradicts the risk compensation hypothesis. Its results are suggestive of a positive effect of masks on maintaining physical distancing in public spaces, acting through social signals sent by wearing a mask. One of the points still in question, however, is how the mask may influence the behaviour of the subject wearing it. While observational evidence from the field indicates that, on average, mask wearers would not stand closer to an experimenter than non-mask wearers, these results cannot be used for the identification

---

[2] This specific tool was chosen to minimise the likelihood that the subject would notice the measurement taking place, which might have otherwise biased the final result.

of a causal mechanism. As the choice of wearing (or not wearing) a mask is endogenous and not part of a treatment, it might be caused by individual preferences that, in turn, influence distancing. Another experimental design would be needed to provide an answer to this question. Furthermore, the study acknowledges that the signal sent by wearing a mask might be dependent on other characteristics of the individual (age, gender, appearance) and, quite relevantly for policy decisions, on the type of mask or PPE worn. The confederates were wearing FFP2 masks.[3] Would different effects have emerged had they chosen a different type of mask or PPE?

A second study, published as a pre-print only at a few days' distance, focuses on these potential heterogeneous effects. The work of Marchiori (2020) tested the effects of different types of PPE on distancing in the Venice metropolitan area in Italy. The main motivation behind this work is the lack of available data on social distancing and, as a consequence, great uncertainty on people's behaviour in a pandemic, according to the author, greatly limits the effectiveness of mathematical and epidemiological models, leading to inaccurate predictions. In the first steps of the pandemic, these inaccuracies led to gaps between the expected efficacy of policies and the results observed after their implementation (see, e.g., Ahmed et al., 2018; Kelso et al., 2009; Ngonghala et al., 2020). Rather than approaching a specific hypothesis, Marchiori's effort was explorative in nature. To provide this much-needed data, the study drew on previous expertise in the realm of sensor-based equipment to develop a distance-measuring belt.[4] Data collection was conducted over a period of two months (from the end of February to the end of April 2020) and focused on distancing behaviour on sidewalks. The researchers selected several sidewalks of different sizes and collected distancing data in five different experimental treatments characterised by the

[3] The decision on the mask to use by the confederates in the experiment was made based on availability, as surgical masks were in short supply at the time.
[4] In this case too, the authors acknowledge the importance of a concealed measurement. The measuring tool is therefore built to appear as a belt pouch.

type of protective equipment worn by the confederate: unmasked, commercial mask, DIY (do-it-yourself) mask, commercial mask and goggles, or DIY mask and goggles. The findings highlight peculiarities in behaviour (what the author calls a *paradoxical default behaviour*): there was an inverse relationship between the risk of the situation and the distance maintained. Regardless of the space available, a pedestrian walked closer to the experimenter if the latter was not wearing any protective equipment (with an average distance maintained of 29.4 cm). The introduction of a mask, whether DIY or commercial, significantly shifted the average distance to 69 or 59 cm, respectively. In line with this trend, the further addition of protective goggles increased average distancing to 80 cm if associated with a commercial mask and to 92 cm if associated with a DIY mask. The author hypothesises that this paradoxical effect is triggered by an innate tendency of the individuals towards social proximity. Protective equipment, providing a visual stimulus, turns this instinctive tendency towards proximity into a conscious tendency towards distancing, reminding them of the potential danger of infection. Although the article does not investigate this mechanism and presents it as a speculative description, this result appears consistent with the survey findings from Seres et al. (2021a). Social distancing behaviour therefore appears to follow similar patterns in different areas, suggesting that at least part of the results presented may not be geographically specific. However, similar to the first study, the field experiment by Marchiori (2020) was conducted before any actual policies on mask-wearing were introduced and the sight of a face mask was not as ubiquitous as it later became.

Indeed, as the pandemic progressed, masks became a more common sight in cities across the world, with their use either recommended or mandated by governments and health authorities. As acknowledged by Seres et al. (2021a), the results observed when masking is entirely voluntary might not necessarily apply to an environment where mask use is mandated. More specifically, the power of masks to signal a preference for larger distances suggested by the previous two studies might be lost in a situation where masks are pervasive in public areas. A replication in Berlin of the original experiment by Seres et al. (2021a) observed how distancing behaviour changes after the introduction of mandatory masking in all closed public spaces. The replication (Seres et al., 2021b) took place in May 2020, adopting the same protocol. The authors point out how other relevant situational changes happened on top of the introduction of mandatory masking. In particular, in Berlin, the period between March and April 2020 was characterised by very tight restrictions. At the beginning of May, however, retail shops, bars, and restaurant reopened, albeit with reduced capacity, and gatherings until fifty people were allowed again. The study compares the distancing data collected before the introduction of mandatory masking and the relaxation of shops with data collected afterwards, testing the persistence of the positive effects of masks on distancing. The results show that, on average, distances between individuals dropped significantly in the second period. However, when accounting for the presence of open restaurants and bars around the measurement area, this does not appear to be driven by the mandatory masking policy per se but rather by the relaxation of measures. Furthermore, the positive effect of masks on distancing remained constant before and after the mask mandate.

Also focusing on the context of public venues and cultural events, Blanken et al. (2021) study how to foster physical distancing among individuals in Amsterdam, Netherlands, in August 2020. The authors look at how walking directions (unidirectional, bidirectional, or absence of walking directions) and supplementary interventions (face masks and a buzzer feedback when not respecting the 150 cm distancing recommendation) affected the distance maintained among visitors of a fair and the number of close contacts they engage in. The authors do not provide a continuous distance measure but rather the number of times a subject came in close proximity with other individuals, making comparison with other results difficult. Nevertheless, they find that face masks did not affect violations of the 150 cm recommendation in any significant way.

Although the studies reported so far speak in favour of recommendations for widespread mask use or even mandatory masking policies, a study by Aranguren (2021) provides some evidence of risk compensation in the field. The experiment, conducted in Paris in two waves (June and September 2020), consists of a confederate asking for directions in front of a traffic light. In the experimental treatments the confederate wore a surgical mask either correctly or exposing the nose or exposing both nose and mouth or, finally, did not wear a mask at all. The suggested social status of the experimenter is also experimentally varied (by wearing a more formal or less formal attire). Finally, the confederates are recognisable as black (50 per cent) and white (50 per cent) men. The results provide conditional support to the risk compensation hypothesis, albeit with heterogeneous effects based on the gender of the subject. Men, when confronted with a confederate wearing a face mask, are less likely to comply with the 100 cm distancing recommendation in force in Paris in both time periods. This effect is stronger when the confederate wears clothes that signal high social status. Women, instead, show risk-compensating tendencies in the presence of a mask only in the second wave of the experiment but not during the first. A straightforward comparison between this experiment and the previous ones is made difficult by the different outcome variable considered: the researchers do not measure the distance maintained between the subjects in the interaction but rather a binary variable indicating if they are complying with the 100 cm distancing rule or not. Moreover, although considerations on the heterogeneity of the effects of face masks in distancing are in themselves interesting, the lack of female experimenters makes it impossible to understand the extent of the gender effects reported. Finally, while the experimental setting aims at replicating real interactions, this makes it especially subject to contextual variations (e.g., background noise), given the verbal interaction taking place between confederates and participants. Nevertheless, it is interesting to observe that some support suggesting the presence of risk-compensating behaviour caused by face masks in France is found also in a survey by

Cartaud et al. (2020). Notwithstanding the larger evidence pointing to the contrary, it cannot be excluded that some form of country-, time-, or situation-specific risk compensation might occur.

5.4 FURTHER BEHAVIOURAL STUDIES

Beyond field experiments, other behavioural studies provided evidence on the claim of a false sense of security accompanying the use of masks. Unlike the work presented in the previous section, most of these studies look at a larger set of issues that include, but are not limited to, the effect of face masks on physical distancing. Guenther et al. (2021) conducted two pre-registered online studies during the early 2020 lockdown in the United Kingdom (March to May 2020) involving a total of 1,254 residents. Participants in the second study (299 from a representative UK sample), in addition to specific risk-taking tasks, answered a range of questions about COVID-19-related risky behaviours. While this work does not focus specifically on distancing behaviour, the authors include questions on engagement in close-range contacts. To test the risk compensation hypothesis, the authors identified whether participants were more or less likely to engage in COVID-19-related risky behaviours when wearing a mask. They found no evidence in support of the risk compensation hypothesis, both in general and in relation to engaging in close physical contacts. Their findings also do not suggest any gender- or age-related differences in the propensity to engage in risky behaviours when wearing a mask.

Liebst et al. (2022) conducted two studies based on video-observational records of public mask-wearing in Amsterdam and Rotterdam, taken between May and June 2020, to test whether face mask-wearing was negatively associated with social distancing compliance. In the second study they combined video observations with a natural experiment to evaluate the effect of an area-based mask mandate. They find that mask-wearing does not reduce social distancing or increase crowding, neither under voluntary nor under mandatory conditions. Nevertheless, they find a positive link between crowding and social distancing violations. These results suggest that *situational opportunity* might be a large predictor of violations of the physical distancing recommendation. This is in line with what Seres et al. (2021b) highlight in the German context. The authors further suggest that possibly too much attention might have been given to individual-level predictors of social distancing (age, norms, gender, and potentially also risk compensation), while effective interventions may more prominently focus on creating situations where less obstacles to physical distancing are in place.

Luckman et al. (2021) conducted an online survey and experiment in June and July 2020. The participants to the experiment consider a potential interaction between themselves and a stranger and, in a distancing preference task, indicate what is the closest acceptable distance they would keep from them. Both the participant and the stranger are represented in stylised scenarios either wearing or not wearing a mask. The results are suggestive of risk compensation preferences among the participants, with this effect being mediated by their beliefs on the effectiveness of face masks. Participants who believed masks to be effective at preventing the spread of COVID-19 were preferring shorter distances. Moreover, younger participants (eighteen to forty years) reported being more comfortable with maintaining shorter distances than older participants (sixty-five-plus years). The authors, rather than suggesting the avoidance of mask mandates and recommendations altogether, draw the attention to the importance of clear guidance from governments and health institutions to avoid these effects.

5.5   CONCLUSION

This chapter presents a body of behavioural work that analyses the relationship between face mask use and social distancing. The majority of these studies does not find evidence of a negative effect of mask-wearing on distancing. This evidence, however, might not yet be definitive, as there seem to be exceptions. These exceptions are not sufficient to justify the delay in the implementation of masking policies and recommendation during the pandemic but raise interesting questions as to where this heterogeneity may come from. These insights could, in turn, extend to the general discussion on the almost-fifty-year-old topic of risk compensation.

Aranguren (2021) suggests that this heterogeneity in effect might be explained by national differences. The observation of a negative effect of face masks on distancing is consistent with the study by Cartaud et al. (2020), also conducted on a French sample. Aranguren also highlights how Luckman et al. (2021) and Jørgensen et al. (2021) find evidence of a similar effect on a British and Danish population, respectively. The underlying effect might then perhaps be driven by mandatory masking policies in specific contexts or other similar situational settings. There is indeed evidence for national and contextual differences: a prominent example is the strong political meaning connected with mask use in the United States. Kahane (2021) shows how partisan political influences have a strong correlation with behaviour in the pandemic. If contextual aspects are behind these heterogeneous aspects, there is some potential value in understanding them. However, the majority of studies does not find any risk-compensating effect (Mantzari et al., 2020), and of those who do, most look at intentions rather than behaviour. Most evidence from the field, on the contrary, tends to point towards the absence of risk compensation. This hints at the presence of an intention–behaviour gap: as Luckman et al. (2021) point out, intentions may reflect people's *cool and reflective judgements*, while in real-world situations, specific factors could override these judgements. A final point of pivotal importance for policy action concerns the costs and benefits of face mask-wearing compared with those of physical distancing. Even assuming the presence of risk compensation in specific physical or social situations, would this be enough to offset the mitigating effect of masks on contagion? To understand this, epidemiological studies are needed: a meta-analysis by Chu et al. (2020) highlights a strong reduction in transmission of SARS-CoV-2 associated with face mask use that would not be offset by moderate reductions in distancing.

The pandemic had brought forward new challenges and posed questions that had to be answered swiftly to provide insights for policymakers. In the past few years, an overwhelming amount of research has been conducted in relation to COVID-19 (Laine et al., 2020), and evidence on these matters is now starting to pile up. The work presented here is only a partial summary of the evidence on the potential interaction between face masks and physical distancing and a very tiny portion of all behavioural studies tackling COVID-19 and its consequences. Thanks to these timely efforts, the first systematic reviews and meta-analyses could combine insights from multiple studies and find hardly any evidence supporting the hypothesis of risk-compensating behaviour. As appealing as it may be as an example of a peculiar behavioural process, then, it should not be used as an excuse to not implement sound health interventions. As Mantzari et al. (2020) argue in their review, the concept of risk compensation, with the obstacles it poses to timely policy action, appears to be a greater threat than risk compensation per se.

REFERENCES

Adams, J., & Hillman, M. (2001). The risk compensation theory and bicycle helmets. *Injury Prevention, 7*(2), 89–91.

Ahmed, F., Zviedrite, N., & Uzicanin, A. (2018). Effectiveness of workplace social distancing measures in reducing influenza transmission: A systematic review. *BMC Public Health, 18*(1), 1–13.

Alvarez, F., Argente, D., & Lippi, F. (2021). A simple planning problem for COVID-19 lockdown, testing, and tracing. *American Economic Review: Insights, 3*(3), 367–382.

Aranguren, M. (2021). Face mask use conditionally decreases compliance with physical distancing rules against COVID-19: Gender differences in risk compensation pattern. *Annals of Behavioral Medicine, 5*(4), 332–346. https://doi.org/10.1093/abm/kaab072

Auger, K. A., Shah, S. S., Richardson, T., Hartley, D., Hall, M., Warniment, A., et al. (2020). Association between statewide school closure and COVID-19 incidence and mortality in the US. *JAMA, 324*(9), 859–870.

Blanken, T. F., Tanis, C. C., Nauta, F. H., Dablander, F., Zijlstra, B. J., Bouten, R. R., et al. (2021). Promoting physical distancing during COVID-19: A systematic approach to compare behavioral interventions. *Scientific Reports, 11*(1), 1–8.

Cartaud, A., Quesque, F., & Coello, Y. (2020). Wearing a face mask against COVID-19 results in a reduction of social distancing. *PloS One*, 15(12), e0243023.

Chu, D. K., Akl, E. A., Duda, S., Solo, K., Yaacoub, S., Schünemann, H. J., et al. (2020). Physical distancing, face masks, and eye protection to prevent person-to-person transmission of SARS-CoV-2 and COVID-19: a systematic review and meta-analysis. *The Lancet*, 395(10242), 1973–1987.

Cohen, A., & Einav, L. (2003). The effects of mandatory seat belt laws on driving behavior and traffic fatalities. *Review of Economics and Statistics*, 85(4), 828–843.

Dehning, J., Zierenberg, J., Spitzner, F. P., Wibral, M., Neto, J. P., Wilczek, M., & Priesemann, V. (2020). Inferring change points in the spread of COVID-19 reveals the effectiveness of interventions. *Science*, 369(6500), eabb9789(2020). DOI:10.1126/science.abb9789.

Eaton, L. A., & Kalichman, S. C. (2007). Risk compensation in HIV prevention: Implications for vaccines, microbicides, and other biomedical HIV prevention technologies. *Current HIV/AIDS Reports*, 4(4), 165–172.

Evans, W. N., & Graham, J. D. (1991). Risk reduction or risk compensation? The case of mandatory safety-belt use laws. *Journal of Risk and Uncertainty*, 4(1), 61–73.

Feng, S., Shen, C., Xia, N., Song, W., Fan, M., & Cowling, B. J. (2020). Rational use of face masks in the COVID-19 pandemic. *The Lancet Respiratory Medicine*, 8(5), 434–436.

Gatto, M., Bertuzzo, E., Mari, L., Miccoli, S., Carraro, L., Casagrandi, R., & Rinaldo, A. (2020). Spread and dynamics of the COVID-19 epidemic in Italy: Effects of emergency containment measures. *Proceedings of the National Academy of Sciences*, 117(19), 10484–10491.

Guenther, B., Galizzi, M. M., & Sanders, J. G. (2021). Heterogeneity in risk-taking during the COVID-19 pandemic: Evidence from the UK lockdown. *Frontiers in Psychology*, 12, 852.

Haug, N., Geyrhofer, L., Londei, A., Dervic, E., Desvars-Larrive, A., Loreto, V., et al. (2020). Ranking the effectiveness of worldwide COVID-19 government interventions. *Nature Human Behaviour*, 4(12), 1303–1312.

Houston, D. J., & Richardson, L. E. (2007). Risk compensation or risk reduction? Seatbelts, state laws, and traffic fatalities. *Social Science Quarterly*, 88(4), 913–936.

Jørgensen, F., Lindholt, M. F., Bor, A., & Petersen, M. B. (2021). Does face mask use elicit risk-compensation? Quasi-experimental evidence from Denmark during the SARS-CoV-2 pandemic. *European Journal of Public Health*, 31(6), 1259–1265.

Kahane, L. H. (2021). Politicizing the mask: Political, economic and demographic factors affecting mask wearing behavior in the USA. *Eastern Economic Journal*, 47(2), 163–183.

Kasting, M. L., Shapiro, G. K., Rosberger, Z., Kahn, J. A., & Zimet, G. D. (2016). Tempest in a teapot: A systematic review of HPV vaccination and risk compensation research. *Human Vaccines & Immunotherapeutics*, 12(6), 1435–1450.

Kelso, J. K., Milne, G. J., & Kelly, H. (2009). Simulation suggests that rapid activation of social distancing can arrest epidemic development due to a novel strain of influenza. *BMC Public Health*, 9(1), 1–10.

Laine, C., Taichman, D. B., Guallar, E., & Mulrow, C. D. (2020). Keeping up with emerging evidence in (almost) real time. *Annals of Internal Medicine*, 173(2), 153–154.

Liebst, L. S., Ejbye-Ernst, P., de Bruin, M., Thomas, J., & Lindegaard, M. R. (2022). No evidence that mask-wearing in public places elicits risk compensation behavior during the COVID-19 pandemic. *Scientific Reports*, 12(1), 1511. https://doi.org/10.1038/s41598-022-05270-3

Luckman, A., Zeitoun, H., Isoni, A., Loomes, G., Vlaev, I., Powdthavee, N., & Read, D. (2021). Risk compensation during COVID-19: The impact of face mask usage on social distancing. *Journal of Experimental Psychology: Applied*, 27(4), 722.

Mantzari, E., Rubin, G. J., & Marteau, T. M. (2020). Is risk compensation threatening public health in the COVID-19 pandemic? *British Medical Journal*, 370. DOI: https://doi.org/10.1136/bmj.m2913

Marchiori, M. (2020). Covid-19 and the social distancing paradox: Dangers and solutions. arXiv Preprint. https://doi.org/10.48550/arXiv.2005.12446

Marcus, J. L., Glidden, D. V., Mayer, K. H., Liu, A. Y., Buchbinder, S. P., Amico, K. R., et al. (2013). No evidence of sexual risk compensation in the iPrEx trial of daily oral HIV preexposure prophylaxis. *PloS One*, 8(12), e81997.

Mitze, T., Kosfeld, R., Rode, J., & Wälde, K. (2020). Face masks considerably reduce COVID-19 cases in Germany. *Proceedings of the National Academy of Sciences*, 117(51), 32293–32301.

Ngonghala, C. N., Iboi, E., Eikenberry, S., Scotch, M., MacIntyre, C. R., Bonds, M. H., & Gumel, A. B. (2020). Mathematical assessment of the impact of non-pharmaceutical interventions on curtailing the 2019 novel Coronavirus. *Mathematical Biosciences*, 325, 108364.

Noland, R. B. (1995). Perceived risk and modal choice: Risk compensation in transportation systems. *Accident Analysis & Prevention*, 27(4), 503–521.

Orben, A., Tomova, L., & Blakemore, S.-J. (2020). The effects of social deprivation on adolescent development and mental health. *The Lancet Child & Adolescent Health*, 4(8), 634–640.

Peltzman, S. (1975). The effects of automobile safety regulation. *Journal of Political Economy*, 83(4), 677–725.

Pless, B. (2016). Risk compensation: Revisited and rebutted. *Safety*, 2(3), 16.

Radun, I., Radun, J., Esmaeilikia, M., & Lajunen, T. (2018). Risk compensation and bicycle helmets: A false conclusion and uncritical citations. *Transportation Research Part F: Traffic Psychology and Behaviour*, 58, 548–555.

Rengasamy, S., Eimer, B., & Shaffer, R. E. (2010). Simple respiratory protection: Evaluation of the filtration performance of cloth masks and common fabric materials against 20–1000 nm size particles. *Annals of Occupational Hygiene*, 54(7), 789–798.

Seres, G., Balleyer, A. H., Cerutti, N., Danilov, A., Friedrichsen, J., Liu, Y., & Süer, M. (2021a). Face masks increase compliance with physical distancing recommendations during the COVID-19 pandemic. *Journal of the Economic Science Association*, 7(2), 139–158.

Seres, G., Balleyer, A., Cerutti, N., Friedrichsen, J., & Süer, M. (2021b). Face mask use and physical distancing before and after mandatory masking: No evidence on risk compensation in public waiting lines. *Journal of Economic Behavior & Organization*, 192, 765–781.

Suess, T., Remschmidt, C., Schink, S. B., Schweiger, B., Nitsche, A., Schroeder, K., et al. (2012). The role of facemasks and hand hygiene in the prevention of influenza transmission in households: Results from a cluster randomised trial; Berlin, Germany, 2009–2011. *BMC Infectious Diseases*, 12(1), 1–16.

Thunström, L., Newbold, S. C., Finnoff, D., Ashworth, M., & Shogren, J. F. (2020). The benefits and costs of using social distancing to flatten the curve for COVID-19. *Journal of Benefit-Cost Analysis*, 11(2), 179–195.

Tull, M. T., Edmonds, K. A., Scamaldo, K. M., Richmond, J. R., Rose, J. P., & Gratz, K. L. (2020). Psychological outcomes associated with stay-at-home orders and the perceived impact of COVID-19 on daily life. *Psychiatry Research*, 289:113098.

Van der Sande, M., Teunis, P., & Sabel, R. (2008). Professional and home-made face masks reduce exposure to respiratory infections among the general population. *PloS One*, 3(7), e2618.

WHO (2020). Advice on the use of masks in the context of COVID-19: Interim guidance. https://iris.who.int/handle/10665/332293

6 Preparing for the Next Pandemic

The Role of Behavioural Economics in Advance Care Planning

Juliet Hodges

6.1 INTRODUCTION

As the SARS-CoV-2 virus began to spread, it quickly became apparent that unprecedented numbers of people were going to become seriously ill and die from COVID-19. Helping people navigate and document their choices in case the worst should happen became of utmost importance (Bender et al., 2021), but local lockdowns and social distancing rules made these sensitive conversations even more difficult. Families were unable to visit their loved ones in hospitals or care homes, non-essential appointments were cancelled or took place over the phone, and any in-person treatment was delivered through dehumanising personal protective equipment. Worse still, in some parts of the United Kingdom, decisions were taken that removed choice from the individuals entirely. Due to fears over National Health Service (NHS) capacity, blanket Do Not Resuscitate (DNR) decisions were applied to groups of people, particularly those in care homes (Care Quality Commission, 2021). The British Institute of Human Rights found that a third of health and social care workers reported feeling under pressure to put DNRs in place without consulting the individual or their families (Hosali, 2020). One General Practitioner surgery in Wales even sent letters to its vulnerable patients, imploring them to complete DNR forms in case they contracted coronavirus, so that the 'young and fit' could be prioritised (Coronavirus: GP surgery apology over 'do not resuscitate' form, 2020). It is unclear how many people were impacted by these decisions or how many unlawful

DNR orders were followed before the issue was investigated and rectified. But this scandal reinforces some negative misconceptions around advance care planning (ACP): that it can be used as a tool to deny care and save money, particularly discriminating against older patients and those with complex medical needs.

At its best, ACP can increase quality of life, help patients to feel more empowered, increase the likelihood of goal-concordant care, and even reduce depression and anxiety for the loved ones they leave behind (Halpern et al., 2013; Mullick et al., 2013). This could include anything from a DNR order for specific situations to an advance directive (AD) stipulating goals of care more broadly or a lasting power of attorney identifying a surrogate decision-maker. Although the main benefit of this planning can be the increased intimacy and understanding through conversations between a patient, their family, and their healthcare provider (Jimenez et al., 2018), a substantial majority do not have any documented preferences for their end-of-life care. One study from 2016 found that just 4 per cent of people in England, and 2 per cent in Wales, had completed any kind of AD (Kitzinger & Kitzinger, 2016). This is also reflected in patient outcomes; although evidence suggests that most people would rather pursue treatments that prioritise their comfort and die at home, the majority of people die in hospital and invasive interventions at the end of life are increasing (Mohammed et al., 2019).

Encouraging more people to engage with this type of planning is vital to improve patient care at end of life, particularly in a post-COVID-19 world. This chapter will explore ACP from the perspective of patients and healthcare providers, as well as how behavioural economics principles could be used to encourage more people to engage with it.

6.2 WHY DO SO FEW PEOPLE ENGAGE IN ACP?

There are no hard and fast rules when it comes to ACP, and variations within local provision and even individual physicians' skills and attitudes mean that patients' experiences will vary (Courtright et al., 2018). As a result, many people who were classed as vulnerable to COVID-19 may not have had any conversations about resuscitation options or end-of-life care previously. This is especially the case for people with chronic but not terminal conditions, who may not have been seen as a particularly high or imminent risk before the pandemic (Bender et al., 2021). Even for those with a terminal diagnosis and a more predictable disease trajectory, evidence suggests that ACP does not consistently occur. This is due to barriers for patients, barriers for physicians, and system-level barriers.

6.2.1   Barriers for Patients

Despite the benefits of ACP, there are a number of reasons why individuals may not have engaged with it. Naturally there can be discomfort with confronting and discussing the concept of end of life, and people are often reluctant to do so. There are also consistent demographic variables that influence this. Younger people are less likely to have had these conversations, even when they are seriously ill. Wright et al. (2014) studied the treatment choices and outcomes of patients with metastatic cancers and found that those who were younger and better educated were more likely to be receiving chemotherapy in the last months of their life. They were also less likely to have accepted that their illness was terminal and, correspondingly, less likely to have engaged in any ACP with their doctor. As a result, they were more likely to receive intensive care (such as mechanical ventilation or cardiopulmonary resuscitation) in the last month of their lives and to die in hospital rather than at home. There are also racial differences in rates of ACP completion, likely driven by a lack of trust in the health system, following experiences of discrimination towards Black, Asian, and minority ethnic people (Williamson et al., 2019). Ethnic minorities are significantly less likely to have documented their wishes, although some studies suggest they are more likely to nominate a surrogate decision-maker (Halpern et al., 2011). Unfortunately, this leads to increased stress on the part of the surrogate and may even lead to care that is not consistent with goals: studies show surrogates are incorrect about the patient's wishes around one-third of the time (Shalowitz et al., 2006). This has been further compounded during the pandemic, as ethnic minorities are at higher risk from COVID-19 (Gupta et al., 2021).

On an interpersonal level, there can also be concerns about how their family or loved ones might react and a desire not to burden them with discussing or making these decisions. The family themselves may also not want to do all they can to preserve hope, to give them motivation to 'fight' the disease as part of the bravery narrative that is often applied to those dealing with a serious illness (Dolan, 2019). Conversely, people may choose to have informal discussions with their families rather than formally documenting their wishes, which can make it difficult for their healthcare provider to deliver the right care (Risk et al., 2019). In some cases, there may be potential conflict that the patient wants to avoid. A patient's relationship with their physician is also key, with a caring and trusting relationship associated with better outcomes (Risk et al., 2019). When that is lacking, patients may not trust that their wishes will be followed, even if they are discussed or documented. In a vignette study, information from the family about the patient's wishes, such as 'She's a fighter', did not affect the doctor's decisions about life support conversations (Turnbull et al., 2014). In fact, de Haes and Koedoot (2003) found that the biggest predictor of a patient receiving care in line with their wishes was their physician agreeing with the approach.

Patients and their families may sometimes want to defer to a clinician's opinion though, as they do not always feel equipped to make these decisions themselves. There is evidence to suggest that often people may not fully understand the severity of their condition or the reality of available treatments. For example, Weeks et al. (2012) found that 69 per cent of patients with metastatic lung cancer and 81 per cent of patients with metastatic colorectal cancer did not understand that their palliative chemotherapy was to manage their symptoms and not at all likely to cure their disease. Further, there are misconceptions about what life-sustaining care entails and what the likely outcomes are. This may be attributable in part to popular culture, as demonstrated by an analysis of almost 100 episodes of the medical dramas *Grey's Anatomy* and *House* (Portanova et al., 2015). Of the 46 depictions of cardiopulmonary resuscitation, 70 per cent of the patients survived. In real life, this figure is only 10 per cent, and survival is often accompanied by neurological or other impairments. Jacobsen et al. (2020) reported similar misconceptions during the pandemic, with patients asking if they would be able to walk around whilst on a ventilator. Given these limitations, it is unsurprising that many patients feel a sense of relief when they do not have to make these decisions themselves and might prefer to take a passive role (de Haes & Koedoot, 2003). Informed assent, a model of care where the physician assumes responsibility for making treatment decisions with the consent of the patient or their family, has become more common as a result of COVID-19 (Curtis et al., 2020).

The most critical factor may be physicians initiating the conversation. One survey found this was the most frequently cited barrier for patients (Emanuel et al., 1991). In the United Kingdom, 60 per cent of patients surveyed said they would discuss ACP only if their doctor brought it up, and that was the most important predictor of whether they had completed any kind of planning (Musa et al., 2015). Unfortunately, physicians have their own reasons to not initiate end-of-life care conversations and may themselves be waiting for the patient to bring it up first (Risk et al., 2019).

6.2.2   Barriers for Physicians

Although estimates suggest that as many as 99 per cent of physicians think ACP is important (Fulmer et al., 2018), this does not always translate into their behaviour. Firstly, they may feel ill-equipped to initiate and discuss such a sensitive topic. Less than a third of the physicians Fulmer et al. (2018) surveyed reported having any formal training in this area at all. As a result, there can be inconsistency across clinicians, and there is a strong relationship between a physician's comfort with end-of-life care and their attitude towards making palliative care referrals (Hui et al., 2016). Those who are less comfortable may just continue suggesting different treatment options rather than broaching the topic, expecting another healthcare provider to do so or that the patient will intervene when they want to stop (Halpern et al., 2013).

Secondly, finding the best time to have a conversation is also a challenge, as a person's goals for end-of-life care may change between being recorded and the care actually being delivered. For some conditions, such as Chronic Obstructive Pulmonary Disease (COPD) or heart failure, it can be difficult to know when to initiate such conversations, as the prognosis is unclear (Wichmann et al., 2018). A systematic review of the available literature on end-of-life preferences found that they tended to be stable over time, particularly for patients with serious illnesses and those who had engaged in ACP (Auriemma et al., 2014). But this may not apply in the case of a pandemic, where a new and sudden threat to life emerges. A number of studies have demonstrated that cancer patients are more willing to accept radical treatments than the general public or healthcare professionals (Slevin et al., 1990). For example, Bremnes et al. (1995) found that cancer patients aged under forty were more likely to accept treatment with only a 7 per cent chance of a cure, 8 per cent chance of symptom reduction, and an additional three months of life than a matched sample of health professionals and healthy participants. One study of cancer patients receiving palliative care found that their desire to live fluctuated up to 30 per cent over the course of a day, depending on the symptoms they were experiencing, such as pain, nausea, and anxiety (Chochinov et al., 1999). Loewenstein (2005) links this pattern of results to projection bias: people may feel very differently when they are healthy than when they are facing the prospect of their own mortality. Therefore, it is possible that a serious or terminal diagnosis, or a pandemic, could change people's priorities for end-of-life care.

Thirdly, some clinicians avoid discussing ACP because they believe that confronting patients with their prognosis could depress them or remove any hope they have (Mack & Smith, 2012). However, this is not the case: Smith et al. (2010) measured patients' levels of hope before and after bad news was delivered and found no significant difference, while Tierney et al. (2001) found patient satisfaction with their primary care visit increased when ACP had been discussed. In fact, open and honest communication with their physician can make patients feel more hopeful and empowered, while the absence of these frank discussions can lead to patients fearing the worst (Mack & Smith, 2012). In contrast, when it comes to their own care, clinicians may have quite different expectations for themselves than they have for their patients. For example, 98 per cent agreed they would want to know about their own terminal diagnosis, while the same group indicated that they thought only 26 per cent of their patients would want that information (Bruera et al., 2000). There is also evidence to suggest that when physicians get ill themselves they receive less aggressive treatments and are less likely to die in hospital (Blecker et al., 2016; Weissman et al., 2016).

Finally, in addition to concerns for the patient, the clinician may also have more personal reasons not to introduce the idea of ACP. Just as patients may wish to seem 'brave' by continuing treatment, the doctor might not wish to entertain the possibility of death for fear of seeming like a failure (Gawande, 2016). A qualitative study in a German hospital found that the majority of reasons for administering futile treatments were personal: the clinician felt guilty, felt hopeless, had injured pride, or was just hoping for a miracle (Jox et al., 2012). In some cases, clinicians had fears about the reaction of the patient and their family, or even the risk of legal action, if they refused the treatment. When faced with these emotions, it can seem easier to keep offering interventions.

6.2.3   Systemic Barriers

There are also more structural issues. Use of palliative or hospice care tends to depend on the local provision of such services (e.g.,

Lancaster et al., 2018). For example, Burke et al. (2020) implemented a standardised palliative care approach with a specialised team in a Louisiana hospital during the early months of COVID-19. They reflected that expecting doctors who were not specialised in palliative care to take that role was not viable; they could not spare the time to communicate effectively with patients and their families or engage with the educational material that had been provided. Without trained teams in place, it can be much more difficult to have these conversations and make the right referrals. This is also the case in the United Kingdom, where a new process called the Recommended Summary Plan for Emergency Care and Treatment is being implemented but is not yet available across all localities (Straw et al., 2021).

Without dedicated systems and healthcare professionals in place, the time to do so may simply not be available. With only ten minutes allotted to each patient for routine GP appointments in the NHS (Lancaster et al., 2018), finding the time to have an ACP conversation is difficult. Further, patients are likely to want multiple conversations over time as they weigh up the issues; it could take over six months for patients to feel prepared to complete any documentation (Hemsley et al., 2019).

There may also be a financial benefit to the clinician to continue treatment. Keating et al. (2010) found that cancer patients received more aggressive chemotherapy in the last weeks of their lives when their doctors were working on a fee-for-service basis. Differences in care have also been observed in the NHS and the private sector in the United Kingdom: for example, prostate cancer patients are more likely to receive surgery than radiotherapy in a private setting, which might reflect the greater cost (and potential payoff) associated with surgery (Barbiere et al., 2012; Warren et al., 2008). The financial context may even influence what patients choose, with some providers in the privatised US market requiring patients to forgo any potentially curative treatments in order to receive palliative care (Morrison, 2013).

6.3   HOW CAN BEHAVIOURAL ECONOMICS HELP?

Courtright et al. (2018) suggest that insights from behavioural economics might hold the key to changing clinician behaviour in end-of-life care, encouraging them to initiate conversations with patients and make referrals to palliative care teams. These interventions have been used to influence a range of behaviours in a clinical setting, from reducing prescriptions of opioids to improving hand hygiene in hospitals (King et al., 2016; Michael et al., 2018). This has already been tested in end-of-life decision-making on the patient side. Halpern et al. (2013) and Loewenstein et al. (2015) demonstrated that an existing default of comfort care or life-prolonging care can influence choices on an AD. However, this approach tends to be more effective at nudging a specific behaviour than a more intricate series of behaviours or outcomes. As such, detailed shared decision-making and ACP might prove too complex for a behavioural intervention, especially as facilitating these conversations well requires skill and training (Mathew et al., 2019). Moreover, clinicians may report that they have engaged the patient in shared decision-making for their treatment options, when the patient's perspective on how much involvement they have had is very different (Stiggelbout et al., 2015). However, existing palliative care teams are already trained and equipped to have these conversations; they just are not being involved at the right time (Gawande, 2016). Therefore, the targeted behaviour could simply be a timely referral to a palliative care service. One-off behaviours tend to respond far better to nudge interventions, for example, getting vaccinated versus repeated visits to the gym (Vlaev et al., 2019).

6.3.1   Prompts

As outlined earlier, the biggest predictor of having engaged in any kind of ACP is whether the patient has been asked about it by their healthcare provider. Simple reminders at the point of decision-making for physicians can be an effective way of ensuring the desired behaviour is enacted, and the widespread adoption of electronic medical records has made this type of intervention very easy and scalable to administer. For example, rates of flu vaccination were increased by 37.2 per cent in one study where physicians received a prompt to order the vaccine for every eligible patient they saw (Patel et al., 2017). This can be made even more effective with an accountability nudge, requiring clinicians who answer no to explain why (Meeker et al., 2016).

Prompts for ACP have already been trialled with providers and their patients with mixed results. Manz et al. (2020) found a four-fold increase in these conversations when clinicians were reminded by a text message on the day they were seeing high-risk patients. However, these were oncology patients, and the reminder was prompted by a machine learning tool that could predict patient mortality risk. Interventions targeting a more general patient population (e.g., those aged over seventy or over fifty with a chronic condition; Heiman et al., 2004) have had less success.

Where there is no access to such detailed forecasting, other prompts might help clinicians decide to raise the issue. The 'surprise' question has been used as a tool to assess the right moment to introduce palliative care, which is: 'Would I be surprised if this patient were to die in the next 12 months?' (Pattison & Romer, 2001). This question has been criticised for not being sensitive enough, as many patients who live much longer can also be included. Weijers et al. (2018) have suggested adding 'Would I be surprised if this patient is still alive after 12 months?' to improve accuracy, which was found to be effective in a vignette-based study. In another vignette study, Turnbull et al. (2014) found that prompting intensive care doctors to consider a patient's functional outcome after three months encouraged them to broach the topic of turning off life support with a patient's family. In light of COVID-19, this could be updated to ask specifically about risk from a novel or existing respiratory disease.

Prompting the patients themselves also has potential and does not need to be only in the context of a medical consultation. Josephs et al. (2018) tested an active choice intervention, making completing an AD part of the online onboarding process for new employees. When participants chose between completing an AD or a form to decline doing so, they were almost twice as likely to complete one as those who could simply skip the task. This must be combined with further discussions with a healthcare provider to avoid simply being a 'tick box' exercise, however. Providing patients with information and an AD template prior to their GP appointment, combined with a prompt for the physician, increases the likelihood they will complete it (Heiman et al., 2004). This suggests that where physician prompts have been unsuccessful, it may be due to the patient not being receptive to the conversation, rather than the physician not initiating it. This would be consistent with evidence that patients need time to think and make decisions, so may not be immediately ready for the conversation, particularly if they are not currently ill (Hemsley et al., 2019).

6.3.2   Framing

In addition to prompting patients to think about end-of-life choices, it is important to consider how these choices are framed, as this can have a significant impact on whether people engage and what they decide to do (e.g., Tversky & Kahneman, 1981).

In the case of AD forms, there are several ways this can be done. A first step could be simplifying the language, which can be complex and laden with medical jargon. Sudore et al. (2007) redesigned standard AD forms to meet a greater number of adults' literacy levels and found that more of their participants preferred the new version and had completed it in the six months following their study.

A second consideration is how the choices on the form are framed. Halpern et al. (2013) found that preferences were swayed towards life-prolonging or comfort-oriented care in a US patient population depending on which option was presented as the default. In other words, patients were more likely to choose whichever option had been pre-selected for them. In a later study, this effect was replicated, even when the participants were explicitly informed, they were being opted into one or the other and given the opportunity to change their minds (Loewenstein et al., 2015). The effect of defaults can be so strong that it is important to avoid influencing people's choices in this way.

A third, related, issue is the wording used to describe each option. In standard US ADs, the choice is presented neutrally between comfort-oriented care and life-prolonging care. However, in the United Kingdom, a patient might be asked to complete an advance decision to refuse treatment, which frames comfort care as refusing treatment altogether. As patients tend to prefer taking action over doing nothing (de Haes & Koedoot, 2003), this framing seems likely to deter them from choosing comfort care. This was demonstrated in a study by Hodges et al. (2023), where participants choosing treatment options were 18.5 per cent more likely to choose life-prolonging care when comfort care was framed as refusing treatment. These nuances may seem trivial on the surface, but it could be enough to stop people engaging with the decision-making and getting the outcome that they want.

This could also be relevant for how physicians themselves communicate. In a simulation study, Lu et al. (2015) demonstrated that most physicians framed life-sustaining care as the default, or even as a requirement. They mentioned comfort or palliative options only once the patient expressed their wish to avoid more aggressive treatment methods. Taken together, with a physician who is promoting prolonging life through invasive treatments and an alternative that sounds like abandoning treatment altogether, it is unsurprising that people choose not to engage or to document their wishes.

6.3.3 Salience

One difficulty with introducing ACP conversations earlier is that they feel less relevant to the patient, who is less likely to engage with them. Conversations about specific medical conditions or treatments can be alienating, particularly for those with limited knowledge or experience of them. As discussed earlier, patients may not understand the implications of having mechanical ventilation or other life-sustaining treatments over a long period of time (Jacobsen et al., 2020). It is also difficult to imagine significant changes to quality of life and capabilities from a position of relatively good health (Loewenstein, 2005). Therefore, focusing early conversations on a patient's goals and values or future planning more broadly can be a helpful starting point (Hemsley et al., 2019).

Even having personal experience with severe illness and surgical interventions is not necessarily enough for a patient to feel ready to take this step. However, one consistent factor that increases a patient's likelihood of engaging with ACP is having experienced the death of a loved one (Amjad et al., 2014). This was especially true when they had had to make decisions on behalf of the decedent. While this experience cannot be replicated in the form of an intervention, it may be that the COVID-19 pandemic provides a reference point for a greater number of people. Firstly, with over 150,000 people in the United Kingdom alone having died of COVID-19, it is likely that many more people have had this experience. Secondly, even without personal experience of bereavement during the pandemic, living through this time may make these inevitabilities feel more immediate and concrete. Physicians often use hypothetical scenarios as a tool to explore patients' preferences, such as hospital beds not being available or going into cardiac arrest (Land et al., 2019). COVID-19 might provide a more relatable hypothetical scenario for the next generations, supporting earlier ACP conversations before people are facing serious illness or frailty.

6.3.4 Non-monetary Incentives

In order to address the perverse incentivisation around end-of-life care, the nationalised US health insurer Medicare started reimbursing clinicians for ACP conversations in January 2016 (Pelland et al., 2019). This was greeted positively by clinicians, with 75 per cent of respondents in one survey agreeing that this change would make them more likely to talk to their patients about ACP (Fulmer et al.,

2018). But it was not reflected in practice: analysis from the first year of this benefit found its impact was underwhelming, and two-thirds of hospice and palliative care physicians did not bill on these ACP codes at all (Belanger et al., 2019). This is consistent with much of the pay-for-performance literature, which frequently demonstrates little or no impact of financial incentives on clinical behaviour (Himmelstein et al., 2014). However, interventions from behavioural science could offer a non-financial incentive for physicians to initiate ACP conversations.

Firstly, a widely used technique in the evaluation and feedback of clinician performance is comparison with their peers. This can be done at an organisational level, targeting specific sites or trusts that are underperforming, or at an individual level, ranking the clinicians in a certain population. For example, Hallsworth et al. (2016) targeted general practices prescribing more antibiotics than 80 per cent of practices in their local area, reducing prescriptions by 3.3 per cent relative to controls. Meeker et al. (2016) took the individual approach, informing clinicians whether or not their personal performance was in the top 10 per cent, which reduced antibiotic prescriptions by 16 percentage points. This could be applied to ACP by reviewing the percentage of a physician's patients who have documented their preferences and retrospectively reviewing care of to condition-specific guidelines (e.g., Earle et al., 2008).

Secondly, people like to act consistently with promises they have made, so making a commitment to do something – particularly publicly – makes it more likely to happen. This has also been used successfully to reduce antibiotic prescribing, where physicians across five outpatient clinics signed a letter committing to follow guidelines for antibiotic prescriptions (Meeker et al., 2014). The letter was printed in a large size featuring a photograph of the clinician and displayed in the patient examination rooms. Over the course of twelve weeks, this intervention reduced the number of prescriptions by around 20 per cent. For end-of-life care, a similar intervention could also be effective, encouraging clinicians to make a public commitment to ensuring they have fully explored and understood their patients' wishes and engaged with all the relevant support that is available to them.

6.4   CONCLUSION

The COVID-19 pandemic has shown at a global scale how quickly a person's health can change and leave them unable to communicate or make decisions about their care, bringing home the importance of ACP discussions and having wishes known. While there are multiple barriers to having these conversations, for patients, physicians, and the systems they operate in, behavioural economics provides a framework for potential interventions that can help to overcome them. In the wake of this global pandemic, we have an opportunity to raise these conversations earlier, giving patients the opportunity to reflect, discuss, and feel more prepared.

REFERENCES

Amjad, H., Towle, V., & Fried, T. (2014). Association of experience with illness and end-of-life care with advance care planning in older adults. *Journal of the American Geriatrics Society*, 62(7), 1304–1309. https://doi.org/10.1111/jgs.12894

Auriemma, C. L., Nguyen, C. A., Bronheim, R., Kent, S., Nadiger, S., Pardo, D., & Halpern, S. D. (2014). Stability of end-of-life preferences: A systematic review of the evidence. *JAMA Internal Medicine*, 174(7), 1085–1092. https://doi.org/10.1001/jamainternmed.2014.1183

Barbiere, J. M., Greenberg, D. C., Wright, K. A., Brown, C. H., Palmer, C., Neal, D. E., & Lyratzopoulos, G. (2012). The association of diagnosis in the private or NHS sector on prostate cancer stage and treatment. *Journal of Public Health*, 34(1), 108–114. https://doi.org/10.1093/pubmed/fdr051

Belanger, E., Loomer, L., Teno, J. M., Mitchell, S. L., Adhikari, D., & Gozalo, P. L. (2019). Early utilization patterns of the new Medicare procedure codes for advance care planning. *JAMA Internal Medicine*, 179(6), 829–830. https://doi.org/10.1001/jamainternmed.2018.8615

Bender, M., Huang, K.-N., & Raetz, J. (2021). Advance care planning during the COVID-19 pandemic. *Journal of the American Board of Family Medicine*, 34(Suppl), S16–S20. https://doi.org/10.3122/jabfm.2021.S1.200233

Blecker, S., Johnson, N. J., Altekruse, S., & Horwitz, L. I. (2016). Association of occupation as a physician with likelihood of dying in a hospital. *JAMA*, 315(3), 301–303. https://doi.org/10.1001/jama.2015.16976

Bremnes, R. M., Andersen, K., & Wist, E. A. (1995). Cancer patients, doctors and nurses vary in their willingness to undertake cancer chemotherapy. *European Journal of Cancer*, 31(12), 1955–1959. https://doi.org/10.1016/0959-8049(95)00513-7

Bruera, E., Neumann, C. M., Mazzocato, C., Stiefel, F., & Sala, R. (2000). Attitudes and beliefs of palliative care physicians regarding communication with terminally ill cancer patients. *Palliative Medicine*, 14(4), 287–298. https://doi.org/10.1191/026921600674582192

Burke, R. V., Rome, R., Constanza, K., Amedee, M., Santos, C., & Leigh, A. (2020). Addressing palliative care needs of COVID-19 patients in New Orleans, LA: A team-based reflective analysis. *Palliative Medicine Reports*, 1(1), 124–128. https://doi.org/10.1089/pmr.2020.0057

Care Quality Commission. (2021). Protect, respect, connect: Decisions about living and dying well during COVID-19. www.cqc.org.uk/publications/themed-work/protect-respect-connect-decisions-about-living-dying-well-during-covid-19

Chochinov, H. M., Tataryn, D., Clinch, J. J., & Dudgeon, D. (1999). Will to live in the terminally ill. *The Lancet*, 354(9181), 816–819. https://doi.org/10.1016/S0140-6736(99)80011-7

Coronavirus: GP surgery apology over 'do not resuscitate' form. (2020). BBC News. 1 April. www.bbc.com/news/uk-wales-52117814

Courtright, K. R., Cassel, J. B., & Halpern, S. D. (2018). A research agenda for high-value palliative care. *Annals of Internal Medicine*, 168(1), 71–72. https://doi.org/10.7326/M17-2164

Curtis, J. R., Kross, E. K., & Stapleton, R. D. (2020). The importance of addressing advance care planning and decisions about do-not-resuscitate orders during Novel Coronavirus 2019 (COVID-19). *JAMA*, 323(18), 1771–1772. https://doi.org/10.1001/jama.2020.4894

de Haes, H., & Koedoot, N. (2003). Patient centered decision making in palliative cancer treatment: A world of paradoxes. *Patient Education and Counseling*, 50(1), 43–49. https://doi.org/10.1016/S0738-3991(03)00079-X

Dolan, P. (2019). *Happy Ever After – A Radical New Approach to Living Well*. Penguin.

Earle, C. C., Landrum, M. B., Souza, J. M., Neville, B. A., Weeks, J. C., & Ayanian, J. Z. (2008). Aggressiveness of cancer care near the end of life: Is it a quality-of-care issue? *Journal of Clinical Oncology*, 26(23), 3860–3866. https://doi.org/10.1200/JCO.2007.15.8253

Emanuel, L. L., Barry, M. J., Stoeckle, J. D., Ettelson, L. M., & Emanuel, E. J. (1991). Advance directives for medical care: A case for greater use. *New England Journal of Medicine*, 324(13), 889–895. https://doi.org/10.1056/NEJM199103283241305

Fulmer, T., Escobedo, M., Berman, A., Koren, M. J., Hernández, S., & Hult, A. (2018). Physicians' views on advance care planning and end-of-life care conversations. *Journal of the American Geriatrics Society*, 66(6), 1201–1205. https://doi.org/10.1111/jgs.15374

Gawande, A. (2016). Quantity and quality of life: Duties of care in life-limiting illness. *JAMA*, 315(3), 267–269. https://doi.org/10.1001/jama.2015.19206

Gupta, A., Bahl, B., Rabadi, S., Mebane, A., Levey, R., & Vasudevan, V. (2021). Value of advance care directives for patients with serious illness in the era of COVID pandemic: A review of challenges and solutions. *American Journal of Hospice and Palliative Medicine*, 38(2), 191–198. https://doi.org/10.1177/1049909120963698

Hallsworth, M., Chadborn, T., Sallis, A., Sanders, M., Berry, D., Greaves, F., et al. (2016). Provision of social norm feedback to high prescribers of antibiotics in general practice: A pragmatic national randomised controlled trial. *The Lancet*, 387(10029), 1743–1752. https://doi.org/10.1016/S0140-6736(16)00215-4

Halpern, N. A., Pastores, S. M., Chou, J. F., Chawla, S., & Thaler, H. T. (2011). Advance directives in an oncologic intensive care unit: A contemporary analysis of their frequency, type, and impact. *Journal of Palliative Medicine*, 14(4), 483–489. https://doi.org/10.1089/jpm.2010.0397

Halpern, S. D., Loewenstein, G., Volpp, K. G., Cooney, E., Vranas, K., Quill, C. M., et al. (2013). Default options in advance directives influence how patients set goals for end-of-life care. *Health Affairs*, 32(2), 408–417. https://doi.org/10.1377/hlthaff.2012.0895

Heiman, H., Bates, D. W., Fairchild, D., Shaykevich, S., & Lehmann, L. S. (2004). Improving completion of advance directives in the primary care setting: A randomized controlled trial. *The American Journal of Medicine*, 117(5), 318–324. https://doi.org/10.1016/j.amjmed.2004.03.027

Hemsley, B., Meredith, J., Bryant, L., Wilson, N. J., Higgins, I., Georgiou, A., et al. (2019). An integrative review of stakeholder views on Advance Care Directives (ACD): Barriers and facilitators to initiation, documentation, storage, and implementation. *Patient Education and Counseling*, 102(6), 1067–1079. https://doi.org/10.1016/j.pec.2019.01.007

Himmelstein, D. U., Ariely, D., & Woolhandler, S. (2014). Pay-for-performance: Toxic to quality? Insights from behavioral economics. *International Journal of Health Services*, 44(2), 203–214. https://doi.org/10.2190/HS.44.2.a

Hodges, J., Stoyanova, L., & Galizzi, M. M. (2023). End-of-life preferences: a randomised trial of framing comfort care as refusal of treatment in the context of COVID-19. *Medical Decision Making*, 43(6), 631–641.

Hosali, S. (2020). Evidence from staff working in health, care and social work. The Joint Committee on Human Rights Inquiry into the human rights implications of the UK Government's Covid-19 response: Evidence from staff working in health, care and social work. The British Institute for Human Rights. bihr-jchr-evidence-submission-staff-2020.pdf

Hui, D., Cerana, M. A., Park, M., Hess, K., & Bruera, E. (2016). Impact of oncologists' attitudes toward end-of-life care on patients' access to palliative care. *The Oncologist*, 21(9), 1149–1155. https://doi.org/10.1634/theoncologist .2016-0090

Jacobsen, J. C., Tran, K. M., Jackson, V. A., & Rubin, E. B. (2020). Case 19-2020: A 74-year-old man with acute respiratory failure and unclear goals of care. *New England Journal of Medicine*, 382(25), 2450–2457. https://doi .org/10.1056/NEJMcpc2002419

Jimenez, G., Tan, W. S., Virk, A. K., Low, C. K., Car, J., & Ho, A. H. Y. (2018). Overview of systematic reviews of advance care planning: Summary of evidence and global lessons. *Journal of Pain and Symptom Management*, 56(3), 436–459 E25. https://doi.org/10.1016/j.jpainsymman.2018.05.016

Josephs, M., Bayard, D., Gabler, N. B., Cooney, E., & Halpern, S. D. (2018). Active choice intervention increases advance directive completion: A randomized trial. *MDM Policy & Practice*, 3(1), 2381468317753127. https://doi.org/ 10.1177/2381468317753127

Jox, R. J., Schaider, A., Marckmann, G., & Borasio, G. D. (2012). Medical futility at the end of life: The perspectives of intensive care and palliative care clinicians. *Journal of Medical Ethics*, 38(9), 540–545. https://doi.org/10.1136/ medethics-2011-100479

Keating, N. L., Landrum, M. B., Lamont, E. B., Earle, C. C., Bozeman, S. R., & McNeil, B. J. (2010). End-of-life care for older cancer patients in the Veterans Health Administration versus the private sector. *Cancer*, 116(15), 3732–3739. https://doi.org/10.1002/cncr.25077

King, D., Vlaev, I., Everett-Thomas, R., Fitzpatrick, M., Darzi, A., & Birnbach, D. J. (2016). 'Priming' hand hygiene compliance in clinical environments. *Health Psychology*, 35(1), 96–101. https://doi.org/10.1037/hea0000239

Kitzinger, J., & Kitzinger, C. (2016). Increasing understanding and uptake of advance decisions to refuse treatment in Wales. www.wcpp.org.uk/publication/ increasing-understanding-and-uptake-of-advance-decisions-to-refuse- treatment-in-wales/

Lancaster, H., Finlay, I., Downman, M., & Dumas, J. (2018). Commissioning of specialist palliative care services in England. *BMJ Supportive & Palliative Care*, 8(1), 93–101. https://doi.org/10.1136/bmjspcare-2016-001119

Land, V., Parry, R., Pino, M., Jenkins, L., Feathers, L., & Faull, C. (2019). Addressing possible problems with patients' expectations, plans and decisions for the future: One strategy used by experienced clinicians in advance care planning conversations. *Patient Education and Counseling*, 102(4), 670–679. https://doi.org/10.1016/j.pec.2018.11.008

Loewenstein, G. (2005). Projection bias in medical decision making. *Medical Decision Making*, 25(1), 96–105. https://doi.org/10.1177/0272989X04273799

Loewenstein, G., Bryce, C., Hagmann, D., & Rajpal, S. (2015). Warning: You are about to be nudged. *Behavioral Science & Policy*, 1(1), 35–42.

Lu, A., Mohan, D., Alexander, S. C., Mescher, C., & Barnato, A. E. (2015). The language of end-of-life decision making: A simulation study. *Journal of Palliative Medicine*, 18(9), 740–746. https://doi.org/10.1089/jpm.2015.0089

Mack, J. W., & Smith, T. J. (2012). Reasons why physicians do not have discussions about poor prognosis, why it matters, and what can be improved. *Journal of Clinical Oncology*, 30(22), 2715–2717. https://doi.org/10.1200/JCO.2012.42.4564

Manz, C. R., Parikh, R. B., Small, D. S., Evans, C. N., Chivers, C., Regli, S. H., et al. (2020). Effect of integrating machine learning mortality estimates with behavioral nudges to clinicians on serious illness conversations among patients with cancer: A stepped-wedge cluster randomized clinical trial. *JAMA Oncology*, 6(12), e204759. https://doi.org/10.1001/jamaoncol.2020.4759

Mathew, R., Weil, A., Sleeman, K. E., Bristowe, K., Shukla, P., Schiff, R., et al. (2019). The second conversation project: Improving training in end of life care communication among junior doctors. *Future Healthcare Journal*, 6(2), 129–136. https://doi.org/10.7861/futurehosp.6-2-129

Meeker, D., Knight, T. K., Friedberg, M. W., Linder, J. A., Goldstein, N. J., Fox, C. R., et al. (2014). Nudging guideline-concordant antibiotic prescribing: A randomized clinical trial. *JAMA Internal Medicine*, 174(3), 425–431. https://doi.org/10.1001/jamainternmed.2013.14191

Meeker, D., Linder, J. A., Fox, C. R., Friedberg, M. W., Persell, S. D., Goldstein, N. J., et al. (2016). Effect of behavioral interventions on inappropriate antibiotic prescribing among primary care practices: A randomized clinical trial. *JAMA*, 315(6), 562–570. https://doi.org/10.1001/jama.2016.0275

Michael, S. S., Babu, K. M., Androski, C., & Reznek, M. A. (2018). Effect of a data-driven intervention on opioid prescribing intensity among emergency department providers: A randomized controlled trial. *Academic Emergency Medicine*, 25(5), 482–493. https://doi.org/10.1111/acem.13400

Mohammed, A. A., Al-Zahrani, O., Salem, R. A., & Elsayed, F. M. (2019). Aggressive care at the end of life; where are we? *Indian Journal of Palliative Care*, 25(4), 539–543. https://doi.org/10.4103/IJPC.IJPC_59_19

Morrison, R. S. (2013). Models of palliative care delivery in the United States. *Current Opinion in Supportive and Palliative Care*, 7(2), 201–206. https://doi.org/10.1097/SPC.0b013e32836103e5

Mullick, A., Martin, J., & Sallnow, L. (2013). An introduction to advance care planning in practice. *British Medical Journal*, 347, f6064. https://doi.org/10.1136/bmj.f6064

Musa, I., Seymour, J., Narayanasamy, M. J., Wada, T., & Conroy, S. (2015). A survey of older peoples' attitudes towards advance care planning. *Age and Ageing*, 44(3), 371–376. https://doi.org/10.1093/ageing/afv041

Patel, M. S., Volpp, K. G., Small, D. S., Wynne, C., Zhu, J., Yang, L., et al. (2017). Using active choice within the electronic health record to increase influenza vaccination rates. *Journal of General Internal Medicine*, 32(7), 790–795. https://doi.org/10.1007/s11606-017-4046-6

Pattison, M., & Romer, A. L. (2001). Improving care through the end of life: Launching a primary care clinic-based program. *Journal of Palliative Medicine*, 4(2), 249–254. https://doi.org/10.1089/109662101750290335

Pelland, K., Morphis, B., Harris, D., & Gardner, R. (2019). Assessment of first-year use of Medicare's advance care planning billing codes. *JAMA Internal Medicine*, 179(6), 827–829. https://doi.org/10.1001/jamainternmed.2018.8107

Portanova, J., Irvine, K., Yi, J. Y., & Enguidanos, S. (2015). It isn't like this on TV: Revisiting CPR survival rates depicted on popular TV shows. *Resuscitation*, 96, 148–150. https://doi.org/10.1016/j.resuscitation.2015.08.002

Risk, J., Mohammadi, L., Rhee, J., Walters, L., & Ward, P. R. (2019). Barriers, enablers and initiatives for uptake of advance care planning in general practice: A systematic review and critical interpretive synthesis. *BMJ Open*, 9(9), e030275. https://doi.org/10.1136/bmjopen-2019-030275

Shalowitz, D. I., Garrett-Mayer, E., & Wendler, D. (2006). The accuracy of surrogate decision makers: A systematic review. *Archives of Internal Medicine*, 166(5), 493–497. https://doi.org/10.1001/archinte.166.5.493

Slevin, M. L., Stubbs, L., Plant, H. J., Wilson, P., Gregory, W. M., Armes, P. J., & Downer, S. M. (1990). Attitudes to chemotherapy: Comparing views of patients with cancer with those of doctors, nurses, and general public. *British Medical Journal*, 300(6737), 1458–1460. https://doi.org/10.1136/bmj.300.6737.1458

Smith, T. J., Dow, L. A., Virago, E., Khatcheressian, J., Lyckholm, L. J., & Matsuyama, R. (2010). Giving honest information to patients with advanced cancer maintains hope. *Oncology (Williston Park, N.Y.)*, 24(6), 521–525.

Stiggelbout, A. M., Pieterse, A. H., & De Haes, J. C. J. M. (2015). Shared decision making: Concepts, evidence, and practice. *Patient Education and Counseling*, 98(10), 1172–1179. https://doi.org/10.1016/j.pec.2015.06.022

Straw, S., McGinlay, M., Drozd, M., Slater, T. A., Cowley, A., Kamalathasan, S., et al. (2021). Advanced care planning during the COVID-19 pandemic: Ceiling of care decisions and their implications for observational data. *BMC Palliative Care*, 20(1), 10. https://doi.org/10.1186/s12904-021-00711-8

Sudore, R. L., Landefeld, C. S., Barnes, D. E., Lindquist, K., Williams, B. A., Brody, R., & Schillinger, D. (2007). An advance directive redesigned to meet the literacy level of most adults: A randomized trial. *Patient Education and Counseling*, 69(1), 165–195. https://doi.org/10.1016/j.pec.2007.08.015

Tierney, W. M., Dexter, P. R., Gramelspacher, G. P., Perkins, A. J., Zhou, X.-H., & Wolinsky, F. D. (2001). The effect of discussions about advance directives on patients' satisfaction with primary care. *Journal of General Internal Medicine*, 16(1), 32–40. https://doi.org/10.1111/j.1525-1497.2001.00215.x

Turnbull, A. E., Krall, J. R., Ruhl, A. P., Curtis, J. R., Halpern, S. D., Lau, B. M., & Needham, D. M. (2014). A scenario-based, randomized trial of patient values and functional prognosis on intensivist intent to discuss withdrawing life support. *Critical Care Medicine*, 42(6), 1455–1462. https://doi.org/10.1097/CCM.0000000000000227

Tversky, A., & Kahneman, D. (1981). The framing of decisions and the psychology of choice. *Science*, 211(4481), 453–458. https://doi.org/10.1126/science.7455683

Vlaev, I., King, D., Darzi, A., & Dolan, P. (2019). Changing health behaviors using financial incentives: A review from behavioral economics. *BMC Public Health*, 19(1), 1059. https://doi.org/10.1186/s12889-019-7407-8

Warren, J. L., Yabroff, K. R., Meekins, A., Topor, M., Lamont, E. B., & Brown, M. L. (2008). Evaluation of trends in the cost of initial cancer treatment. *Journal of the National Cancer Institute*, 100(12), 888–897. https://doi.org/10.1093/jnci/djn175

Weeks, J. C., Catalano, P. J., Cronin, A., Finkelman, M. D., Mack, J. W., Keating, N. L., & Schrag, D. (2012). Patients' expectations about effects of chemotherapy for advanced cancer. *New England Journal of Medicine*, 367(17), 1616–1625. https://doi.org/10.1056/NEJMoa1204410

Weijers, F., Veldhoven, C., Verhagen, C., Vissers, K., & Engels, Y. (2018). Adding a second surprise question triggers general practitioners to increase the thoroughness of palliative care planning: Results of a pilot RCT with case vignettes. *BMC Palliative Care*, 17(1), 64. https://doi.org/10.1186/s12904-018-0312-6

Weissman, J. S., Cooper, Z., Hyder, J. A., Lipsitz, S., Jiang, W., Zinner, M. J., & Prigerson, H. G. (2016). End-of-life care intensity for physicians, lawyers, and the general population. *JAMA*, 315(3), 303–305. https://doi.org/10.1001/jama.2015.17408

Wichmann, A. B., van Dam, H., Thoonsen, B., Boer, T. A., Engels, Y., & Groenewoud, A. S. (2018). Advance care planning conversations with palliative patients: Looking through the GP's eyes. *BMC Family Practice*, 19(1), 184. https://doi.org/10.1186/s12875-018-0868-5

Williamson, L. D., Smith, M. A., & Bigman, C. A. (2019). Does discrimination breed mistrust? Examining the role of mediated and non-mediated discrimination experiences in medical mistrust. *Journal of Health Communication*, 24(10), 791–799. https://doi.org/10.1080/10810730.2019.1669742

Wright, A. A., Zhang, B., Keating, N. L., Weeks, J. C., & Prigerson, H. G. (2014). Associations between palliative chemotherapy and adult cancer patients' end of life care and place of death: Prospective cohort study. *British Medical Journal*, 348, g1219. https://doi.org/10.1136/bmj.g1219

7   Human Challenge Trials for Research on COVID-19 and Beyond

The Case of 1Day Sooner

Jupiter Adams-Phipps, Steffen Kamenicek, and Virginia Schmit

7.1   INTRODUCTION

After the emergence of the COVID-19 pandemic in late 2019 and early 2020, the need for a vaccine became evident. Early on, substantial interest was generated around the idea of using human challenge trials (HCTs) as a possible way of speeding up vaccine development. HCTs (also known as 'controlled human infection models' or CHIMs) are trials in which volunteers are intentionally exposed to infectious disease-causing organisms for the purpose of testing novel vaccines or treatments, as well as to study the progression of the disease in a controlled environment. The practice of systematically infecting individuals with pathogens of interest has been recorded since the eighteenth century, although in most cases these infections did not meet the ethical standards that are in place today (Jamrozik & Selgelid, 2021). With the rise of modern research ethics in the 1970s and the wider implementation of these standards by the 1980s, HCTs that have been conducted more recently have been used to safely study a wide variety of pathogens (Adams-Phipps et al., 2023) and speed up the development of vaccines for typhoid (Jin et al., 2017) and cholera (Tacket et al., 1999). Despite this historical precedent, the

Special thanks to Mabel Rosenheck for her input on structure and content prior to writing, as well as for reviewing the draft and giving valuable insights and suggestions throughout. Additional thanks to the following members of the 1Day Sooner Research Team for their assistance in reviewing the draft: David Manheim, Witold Więcek, Keller Scholl, and James Wilkinson.

idea of conducting an HCT with SARS-CoV-2 (the causative agent of COVID-19) faced ethical and practical challenges, including the lack of any known rescue treatment for the disease and uncertainty around the potential long-term effects that volunteers exposed to the pathogen might someday experience (Sulmasy, 2021; World Health Organization, 2020b).

In March 2020, Eyal et al. published an article in *The Journal of Infectious Diseases* that examined the ethics of a potential COVID-19 HCT and argued that the risks associated with such a study could be acceptable. In response to the enthusiasm that many members of the general public had for the idea, the non-profit advocacy organisation 1Day Sooner was founded in April 2020. The organisation began recruiting volunteers who expressed interest in participating in a hypothetical COVID-19 HCT and eventually created an international database of nearly 40,000 prospective trial volunteers. By May 2020, the World Health Organization (WHO) released a report titled 'Key criteria for the ethical acceptability of COVID-19 human challenge studies' (World Health Organization, 2020a). The report did not aim to advocate for or against COVID-19 HCTs; rather, it presented guidelines that an eventual study would need to consider. In June 2020, a WHO advisory group released a draft of another report examining the feasibility, potential value, and limitations of a COVID-19 HCT, which was eventually published in December 2020 (World Health Organization, 2020b).

1Day Sooner continued investigation of the topic and established several areas of focus, with the goal of advocating on behalf of those interested in volunteering to participate in high-impact medical trials. The communications team amplified the voices of research volunteers in academic literature and public discourse by supporting the publication of over two dozen op-eds and numerous news articles on the topics of research trials and research participants. The organising team worked to answer potential volunteers' questions about HCTs and connect them with relevant trial opportunities, and the advocacy team engaged with regulators and lawmakers on projects that volunteers supported. Lacking direct and prior experience with HCTs and finding itself needing to inform these initiatives and the work of the organisation as a whole, 1 Day Sooner also established an independent research team to evaluate and produce information related to HCTs and the COVID-19 pandemic in general. In this chapter, we present these research projects in the context of the pandemic and discuss how these findings may be relevant to pandemic preparedness efforts in the future.

7.2   USE CASES FOR HCTS

In July 2021 Nguyen et al. (2021). published an article in *Clinical Infectious Diseases* that identified and discussed potential use cases for HCTs in the COVID-19 pandemic. Considering that the first US FDA-approved cholera vaccine was licensed in part on the basis of HCT efficacy data, Nguyen et al. suggested that COVID-19 HCTs could likewise be used to evaluate vaccine efficacy. The authors argued that there was potential for HCTs, used alongside an expanded safety trial, to replace phase 3 trials or, alternatively, in conjunction with phase 3 trials to provide expedited efficacy data in advance of phase 3 results. Furthermore, the authors highlighted that HCTs could be used to identify or verify correlates of protection (CoPs), biomarkers that correlate with vaccine-induced protection against specific infection outcomes. These CoPs could then be used as surrogate endpoints in clinical trials instead of clinical endpoints (such as observing symptoms of COVID-19), thus accelerating the approval of new vaccines. Nguyen et al. identified precedents for this approach: vaccines against hepatitis B, H5N1 influenza, and Japanese encephalitis were approved based on CoPs. The authors also suggested that HCTs could play a role in understanding the disease progression of COVID-19, including early stages of pathogenesis and the human immune system response. In the case of influenza, for example, HCTs have elucidated the evolutionary dynamics of influenza populations within a host. While recognising limitations of HCTs (such as problems with the generalizability of results due to differences between HCTs and real-world infection scenarios) and also paying heed to ethical aspects in light of appreciable risks to study participants, Nguyen et al. nonetheless concluded that there were many scenarios in which the benefits generated by HCTs would likely outweigh their risks.

7.3 ETHICAL PAYMENT TO HCT PARTICIPANTS

1Day Sooner commissioned an independent report that aimed to develop an ethical framework for financial compensation for HCT volunteers that was released in August 2020 (Lynch et al., 2020), with a peer-reviewed article discussing the report published in February 2021 (Lynch et al., 2021). The report did not consider whether COVID-19 HCTs met the relevant ethical standards at the time, but assumed that they could be deemed ethical eventually, and focused on offering guidance regarding compensation for volunteers in such a scenario. The working group behind this report determined that the issues of paying volunteers and relevant ethical concerns for participating in HCTs are similar to those raised around participating in other types of clinical research. Consequently, the group concluded that the same basic ethical payment framework consisting of reimbursement, compensation, and incentives used in other clinical research involving human volunteers could be applied to HCTs. Although a payment framework unique to HCTs was deemed unnecessary, the group did identify several factors they found to be particularly relevant to HCTs, and especially to HCTs for COVID-19. Considering the length and intensity of isolation and confinement that may be required to prevent unintentional disease transmission during the course of an HCT, the group argued that a payment framework should fully account for these burdens and that volunteers must be educated on trial procedures to ensure they are capable of giving proper informed consent. The group also suggested that a payment framework should compensate for other discomforts and risks associated with participation, including by providing volunteers with comprehensive no-fault insurance for riskier HCTs such as those for COVID-19. The group believed that HCT volunteers would likely be motivated by altruism, thus reducing the need for incentive payments, but cautioned that it must be ensured that volunteers are not confused by mistaken beliefs about the potential impact of the research or expectations of direct medical benefit as a result of participating. The group also considered issues around recruitment diversity and stigma associated with participation in HCTs and discussed how a payment framework might account for them. Finally, the group recommended independent ethical approval from ethics review boards that are familiar with HCTs. Although concerns have been raised over the offer of high payments for participation in clinical research, Lynch et al. (2021) suggested that substantial payment can be ethically appropriate and argued that there are comparable ethical concerns associated with payments being too low. As part of their report, the working group released a worksheet designed to 'help sponsors, researchers, and ethics reviewers systematically develop and assess ethically justifiable payment amounts' for COVID-19 HCTs (Lynch et al., 2021: 12).

7.4   RISK MODEL FOR COVID-19 HCTS

A SARS-CoV-2 dosing study would be necessary to determine the appropriate viral dose for any further HCTs, such as one investigating vaccine efficacy. Seeking to explore some of the risks that volunteers would face in a dosing study, Manheim et al. (2021) developed an interactive model that uses a Bayesian meta-analysis of data on infection fatality risks (IFRs) and hospitalisation in order to infer these risks in dosing study participants. By quantifying the risk of COVID-19 mortality and simulating the risk of a study, a publicly available web tool (Risk Model for Human Challenge Trials, 2021) allows users to interactively explore risks either to an individual or from participating in a study. By combining age- and location-specific SARS-CoV-2 seroprevalence data from thirty-four studies with corresponding mortality data, the model generates estimates of both IFR (the probability that a person infected with COVID-19 would die, accounting for age) and hospitalisation risk. The risk to an individual participating in a study is uncertain, being dependent on the dose of virus they are given. As such, the model is restricted to give an upper bound estimate for the risk of mortality and hospitalisation. Taking into account this uncertainty and the study design, the probability of any individual experiencing severe disease or death in such a trial is calculated as a function of each individual's risk (as estimated by the risk model) and the number of participants in the trial. Using OpenSAFELY data (Williamson et al., 2020), the model estimates that the average mortality risk in healthy twenty- to twenty-nine-year-olds is 1.9 times lower than in the general population. Applying this estimate to a study involving fifty people, the probability of at least one death occurring is 0.13 per cent, and the probability of at least one hospitalisation occurring is 1.1 per cent. However, the model is unable to include estimates of longer-term risks due to a lack of reliable data on these risks being available at the time of its creation, leading 1Day Sooner to address this topic further on its website with additional information as it has been published. The model is designed to be adapted and expanded in the future, and additional data from new and updated studies can be added as it becomes available. Seroprevalence and mortality data from low- and middle-income countries would be of particular interest to incorporate.

7.5 SYSTEM REVIEW OF PAST HCTS

To better inform discussion around the use of HCTs throughout history, Adams-Phipps et al. (2023) conducted a systematic review of HCTs published between 1980 and 2021, with the goal of assessing the reporting of clinical outcomes, adverse events (AEs), and risk mitigations. After searching the PubMed Central and PubMed databases and reviewing the reference lists of several prior reviews and studies, more than 2,800 articles were screened to identify 308 studies that described 15,046 challenged volunteers. With zero deaths or cases of permanent damage, and only 24 challenged volunteers with serious adverse events (SAEs), this review found that HCTs have been used to safely study at least 28 different categories of infectious disease organisms. However, the review also found significant inconsistencies in the definition and reporting of AEs: 56.7 per cent of included studies did not define AEs, and 33.1 per cent and 34.2 per cent of included studies failed to report AE and SAE data, respectively. Additionally, issues around the definition and self-identification of challenges both within and across studies, as well as an incomplete use of clinical trial registries and databases, made it difficult to collect and compare data consistently across different studies. The authors highlighted risk mitigations in HCTs as a topic in need of further review and also suggested that efforts should be made to standardise definitions and AE data reporting across published HCTs.

7.6   MOTIVATIONS OF POTENTIAL HCT VOLUNTEERS

In response to concerns raised about the potential for invalid consent and exploitation in HCTs, Marsh et al. (2022) conducted a study measuring altruistic motivations, values, and behaviours, as well as risk preferences and behaviours, in 1,911 potential volunteers for COVID-19 HCTs. 1Day Sooner queried a set of volunteers from their database and compared their answers with individuals from the general public. Questions were developed for the HEXACO and Domain-Specific Risk Taking (DOSPERT) paradigms: HEXACO investigates dimensions of personality (Honesty–Humility, Emotionality, eXtraversion, Agreeableness, Conscientiousness, and Openness to Experience), while DOSPERT investigates domain-specific risk-taking tendencies. The results of the project indicated that HCTs for COVID-19 attract volunteers with altruistic attitudes and with no heightened risk-taking tendencies over controls,[1] which, taken together, may alleviate some ethical concerns over volunteers for these HCTs.

---

[1] For the study, 999 control participants were recruited to be reflective of the US population distribution according to the 2019 census.

7.7   WEBSITE INITIATIVES AND RESOURCES

In addition to contributing to the scientific corpus of knowledge on HCTs throughout the COVID-19 pandemic, another aim of 1Day Sooner has been to educate and inform the general public by assembling accessible explanations regarding HCTs and COVID-19 on its website (1Day Sooner, n.d.). To provide information about risks for potential HCT volunteers that could not be incorporated in the risk model developed by Manheim et al. (2021), the website hosts a Frequently Asked Questions (FAQ) section discussing the long-term effects of COVID-19, as well as a database of additional resources on the topic. Various other research repositories are also available, including literature on treatments for COVID-19 and ethical aspects of HCTs. These referenced and frequently updated resources are also intended to help combat the deluge of misinformation surrounding COVID-19 that can be found elsewhere online.

7.8   HCTS FOR COVID-19 AND FUTURE PANDEMICS

1Day Sooner's initial approach to the COVID-19 pandemic was to mobilise volunteers around the idea that HCTs were both ethically justifiable and necessary to speed up vaccine development and accelerate our understanding of the virus in order to help end the pandemic as quickly as possible. One of the key benefits of using an HCT during the COVID-19 pandemic would have been the ability to obtain results quickly, but the lack of an existing challenge model or challenge strain and the lack of consensus over whether and how to use HCTs delayed their use significantly and largely erased that benefit. When numerous effective vaccines were developed by the end of 2020, the overall 'social value' of COVID-19 HCTs decreased to the point where many who had considered conducting them no longer believed that they were worth the risk (Rosenheck,2022). For example, Johnson & Johnson and the US National Institutes of Health (NIH) both considered using HCTs for SARS-CoV-2 vaccine development but did not pursue them further once it became clear that phase 3 trials would be sufficient for developing first-generation vaccines (Rosenheck, 2022). The funding and support that vaccine development and manufacturing received from Operation Warp Speed and the federal government in the United States, the US NIH's efforts to coordinate and overlap phases of clinical trials, and the lacklustre public health response in the United Kingdom and the United States were among a myriad of factors that precluded the use of COVID-19 HCTs (Rosenheck, 2022).

The private HCT service provider hVIVO conducted a dose optimisation HCT in the United Kingdom in early 2021 (Killingley et al., 2022). In simply moving forward with an HCT using a newly emerged infectious organism, hVIVO and their UK partners have helped demonstrate that these trials can be run safely and ethically, even in an emergent pandemic environment. As the first COVID-19 HCT, it is an example of a successful deployment of this investigative technique and a model for both lessons learned and successful accomplishments. However, in order for HCTs to have a greater impact in any future pandemic, frameworks must be developed before that situation arises. By developing challenge model protocols and establishing the infrastructure needed to rapidly institute them, it becomes possible to answer questions of when and how to use HCTs far more quickly, based on what is known about the specific pathogen. Transparency and availability of results are crucial ethical prerequisites for any research involving human subjects (World Medical Association, 2013), and 1Day Sooner strongly recommends that all protocols for HCTs be made available publicly following ethical and IRB approval.

It also must be recognised that HCTs are not necessarily an appropriate response to every pathogen under every circumstance. For example, a 2017 report on ethical considerations for Zika virus HCTs determined that such a trial would have been difficult to justify at the time but 'could be ethically justified if certain conditions were met' (Shah et al., 2017). During the COVID-19 pandemic, several concerns were raised against the use of HCTs, and similar issues in a future pandemic would need clear and pandemic-specific responses, ideally based on clear guidelines that could be made in advance.

7.9 CONCLUSION

Although COVID-19 HCTs were not used to the extent that 1Day Sooner hoped they would be, in part because vaccines were available far faster than most expected, the work done by the organisation throughout the COVID-19 pandemic still yielded relevant insights and should be extended to inform potential approaches in the future. Investigating ethical payment for HCT volunteers was an important step in proposing practical guidelines for standardisation of payment, and by conducting a systematic review of past HCTs, 1Day Sooner's research team informed both the advocacy organisation and the general public about the use of HCTs throughout history. The use cases for HCTs identified by Nguyen et al. (2021) can also be generalised to other pathogens, and many of the arguments presented in favour of using HCTs in the context of a pandemic are likely to remain relevant in the future. Awareness of HCTs has expanded, particularly amongst policymakers, and the study conducted by Marsh et al. (2022) shows that potential HCT volunteers with altruistic motivations are eager to participate in responding quickly to global pandemic-level threats. 1Day Sooner's efforts to educate the general public about COVID-19 and provide resource collections through its website were also valuable initiatives that could be replicated in a future pandemic to help combat misinformation. Creating models to characterise the risks associated with conducting an HCT (such as the model developed by Manheim et al., 2021) is crucial for educating future participants and addressing concerns regarding involvement in HCTs. Using the approaches and tools developed during the COVID-19 pandemic to inform strategies in the future, 1Day Sooner believes that HCTs remain an important strategy to consider for pandemic preparedness efforts.

REFERENCES

1Day Sooner. (n.d.). 1Day Sooner. www.1daysooner.org

Adams-Phipps, J., Toomey, D., Więcek, W., Schmit, V., Wilkinson, J., Scholl, K., et al. (2023). A systematic review of human challenge trial designs and their safety. *Clinical Infectious Diseases*, 76(4), 609–619.

Eyal, N., Lipsitch, M., & Smith, P. G. (2020). Human challenge studies to accelerate coronavirus vaccine licensure. *Journal of Infectious Diseases*, 221(11), 1752–1756. https://doi.org/10.1093/infdis/jiaa152

Jamrozik, E., & Selgelid, M. J. (2021). *Human Challenge Studies in Endemic Settings: Ethical and Regulatory Issues.* Springer Nature. https://doi.org/10.1007/978-3-030-41480-1

Jin, C., Gibani, M. M., Moore, M., Juel, H. B., Jones, E., Meiring, J., et al. (2017). Efficacy and immunogenicity of a Vi-tetanus toxoid conjugate vaccine in the prevention of typhoid fever using a controlled human infection model of Salmonella Typhi: A randomised controlled, phase 2b trial. *The Lancet*, 390(10111), 2472–2480. https://doi.org/10.1016/S0140-6736(17)32149-9

Killingley, B., Mann, A., Kalinova, M., Boyers, A., Goonawardane, N., Zhou, J., et al. (2022). Safety, tolerability and viral kinetics during SARS-CoV-2 human challenge in young adults. *Nature Medicine*, 28, 1031–1041. https://doi.org/10.1038/s41591-022-01780-9.

Lynch, H. F., Darton, T., Largent, E., Levy, J., McCormick, F., Ogbogu, U., et al. (2020). Ethical payment to participants in human infection challenge studies, with a focus on SARS-CoV-2: Report and recommendations. Scholarly Paper 3674548. Social Science Research Network. https://doi.org/10.2139/ssrn.3674548

Lynch, H. F., Darton, T. C., Levy, J., McCormick, F., Ogbogu, U., Payne, R. O., et al. (2021). Promoting ethical payment in human infection challenge studies. *The American Journal of Bioethics*, 21(3), 11–31. https://doi.org/10.1080/15265161.2020.1854368

Manheim, D., Więcek, W., Schmit, V., Morrison, J., & 1Day Sooner Research Team. (2021). Exploring risks of human challenge trials for COVID-19. *Risk Analysis*, 41(5), 710–720. https://doi.org/10.1111/risa.13726

Marsh, A. A., Magalhaes, M., Peeler, M., Rose, S. M., Darton, T. C., Eyal, N., et al. (2022). Characterizing altruistic motivation in potential volunteers for SARS-CoV-2 challenge trials. *PLoS ONE*, 17(11), e0275823.

Nguyen, L. C., Bakerlee, C. W., McKelvey, T. G., Rose, S. M., Norman, A. J., Joseph, N., et al. (2021). Evaluating use cases for human challenge trials in accelerating SARS-CoV-2 vaccine development. *Clinical Infectious Diseases*, 72(4), 710–715. https://doi.org/10.1093/cid/ciaa935

Risk Model for Human Challenge Trials. (2021). https://1daysooner.shinyapps.io/Riskmodel/

Rosenheck, M. (2022). Risk, benefit, and social value in Covid-19 human challenge studies: Pandemic decision making in historical context. *Monash Bioethics Review*, 40(2), 188–213. https://doi.org/10.1007/s40592-022-00156-6.

Shah, S., Kimmelman, J., Drapkin Lyerly, A., Fernandez Lynch, H., McCutchan, F., Miller, F., et al. (2017). Ethical considerations for Zika virus human challenge trials: Report & recommendations. www.niaid.nih.gov/sites/default/files/EthicsZikaHumanChallengeStudiesReport2017.pdf

Sulmasy, D. P. (2021). Are SARS-CoV-2 human challenge trials ethical? *JAMA Internal Medicine*, 181(8), 1031–1032. https://doi.org/10.1001/jamainternmed.2021.2614

Tacket, C. O., Cohen, M. B., Wasserman, S. S., Losonsky, G., Livio, S., Kotloff, K., et al. (1999). Randomized, double-blind, placebo-controlled, multicentered trial of the efficacy of a single dose of live oral cholera vaccine CVD 103-HgR in preventing cholera following challenge with *Vibrio cholerae* O1 El Tor Inaba three months after vaccination. *Infection and Immunity*, 67(12). https://doi.org/10.1128/IAI.67.12.6341-6345.1999

Williamson, E. J., Walker, A. J., Bhaskaran, K., Bacon, S., Bates, C., Morton, C. E., et al. (2020). Factors associated with COVID-19-related death using OpenSAFELY. *Nature*, 584(7821), 430–436. https://doi.org/10.1038/s41586-020-2521-4

World Health Organization. (2020a). Key criteria for the ethical acceptability of COVID-19 human challenge studies. https://apps.who.int/iris/bitstream/handle/10665/331976/WHO-2019-nCoV-Ethics_criteria-2020.1-eng.pdf

World Health Organization. (2020b). Feasibility, potential value and limitations of establishing a closely monitored challenge model of experimental COVID-19 infection and illness in healthy young adult volunteers. www.who.int/publications/m/item/feasibility-potential-value-and-limitations-of-establishing-a-closely-monitored-challenge-model-of-experimental-covid-19-infection-and-illness-in-healthy-young-adult-volunteers

World Medical Association. (2013). World Medical Association Declaration of Helsinki: Ethical principles for medical research involving human subjects. *JAMA*, 310(20), 2191–2194. https://doi.org/10.1001/jama.2013.281053

8 Do the Public Support 'Hard' or 'Soft' Public Policies?

Trends during COVID-19 and Implications for the Future

Sanchayan Banerjee, Manu Savani, and Ganga Shreedhar

8.1 INTRODUCTION

Policymakers have several types of policy instruments at their disposal to achieve societal goals by changing behaviour. Directive and top-down policy instruments include mandates, laws, regulations, taxes, and subsidies (John, 2011; Schneider & Ingram, 1990). These can be described as 'harder' policies (Zehavi, 2012). In contrast, 'softer' policies aim to persuade and leave the final choice of behaviour to the individual; for example, preference-based or information-based policies (Galizzi, 2014) that promote awareness and personal choice. Nudges are increasingly popular as a 'soft' policy instrument amongst policymakers, and it is easy to see why. After all, nudges do not restrict choice (like mandates) or explicitly alter the overall costs and benefits through financial costs on the target audience (as economic regulatory tools such as taxes or fines might) or through financial incentives (such as grants or subsidies) (Thaler & Sunstein, 2009). They may also be cost-effective compared to 'hard' instruments (Benartzi et al., 2017). In contrast, 'hard' instruments like taxes and rules can be unpopular. Recent studies confirm that there is much public support for using nudges as a behavioural policy instrument in various domains including public health (Diepeveen et al., 2013; Reisch & Sunstein, 2016; Sunstein, 2016).

It was rather striking, then, the extent to which the public accepted unprecedented 'hard' policy measures during the early months of the pandemic, more so than decision-makers may have expected (Duffy & Allington, 2020). This appeared to contradict the findings of recent work that people prefer to be nudged rather than mandated (Diepeveen et al., 2013; Sunstein et al., 2018). These trends prompted us to review public support for 'hard' versus 'soft' COVID-19 policy measures (Banerjee et al., 2021). We found evidence of widespread support for harder measures, both in the United Kingdom and globally. Respondents from fifteen Western European countries were more satisfied once their governments introduced measures such as lockdowns to curb COVID-19 (Genie et al., 2020). Findings from Hungary also indicated broad support for both nudges and regulatory measures relating to health behaviours, based on a survey fielded in November 2020 (Dudás & Szántó, 2021).

When we examined *what drives preferences for 'soft' and 'hard' policies*, in the context of both COVID-19 and other health and environmental policy issues, we found a range of possible determinants, including individual-level factors (e.g., socio-demographic factors like age and gender) and contextual factors (e.g., national context, framing effects). We also found several gaps in the literature, such as a dearth of rigorous empirical evidence on studies examining the stability of support for soft versus hard policies over time, as well as implications for support for policy action on other issues like environmental and climate change. We therefore proposed a research agenda that paid more attention to cross-country survey evidence and experimental techniques to measure COVID-19 policy preferences; that delved further into socio-demographic characteristics and psychological attitudes as predictors of preference; and that considered change over time in preferences, as well as spillovers in preferences for 'hard' policies to other policy domains (for details, see Banerjee et al., 2021, Table 2).

Using our previous work as a starting point (Banerjee et al., 2021), we have two main goals in this chapter. The first is to examine the evidence on whether public support for hard policies has persisted over the duration of the pandemic. We now have more information and experience of the policies that were implemented across countries. Section 8.2 revisits empirical data on public support for various examples of 'hard' COVID-19 policies. Our second goal is to revisit the scholarly literature on drivers of support for hard versus soft COVID-19 policies and potential spillover effects for environmental policy. We report in Section 8.3 on new developments in the literature on policy preferences. We find that recent work has begun to address some of the gaps we identified. The evidence base now sheds more light on individual factors, like political partisanship (Duren et al., 2021; Gadarian et al., 2021), and risk perceptions (Dudás & Szántó, 2021), in explaining public support for different types of policy measures. While these developments are welcome, we conclude with our reflections on outstanding gaps in our knowledge and where the research agenda should go next.

8.2   TRENDS IN PUBLIC POLICY SUPPORT FOR 'HARD' COVID-19 POLICIES

Governments have deployed a wide range of 'hard' public policy measures since March 2020. Measures to contain the spread of the virus have ranged from closure of schools and workplaces to cancellations of social events and bans against travel, both domestically and internationally. Unlike what we had seen in the pre-pandemic period,[1] harder measures to mitigate COVID-19 seem to have garnered strong public support globally (Banerjee et al., 2021; Dudás & Szántó, 2021). Duren et al. (2021) report broad levels of support across the United States for measures such as social distancing on public transport and wearing masks in indoor public spaces. Residents of Australia experienced one of the toughest lockdown regimes in the world. They nonetheless largely agreed in July–August 2020 that their borders should stay closed (76 per cent of respondents) and largely disagreed that the government's restrictions were excessive (65 per cent) (Manipis et al., 2021).

---

[1] People have been shown to prefer softer libertarian policies over taxes and bans; for details, see Sunstein (2016), Reisch and Sunstein (2016).

What is unclear is whether this widespread support is indicative of a more enduring trend in public preferences in favour of harder policies or a one-off change that might wane over time.

There remains little time-series analysis in the scholarly literature that addresses this question directly. To shed some light on how public support for hard policies may have evolved over time, we draw upon public opinion polling gathered by YouGov's COVID-19 Public Monitor (2022).[2] We pool data from nineteen countries drawing on polls run from 21 February 2020 to 31 December 2021. The public opinion tracker asks respondents about a range of 'hard' and 'soft' policies including: (i) quarantining anyone who has been in contact with a contaminated patient, (ii) quarantining any location that a contaminated patient has lived in, (iii) free provision of face masks, (iv) working from home measures, (v) temporarily suspending schools, (vi) cancelling large events, (vii) cancelling routine hospital procedures, (viii) banning all inbound flights, and (ix) quarantining all inbound passengers. We classify the provision of free face masks and working from home as 'soft' COVID-19 measures and the remainder as 'hard' policies. These questions are summarised in Table A.1.

In Figure 8.1 we present public support in percentage terms over eight quarterly time periods spanning February 2020 to December 2021. A higher percentage indicates more public support. We find that levels of support for all nine policies in our dataset have consistently decreased over time but that support for 'hard' policies has declined more sharply over time. For example, measures such as cancelling large events, hospital procedures, school closures, and cancelling air travel all demonstrate a marked decline in public support from Q1 to Q8. In contrast, support for free provision of masks, a relatively 'soft' policy, barely changed over the same period. Public support for all 'hard' COVID-19 measures is significantly higher in Vietnam, Malaysia, and Philippines, relative to the United Kingdom.

---

[2] While online opinion polling may be critiqued as not being fully representative, or subject to measurement error, we find this data one of the few available ways to examine public attitudes over this period with an international sample.

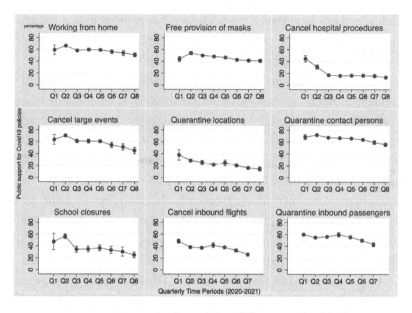

FIGURE 8.1 International trends in public support for COVID-19 measures over 2020–2021
Note: Pooled public support for different COVID-19 containment measures from nineteen countries, from quarter 1 of 2020 (labelled Q1) to quarter 4 of 2021 (labelled Q8). The first quarter of 2021 is Q5. Data is limited to Q1–Q7 for policy support on cancellation of inbound flights and quarantining of inbound passengers. For details, see Table A.2.
Source: YouGov Plc 2022 © All rights reserved.

Further, on average, public support for provision of free masks in the United Kingdom is significantly lower than all other countries in the dataset (for details, see Table A.2). The period includes successive waves of COVID variants including the Delta and Omicron waves, but these events do not appear especially influential in slowing the decline in support. Overall, then, the data suggests that preference shifts towards 'harder' policy measures varies across countries and in the immediate aftermath of the COVID-19 are not likely to be sustained over time.

We also plot trends in UK public policy preferences in Figure 8.2. While the overall support for both hard and soft measures decrease

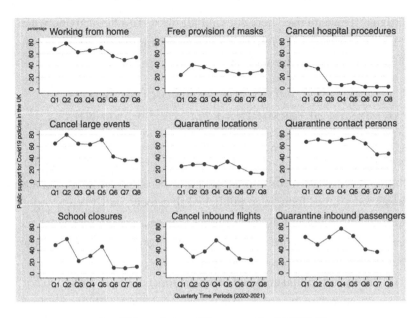

FIGURE 8.2 UK trends in public support for COVID-19 measures over 2020–2021
Note: Public support for COVID-19 containment measures from the United Kingdom, from quarter 1 of calendar year 2020 (labelled Q1) to quarter 4 of 2021 (labelled Q8). The start of 2021 is labelled Q5.
Source: YouGov Plc 2022 © All rights reserved.

over time, there are two distinct peaks for the United Kingdom. After the first peak in Q2 (2020 quarter 2), the second peak of public support is evident in Q5 (2021 quarter 1), particularly for policies such as cancelling large events and school closures. The timing corresponds with the winter lockdown imposed by the government in early 2021. Public support for both hard and soft policies increase during periods of rising and high infection rates that were marked by national lockdowns in the United Kingdom (see Q4–Q5 in Figure 8.2, covering the winter season 2020/2021). However, after this period, support gradually wanes, even during later waves of infection associated with new variants of the coronavirus (Q8). This may be in response to the outbreak being more effectively contained with the vaccination effort, and the perception of risk falling, or perhaps due to compliance 'fatigue'. The data used here does not allows us to adjudicate between these factors but raises important questions around the shifts in public preferences over the short and medium term.

8.3 THE ROLE OF INDIVIDUAL AND CONTEXTUAL FACTORS IN DETERMINING POLICY SUPPORT: WHAT MORE HAVE WE LEARNED?

In the short time since our state-of-the-art review on public preferences for health and environmental policies, several compelling and insightful studies have been published that focus on COVID-19 policies and how the public view them. This section reviews what we learn from these studies and to what extent gaps remain against our earlier call on directions for research.

Many individual and contextual factors have been linked to policy preferences, as discussed in Banerjee et al. (2021). Political ideology has been linked to support for certain policy instruments relating to environmental protection, welfare policy, and obesity reduction (Haselswerdt & Bartels, 2015; Mazzocchi et al., 2015; Owen et al., 2012). New evidence adds COVID-19 policies to that list, as Gadarian et al. (2021) investigate the role of partisanship in the United States. The handling of COVID-19 in the United States, particularly in terms of messaging and communications in 2020, quickly became synonymous with partisan divergence. Face masks were the new and highly visual political dividing line, a further source of polarisation after a fraught election race and outcome (Kahane, 2021; Lang et al., 2021).

Gadarian et al. (2021) surveyed 3,000 US residents in March 2020 and defined partisanship based on measures of party affiliation, ideological position, and intended vote in the US 2020 presidential election. Twenty different policies, ten relating to COVID-19 (such as free testing) and ten more relating to wider public policy with impacts on the pandemic (such as travel bans for China), were put to respondents to assess support or opposition. They found that partisanship successfully explains differences in policy preferences, even controlling for other individual characteristics (education and income) and context (local COVID-19 deaths and news consumptions). For some policies, partisanship was not a source of difference, including whether states should take the lead on COVID-19 policies and whether firms should be compensated. On others, there were strong differences based on partisanship. Democrats were much more strongly in support of measures we would place on the 'hard' end of the policy instrument spectrum, involving considerable spending or mandates, such as providing paid sick leave, cancelling public events, waiving treatment costs, and providing free testing. The timing of the Gadarian et al. (2021) survey is important. It gives us direct insights into how entrenched partisanship was from the very beginning of the pandemic. Republicans reported less concern and less compliance with recommended health behaviours. Partisanship was found to be the single most effective predictor of differences in behaviours, attitudes, and policy preferences during the first month of COVID-19 and 'the deepest cleavage' (2021: 10).

We should take care, however, not to overstate the importance of partisanship. In a survey of over 2,000 people designed to analyse variation across US states, Duren et al. (2021) report a surprising degree of consensus across US states in support of social distancing on public transport and masks in public spaces. This study does not directly contrast soft and hard policy measures, and the eight policies put to respondents all relate to regulations and laws in one form or another. But it is valuable for our argument in cautioning against framing the United States in overly simplistic terms. Although there were high-profile cases of people refusing to wear masks, in every state most respondents supported mask mandates in public and on public transport (Duren et al., 2021: 3).

While we should try to understand sub-national policy preferences, the authors suggest that states may be less meaningful units of analysis as they cannot precisely capture population density and rural–urban characteristics. It appears a limitation of the current literature that research on partisanship and ideology has been focused on the United States, despite the potential for learning from other countries in Europe and the world. Further, relatively stable factors such as political ideology may explain some differences across geographies but are not as useful for understanding significant change over time within a country. We agree with the authors' suggestions that further work needs to consider comparative cases across countries and more micro-level geographies to understand differences across communities, including based on social cohesion or norms.

A further factor that has received attention in the literature relates to risk perceptions. We welcome this development, as it responds to our earlier call for more work on psychological and behavioural variables. Dudás and Szántó (2021) investigate the importance of risk perceptions drawing on survey data from Hungary. They use a risk perceptions index developed by Dryhurst et al. (2020), who report that risk perceptions predicted the adoption of health behaviours across ten countries. The earlier work did not ask about preferences for policy, only compliance with advised health behaviours. Dudás and Szántó aim to address that gap by applying the risk perceptions index to public preferences. They consider three preventative public health policies – hand hygiene, social distancing, and mask-wearing – that could be implemented using nudges or stronger regulations. While on average there were no marked differences between the level of support for softer and harder policy measures, there were statistically significant (but modest) correlations between risk perception and policy preferences: 'people with a higher level of risk perception favour regulatory approaches slightly more' (2021: 9).

Somewhat related to the perception of risk are self-interest and personal experience, which have also been suggested as important variables determining preferences for policy measures (Owen et al., 2012; Umit & Schaffer, 2020). Past research shows that people who are personally affected by heat waves or drought – environmental risks – are more likely to support environmental laws. Taking this logic to the COVID-19 policy domain suggests that people who have personally been affected by the virus may be more likely to support harder measures to curb its transmission. Dudás and Szántó (2021) find the opposite. Direct experience of COVID-19 is statistically significant but *negatively* related to support for regulatory policies. The authors speculate that people who have recovered from infection may feel more protected by their natural immunity and are less willing to trade off their personal freedom for the good of the wider public.

Their study suffers from a key limitation of not including the over-sixty-fives in the survey sample, thereby excluding older and more vulnerable people whose risk perceptions are also important to consider. But it raises important questions for future research. Would policy preferences shift over time as caseloads increase and more people register direct experience of COVID-19? If this affects risk perceptions and the willingness to accept harder measures, would we see waning support for regulations and laws moving forward? And would this effect be moderated by new variants that might leave even those with direct experience of COVID-19 concerned about being infected with a new strain of the virus?

A final area of work that we welcome are studies that consider the issue of trade-offs and policy preferences. Discrete choice experiments are uniquely well-suited to investigate how people balance the positive health effects of harsher restrictions with the negative social and economic effects and vice versa. In their survey of 1,046 Australian respondents, Manipis et al. (2021) present a series of scenarios that respondents must choose from. Respondents select their preferred policy approaches based on the level of restrictions (low, medium, and high), tracking approaches, and the duration of lockdowns, which are set against potential policy outcomes in terms of COVID infections and deaths, unemployment, government spending, and personal tax increases. In general, people preferred shorter duration of restrictions and for people to be tracked with a tracking bracelet or mobile phone (versus no tracking) and prioritised the avoidance of infections and deaths. Within the sample, two broad groups emerged. Class 1 were younger, were more likely to have had direct experience of COVID-19 restrictions, and reported excellent health. This group preferred medium to low control measures, tracking bracelets, and 3 per cent or even 5 per cent personal tax levies relative to the 1 per cent options, and they prioritised fewer deaths. Class 2 were older and more likely to report poor health. They preferred the highest set of control measures and six months of restrictions rather than a one-month duration, and they had strong preferences for policies that reduced the burden of disease.

The findings demonstrate a clear willingness to relinquish personal freedom, to accept higher taxes, and to prescribe electronic tracking to 'flatten the curve' and preserve public health. Even younger people preferred medium rather than low control measures, for example. This study challenges the fears of 'lockdown fatigue', with the authors highlighting 'an alignment between what the public were willing to endure and what they have been compelled to endure' (Manipis et al., 2021: 369). The virtue of this method is to highlight where the balance is struck between health, social, and economic objectives and what the public are willing to accept. As with any individual experimental study, the design of the choice tasks will be highly specific to the study setting. It may not be possible to extrapolate findings over time or space. Nonetheless this research design is a valuable way of assessing policy preferences. We have come across a relatively small number of discrete choice experiments (Chorus et al., 2020; Genie et al., 2020) but expect them to grow in number as policy discourse increasingly asks questions of how far COVID-19 policies can go and what 'living with COVID' should look like.

To summarise, the current body of work provides important new insights. Public health behaviours and attitudes can be polarised across partisan lines; this appears to have happened very early on in the pandemic in places like the United States (Gadarian et al., 2021). Age and direct experience of COVID-19 policies represent important social cleavages that predict policy preferences (Manipis et al., 2021), including through varied risk perceptions (Dudás & Szántó,

2021). Country-level experiences and degree of success in 'flattening the curve' may also play a role in shaping preferences for harder measures – consider Australia in late 2020 – although there is relatively little cross-country evidence to test this further. While these single studies provide thought-provoking insights, there are few cross-country studies or panel studies that incorporate change over time. This remains an important gap in the scholarly literature.

8.4 IMPLICATIONS FOR ENVIRONMENTAL POLICY SUPPORT: EVIDENCE OF SPILLOVERS OR CROWDING OUT?

In Banerjee et al. (2021), we had noted that there is much potential for work at the intersection of health and environmental policies. In particular, we remarked that exploring how the pandemic and COVID-19 policies may have unintended or spillover effects onto support for environmental action and preferences for different pro-environmental policies may be fruitful. Past evidence showed that the pandemic can not only impact concern for environmental issues like biodiversity conservation and air pollution (Shreedhar & Mourato, 2020) but also influence public support for 'hard' and 'soft' environmental policies (Shreedhar & Mourato, 2020). The question is therefore whether public preferences for COVID-19 policy may generate spillovers for environment policy, either positive or negative. New evidence casts further light, firstly, on whether the pandemic 'crowds out' concern and private action on other social issues like climate change (which in turn may influence environmental policy support) and, secondly, on whether public support for environmental policies have shifted during the pandemic.

Turning to the question of whether the pandemic has impacted support for environmental action, Evensen et al. (2021: 1) investigate the idea of there being a 'finite pool of worry', where concerns over COVID-19 might crowd out concerns over climate change. In their repeated survey of a longitudinal panel survey of 1,858 UK residents in April 2019 and June 2020, they report little change in

beliefs about the seriousness of climate change. The apparent stability of attitudes and beliefs towards climate change might reflect
the public's growing familiarity with the issues. Blanco et al. (2021)
also investigate the potential for COVID-19 to have caused a shift in
social preferences for other priority issues (climate change and poverty alleviation). The authors draw on an online experiment with
1,762 Austrian participants, using incentivised donation tasks, collected between April 2020 and January 2021. Introducing the option
to donate to the World Health Organization's COVID-19 Solidarity
Response Fund significantly reduces the sum of donations to other
charities working on environmental and social protection issues,
although overall giving remains stable. Overall, their results indicated that donations to the COVID-19 fund partly substitute concerns for other issues.

The question of political partisanship in driving preferences
for types of policies that has been discussed in the previous section
is also relevant for understanding support for climate change policies. Pre-pandemic studies have demonstrated that there can be
polarisation based on political party affiliation and identity (Doell
et al., 2021). Kenward and Brick (2021) examine the balance between
public prioritisation of environment and economy in the light of
the pandemic using a nationally representative YouGov sample of
1,654 UK adults. Respondents were presented with two political
speeches, either linking COVID-19 to climate and prioritising environment as part of planned economic recovery or separating the
issues and stating that environmental prioritisation is now unaf-
fordable and then elicited stated attitudes towards the speeches.
Most participants were positive towards the environmental speech,
including 62 per cent of Conservative voters (with 50 per cent positive towards the other speech). Consistent with these results is the
suggestion that environmental concern in the United Kingdom is
becoming less tied to social identity and more tied to concern for
personal well-being. Despite lacking evidence from the pre-crisis
period, these findings suggest that foregrounding environmental

concerns in post-COVID-19 economic policy is feasible to garner public support.

Another strand of literature examines whether support for specific environmental policies change over time. Hynes et al. (2021) test the stability of environmental preferences and willingness to pay (WTP) values using a discrete choice experiment (DCE) across Canada, Scotland, and Norway with 3,015 respondents. The DCE examined preferences for alternative environmental management plans on the high seas, in the area of the Flemish Cap, in late 2019, which was rerun in early May 2020 shortly after the COVID-19 pandemic had 'peaked' in the three countries. The same choice set sequence is tested across the two periods, using nationally representative cross-sectional samples. The results suggest that both preferences and WTP values remain relatively stable in the face of a major public health crisis and economic upheaval, providing support for the idea that environmental policy support remained unchanged. Finally, Wunsch et al. (2022) studied the stability over time of preferences for coastal adaptation policies, using a choice experiment approach with German respondents fielded in two waves five months apart. Valuations of different aspects of adaptation policies grouped into 'safety', 'recreation' and 'access to nature' varied from the first wave to the next, with estimates of support for the 'safety' scenario increasing, while that for the 'recreation' scenario decreasing by half. The authors suggest that, in times of uncertainty, policy discussion and decision-making should be wary of relying on one valuation or set of preferences alone.

These studies focus on preferences towards a policy's attributes rather than support for types of 'hard' versus 'soft' climate policies per se. Duren et al. (2021), however, found that there was much lower stated support for reducing speed limits, staggering work times to make commuting less crowded, and giving more space to cycling and walking, suggesting limited spillover of policy support from COVID-19 to wider environmentally relevant transport policies with health impacts.

In sum, we did not come across any studies that looked at whether preferences for a range of environmental policies shifted over time (e.g., mandates to nudges) during a period where 'hard' policies were supported. This remains a significant gap in the literature. The limited evidence on revealed actions such as charitable donations suggest some partial substitution towards COVID-19 causes but no systematic trends over time. Turning to self-reported concern and policy support, the results are limited and mixed. In some cases, support was higher when there was a clearer link between COVID-19 and the environmental issue at hand (e.g., biodiversity conservation, air pollution) but not in other cases (including active travel and public commuting). In other policy arenas where the interlinkages are less clear (such as coastal conservation planning), policy preferences seem to remain relatively stable (if not marginally more in favour of environmental policy action). There seems to be support across the political spectrum in some regions like the United Kingdom. On a positive note, there is no systematic evidence of crowding out of environmental policy preferences by the pandemic.

8.5   CONCLUSION

The shared experience of the pandemic, and the policy responses it has necessitated, means it is more important than ever to investigate public acceptance of policy measures. COVID-19 has ushered in a raft of relatively interventionist policy measures to contain the spread of infections and protect public health. We can point to 'hard' policy measures now in place that would once have been considered only in the hypothetical. How have people responded to these policies? What do we learn about preferences for harder and softer measures in the context of public health crises?

Findings can be distilled into three points: (1) public support for harder public health measures has waned over time for some measures; (2) we have learned more about the factors that predict policy preferences, particularly in relation to partisanship and risk perceptions; and (3) sophisticated research designs including discrete choice experiments are beginning to address gaps in our understanding of preferences when people are faced with complex trade-offs.

But there remain gaps in measuring preferences over time through longitudinal or panel datasets and in measuring cultural or values-based drivers of preferences using cross-country surveys. Several research questions remain in need of investigation. Why do these preferences for policy measures shift over time? How can we reconcile prominent examples of citizen protest (e.g., Austria) after a period of relative compliance? Why do some countries appear to accept further hard measures to come (e.g., Germany)? How do wider contextual factors such as leadership, trust, and social cohesion play a role?

As the pandemic evolves, so too do policy responses. A key step in high-income countries has been the roll-out of vaccines, and we have no doubt that forthcoming research will continue to provide compelling insights about how policy preferences have responded in the context of vaccine availability. With policymakers aiming for 'COVID-normal' societies, we still have much to learn about how public preferences for policy action will shape up as we continue to trade-off normality with public health protections.

APPENDIX

Table A.1 *List of opinion poll questions as available on YouGov (2022)*

Label	Public policy type	Question description
Provision of free masks	Soft	Percentage of people in each market who say they are supporting providing free masks for all people in the country
Working from home	Soft	Percentage of people in each territory who say they are supporting their government encouraging companies to allow people to work from home.

Table A.1 (*cont.*)

Label	Public policy type	Question description
Quarantine contact persons	Hard	Percentage of people in each market/region who say they would support their government: Quarantining anyone who has been in contact with a contaminated patient.
Quarantine locations	Hard	Percentage of people in each market/region who say they would support their government quarantining any location in [country] that a contaminated patient has been in.
School closures	Hard	Percentage of people in each territory who say they are supporting their government temporarily closing schools.
Cancel large events	Hard	Percentage of people in each territory who say they are supporting their government cancelling large sporting events, concerts, or other large events.
Cancel hospital procedures	Hard	Percentage of people in each territory who say they are supporting their government cancelling routine hospital appointments and operations.
Cancel inbound flights	Hard	Percentage of people in each market/region who say they would support their government stopping all inbound flights coming into the country/region.
Quarantine passenger	Hard	Percentage of people in each market/region who say they would support their government quarantining all passengers on all flights coming into a country/region

Source: COVID-19: Level of support for actions governments could take, YouGov Plc 2022 © All rights reserved.

Table A.2 Support for different policies across countries and over time

Outcome measure	Working from home	Free provision of masks	Cancel hospital procedures	Cancel large events	Quarantine locations	Quarantine contact persons	School closures	Cancel inbound flights	Quarantine inbound passengers
Country fixed effects									
Australia	3.220	14.533***	5.080	6.467	10.925***	8.222	16.880***	19.255***	
Canada	0.326	7.588***	9.720**	7.272	6.815*	15.584*	6.601	6.278	
France	-8.298**	16.701***	-2.804	-10.305*	0.558	-11.583***	-5.852	-8.523*	-10.777**
Germany	-9.127***	11.948***	1.740	0.102	-10.075**	-7.321*	-1.665	-14.434***	-10.893**
Hong Kong	-7.075**	12.398***	15.654***	4.300	1.180	11.814*	-2.407	0.351	
India	2.685	22.338***	11.425**	5.978	3.773	24.070***	6.134	5.065	
Indonesia	-12.814***	21.770***	10.331***	-10.791*	0.001	9.789	6.466	-3.397	
Italy	-12.712**	18.189***	1.430	-11.735	5.559	0.532	1.797	-12.851**	-19.966***
Japan	-13.815***	-5.984	-11.591***	3.931	-12.216**	5.429			
Malaysia	1.684	21.081***	8.793***	15.821**	15.400***	24.532**	19.590***	15.294***	
Mexico	1.452	13.416***	3.026	13.811**	7.551**	22.870***	4.811	-11.266**	
Philippines	4.511	27.302***	12.873***	11.117*	12.757***	24.937***	11.114**	10.367**	
Singapore	4.425	21.323***	9.120***	6.017	7.469*	-4.555	-9.284*	-1.033	
Spain	-6.607	26.755***	4.762	5.377	6.256*	4.429	-0.445	-11.082**	-12.468**
Taiwan	-14.892**	-5.461*	17.156***	2.311	0.841	-0.749	-3.853	-2.078	

(cont.)

Table A.2 *(cont.)*

Outcome measure	Working from home	Free provision of masks	Cancel hospital procedures	Cancel large events	Quarantine locations	Quarantine contact persons	School closures	Cancel inbound flights	Quarantine inbound passengers
Thailand	-9.695**	28.195***	17.855***	0.070	1.902	9.469	8.149*	4.705	
UK	(base)	(base)	(base)	(base)	(base)	(base)	(base)	(base)	(base)
USA	-13.172***	8.363***	2.629	-12.968**	-13.311***	2.341	-15.389***	-25.229***	
Vietnam	-0.013	20.378***	31.329***	12.109*	13.490***	28.256***	15.226***	10.693**	
Time fixed effects									
2020Q1	-7.267	-10.098***	13.898***	-6.761	9.444*	-3.676	-9.016	10.111***	4.849***
2020Q2	(base)	(base)	(base)	(base)	(base)	(base)	(base)	(base)	(base)
2020Q3	-8.422***	-4.126*	-13.675***	-9.328***	-3.268	-4.539***	-22.026***	-1.019	1.080
2020Q4	-6.805***	-5.811**	-14.836***	-9.530***	-6.857***	-5.179***	-21.605***	3.490	4.593*
2021Q1	-7.387***	-7.514***	-14.496***	-9.786***	-3.779	-5.960***	-19.788***	-0.139	0.437
2021Q2	-10.374***	-11.296***	-14.424***	-16.267***	-7.967***	-7.960***	-23.193***	-5.270**	-5.064**
2021Q3	-12.441***	-12.539***	-15.144***	-19.367***	-12.296***	-12.489***	-25.838***	-12.172***	-11.886***
2021Q4	-15.710***	-13.009***	-17.462***	-25.344***	-13.932***	-16.201***	-31.468***		
Constant	71.615***	38.133***	21.991***	69.069***	28.179***	69.620***	48.771***	38.078***	56.416***

*** $p<.01$, ** $p<.05$, * $p<.1$

REFERENCES

Banerjee, S., Savani, M., & Shreedhar, G. (2021). Public support for 'soft' versus 'hard' public policies: Review of the evidence. *Journal of Behavioral Public Administration*, 4(2), 1–24. https://doi.org/10.30636/jbpa.42.220

Benartzi, S., Beshears, J., Milkman, K. L., Sunstein, C. R., Thaler, R. H., Shankar, M., et al. (2017). Should governments invest more in nudging? *Psychological Science*, 28(8), 1041–1055. https://doi.org/10.1177/0956797617702501

Blanco, E., Baier, A., Holzmeister, F., Jaber-Lopez, T., Struwe, N. (2021). Long term effects of the COVID-19 pandemic on social concerns. *Frontiers in Psychology*, 12, 1–14. DOI 10.3389/fpsyg.2021.743054.

Chorus, C., Sandorf, E. D., & Mouter, N. (2020). Diabolical dilemmas of COVID-19: An empirical study into Dutch society's trade-offs between health impacts and other effects of the lockdown. *PLOS ONE*, 15(9), e0238683. https://doi.org/10.1371/journal.pone.0238683

Diepeveen, S., Ling, T., Suhrcke, M., Roland, M., & Marteau, T. M. (2013). Public acceptability of government intervention to change health-related behaviours: A systematic review and narrative synthesis. *BMC Public Health*, 13(1), 756. https://doi.org/10.1186/1471-2458-13-756

Doell, K. C., Conte, B., & Brosch, T. (2021). Interindividual differences in environmentally relevant positive trait affect impacts sustainable behavior in everyday life. *Scientific Reports*, 11(1), 20423. https://doi.org/10.1038/s41598-021-99438-y

Dryhurst, S., Schneider, C. R., Kerr, J., Freeman, A. L. J., Recchia, G., van der Bles, A. M., et al. (2020). Risk perceptions of COVID-19 around the world. *Journal of Risk Research*, 23(7–8), 994–1006. https://doi.org/10.1080/13669877.2020.1758193

Dudás, L., & Szántó, R. (2021). Nudging in the time of coronavirus? Comparing public support for soft and hard preventive measures, highlighting the role of risk perception and experience. *PLOS ONE*, 16(8), e0256241. https://doi.org/10.1371/journal.pone.0256241

Duffy, B., & Allington, D. (2020). The three groups reacting to life under lockdown. www.kcl.ac.uk/news/the-three-groups-reacting-to-life-under-lockdown

Duren, M., Corrigan, B., Ehsani, J., & Michael, J. (2021). Modeling state preferences for Covid-19 policies: Insights from the first pandemic summer. *Journal of Transport & Health*, 23, 101284. https://doi.org/10.1016/j.jth.2021.101284

Evensen, D., Whitmarsh, L., Bartie, P., Devine-Wright, P., Dickie, J., Varley, A., et al. (2021). Effect of 'finite pool of worry' and COVID-19 on UK climate change perceptions. *Proceedings of the National Academy of Sciences*, 118(3), e2018936118. https://doi.org/10.1073/pnas.2018936118

Gadarian, S. K., Goodman, S. W., & Pepinsky, T. B. (2021). Partisanship, health behavior, and policy attitudes in the early stages of the COVID-19 pandemic. *PLOS ONE*, 16(4), e0249596. https://doi.org/10.1371/journal.pone.0249596

Galizzi, M. M. (2014). What is really behavioral in behavioral health policy? And does it work? *Applied Economic Perspectives and Policy*, 36(1), 25–60. https://doi.org/10.1093/aepp/ppt036

Genie, M. G., Loría-Rebolledo, L. E., Paranjothy, S., Powell, D., Ryan, M., Sakowsky, R. A., & Watson, V. (2020). Understanding public preferences and trade-offs for government responses during a pandemic: A protocol for a discrete choice experiment in the UK. *BMJ Open*, 10(11), e043477. https://doi.org/10.1136/bmjopen-2020-043477

Haselswerdt, J., & Bartels, B. L. (2015). Public opinion, policy tools, and the status quo: Evidence from a survey experiment. *Political Research Quarterly*, 68(3), 607–621. https://doi.org/10.1177/1065912915591217

Hynes, S., Armstrong, C. W., Xuan, B. B., Ankamah-Yeboah, I., Simpson, K., Tinch, R., & Ressurreição, A. (2021). Have environmental preferences and willingness to pay remained stable before and during the global Covid-19 shock? *Ecological Economics*, 189, 107142. https://doi.org/10.1016/j.ecolecon.2021.107142

John, P. (2011). *Making Policy Work*. Routledge.

Kahane, L. H. (2021). Politicizing the mask: Political, economic and demographic factors affecting mask wearing behavior in the USA. *Eastern Economic Journal*, 47(2), 163–183. https://doi.org/10.1057/s41302-020-00186-0

Kenward, B., & Brick, C. (2021). Even conservative voters want the environment to be at the heart of post-COVID-19 economic reconstruction in the UK. *Journal of Social and Political Psychology*, 9(1), 321–333.

Lang, J., Erickson, W. W., & Jing-Schmidt, Z. (2021). #MaskOn! #MaskOff! Digital polarization of mask-wearing in the United States during COVID-19. *PLOS ONE*, 16(4), e0250817. https://doi.org/10.1371/journal.pone.0250817

Manipis, K., Street, D., Cronin, P., Viney, R., & Goodall, S. (2021). Exploring the trade-off between economic and health outcomes during a pandemic: A discrete choice experiment of lockdown policies in Australia. *The Patient: Patient-Centered Outcomes Research*, 14(3), 359–371. https://doi.org/10.1007/s40271-021-00503-5

Mazzocchi, M., Cagnone, S., Bech-Larsen, T., Niedźwiedzka, B., Saba, A., Shankar, B., et al. (2015). What is the public appetite for healthy eating policies? Evidence from a cross-European survey. *Health Economics, Policy and Law*, 10(3), 267–292. https://doi.org/10.1017/S1744133114000346

Owen, A. L., Conover, E., Videras, J., & Wu, S. (2012). Heat waves, droughts, and preferences for environmental policy. *Journal of Policy Analysis and Management*, 31(3), 556–577. https://doi.org/10.1002/pam.21599

Reisch, L. A., & Sunstein, C. R. (2016). Do Europeans like nudges? *Judgment and Decision Making*, 11(4), 310–325.

Schneider, A., & Ingram, H. (1990). Behavioral assumptions of policy tools. *The Journal of Politics*, 52(2), 510–529. https://doi.org/10.2307/2131904

Shreedhar, G., & Mourato, S. (2020). Linking human destruction of nature to COVID-19 increases support for wildlife conservation policies. *Environmental and Resource Economics*, 76(4), 963–999. https://doi.org/10.1007/s10640-020-00444-x

Sunstein, C. R. (2016). Do people like nudges? *Administrative Law Review*, 68(2), 177–232.

Sunstein, C. R., Reisch, L. A., & Rauber, J. (2018). A worldwide consensus on nudging? Not quite, but almost. *Regulation & Governance*, 12(1), 3–22. https://doi.org/10.1111/rego.12161

Thaler, R. H., & Sunstein, C. R. (2009). Nudge: Improving Decisions about Health, Wealth and Happiness, rev. ed. Penguin. https://app.kortext.com/borrow/409551

Umit, R., & Schaffer, L. M. (2020). Attitudes towards carbon taxes across Europe: The role of perceived uncertainty and self-interest. *Energy Policy*, 140, 111385. https://doi.org/10.1016/j.enpol.2020.111385

Wunsch, A., Meyerhoff, J., & Rehdanz, K. (2022). A test–retest analysis of stated preferences in uncertain times. *Economic Analysis and Policy*, 73, 725–736. https://doi.org/10.1016/j.eap.2021.12.021

YouGov. (2022). COVID-19 Public Monitor. YouGov. https://yougov.co.uk/covid-19

Zehavi, A. (2012). New governance and policy instruments: Are governments going 'soft'? In D. Levi-Faur (ed.), *The Oxford Handbook of Governance* (pp. 242–254). Oxford Handbooks Online. https://doi.org/10.1093/oxfordhb/9780199560530.013.0017

9 One Size Does Not Fit All

Behavioural Interventions to Promote Vaccination

Ilana Brody, Silvia Saccardo, and Hengchen Dai

9.1 INTRODUCTION

Two years into the COVID-19 pandemic, the evidence from the US Centers for Disease Control and Prevention concluded that 'the risks for SARS-CoV-2 infection and COVID-19-associated hospitalisation are lower among fully vaccinated than among unvaccinated persons; this reduction is even more pronounced among those who have received additional or booster doses' (Danza et al., 2022: 177). Despite these benefits, a non-negligent proportion of individuals remain unvaccinated for COVID-19, and the majority of the fully vaccinated population (65.8 per cent) has not received a booster shot long after becoming eligible, as of 10 March 2022 (CDC, 2022). As a result, finding public health strategies to encourage vaccinations is critical for containing and ending the COVID-19 pandemic. Even before the pandemic, vaccine hesitancy had been deemed a top ten global health threat by the World Health Organization (2019). While government and institution-led mandates and regulations play an important role in improving vaccination take-up rates for COVID-19 and other infectious diseases, it is also critical to consider individual-level barriers that stand in the way of vaccine uptake and devise interventions accordingly.

In this chapter, we first review factors that may either produce vaccine hesitancy or lead people with favourable attitudes towards a vaccine to not get vaccinated soon enough. Then we propose behavioural science strategies for tackling these barriers to vaccine uptake and demonstrate that effective solutions vary based on individuals' existing motivation to get vaccinated. This chapter ultimately seeks to synthesise behavioural science insights about promoting vaccinations and to highlight that aligning the intervention to the cause of individuals' vaccination problem is key for effectively moving the needle for everyone.

9.2 KEY DETERMINANTS OF VACCINE UPTAKE

To understand how to best promote vaccination, it is important to consider two categories of barriers to vaccine uptake. First, individuals may have low or no **intentions** to vaccinate, due to a variety of beliefs and attitudes about a vaccine and the disease it protects them against. Imagine that Sam is this type of person. An effective intervention to motivate Sam may aim to change her intentions by addressing why she is uncertain or even resistant about receiving the vaccine. Other individuals, like Alex, may already have intentions to get the vaccine but fail to follow through on their good intentions when the time comes. Alex does not need additional information to convince her of the importance of getting vaccinated, but she can benefit from tools that help her close **the gap between intentions and action**. Although the goals of vaccination promotion interventions are the same, an effective intervention for Sam may look vastly different from an effective intervention for Alex. Next, we review the determinants of intentions and the gap between intention and action in the context of vaccinations.

9.2.1 Intentions

Intentions refer to people's inherent willingness to exert the effort to perform a behaviour (Ajzen, 1991). For a planned behaviour like obtaining a vaccine, intentions are a key antecedent of execution (Ajzen, 1991). In the vaccination context, intentions may be informed, among other factors, by a valuation of the costs and benefits of vaccination and one's normative beliefs about whether vaccination is right or wrong (Brewer et al., 2017). Next, we highlight key factors that inform whether vaccination intentions may or may not be in place.

9.2.2 Risk Appraisals and Vaccine Confidence

Two important antecedents of vaccination intentions are risk apprais-als and vaccine confidence, which are sets of beliefs and attitudes that inform the trade-off between the costs and benefits of vaccination. **Risk appraisals** refer to individuals' perceptions of risks associated with an infectious disease, often including the perceived likelihood of getting infected, the chance of spreading the disease to others, and the perceived severity of the illness (Brewer et al., 2007, 2017; Schmid et al., 2017). A meta-analysis by Brewer et al. (2007) finds that individuals who perceive a greater likelihood of getting infected with a disease are more likely to receive the pertinent vaccine ($r = .26$ across twelve studies). The pattern is similar, albeit weaker, for the relationship between perceived severity of the infection and vaccina-tion intentions ($r = .16$ across thirty-two studies; Brewer et al., 2007). Perceptions of personal susceptibility to the illness (i.e., perceived vulnerability) may be considered a separate informant of risk apprais-als and are similarly associated with vaccination intentions ($r = .24$ across fifteen studies; Brewer et al., 2007). Similarly, anticipating that one would regret not getting vaccinated, which captures both affective and cognitive reactions to the risks of getting a disease, posi-tively predicts vaccination intentions ($r = .27$ across eighteen studies; Brewer et al., 2016). In the context of COVID-19, compared to people who fully intend to vaccinate, those who were uncertain about the COVID-19 vaccine view themselves as having a lower likelihood of catching COVID-19 without receiving the vaccine, feel less vulnera-ble to COVID-19, and are less worried about transmission (Dai et al., 2021). Furthermore, individuals with lower (vs higher) intentions to get vaccinated against COVID-19 perceive the virus as less threaten-ing (Fridman et al., 2021; Galasso et al., 2022).

Vaccine confidence refers to beliefs and attitudes about the vac-cine's effectiveness in preventing an illness as well as its own safety and side effects (Brewer et al., 2017). These beliefs affect individ-uals' willingness to vaccinate (Kreps et al., 2020; MacDonald, 2015).

For example, people are more willing to take vaccines that could provide better protection against COVID-19 and that have a lower probability of causing a serious adverse reaction (Kaplan & Milstein, 2021). For influenza vaccinations, common beliefs held by unvaccinated healthcare workers include feeling that the vaccine is ineffective, that the vaccine would make them unwell, or that they are at low risk for catching influenza and thus do not need the vaccine (Heinrich-Morrison et al., 2015).

Notably, one's risk appraisals and vaccine confidence may be inaccurate, for example because individuals lack access to or are miscalibrated about factual statistics and information. But even when presented with facts (e.g., data collected by scientists and reviewed by the US Food and Drug Administration and the US Centers for Disease Control and Prevention), individuals' **trust** in scientists, government, healthcare systems, and medical experts heavily influences whether they believe it is necessary, useful, and safe to receive a vaccine, thus shaping their vaccination intentions (Galasso et al., 2022; Jennings et al., 2021; McLamore et al., 2022; Murphy et al., 2021). Trust may help explain differences in vaccination intentions across social and demographic groups. For example, relative to liberals, conservatives in the United States tend to distrust scientific institutions and medical professionals, thus expressing less concerns about contracting COVID-19 and lower willingness to comply with COVID-19-related health guidelines (McLamore et al., 2022). Also, higher prevalence of hesitancy among Black American respondents has been partly attributed to their low trust in government and health institutions in the United States (Bogart et al., 2021; Razai et al., 2021).

Trust in scientific and medical authorities could be undermined by the prevalence of online and offline **misinformation** (Agley & Xiao, 2021). Since the start of the pandemic, misinformation about COVID-19 has proliferated (Kouzy et al., 2020; Mian & Khan, 2020), and misinformation surrounding the importance, safety, or efficacy of vaccines may fuel vaccine hesitancy (Jaiswal et al., 2020). Indeed, exposure to COVID-19 vaccine misinformation, particularly misinformation that sounds scientific, has been shown to lower COVID-19 vaccination intentions across all levels of pre-exposure intent, even among those who initially stated that they would definitely accept a vaccine (Loomba et al., 2021). Blind trust in those who disseminate misinformation could strengthen the power of misinformation (Kahan et al., 2012; Xiao et al., 2021) and motivate people from certain socio-political groups to selectively focus on channels that spread or reinforce misinformation (Kahan, 2017). For example, Fridman et al. (2021) find differences in news consumption sources among Democrats and Republicans, with the latter primarily watching news from Fox News (as opposed to CNN). Since Fox News (vs CNN) consumers are more likely to believe that COVID-19 risks have been exaggerated by the media (Jurkowitz & Mitchell, 2020), differential exposure to news sources may explain why Fridman et al. (2021) also find that survey respondents who identify as Republicans (but not those as Democrats) show a decline in perceived COVID-19 threat and COVID-19 vaccination intentions between March and August 2020.

Beyond risk perceptions of an illness and the perceived benefits and costs of getting vaccinated, **identity, moral values, and social considerations** may also inform vaccination intentions. Individuals care about how their own behaviour reflects their identity and take actions to maintain a positive self-view (Bem, 1972; Bénabou & Tirole, 2006). In the context of vaccination, the desire to preserve a positive identity might lead individuals to behave in line with the traits and values they would like to uphold, including getting vaccinated to 'do the right thing' or refraining from it to avoid spiritual contamination (Amin et al., 2017). For instance, individuals may care to uphold a pro-social identity. Since vaccination is, in part, a pro-social act, the desire to view oneself as 'pro-social' could boost intentions to get vaccinated. Indeed, pro-social reasons have been found to predict vaccination intentions (Böhm & Betsch, 2022; Heinrich-Morrison et al., 2015), and general pro-sociality predicts other COVID-19 prevention behaviours (Campos-Mercade et al., 2021b). Similarly, people may decide whether to get vaccinated based on other moral values they want to uphold. For example, Reimer et al. (2021) document that vaccination rates in the United States are positively correlated with county-level values of fairness and loyalty and negatively correlated with county-level values of bodily and spiritual purity. Additionally, Korn et al. (2020) provide evidence in line with the idea that individuals consider getting vaccinated as a moral obligation.

The desire to do the right thing could be intensified when behaviour is visible. This is because individuals strive to be well-regarded by others (Bénabou & Tirole, 2006, 2011) and take actions to signal a positive image to observers (see, e.g., Bursztyn & Jensen, 2017). Thus, social image concerns could boost vaccination intentions when individuals' vaccination status is observed by others, such as at the workplace or within a circle of friends. Considerations about signalling one's identity may become stronger when individuals desire to conform to the norms and behaviours of social groups they identify with (Akerlof & Kranton, 2000; Falomir-Pichastor et al., 2009), which may explain why political, religious, or professional identity can influence behaviour beyond other determinants of intentions such as risk perceptions or trust (Bénabou & Tirole, 2011; Huynh et al., 2021).

9.2.3 Intention–Action Gap

Intentions are necessary but insufficient for action to take place (Gollwitzer & Sheeran, 2009). Next, we discuss why well-intended individuals sometimes fail to follow through on their intentions, which is known as the **intention–action gap** (Sheeran & Webb, 2016). Failures to translate intentions into action often originate from failures to initiate a given goal (Sheeran & Webb, 2016), such as failures to choose a vaccine clinic or schedule an appointment in the vaccination context. Even when goals are initiated, sometimes individuals struggle to complete them. For example, after scheduling an appointment, patients may fail to show up and, as a result, not receive the vaccine despite intending to get vaccinated. Failures to initiate or complete goals may stem from a variety of behavioural barriers.

Goal salience. In some occasions, individuals with favourable intentions towards a goal fail to enact such intentions because the goal is not salient at the right time. This is because cognitive resources are limited (Kahneman, 1973), and multiple goals simultaneously compete for individuals' attention (Kruglanski et al., 2002; Shah & Kruglanski, 2002). As a result, individuals can attend to only a few goals at a time and are more likely to be drawn to goals that are more salient (Congdon et al., 2011; Fishbach et al., 2003, 2006). Such limited attention has been shown to affect behaviour in a variety of domains – from consumption decisions to financial and health-related choices (see, e.g., Gabaix, 2019). On top of inattention, lack of goal salience could also stem from memory failures: information that was once salient can be quickly forgotten over time (Ebbinghaus, 2013). Both inattention and memory failures matter to the act of getting a vaccine. For example, individuals with favourable intentions to get vaccinated may not book appointments because the goal of vaccination fails to compete for their attention on their busy days. They may also miss the opportunities to get vaccinated because they simply forget their appointments or forget the day when their employer offers an on-site vaccine clinic.

Time-inconsistent preferences. Failures to enact a given goal can also stem from time-inconsistent preferences. Individuals with intentions in place may plan to take up a given behaviour in the future but fail to take action when the time arrives. Such patterns of time inconsistency often arise because of present-focused preferences (Ericson & Laibson, 2019; Laibson, 1997) – that is, individuals' tendency to overweight immediate utility. Such preferences can lead individuals to choose more impatiently for the present than they do for the future and to sub-optimally procrastinate on behaviours that involve some immediate costs but larger long-term rewards (O'Donoghue & Rabin, 1999). In the domain of vaccination, two main types of immediate costs could make individuals put off getting a vaccine that provides health benefits in the long run. The first type of cost involves physical and mental discomfort associated with getting an injection or with experiencing minor short-term side effects after receiving the vaccine. Anticipating such discomfort (e.g., fearing that the injection will be painful or that the vaccine could cause headache) could lead individuals with vaccination intentions to procrastinate (e.g., Falagas & Zarkadoulia, 2008). Notably, though anxiety about severe adverse reactions to the COVID-19 vaccine reduces vaccination intentions, minor side effects are shown to not affect vaccination intentions (Kaplan & Milstein, 2021); instead, minor side effects are likely to cause people with favourable intentions to put off getting the vaccine. The second form of cost involves the time and effort associated with completing the steps needed to get vaccinated. Such hassle costs include the inconvenience and time investment arising from locating a clinic that offers vaccinations, booking an appointment, and traveling to and back from the appointment. They can also include the cognitive efforts associated with information or choice overload (Iyengar & Lepper, 2000; Scheibehenne et al., 2010), which could arise when individuals are confronted with too many vaccination sites or time slots to choose from. Even when small, these hassle costs have been shown to have large detrimental effects on the uptake of beneficial behaviours (Bertrand et al., 2006; Bhargava & Manoli, 2015) and could intensify the tendency to procrastinate if individuals underestimate their time demands in the future (Zauberman & Lynch Jr, 2005).

9.3 INTERVENTION EFFORTS TO IMPROVE VACCINE UPTAKE

So far we have reviewed factors that drive vaccination intentions as well as contributors to the intention–action gap, all of which influence whether and when people receive a necessary vaccine. Interventions based on behavioural science insights usually either aim to increase individuals' intentions to vaccinate or encourage action by facilitating follow-through, assuming that intentions are already in place. We next review interventions that operate via either of these mechanisms.

9.3.1 *Interventions That Target Intentions*

This section presents evidence from COVID-19 and other vaccination contexts to highlight examples of interventions that target individuals' intentions to vaccinate. Some of the studies in our review report direct evidence for changes in vaccination intentions, while others provide indirect evidence by showing changes in actual vaccination behaviour. For a more detailed review of studies outside of the COVID-19 domain see Brewer et al. (2017) and Betsch et al. (2015).

Risk appraisals and vaccine confidence. Since risk appraisals and vaccine confidence inform vaccination intentions, a natural way to elevate such intentions is to adjust these beliefs and perceptions via information provision interventions. Information provision interventions have been employed in a variety of domains to effectively correct misbeliefs and misperceptions as well as change attitudes (see Haaland et al., 2020, for a review). In the vaccination context, this involves presenting information (e.g., statistics, scientific knowledge, experts' statements, narratives about victims of a disease) to elevate one's perceived risk or harm of contracting the illness and one's beliefs in the efficacy and safety of the vaccine. For example, in an online experiment, using information provided by the US Centers for Disease Control and Prevention, Horne et al. (2015) countered people's anti-vaccination attitudes by making them recognise the consequences of failing to vaccinate their children. In the COVID-19 context, short videos or brief text messages that communicate the risk of remaining unvaccinated and/or the efficacy and safety of the vaccines have been shown to successfully increase vaccination intentions (Berliner Senderey et al., 2021; Chang et al., 2021; Jensen et al., 2022); also, information that contextualised the risks of the vaccine by comparing it to the risks of contracting the virus itself appears effective as well (Santos et al., 2021). Besides providing factual information to elevate risk appraisals, calling attention to one's own past experiences with a related illness can help increase vaccination rates among those who may not already appreciate the benefits of vaccination (Brody et al., 2022b).

However, the evidence on the impact of interventions that aimed to change risk appraisals and vaccine confidence is mixed. Taking risk appraisals as an example, the meta-analysis by Sheeran et al. (2014) reports a moderate-sized boost of vaccination intentions as a result of interventions that sought to change risk appraisals. But this meta-analysis includes only interventions that successfully changed any form of risk appraisals, and therefore the estimated overall effect on intentions is biased upwards. Another meta-analysis that reviews interventions containing risk messages, regardless of whether they altered risk appraisals, reports small and non-significant effects of such interventions on vaccination intentions (Parsons et al., 2018). Many of the interventions reviewed by Parsons et al. (2018) involved simple risk messages and simple information about health consequences, but even more heavy-handed educational campaigns have seen mixed evidence, with some studies showing discouraging results (Kaufman et al., 2018), some influencing only intentions or vaccine-related attitudes but not behaviour (Brewer et al., 2017; Schoeppe et al., 2017; Williams, 2014; Williams et al., 2013), and some documenting promising evidence for behaviours (Jackson et al., 2011; Pandey et al., 2007).

Notably, trying to convince people of the absence of side effects can backfire in some cases. For example, efforts to refute claims connecting autism and vaccinations for children have been shown to unfortunately *reduce* parents' intentions to vaccinate their children among those with the least favourable attitudes towards the vaccine (Nyhan & Reifler, 2015); moreover, strong statements (vs weak statements) that vaccines do not cause harm actually increase the perceived harm of vaccines when the source of the information is a pharmaceutical company (Betsch & Sachse, 2013). Experimental evidence from Horne et al. (2015) suggests that fighting vaccine myths may be less effective than diffusing information about why vaccines are useful. This finding is in line with prior research that has corrected erroneous beliefs in other settings by replacing incorrect elements of these beliefs with new factual information (as opposed to simply refuting these elements; Lewandowsky et al., 2012). This approach – providing an alternative narrative to replace the retracted misinformation – may be broadly applied to the battle against misinformation about COVID-19 and vaccinations. Another general lesson from research that seeks to reduce the prevalence of misinformation is to shift individuals' attention from naturally occurring motives on social media (e.g., the desire to attract and please followers/friends) to news accuracy (Pennycook et al., 2021) – a strategy that has been shown to reduce the sharing of misinformation about COVID-19 (Pennycook et al., 2020).

An important aspect to consider when seeking to shift beliefs is the messenger of vaccine-related information. For example, in societies where medical doctors are a highly trusted group, information provision interventions that capitalise on people's trust in doctors may be useful. In the Czech Republic, where trust in doctors is high, truthfully informing individuals that the vast majority of doctors recommended getting the COVID-19 vaccine updated participants' misbeliefs about doctors' endorsements of the vaccine and thus increased vaccination intentions (Bartoš et al., 2022). More broadly, interventions that make messengers appear more trustworthy to the listeners can increase listeners' openness to change their attitudes towards vaccines. One approach for building trust in messengers is to highlight shared values with the listeners. For instance, when unvaccinated American Christians were told (vs not told) that the prominent medical expert featured in an educational video was a Christian and that many medical experts were people of faith, they expressed higher trust in medical experts as well as greater intentions to both receive the COVID-19 vaccine themselves and promote vaccination to close others (Chu et al., 2021). The researchers confirmed that this strategy indeed operated through enhancing perceptions of shared values with the featured medical expert endorsing the COVID-19 vaccine and worked the best among the most religious participants (Chu et al., 2021).

Relatedly, aligning race between the messenger and listeners has also been proposed as a strategy to establish trust in COVID-19 vaccines among Black Americans (Bajaj & Stanford, 2021). This strategy is motivated by recent research showing that treatment by a race-concordant physician in an in-person setting (e.g., a doctor consultation, childbirth) can increase demand for preventive care as well as improve health outcomes among Black American patients (e.g., Alsan et al., 2019; Greenwood et al., 2020). The evidence for implementing this strategy in communication from physicians has been mixed in the COVID-19 context: in one online experiment, watching an educational video featuring a race-concordant physician increased information-seeking behaviours among Black respondents (Alsan et al., 2021), but other experiments by the same set of authors did not detect benefits of having Black respondents receive information from a race-concordant medical expert (Alsan & Eichmeyer, 2021; Torres et al., 2021).

The actions of well-known and influential figures who are not medical experts may also affect vaccination intentions. It is theorised that thousands of young people were motivated to adopt the polio vaccine after Elvis Presley accepted his vaccine on a popular television show (Hershfield & Brody, 2021). Evidence from before the coronavirus pandemic suggests that celebrity endorsements (as compared to the endorsement of ordinary individuals) on social media (e.g., Twitter) can positively affect vaccine attitudes (Alatas et al., 2019). Similar strategies have been attempted with the COVID-19 response, where the US government partnered with some of the most popular young social media stars to encourage their fans to get the vaccine (Lorenz, 2021). Even when there is already an abundance of messaging during the COVID-19 crisis, messages from influential figures could further help: relative to a message pointing people to government information, video clips delivered by a respected public intellectual figure and sent via a text message increased health-preserving behaviour (e.g., reporting health symptoms to community health workers, washing hands, wearing masks) – a benefit that diffused even to people who did not directly receive the video clips (Banerjee et al., 2020). Also, political leaders can be a powerful source of influence. A difference-in-differences analysis found that a presidential address from French president Emmanuel Macron, which transmitted scientific insights via a clear message, led to a 5-percentage-point increase in COVID-19 vaccinations in France, suggesting that leadership communication can be harnessed to increase vaccination intentions (Klotz, 2022). Political leaders who share the viewers' socio-political identity have been demonstrated to shift attitudes among the most reluctant: watching video-based vaccine endorsements from former US president Donald Trump and other Republican leaders (relative to watching endorsement from Democratic leaders or no endorsement) boosted Republican respondents' beliefs that Republican politicians wanted them to receive COVID-19 vaccine and, as a result, increased their vaccination intentions (Pink et al., 2021).

Identity: moral values and social considerations. Another angle for elevating vaccination intentions is to harness individuals' desire to view themselves as pro-social. There is some evidence that highlighting the pro-social benefits of getting vaccinated can increase vaccination intentions (Böhm & Betsch, 2022). For instance, Böhm et al. (2019) find that an intervention that described vaccination as a way to protect others who are willing but unable to vaccinate increased vaccination intentions for a fictitious disease. In the context of influenza vaccination, providing information describing potential flu victims who may suffer if others fail to vaccinate increased sympathy and pro-social motivation to vaccinate, as compared to not providing such information (Li et al., 2016). Similarly, in the context of COVID-19 vaccination, an empathy-inducing intervention about those who were suffering most from COVID-19 increased vaccination intentions (Pfattheicher et al., 2021). When capitalising on pro-social motives, crafting messages that tap into the societal values of a targeted population may be important. For example, highlighting that vaccinations protect the health of the community increased vaccination intentions and behaviour among people from the European

Union, whereas highlighting the importance of vaccinating to protect the economy and prevent unemployment was effective in the United States (Galasso et al., 2022). Further, Rabb et al. (2021a) suggest that highlighting the protection COVID-19 vaccine provides for one's community may work less well than highlighting the protection for one's family in the United States.

Some interventions tap into pro-social motives by explaining the concept of herd immunity and its benefits. For example, Betsch et al. (2017) find that communicating the concept of herd immunity improves the hypothetical intentions to vaccinate against a fictitious disease. In the COVID-19 context, relative to those who read only about the vaccine's efficacy, people who additionally read about the necessary coverage rate of vaccination to achieve herd immunity indicated greater eagerness to get the vaccine (Trueblood et al., 2022). Though these articles suggest that drawing attention to herd immunity could boost vaccination intentions, a review article reports mixed effects of helping people understand herd immunity, with such interventions increasing favourable attitudes towards vaccinations in some but not all studies (Hakim et al., 2019). For instance, such interventions are ineffective when the perceived risks of adverse events arising from getting vaccinated are high (Böhm & Betsch, 2022).

While pro-social messaging has often been employed as a strategy for promoting vaccination, not all studies find a conclusive impact of pro-social messaging. In a study aiming to encourage COVID-19 vaccination in the United States, messages highlighting personal benefits of getting vaccinated actually led to higher vaccination intentions than messages highlighting pro-social benefits (Ashworth et al., 2021). In addition, recent randomised controlled trials find no detectable difference between highlighting the personal or pro-social benefits of getting vaccinated in terms of their impact on vaccination behaviours (Saccardo et al., 2022, and Rabb et al., 2022, in the context of COVID-19; Hoffmann et al., 2020, and Milkman et al., 2021b, in the context of influenza).

Since individuals who strive to 'do the right thing' often infer the appropriateness of a given action from others' behaviours or recommendations, vaccination intentions can also be elevated by informing individuals of similar others' behaviours or endorsement. In an experiment with participants from twenty-three different countries, providing accurate information about the percentage of others in one's country who planned to take the vaccine on average boosted COVID-19 vaccination intentions, and this normative information treatment partially worked through correcting underestimated beliefs about how many other people would accept a vaccine (Moehring et al., 2021). Consistently, several online experiments find that people's vaccination intentions increase with vaccination coverage rates in one's social environment, but only up to a given point after which vaccination intentions actually decrease as vaccination coverage rates continue to move up (Agranov et al., 2021; Galizzi et al., 2022). This result suggests that conveying high population vaccination coverage rates can encourage vaccination due to bandwagoning effects but policymakers need to be careful about the potential free-riding effects that lead people to reduce vaccinations in response to an already high population coverage rate. Besides peers' behaviour, peers' recommendations could also stir up people's motivation. In another experiment that aimed to increase influenza vaccination in a college campus, students who received encouragement emails from another student (vs an office on campus) and read that the student (vs a health institution) thought flu vaccination was a good idea were more likely to seek vaccine-related information; the effect of this peer endorsement intervention was on par with that of a monetary incentive, though the benefits did not translate into vaccination behaviour (Bronchetti et al., 2015).

Individuals' desire to uphold moral values and norms could be strengthened by harnessing their desire to be viewed in a positive light by others. Social image concerns have been shown to affect other types of pro-social behaviours (Bursztyn & Jensen, 2017). One way to leverage social-image concerns in the vaccination context is to increase the visibility of vaccination decisions, which could take the form of handing out to individuals visible signals of their vaccination status (e.g., pins, buttons, stickers, or bracelets) or to publicly recognise vaccinated individuals in other ways. For instance, one study in a US college campus found that messages highlighting the pro-social benefits of getting vaccinated increased influenza vaccination intentions only when individuals received stickers that could visibly display their choice to get vaccinated to others; by contrast, in the absence of stickers, an egoistic appeal was more effective (Pittman, 2020). In the context of childhood immunisation in Sierra Leone, Karing (2019) finds that handing out color-coded bracelets that signal children vaccination status motivated mothers to complete their children's vaccination, partially because visible signals affected mothers' perceived visibility of their own actions and capitalised on parents' desire to maintain a positive social image. However, the effectiveness of this strategy depended on the signals' informativeness, with more informative signals being more effective at ensuring mothers completed the full sequence of vaccinations.

Taken together, the studies reviewed in this section point out several strategies that could elevate vaccination intentions. However, while many of these studies provide evidence for improved vaccination intentions as a result of a tested intervention, only a few assess impact on actual vaccine uptake. Among those that do, increasing intentions alone does not consistently alter vaccination behaviour. For instance, while informational videos that emphasised the importance of safety and the health consequences of not vaccinating boosted COVID-19 vaccination intentions substantially by up to 8.6 percentage points, they had no effect on action (Chang et al., 2021). The fact that shifting intentions may not be enough to move the needle on behaviour suggests that closing the intention–action gap may be important once intentions are in place. Next, we discuss interventions designed to close this gap to encourage vaccination rates.

9.3.2   Interventions That Target the Intention–Action Gap

Goal salience. Tackling goal salience could play an important role in promoting vaccination, because, as reviewed earlier, well-intended individuals may fail to act due to inattention or forgetfulness. The most common intervention for increasing goal salience consists of reminding people of their goals, which, in the context of vaccinations, could take the form of reminding people to schedule or show up for their vaccination appointments. Increasing the salience of vaccination through reminders is one of the most prominent approaches for encouraging vaccinations (Briss et al., 2000; Jacobson Vann et al., 2018). For example, across ten studies conducted in five countries, text message reminders significantly boosted childhood vaccination coverage, especially in low- to middle-income countries (Mekonnen et al., 2019). In the context of influenza vaccination, a mega-study – that is, a large-scale field experiment involving many nested studies that are developed by different research teams and are simultaneously conducted (Milkman et al., 2021a) – tested twenty-two different text-based reminders sent to Walmart pharmacy patients across the United States who had received a flu shot in the prior season (Milkman et al., 2022). This mega-study found that reminders increased vaccinations obtained at Walmart by an average of 2 percentage points, a 6.8 per cent improvement over the 29.4 per cent vaccination rates in the business-as-usual group that received no reminders. Evidence from seventy-five studies about immunisation-focused patient reminder interventions across ten countries suggests that the most effective reminder medium consists of text messages, postcards, and auto-dial phone calls (Jacobson Vann et al., 2018).

Since reminders are generally more effective when individuals have opportunities to act right away (Austin et al., 2006; Sunstein, 2014), policymakers seeking to boost vaccinations should consider sending reminders right before they expect recipients to encounter opportunities to get the vaccine. In line with this idea, a mega-study tested reminders that were sent to patients of two healthcare systems a couple of days before an upcoming primary care visit and encouraged patients to get the flu shot at the visit (Milkman et al., 2021b). The reminders boosted influenza vaccination rates within the healthcare systems by an average of 2.1 percentage points, or 5 per cent over the 42 per cent vaccination rates in the no-reminder control group. In the context of COVID-19, Dai et al. (2021) tested reminders that prompted patients of a large hospital to act right away by including a direct link to schedule a vaccination appointment at the hospital. Their reminders increased appointment rates by an average of 6.07 percentage points, vaccinations at the hospital by 3.57 percentage points, and vaccinations obtained anywhere in California by 2.1 percentage points, amounting to an 84 per cent, 26 per cent, and 6.6 per cent increase over the rates in the no-reminder group (Dai et al., 2021).

Importantly, the language used in reminders matters. For example, not all nineteen reminders tested in the aforementioned mega-study involving patients of two healthcare systems increased vaccination relative to the no-reminder control (Milkman et al., 2021b). Reminders that were congruent with patients' expectations, that is, that matched the language and communication style expected from a healthcare provider, were more effective than reminders that were not. Further, in recent evaluations of reminder tactics, asking people to 'claim their dose' of the vaccine or telling them that the vaccine was 'waiting for you' or 'reserved for you' significantly or directionally outperformed other reminders without this language (Dai et al., 2021, and Keppeler et al., 2021, for COVID-19 vaccinations; Milkman et al., 2021b, and Milkman et al., 2022, for influenza vaccinations). Follow-up online experiments conducted by Dai et al. (2021) suggest that asking patients to claim their dose increases feelings of psychological ownership over the vaccine, while Bogard et al. (2022) find that language such as 'the vaccine is reserved for you' heightens feelings of vaccine exclusivity. Future work could further investigate the mechanisms through which such language effectively induces behaviour change and its moderators.

Apart from reminders, another strategy for increasing goal salience involves leveraging situational cues that are associated with relevant goals. This is because memories can be triggered by associations with certain environments (Kahan et al., 2012), which can make a relevant goal 'top of mind'. A well-known approach to help people mentally associate situational cues with a goal is planning prompts, which guide individuals to form an implementation intention by creating an 'if-then' plan that links specific cues with goal-directed action (Gollwitzer, 1999; Gollwitzer & Sheeran, 2006). Such cues could include specific dates, times, and locations that will prompt behaviour (Milkman et al., 2011) or special locations or attention-grabbing objects individuals anticipate to come across (Rogers & Milkman, 2016). The more concrete one makes their plan and the more vivid/special cues one connects their goal with, the more likely they will be to remember to take action when the cues appear (Milkman, 2021). In the domain of influenza vaccination, Milkman et al. (2011) tested the effectiveness of planning prompts among employees of a large firm who were invited to get vaccinated at an on-site clinic. They found that specific planning prompts that asked employees to think about both a date and a time to get vaccinated increased vaccinations by 4.2 percentage points, as compared to the 33.1 per cent vaccination rates in the no-prompt control condition. Another study similarly found that specifying concretely when, where, and how one plans to get vaccinated encouraged vaccine uptake (Vet et al., 2014). However, in Milkman et al. (2011), prompts that only asked employees to think about a date did not successfully impact vaccinations.

Time-inconsistent preferences. In this section, we discuss strategies to help individuals follow through on their pre-existing intentions when time-inconsistent preferences may lead them to overweight immediate costs associated with getting vaccinated and thus procrastinate. To tackle procrastination, interventions could reduce the hassle costs associated with getting vaccinated. One way to achieve this objective is to make vaccination more convenient, for example, by automatically scheduling vaccination appointments. Chapman et al. (2010) tested this strategy, comparing an 'opt out' condition where individuals were pre-scheduled for an influenza vaccination appointment that they could cancel to an 'opt in' condition where individuals had to actively schedule their appointment. Defaulting people into appointments increased vaccination rates by 12 percentage points, or 36 per cent, relative to the 'opt in' condition (Chapman et al., 2010). Chapman et al. (2016) and Lehmann et al. (2016) provide additional evidence supporting the efficacy of the default strategy. A more structural approach to reduce hassle costs is to reduce physical barriers to getting vaccinated, for example, by improving the accessibility of vaccine clinics or by providing transportation. These strategies may be especially beneficial for Black, Latinx, lower-income, and older individuals who face greater logistic barriers to obtaining the vaccine (Hoffmann et al., 2020; Wong et al., 2022). In a randomised controlled trial involving employees of a bank, allowing the employees to take time off work to get on-site vaccinations during the workweek boosted flu shot take-up rates by an estimated magnitude of 6.7 to 9 percentage points across specifications, relative to assigning them to get vaccinated on Saturday when employees would need to incur additional transportation costs and arrange their weekend schedules to get vaccinated (Hoffmann et al., 2020). This result provides empirical support for the strategy of offering employees paid time off to counter the time costs of getting vaccinated against COVID-19 (including the time needed to travel to and back from a clinic, as well as the time needed to recover from the minor side effects of the vaccine).

When costs cannot be directly reduced, interventions that help individuals stick to their vaccination plans could be effective. Soft commitment strategies like the planning prompts reviewed earlier (e.g., Milkman et al., 2011) might help individuals stay committed to a course of action, because individuals feel guilty about reneging on the promise they have made to themselves. More costly commitment strategies, which capitalise on people's self-awareness of their time-inconsistent preferences, have effectively induced behaviour change in other health domains (Bryan et al., 2010; Rogers et al., 2014) but have not been tested in the domain of vaccinations to the best of our knowledge. When individuals' inertia is driven by logistical costs and the discomfort associated with vaccinations, another potential solution is to pair the undesirable activity of vaccination with a pleasant reward. To effectively overcome the short-term costs of getting vaccinated, which may be overweighted due to present bias, such rewards should be offered as close as possible to the act of getting vaccinated (Gneezy et al., 2020). Allowing people to get something desirable, like a sweet treat, during or immediately after they get the vaccine is a form of temptation bundling, a strategy that has been found to be effective in promoting other health behaviours, like physical exercise (Milkman et al., 2014). During the COVID-19 pandemic, a variety of businesses and organisations had offered free gifts to individuals showing up to vaccination clinics. For instance, the Indiana Department of Health partnered with girl scouts to offer free cookies at vaccination clinics (Delfino, 2021), and several vaccine clinics across the United States had partnered with local breweries to offer free beer to those who agreed to be inoculated (Tan, 2021; Umana, 2021).

9.3.3 Additional Considerations: Combining Intentions and Action

Although our review has separately discussed interventions that attempt to elevate intentions and interventions aimed at closing the intention–action gap, those two sets of interventions should not be considered independent from each other for two reasons. First, there are no clear boundaries between the mechanisms they operate through: sometimes it is unclear whether an intervention targets drivers of intentions, barriers to follow-through, or both. For instance, though we discussed earlier that one way to reduce the inconvenience associated with vaccinations is to automatically schedule vaccination appointments by default for patients (Chapman et al., 2010), this strategy may also convey doctors' implicit recommendation that vaccination is the right and safe thing to do (McKenzie et al., 2006) and thus boost vaccination intentions (Serra-Garcia & Szech, 2021). Similarly, financial or non-financial rewards that are contingent on vaccination could elevate intentions because incentives introduce economic benefits of getting vaccinated beyond personal and community health benefits, altering the cost–benefit considerations people make when deciding whether to get inoculated. At the same time, offering incentives could also offset the immediate costs of getting vaccinated, helping individuals follow through on their intentions, as mentioned earlier (Gneezy et al., 2020). Similar to other domains where incentives have produced mixed results across studies (Gneezy et al., 2020), the evidence for the impact of incentives on both intentions and behaviours is also inconclusive in the domain of vaccinations (Adams et al., 2015; Higgins et al., 2021). Taking COVID-19 as an example, incentives are helpful in some studies (e.g., Klüver et al., 2021, and Serra-Garcia et al., 2021, for intentions; Campos-Mercade et al., 2021a, for behaviour) but not in others (Sprengholz et al., 2021, for intentions; Milkman et al., 2021b, and Chang et al., 2021, for behaviour).

Another reason for not clearly drawing a boundary between interventions targeting intentions and those targeting the intention–action gap is that, on many occasions, interventions that tap onto different mechanisms could be combined to maximise effectiveness. As reviewed earlier, in many instances, interventions that are effective at moving vaccination intentions do not translate such impact into action. Since follow-through barriers may prevent individuals from acting on their intentions, a potentially promising strategy could be to combine interventions that elevate intentions with those that facilitate action. There is some evidence that this approach can pay off. A large-scale evaluation of policy interventions to increase measles vaccine uptake in India found that the most effective strategy is to combine information provision via information hubs (i.e., dedicated individuals in a community in charge of diffusing information) and text-based reminders of upcoming vaccination opportunities (Banerjee et al., 2021). These results underscore the potential benefit of combining interventions that tackle different mechanisms.

9.4   MATCHING INTERVENTIONS WITH THE PROBLEM

9.4.1   *One Size Does Not Fit All*

As we have discussed earlier for some of the reviewed interventions, mixed evidence often exists: an intervention may successfully change vaccination intentions or behaviour in some studies but fail to work in others. For instance, as reviewed earlier, in a large-scale randomised controlled trial, a text message reminder sent to unvaccinated patients of a California hospital in January and February 2021 increased COVID-19 vaccination rates anywhere in California within a month by 2.1 percentage points (Dai et al., 2021). However, in a separate large-scale randomised controlled trial that took place from late May to mid-June 2021, sending a text reminder to Rhode Island residents who had not yet been vaccinated against COVID-19 four to eight weeks after they became eligible had a precisely estimated null effect on vaccination rates within a month (Rabb et al., 2021b). Both randomised controlled trials tested a version of the text reminder that adopted very similar psychological ownership language (e.g., stating that a COVID-19 vaccine is 'available for you' and encouraging people to 'claim your dose'). Whereas this was the most effective reminder tested by Dai et al. (2021), it still had no detectable effect on (and even directionally decreased) vaccination rates in the study by Rabb et al. (2021b). Similarly, studies testing the impact of financial incentives on COVID-19 vaccinations also have presented divergent experimental evidence. Monetary incentive of 200 Swedish kronor (USD 24) increased vaccination rates by 4 percentage points within thirty days right after Swedes became eligible for the COVID-19 vaccine (Campos-Mercade et al., 2021a). However, among people who had not received the vaccine two or three months after they became eligible, offering an incentive of a similar magnitude (USD 10 or 50) did not produce any detectable improvement on vaccination rates (Chang et al., 2021).

One important factor that may partly explain the divergent findings across these examples is people's pre-existing vaccination intent. Across both sets of examples discussed here, the vaccination rates in the holdout group (i.e., people who did not receive the intervention), which could be considered as a proxy of baseline vaccination intentions, were substantially higher among studies that documented benefits of an intervention (31 per cent in Dai et al., 2021, and 71.6 per cent in Campos-Mercade et al., 2021a) than among studies that found null effects of a similar intervention (2 per cent in Rabb et al., 2021b, and 8 per cent in Chang et al., 2021). Thus, the two studies showing promising evidence (Campos-Mercade et al., 2021a; Dai et al., 2021) may have tested their interventions on a much less hesitant population than the other two studies (Chang et al., 2021; Rabb et al., 2021b). These examples not only highlight that policymakers, when seeking to promote vaccine uptake, cannot take the one-size-fits-all approach but also suggest that heterogeneity in individuals' baseline vaccination intentions may be worth considering when policymakers look for the right interventions for a given population. We will elaborate on these points next.

9.4.2 Tailoring Interventions to the Mechanism

We next look at heterogeneity that emerged within studies, highlighting how predictors of vaccination intentions moderate the effectiveness of vaccine interventions. We will first show evidence suggesting that interventions designed to enact intentions tend to work better among people who do not yet have the right intentions in place.

In an online experiment, unvaccinated people were randomly assigned to watch either a control video that described how COVID-19 vaccines work to protect the body or one of four treatment videos designed to influence beliefs and attitudes as crucial drivers of vaccine hesitancy (e.g., attitudes about vaccine safety, attitudes about vaccine efficacy, and normative beliefs of vaccination). The four treatment videos significantly increased vaccination intentions relative to the control video. Importantly, the treatment videos improved willingness to vaccinate among conservatives and moderates as well as people with low trust in the US government and US coronavirus taskforce but not among liberals and more trusting individuals (Jensen et al., 2022). Since the former groups were less prone to get vaccinated than the latter groups at baseline, such heterogeneous responses suggest that these video-based information provisions may be more effective in enhancing vaccination intentions among those who were initially hesitant to vaccinate than those who had intentions at baseline. Another study provides more direct evidence for this argument by testing how the effect of an information provision intervention varies by people's pre-existing vaccine attitudes: in Horne et al. (2015), presenting people with scientific information about the consequences of not vaccinating their children changed attitudes towards vaccines to a more positive degree among people whose pre-intervention attitudes were more negative.

A similar trend emerged for an intervention designed to alter people's risk appraisals about the disease. In a field experiment involving Walmart pharmacy patients in the United States, calling to mind the potential sickness one could face if they did not vaccinate for the flu significantly increased vaccination rates among people who did not get routinely vaccinated against the flu but did not help and even backfired among people who routinely got the flu shot in past years (Brody et al., 2022b). Since prior influenza history is a strong predictor of one's baseline influenza vaccination intentions (Chapman & Coups, 1999), this finding suggests that appeals targeting motivation to vaccinate through elevated virus risk perceptions may more effectively encourage vaccination among those with lower (vs higher) baseline intentions.

Beyond interventions designed to change beliefs and attitudes about a disease and vaccine, interventions aimed to increase vaccination intentions by eliciting pro-social motivation to vaccinate also appear to work better among initially more hesitant populations. In an online experiment launched in eight countries, an intervention that identified potential flu victims who would suffer as a result of others not vaccinating boosted influenza vaccination intentions among participants who did not vaccinate in the previous year but not among those who had vaccinated in the previous year (Li et al., 2016). This result suggests that appealing to pro-social motives may be better at shifting influenza vaccination intentions among those who had lower motivation to act.

On the flip side, interventions designed to facilitate action by addressing the intention–action gap may be more effective among people who already have the intentions to vaccinate but face follow-through barriers. Saccardo et al. (2022) present evidence for this argument both in the COVID-19 vaccination context and in other policy domains. Leveraging data from two large-scale randomised controlled trials that tested the effect of behaviourally informed text reminders (these were the same trials as those reported in Dai et al., 2021, but the data included more variables and more patients in a longer study period), the authors find that these reminders produced a smaller effect on vaccination behaviour among people living in Republican-leaning (vs Democratic-leaning) counties and those who did not receive (vs received) a flu shot in recent years. Political ideology and historical influenza history are reliable predictors of baseline COVID-19 vaccination intentions (Fridman et al., 2021; Kreps et al., 2020). As such, these results suggest that reminders are less effective among hesitant individuals than among individuals with some propensity to get vaccinated. Further, since patients were enrolled in these randomised controlled trials in batches that differed in overall vaccination rates – a proxy of baseline vaccination intentions – and were randomised to conditions within each batch, the authors also find that reminders boosted vaccination rates to a smaller extent when vaccination rate in the holdout arm of a batch was lower (indicating that the patients in that batch were less open to the vaccine). This result is consistent with the idea that the big difference in baseline vaccination motivation between Dai et al. (2021) and Rabb et al.

(2021b) could at least partly explain the discrepancy in their esti-mated effects of text reminders.

Saccardo et al. (2022) further demonstrate the generalisability of this finding leveraging data from 111 randomised controlled trials conducted by either academics or a government agency that eval-uated light-touch behavioural interventions (e.g., reminders, sim-plifications, planning prompts) across a variety of policy areas (e.g., take-up of service and programmes, civic engagement, donations). There, the authors use the take-up rate in the control condition of each study as a proxy for the study sample's baseline motivation. Across the 111 randomised controlled trials, the authors find that the impact of soft-touch behavioural interventions is smaller for low levels of control take-up rates, suggesting that these interventions tend to be less effective among individuals with lower intentions to engage in the targeted behaviour.

Altogether, our review of the heterogeneity emerging across and within intervention efforts suggests that an underlying psychol-ogy about the baseline motivations of individuals may be an impor-tant indicator for the appropriate intervention channel. Thus, a tailored intervention to target the right barriers to vaccination – low intentions or the intention-action gap – may take policymakers one step further towards maximising the impact of behavioural science insights on vaccination efforts. Brody et al. (2022a) provide evidence for the value of customising interventions according to individuals' baseline motivation in the context of influenza vaccination.

Specifically, Brody et al. (2022a) examine two types of interven-tions: (1) a video-based information intervention that provided facts about flu and its vaccine in order to change the related beliefs and thus boost vaccination intentions and (2) a text-message interven-tion that reminded people of the flu season and shared a convenient way for them to get the vaccine soon, thus tackling forgetfulness and hassle costs as follow-through barriers. Across two online experi-ments and a large-scale randomised controlled trial, the information intervention effectively increased vaccination intentions and actual vaccine uptake, but only among those who did not get the flu shot in recent years. By contrast, the follow-through text message increased vaccine uptake, but only among those who received the flu shot in recent years. Taking prior influenza vaccination behaviour as a proxy for current vaccination intentions (Chapman & Coups, 1999), Brody et al. (2022a) suggest that correcting misbeliefs (e.g., underestimation of flu prevalence and vaccine effectiveness) addresses the underlying issue faced by people with low baseline vaccination intentions and thus is more effective among this population. However, facilitating follow-through is more useful for those who already have intentions in place but forget or procrastinate. These results highlight the importance of matching individuals' problem (either lacking intentions or failing to act on intentions) to what an intervention is designed to tackle (either establishing intention or closing the intention–action gap). Such a tailored approach may maximise the power of behavioural science in enhancing the uptake of vaccines as well as other valuable activities.

9.5 CONCLUSION

Individuals differ immensely in their perceptions, beliefs, and barriers associated with vaccinations. As a result, interventions that aim to encourage vaccination must target the appropriate hurdle to either shift individual intentions or to facilitate follow-through on existing intentions. For vaccine hesitant groups, establishing intentions to get the vaccine is a crucial first step. Thus, providing information about the utility of vaccination, elevating trust in such information and its messengers, and combating misinformation may be the best suited approach. However, these tactics may have little effect on those who already intend to vaccinate but face barriers to action. This motivated group of individuals may instead benefit from reminders, planning prompts, simplifications, and other interventions that overcome follow-through barriers, in order to turn their pre-existing intentions into action. Future work could add to the body of literature described in this chapter by uncovering important predictors of intentions to vaccinate and by providing more systematic evidence on the heterogeneous effects of interventions depending on baseline motivation. Such research would join a new and growing movement to design for and predict heterogeneity in behavioural intervention efficacy based on individual-level characteristics (Bryan et al., 2021).

Practitioners and policymakers can directly apply insights from this chapter to assess the baseline motivation in a population of interest using known proxies and tailor interventions accordingly (Balu et al., 2018; Brody et al., 2022a). For example, in the COVID-19 vaccine context, practitioners could analyse the time since the targeted sample became eligible, recent vaccination rates in the targeted population, self-reported intentions to vaccinate, or history of prior influenza vaccination. These indicators of baseline vaccination intent could then point to the appropriate mechanisms to deploy in the intervention effort. Circling back to the example introduced at the beginning of this chapter, if the targeted sample primarily consists of people like Sam, who has relatively low intentions to vaccinate, a tailored intervention could focus on enhancing vaccination intentions. If instead these indicators suggest that the sample consists of many people like Alex, who already has intentions in place but may put off getting the vaccine for a variety of reasons, investing resources in closing the intention–action gap may be more fruitful.

Although in this chapter we have focused on reviewing interventions that directly target individuals, we should note that moving the needle on vaccinations also requires more forceful policies, such as bans, mandates, and regulations that have likely to have a much stronger impact than individual-level interventions (Chater & Loewenstein, 2022). Policy interventions should consider the system-level entities involved, like the service providers of the vaccine (pharmacies and medical centres), the institutions developing and promoting the vaccine (government institutions, research laboratories), and structural aspects (e.g., distance between each community and vaccination centres, schedule of vaccination centres). Although these strategies are important for ensuring high uptake of vaccination, individual-level interventions could be a useful complement in a variety of settings. For instance, while vaccine mandates (e.g., at the workplace) could eventually ensure high take-up of initial doses, individuals may procrastinate on getting the initial shots or choose not to take up booster shots that are not mandatory. Further, in the prevalent contexts where mandates are not in place, convincing the hesitant individuals about the effectiveness of vaccines may be critical. In those situations, individual-level interventions could complement the systemic approach, helping accelerate vaccine uptake efforts even when more forceful strategies are already in place or increase vaccinations whenever more forceful strategies are not feasible.

As policymakers and medical experts increasingly turn to behavioural research to motivate individuals to vaccinate, it is essential for behavioural science experts to transparently identify the contexts in which interventions work and when they do not. This comprehensive understanding of the underlying mechanisms may help to vaccinate individuals across the spectrum of baseline motivation and will be applicable for many behavioural challenges to come.

REFERENCES

Adams, J., Bateman, B., Becker, F., Cresswell, T., Flynn, D., McNaughton, R., et al. (2015). Effectiveness and acceptability of parental financial incentives and quasi-mandatory schemes for increasing uptake of vaccinations in preschool children: Systematic review, qualitative study and discrete choice experiment. *Health Technology Assessment*, 19(94), 1–176.

Agley, J., & Xiao, Y. (2021). Misinformation about COVID-19: Evidence for differential latent profiles and a strong association with trust in science. *BMC Public Health*, 21(1), 89. https://doi.org/10.1186/s12889-020-10103-x

Agranov, M., Elliott, M., & Ortoleva, P. (2021). The importance of social norms against strategic effects: The case of Covid-19 vaccine uptake. *Economics Letters*, 206, 109979. https://doi.org/10.1016/j.econlet.2021.109979

Ajzen, I. (1991). The theory of planned behavior. *Organizational Behavior and Human Decision Processes*, 50(2), 179–211.

Akerlof, G. A., & Kranton, R. E. (2000). Economics and identity. *Quarterly Journal of Economics*, 115(3), 715–753. https://doi.org/10.1162/003355300554881

Alatas, V., Chandrasekhar, A., Mobius, M., Olken, B., & Paladines, C. (2019). When celebrities speak: A nationwide Twitter experiment promoting vaccination in Indonesia. Working Paper 25589. National Bureau of Economic Research. https://doi.org/10.3386/w25589

Alsan, M., & Eichmeyer, S. (2021). Experimental evidence on the effectiveness of non-experts for improving vaccine demand. Working Paper 28593. National Bureau of Economic Research. https://doi.org/10.3386/w28593

Alsan, M., Garrick, O., & Graziani, G. (2019). Does diversity matter for health? Experimental evidence from Oakland. *American Economic Review*, 109(12), 4071–4111.

Alsan, M., Stanford, F. C., Banerjee, A., Breza, E., Chandrasekhar, A. G., Eichmeyer, S., et al. (2021). Comparison of knowledge and information-seeking behavior after general COVID-19 public health messages and messages tailored for Black and Latinx communities: A randomized controlled trial. *Annals of Internal Medicine*, 174(4), 484–492. https://doi.org/10.7326/M20-6141

Amin, A. B., Bednarczyk, R. A., Ray, C. E., Melchiori, K. J., Graham, J., Huntsinger, J. R., & Omer, S. B. (2017). Association of moral values with vaccine hesitancy. *Nature Human Behaviour*, 1(12), 873–880.

Ashworth, M., Thunström, L., Cherry, T. L., Newbold, S. C., & Finnoff, D. C. (2021). Emphasize personal health benefits to boost COVID-19 vaccination rates. *Proceedings of the National Academy of Sciences*, 118(32), e2108225118. https://doi.org/10.1073/pnas.2108225118

Austin, J., Sigurdsson, S. O., & Rubin, Y. S. (2006). An examination of the effects of delayed versus immediate prompts on safety belt use. *Environment and Behavior*, 38(1), 140–149. https://doi.org/10.1177/0013916505276744

Bajaj, S. S., & Stanford, F. C. (2021). Beyond Tuskegee: Vaccine distrust and everyday racism. *New England Journal of Medicine*, 384(5), e12. https://doi.org/10.1056/NEJMpv2035827

Balu, R., Dechausay, N., & Anzelone, C. (2018). An organizational approach to applying behavioral insights to policy: Center for Applied Behavioral Science at MDRC. In K. Ruggeri (ed.), *Behavioral Insights for Public Policy* (pp. 200–217). Routledge.

Banerjee, A., Alsan, M., Breza, E., Chandrasekhar, A., Chowdhury, A., Duflo, E., et al. (2020). Messages on COVID-19 prevention in India increased symptoms reporting and adherence to preventive behaviors among 25 million recipients with similar effects on non-recipient members of their communities. Working Paper 27496. National Bureau of Economic Research. https://doi.org/10.3386/w27496

Banerjee, A., Chandrasekhar, A., Dalpath, S., Duflo, E., Floretta, J., Jackson, M., et al. (2021). Selecting the most effective nudge: Evidence from a large-scale experiment on immunization. Working Paper 28726. National Bureau of Economic Research. https://doi.org/10.3386/w28726

Bartoš, V., Bauer, M., Cahlíková, J., & Chytilová, J. (2022). Communicating doctor's consensus persistently increases COVID-19 vaccinations. *Nature, 606*, 542–549. https://doi.org/10.1038/s41586-022-04805-y

Bem, D. J. (1972). Self-perception theory. In L. Berkowitz (ed.), *Advances in Experimental Social Psychology* (vol. 6, pp. 1–62). Academic Press. https://doi.org/10.1016/S0065-2601(08)60024-6

Bénabou, R., & Tirole, J. (2006). *A Cognitive Theory of Identity, Dignity, and Taboos.* Princeton University Press. www. Econ. Yale. Edu//~ Shiller/Behmacro/2006-11/ Benabou-Tirole. Pdf

Bénabou, R., & Tirole, J. (2011). Identity, morals, and taboos: Beliefs as assets. *The Quarterly Journal of Economics, 126*(2), 805–855.

Berliner Senderey, A., Ohana, R., Perchik, S., Erev, I., & Balicer, R. (2021). Encouraging uptake of the COVID-19 vaccine through behaviorally informed interventions: National real-world evidence from Israel. Social Science Research Network. https://ssrn.com/abstract=3852345 or https://dx.doi.org/10.2139/ssrn.3852345

Bertrand, M., Mullainathan, S., & Shafir, E. (2006). Behavioral economics and marketing in aid of decision making among the poor. *Journal of Public Policy & Marketing, 25*(1), 8–23.

Betsch, C., Böhm, R., & Chapman, G. B. (2015). Using behavioral insights to increase vaccination policy effectiveness. *Policy Insights from the Behavioral and Brain Sciences, 2*(1), 61–73. https://doi.org/10.1177/2372732215600716

Betsch, C., Böhm, R., Korn, L., & Holtmann, C. (2017). On the benefits of explaining herd immunity in vaccine advocacy. *Nature Human Behaviour, 1*(3), 1–6.

Betsch, C., & Sachse, K. (2013). Debunking vaccination myths: Strong risk negations can increase perceived vaccination risks. *Health Psychology, 32*(2), 146–155. https://doi.org/10.1037/a0027387

Bhargava, S., & Manoli, D. (2015). Psychological frictions and the incomplete take-up of social benefits: Evidence from an IRS field experiment. *American Economic Review, 105*(11), 3489–3529. https://doi.org/10.1257/aer.20121493

Bogard, J. E., Fox, C. R., & Goldstein, N. J. (2022). The implied exclusivity effect: Promoting choice through reserved labeling. Unpublished Working Paper.

Bogart, L. M., Dong, L., Gandhi, P., Ryan, S., Smith, T., Klein, D., et al. (2021). *What Contributes to COVID-19 Vaccine Hesitancy in Black Communities, and How Can It Be Addressed?* RAND Corporation. https://doi.org/10.7249/RRA1110-1

Böhm, R., & Betsch, C. (2022). Prosocial vaccination. *Current Opinion in Psychology*, 43, 307–311. https://doi.org/10.1016/j.copsyc.2021.08.010

Böhm, R., Meier, N. W., Groß, M., Korn, L., & Betsch, C. (2019). The willingness to vaccinate increases when vaccination protects others who have low responsibility for not being vaccinated. *Journal of Behavioral Medicine*, 42(3), 381–391.

Brewer, N. T., Chapman, G. B., Gibbons, F. X., Gerrard, M., McCaul, K. D., & Weinstein, N. D. (2007). Meta-analysis of the relationship between risk perception and health behavior: The example of vaccination. *Health Psychology*, 26(2), 136–145. https://doi.org/10.1037/0278-6133.26.2.136

Brewer, N. T., Chapman, G. B., Rothman, A. J., Leask, J., & Kempe, A. (2017). Increasing vaccination: Putting psychological science into action. *Psychological Science in the Public Interest*, 18(3), 149–207. https://doi.org/10.1177/1529100618760521

Brewer, N. T., DeFrank, J. T., & Gilkey, M. B. (2016). Anticipated regret and health behavior: A meta-analysis. *Health Psychology*, 35(11), 1264–1275. https://doi.org/10.1037/hea0000294

Briss, P. A., Rodewald, L. E., Hinman, A. R., Shefer, A. M., Strikas, R. A., Bernier, R. R., et al. (2000). Reviews of evidence regarding interventions to improve vaccination coverage in children, adolescents, and adults. The Task Force on Community Preventive Services. *American Journal of Preventive Medicine*, 18(1 Suppl), 97–140. https://doi.org/10.1016/S0749-3797(99)00118-X

Brody, I., Dai, H., Saccardo, S., Milkman, K., Patel, M., Gromet, D., & Duckworth, A. (2022a). Provide information or encourage follow-through? Effects of behavioral interventions depend on baseline motivation. Unpublished Working Paper.

Brody, I., Hershfield, H., Milkman, K., Patel, M., Gromet, D., & Duckworth, A. (2022b). Leveraging past adversity to increase preventative behavior. Working Paper.

Bronchetti, E. T., Huffman, D. B., & Magenheim, E. (2015). Attention, intentions, and follow-through in preventive health behavior: Field experimental evidence on flu vaccination. *Journal of Economic Behavior & Organization*, 116, 270–291.

Bryan, C. J., Tipton, E., & Yeager, D. S. (2021). Behavioural science is unlikely to change the world without a heterogeneity revolution. *Nature Human Behaviour*, 5, 980–989. https://doi.org/10.1038/s41562-021-01143-3

Bryan, G., Karlan, D., & Nelson, S. (2010). Commitment devices. *Annual Review of Economics*, 2(1), 671–698. https://doi.org/10.1146/annurev.economics.102308.124324

Bursztyn, L., & Jensen, R. (2017). Social image and economic behavior in the field: Identifying, understanding, and shaping social pressure. *Annual Review of Economics*, 9, 131–153.

Campos-Mercade, P., Meier, A. N., Schneider, F. H., Meier, S., Pope, D., & Wengström, E. (2021a). Monetary incentives increase COVID-19 vaccinations. *Science*, 374(6569), 879–882. https://doi.org/10.1126/science.abm0475

Campos-Mercade, P., Meier, A. N., Schneider, F. H., & Wengström, E. (2021b). Prosociality predicts health behaviors during the COVID-19 pandemic. *Journal of Public Economics*, 195, 104367. https://doi.org/10.1016/j.jpubeco.2021.104367

CDC. (2022). COVID Data Tracker. Centers for Disease Control and Prevention. 10 March. https://covid.cdc.gov/covid-data-tracker

Chang, T., Jacobson, M., Shah, M., Pramanik, R., & Shah, S. (2021). Financial incentives and other nudges do not increase COVID-19 vaccinations among the vaccine hesitant. Working Paper w29403. National Bureau of Economic Research. https://doi.org/10.3386/w29403

Chapman, G. B., & Coups, E. J. (1999). Predictors of Influenza vaccine acceptance among healthy adults. *Preventive Medicine*, 29(4), 249–262. https://doi.org/10.1006/pmed.1999.0535

Chapman, G. B., Li, M., Colby, H., & Yoon, H. (2010). Opting in vs opting out of influenza vaccination. *JAMA*, 304(1), 43. https://doi.org/10.1001/jama.2010.892

Chapman, G. B., Li, M., Leventhal, H., & Leventhal, E. A. (2016). Default clinic appointments promote influenza vaccination uptake without a displacement effect. *Behavioral Science & Policy*, 2(2), 40–50.

Chater, N., & Loewenstein, G. (2022). The i-frame and the s-frame: How focusing on the individual-level solutions has led behavioral public policy astray. Scholarly Paper No. 4046264. Social Science Research Network. https://papers.ssrn.com/abstract=4046264

Chu, J., Pink, S. L., & Willer, R. (2021). Religious identity cues increase vaccination intentions and trust in medical experts among American Christians. *Proceedings of the National Academy of Sciences*, 118(49), e2106481118. https://doi.org/10.1073/pnas.2106481118

Congdon, W. J., Kling, J. R., & Mullainathan, S. (2011). *Policy and Choice: Public Finance through the Lens of Behavioral Economics*. Brookings Institution Press.

Dai, H., Saccardo, S., Han, M. A., Roh, L., Raja, N., Vangala, S., et al. (2021). Behavioral nudges increase COVID-19 vaccinations. *Nature*, 1–9. https://doi.org/10.1038/s41586-021-03843-2

Danza, P., Koo, T. H., Haddix, M., Fisher, R., Traub, E., OYong, K., & Balter, S. (2022). SARS-CoV-2 infection and hospitalization among adults aged ≥18 years, by vaccination status, before and during SARS-CoV-2 B.1.1.529 (Omicron) variant predominance – Los Angeles County, California, November 7, 2021– January 8, 2022. *Morbidity and Mortality Weekly Report*, 71(5), 177–181. https://doi.org/10.15585/mmwr.mm7105e1

Delfino, D. (2021, June 24). Incentives for COVID-19 Vaccination: Food, Cash, & Other Perks. Health Topic. GoodRx Health. www.goodrx.com/health-topic/vaccines/covid-19-vaccination-incentives

Ebbinghaus, H. (2013). Memory: A contribution to experimental psychology. *Annals of Neurosciences*, 20(4), 155.

Ericson, K. M., & Laibson, D. (2019). Intertemporal choice. In B. D. Bernheim, S. DellaVigna, D. Laibson (eds.), *Handbook of Behavioral Economics: Applications and Foundations 1* (vol. 2, pp. 1–67). Elsevier. https://doi.org/10.1016/bs.hesbe.2018.12.001

Falagas, M. E., & Zarkadoulia, E. (2008). Factors associated with suboptimal compliance to vaccinations in children in developed countries: A systematic review. *Current Medical Research and Opinion*, 24(6), 1719–1741. https://doi.org/10.1185/03007990802085692

Falomir-Pichastor, J. M., Toscani, L., & Despointes, S. H. (2009). Determinants of flu vaccination among nurses: The effects of group identification and professional responsibility. *Applied Psychology: An International Review*, 58(1), 42–58.

Fishbach, A., Dhar, R., & Zhang, Y. (2006). Subgoals as substitutes or complements: The role of goal accessibility. *Journal of Personality and Social Psychology*, 91(2), 232.

Fishbach, A., Friedman, R. S., & Kruglanski, A. W. (2003). Leading us not into temptation: Momentary allurements elicit overriding goal activation. *Journal of Personality and Social Psychology*, 84(2), 296.

Fridman, A., Gershon, R., & Gneezy, A. (2021). COVID-19 and vaccine hesitancy: A longitudinal study. *PLOS ONE*, 16(4), e0250123. https://doi.org/10.1371/journal.pone.0250123

Gabaix, X. (2019). Behavioral inattention. In B. D. Bernheim, S. DellaVigna, D. Laibson (eds.), *Handbook of Behavioral Economics: Applications and Foundations 1* (vol. 2, pp. 261–343). Elsevier.

Galasso, V., Pons, V., Profeta, P., Becher, M., Brouard, S., & Foucault, M. (2022). From anti-vax intentions to vaccination: Panel and experimental evidence from nine countries. Working Paper No. w29741. National Bureau of Economic Research. https://doi.org/10.3386/w29741

Galizzi, M. M., Lau, K., Miraldo, M., & Hauck, K. (2022). Bandwagoning, free-riding and heterogeneity in influenza vaccine decisions: An online experiment. *Health Economics*, 31(4), 614–646. https://doi.org/10.1002/hec.4467

Gneezy, U., Kajackaite, A., & Meier, S. (2020). Incentive-based interventions. In M. S. Hagger, L. D. Cameron, K. Hamilton, N. Hankonen, & T. Lintunen (eds.), *The Handbook of Behavior Change* (pp. 523–536). Cambridge University Press. https://doi.org/10.1017/9781108677318.036

Gollwitzer, P. M. (1999). Implementation intentions: Strong effects of simple plans. *American Psychologist*, 54(7), 493–503. https://doi.org/10.1037/0003-066X.54.7.493

Gollwitzer, P. M., & Sheeran, P. (2006). Implementation intentions and goal achievement: A meta-analysis of effects and processes. *Advances in Experimental Social Psychology*, 38, 69–119.

Gollwitzer, P. M., & Sheeran, P. (2009). Self-regulation of consumer decision making and behavior: The role of implementation intentions. *Journal of Consumer Psychology*, 19(4), 593–607.

Greenwood, B. N., Hardeman, R. R., Huang, L., & Sojourner, A. (2020). Physician-patient racial concordance and disparities in birthing mortality for newborns. *Proceedings of the National Academy of Sciences*, 117(35), 21194–21200. https://doi.org/10.1073/pnas.1913405117

Haaland, I., Roth, C., & Wohlfart, J. (2020). Designing information provision experiments. Scholarly Paper No. 3638879. Social Science Research Network. https://doi.org/10.2139/ssrn.3638879

Hakim, H., Provencher, T., Chambers, C. T., Driedger, S. M., Dubé, E., Gavaruzzi, T., et al. (2019). Interventions to help people understand community immunity: A systematic review. *Vaccine*, 37(2), 235–247.

Heinrich-Morrison, K., McLellan, S., McGinnes, U., Carroll, B., Watson, K., Bass, P., et al. (2015). An effective strategy for influenza vaccination of healthcare workers in Australia: Experience at a large health service without a mandatory policy. *BMC Infectious Diseases*, 15(1), 42. https://doi.org/10.1186/s12879-015-0765-7

Hershfield, H., & Brody, I. (2021). How Elvis got Americans to accept the Polio Vaccine. *Scientific American*, 18 January www.scientificamerican.com/article/how-elvis-got-americans-to-accept-the-polio-vaccine/

Higgins, S. T., Klemperer, E. M., & Coleman, S. R. M. (2021). Looking to the empirical literature on the potential for financial incentives to enhance adherence with COVID-19 vaccination. *Preventive Medicine*, 145, 106421. https://doi.org/10.1016/j.ypmed.2021.106421

Hoffmann, M., Mosquera, R., & Chadi, A. (2020). Vaccines at work. Discussion Paper No. 12939. Institute of Labor Economics (IZA). https://econpapers.repec.org/paper/izaizadps/dp12939.htm

Horne, Z., Powell, D., Hummel, J. E., & Holyoak, K. J. (2015). Countering antivaccination attitudes. *Proceedings of the National Academy of Sciences*, 112(33), 10321–10324. https://doi.org/10.1073/pnas.1504019112

Huynh, H. P., Zsila, Á., & Martinez-Berman, L. (2021). Psychosocial predictors of intention to vaccinate against the Coronavirus (COVID-19). *Behavioral Medicine*, 1–15. https://doi.org/10.1080/08964289.2021.1990006

Iyengar, S. S., & Lepper, M. R. (2000). When choice is demotivating: Can one desire too much of a good thing? *Journal of Personality and Social Psychology*, 79(6), 995.

Jackson, C., Cheater, F. M., Harrison, W., Peacock, R., Bekker, H., West, R., & Leese, B. (2011). Randomised cluster trial to support informed parental decision-making for the MMR vaccine. *BMC Public Health*, 11(1), 475. https://doi.org/10.1186/1471-2458-11-475

Jacobson Vann, J. C., Jacobson, R. M., Coyne-Beasley, T., Asafu-Adjei, J. K., & Szilagyi, P. G. (2018). Patient reminder and recall interventions to improve immunization rates. *Cochrane Database of Systematic Reviews*, (1). https://doi.org/10.1002/14651858.CD003941.pub3

Jaiswal, J., LoSchiavo, C., & Perlman, D. C. (2020). Disinformation, misinformation and inequality-driven mistrust in the time of COVID-19: Lessons unlearned from AIDS denialism. *AIDS and Behavior*, 24(10), 2776–2780. https://doi.org/10.1007/s10461-020-02925-y

Jennings, W., Stoker, G., Bunting, H., Valgarðsson, V. O., Gaskell, J., Devine, D., et al. (2021). Lack of trust, conspiracy beliefs, and social media use predict COVID-19 vaccine hesitancy. *Vaccines*, 9(6), 593. https://doi.org/10.3390/vaccines9060593

Jensen, U. T., Ayers, S., & Koskan, A. M. (2022). Video-based messages to reduce COVID-19 vaccine hesitancy and nudge vaccination intentions. *PLOS ONE*, 17(4), e0265736. https://doi.org/10.1371/journal.pone.0265736

Jurkowitz, M., & Mitchell, A. (2020). Cable TV and COVID-19: How Americans perceive the outbreak and view media coverage differ by main news source. Pew Research Center.

Kahan, D. M. (2017). Misconceptions, misinformation, and the logic of identity-protective cognition. Scholarly Paper No. 2973067. Social Science Research Network. https://doi.org/10.2139/ssrn.2973067

Kahan, D. M., Peters, E., Wittlin, M., Slovic, P., Ouellette, L. L., Braman, D., & Mandel, G. N. (2012). The polarizing impact of science literacy and numeracy on perceived climate change risks. Scholarly Paper No. 2193133. Social Science Research Network. https://papers.ssrn.com/abstract=2193133

Kahneman, D. (1973). *Attention and Effort*, vol. 1063. Prentice-Hall.

Kaplan, R. M., & Milstein, A. (2021). Influence of a COVID-19 vaccine's effectiveness and safety profile on vaccination acceptance. *Proceedings of the National Academy of Sciences*, 118(10), e2021726118. https://doi.org/10.1073/pnas.2021726118

Karing, A. (2019). Social signaling and health behavior in low-income countries. Doctoral dissertation, UC Berkeley. https://escholarship.org/uc/item/6w70d701

Kaufman, J., Ryan, R., Walsh, L., Horey, D., Leask, J., Robinson, P. et al. (2018). Face to face interventions for informing or educating parents about early childhood vaccination. *Cochrane Database of Systematic Reviews*, 5(5), CD10038. https://doi.org/10.1002/14651858.CD010038

Keppeler, F., Sievert, M., & Jilke, S. (2021). Increasing Covid-19 vaccination intentions through a local government vaccination campaign: A field experiment on psychological ownership. *SSRN Electronic Journal*. https://doi.org/10.2139/ssrn.3905470

Klotz, P. A. (2022). Leadership communication and COVID-19 vaccination hesitancy. MAGKS Papers on Economics 202206. Philipps-Universität Marburg, Faculty of Business Administration and Economics, Department of Economics (Volkswirtschaftliche Abteilung).

Klüver, H., Hartmann, F., Humphreys, M., Geissler, F., & Giesecke, J. (2021). Incentives can spur COVID-19 vaccination uptake. *Proceedings of the National Academy of Sciences*, 118(36).

Korn, L., Böhm, R., Meier, N. W., & Betsch, C. (2020). Vaccination as a social contract. *Proceedings of the National Academy of Sciences*, 117(26), 14890–14899.

Kouzy, R., Abi Jaoude, J., Kraitem, A., El Alam, M. B., Karam, B., Adib, E., et al. (2020). Coronavirus goes viral: Quantifying the COVID-19 misinformation epidemic on Twitter. *Cureus*, 12(3).

Kreps, S., Prasad, S., Brownstein, J. S., Hswen, Y., Garibaldi, B. T., Zhang, B., & Kriner, D. L. (2020). Factors associated with US adults' likelihood of accepting COVID-19 vaccination. *JAMA Network Open*, 3(10), e2025594. https://doi.org/10.1001/jamanetworkopen.2020.25594

Kruglanski, A. W., Shah, J. Y., Fishbach, A., Friedman, R., Chun, W. Y., & Sleeth-Keppler, D. (2002). A theory of goal systems. In *Advances in Experimental Social Psychology* (vol. 34, pp. 331–378). Academic Press. https://doi.org/10.1016/S0065-2601(02)80008-9

Laibson, D. (1997). Golden eggs and hyperbolic discounting. *The Quarterly Journal of Economics*, 112(2), 443–478.

Lehmann, B. A., Chapman, G. B., Franssen, F. M., Kok, G., & Ruiter, R. A. (2016). Changing the default to promote influenza vaccination among health care workers. *Vaccine*, 34(11), 1389–1392. https://doi.org/10.1016/j.vaccine.2016.01.046

Lewandowsky, S., Ecker, U. K. H., Seifert, C. M., Schwarz, N., & Cook, J. (2012). Misinformation and its correction: Continued influence and successful debiasing. *Psychological Science in the Public Interest*, 13(3), 106–131. https://doi.org/10.1177/1529100612451018

Li, M., Taylor, E. G., Atkins, K. E., Chapman, G. B., & Galvani, A. P. (2016). Stimulating influenza vaccination via prosocial motives. *PLOS ONE*, 11(7), e0159780. https://doi.org/10.1371/journal.pone.0159780

Loomba, S., de Figueiredo, A., Piatek, S. J., de Graaf, K., & Larson, H. J. (2021). Measuring the impact of COVID-19 vaccine misinformation on vaccination intent in the UK and USA. *Nature Human Behaviour*, 5(3), 337–348. https://doi.org/10.1038/s41562-021-01056-1

Lorenz, T. (2021). To fight vaccine lies, authorities recruit an 'influencer army'. *The New York Times*, 1 August. www.nytimes.com/2021/08/01/technology/vaccine-lies-influencer-army.html

MacDonald, N. E. (2015). Vaccine hesitancy: Definition, scope and determinants. *Vaccine*, 33(34), 4161–4164. https://doi.org/10.1016/j.vaccine.2015.04.036

McKenzie, C. R., Liersch, M. J., & Finkelstein, S. R. (2006). Recommendations implicit in policy defaults. *Psychological Science*, 17(5), 414–420.

McLamore, Q., Syropoulos, S., Leidner, B., Hirschberger, G., Young, K., Zein, R. A., et al. (2022). Trust in scientific information mediates associations between conservatism and coronavirus responses in the U.S., but few other nations. *Scientific Reports*, 12(1), 3724. https://doi.org/10.1038/s41598-022-07508-6

Mekonnen, Z. A., Gelaye, K. A., Were, M. C., Gashu, K. D., & Tilahun, B. C. (2019). Effect of mobile text message reminders on routine childhood vaccination: A systematic review and meta-analysis. *Systematic Reviews*, 8(1), 1–14.

Mian, A., & Khan, S. (2020). Coronavirus: The spread of misinformation. *BMC Medicine*, 18(1), 89. https://doi.org/10.1186/s12916-020-01556-3

Milkman, K. L. (2021). *How to Change: The Science of Getting from Where You Are to Where You Want to Be*. Portfolio/Penguin, an imprint of Penguin Random House LLC.

Milkman, K. L., Beshears, J., Choi, J. J., Laibson, D., & Madrian, B. C. (2011). Using implementation intentions prompts to enhance influenza vaccination rates. *Proceedings of the National Academy of Sciences*, 108(26), 10415–10420. https://doi.org/10.1073/pnas.1103170108

Milkman, K. L., Gandhi, L., Patel, M. S., Graci, H. N., Gromet, D. M., Ho, H., et al. (2022). A 680,000-person megastudy of nudges to encourage vaccination in pharmacies. *Proceedings of the National Academy of Sciences*, 119(6). https://doi.org/10.1073/pnas.2115126119

Milkman, K. L., Gromet, D., Ho, H., Kay, J. S., Lee, T. W., Pandiloski, P., et al. (2021a). Megastudies improve the impact of applied behavioural science. *Nature*, 600(7889), 478–483. https://doi.org/10.1038/s41586-021-04128-4

Milkman, K. L., Minson, J. A., & Volpp, K. G. M. (2014). Holding the hunger games hostage at the gym: An evaluation of temptation bundling. *Management Science*, 60(2), 283–299. https://doi.org/10.1287/mnsc.2013.1784

Milkman, K. L., Patel, M. S., Gandhi, L., Graci, H. N., Gromet, D. M., Ho, H., et al. (2021b). A megastudy of text-based nudges encouraging patients to get vaccinated at an upcoming doctor's appointment. *Proceedings of the National Academy of Sciences*, 118(20). https://doi.org/10.1073/pnas.2101165118

Moehring, A., Collis, A., Garimella, K., Rahimian, M. A., Aral, S., & Eckles, D. (2021). Surfacing norms to increase vaccine acceptance. PsyArXiv Preprint. https://doi.org/10.31234/osf.io/srv6t

Murphy, J., Vallières, F., Bentall, R. P., Shevlin, M., McBride, O., Hartman, T. K., et al. (2021). Psychological characteristics associated with COVID-19 vaccine hesitancy and resistance in Ireland and the United Kingdom. *Nature Communications*, 12(1), 29. https://doi.org/10.1038/s41467-020-20226-9

Nyhan, B., & Reifler, J. (2015). Does correcting myths about the flu vaccine work? An experimental evaluation of the effects of corrective information. *Vaccine*, 33(3), 459–464. https://doi.org/10.1016/j.vaccine.2014.11.017

O'Donoghue, T., & Rabin, M. (1999). Doing it now or later. *American Economic Review*, 89(1), 103–124.

Pandey, P., Sehgal, A. R., Riboud, M., Levine, D., & Goyal, M. (2007). Informing resource-poor populations and the delivery of entitled health and social services in rural India: A cluster randomized controlled trial. *JAMA*, 298(16), 1867. https://doi.org/10.1001/jama.298.16.1867

Parsons, J. E., Newby, K. V., & French, D. P. (2018). Do interventions containing risk messages increase risk appraisal and the subsequent vaccination intentions and uptake? A systematic review and meta-analysis. *British Journal of Health Psychology*, 23(4), 1084–1106. https://doi.org/10.1111/bjhp.12340

Pennycook, G., Epstein, Z., Mosleh, M., Arechar, A. A., Eckles, D., & Rand, D. G. (2021). Shifting attention to accuracy can reduce misinformation online. *Nature*, 592(7855), 590–595. https://doi.org/10.1038/s41586-021-03344-2

Pennycook, G., McPhetres, J., Zhang, Y., Lu, J. G., & Rand, D. G. (2020). Fighting COVID-19 misinformation on social media: Experimental evidence for a scalable accuracy-nudge intervention. *Psychological Science*, 31(7), 770–780. https://doi.org/10.1177/0956797620939054

Pfattheicher, S., Petersen, M. B., & Böhm, R. (2021). Information about herd immunity through vaccination and empathy promote COVID-19 vaccination intentions. *Health Psychology*, 41(2), 85–93. https://doi.org/10.1037/hea0001096

Pink, S. L., Chu, J., Druckman, J. N., Rand, D. G., & Willer, R. (2021). Elite party cues increase vaccination intentions among Republicans. *Proceedings of the National Academy of Sciences*, 118(32), e2106559118. https://doi.org/10.1073/pnas.2106559118

Pittman, M. (2020). Accountability moderates the effects of egoistic and altruistic appeals in prosocial messages. *Journal of Consumer Marketing*, 37(7), 807–820. https://doi.org/10.1108/JCM-07-2018-2751

Rabb, N., Glick, D., Houston, A., Bowers, J., & Yokum, D. (2021a). No evidence that collective-good appeals best promote COVID-related health behaviors. *Proceedings of the National Academy of Sciences*, 118(14), e2100662118. https://doi.org/10.1073/pnas.2100662118

Rabb, N., Swindal, M., Glick, D., Bowers, J., Tomasulo, A., Oyelami, Z., et al. (2021b). Nudges do not increase COVID-19 vaccinations in a longer-eligible population. Unpublished Working Paper.

Rabb, N., Swindal, M., Glick, D., Bowers, J., Tomasulo, A., Oyelami, Z., et al. (2022). Evidence from a statewide vaccination RCT shows the limits of nudges. *Nature*, 604(7904), E1–E7.

Razai, M. S., Chaudhry, U. A. R., Doerholt, K., Bauld, L., & Majeed, A. (2021). Covid-19 vaccination hesitancy. *British Medical Journal*, n1138. https://doi.org/10.1136/bmj.n1138

Reimer, N. K., Atari, M., Karimi-Malekabadi, F., Trager, J., Kennedy, B., Graham, J., & Dehghani, M. (2021). Moral values predict county-level COVID-19 vaccination rates in the United States. *American Psychologist*, 77(6),743–759. https://doi.org/10.1037/amp0001020.

Rogers, T., & Milkman, K. L. (2016). Reminders through association. *Psychological Science*, 27(7), 973–986.

Rogers, T., Milkman, K. L., & Volpp, K. G. (2014). Commitment devices: Using initiatives to change behavior. *JAMA*, 311(20), 2065–2066. https://doi.org/10.1001/jama.2014.3485

Saccardo, S., Dai, H., Han, M., Roh, L., Raja, N., Vangala, S., et al. (2022). The impact and limits of nudges: Evidence from large-scale RCTs. *SSRN Electronic Journal*. https://doi.org/10.2139/ssrn.3971192

Santos, H. C., Goren, A., Chabris, C. F., & Meyer, M. N. (2021). Effect of targeted behavioral science messages on COVID-19 vaccination registration among employees of a large health system: A randomized trial. *JAMA Network Open*, 4(7), e2118702–e2118702.

Scheibehenne, B., Greifeneder, R., & Todd, P. M. (2010). Can there ever be too many options? A meta-analytic review of choice overload. *Journal of Consumer Research*, 37(3), 409–425. https://doi.org/10.1086/651235

Schmid, P., Rauber, D., Betsch, C., Lidolt, G., & Denker, M.-L. (2017). Barriers of influenza vaccination intention and behavior: A systematic review of Influenza vaccine hesitancy, 2005–2016. *PLOS ONE*, 12(1), e0170550. https://doi.org/10.1371/journal.pone.0170550

Schoeppe, J., Cheadle, A., Melton, M., Faubion, T., Miller, C., Matthys, J., & Hsu, C. (2017). The immunity community: A community engagement strategy for reducing vaccine hesitancy. *Health Promotion Practice*, 18(5), 654–661. https://doi.org/10.1177/1524839917697303

Serra-Garcia, M., & Szech, N. (2021). Choice architecture and incentives increase COVID-19 vaccine intentions and test demand. *SSRN Electronic Journal*. https://doi.org/10.2139/ssrn.3818182

Shah, J. Y., & Kruglanski, A. W. (2002). Priming against your will: How accessible alternatives affect goal pursuit. *Journal of Experimental Social Psychology*, 38(4), 368–383.

Sheeran, P., Harris, P. R., & Epton, T. (2014). Does heightening risk appraisals change people's intentions and behavior? A meta-analysis of experimental studies. *Psychological Bulletin*, 140(2), 511.

Sheeran, P., & Webb, T. L. (2016). The intention–behavior gap. *Social and Personality Psychology Compass*, 10(9), 503–518.

Sprengholz, P., Eitze, S., Felgendreff, L., Korn, L., & Betsch, C. (2021). Money is not everything: Experimental evidence that payments do not increase willingness to be vaccinated against COVID-19. *Journal of Medical Ethics*, 47(8), 547–548. https://doi.org/10.1136/medethics-2020-107122

Sunstein, C. R. (2014). Nudging: A very short guide. *Journal of Consumer Policy*, 37(4), 583–588. https://doi.org/10.1007/s10603-014-9273-1

Tan, S. (2021). Shot and a beer: Erie County partners with breweries for pop-up vaccine clinics. *The Buffalo News*, 8 June. https://buffalonews.com/news/local/shot-and-a-beer-erie-county-partners-with-breweries-for-pop-up-vaccine-clinics/article_99eaf386-a76c-11eb-8841-331e154637ed.html

Torres, C., Ogbu-Nwobodo, L., Alsan, M., Stanford, F. C., Banerjee, A., Breza, E., et al. (2021). Effect of physician-delivered COVID-19 public health messages and messages acknowledging racial inequity on Black and White adults' knowledge, beliefs, and practices related to COVID-19: A randomized clinical trial. *JAMA Network Open*, 4(7), e2117115. https://doi.org/10.1001/jamanetworkopen.2021.17115

Trueblood, J. S., Sussman, A. B., & O'Leary, D. (2022). The role of risk preferences in responses to messaging about COVID-19 vaccine take-up. *Social Psychological and Personality Science*, 13(1), 311–319. https://doi.org/10.1177/1948550621999622

Umana, J. (2021). This COVID-19 vaccine shot comes with a free beer. *WTOP News*, 29 May. https://wtop.com/loudoun-county/2021/05/this-covid-19-vaccine-shot-comes-with-a-free-beer/

Vet, R., Wit, J. B. de, & Das, E. (2014). The role of implementation intention formation in promoting hepatitis B vaccination uptake among men who have sex with men. *International Journal of STD & AIDS*, 25(2), 122–129.

Williams, S. E. (2014). What are the factors that contribute to parental vaccine-hesitancy and what can we do about it? *Human Vaccines & Immunotherapeutics*, 10(9), 2584–2596. https://doi.org/10.4161/hv.28596

Williams, S. E., Rothman, R. L., Offit, P. A., Schaffner, W., Sullivan, M., & Edwards, K. M. (2013). A randomized trial to increase acceptance of childhood vaccines by vaccine-hesitant parents: A pilot study. *Academic Pediatrics*, 13(5), 475–480. https://doi.org/10.1016/j.acap.2013.03.011

Wong, C. A., Pilkington, W., Doherty, I. A., Zhu, Z., Gawande, H., Kumar, D., & Brewer, N. T. (2022). Guaranteed financial incentives for COVID-19 vaccination: A pilot program in North Carolina. *JAMA Internal Medicine*, 182(1), 78–80.

World Health Organization. (2019). Ten threats to global health in 2019. *World Health Organization Newsroom Spotlight*. www.who.int/news-room/spotlight/ten-threats-to-global-health-in-2019

Xiao, X., Borah, P., & Su, Y. (2021). The dangers of blind trust: Examining the interplay among social media news use, misinformation identification, and news trust on conspiracy beliefs. *Public Understanding of Science*, 30(8), 977–992. https://doi.org/10.1177/0963662521998025

Zauberman, G., & Lynch Jr, J. G. (2005). Resource slack and propensity to discount delayed investments of time versus money. *Journal of Experimental Psychology: General*, 134(1), 23.

10 Psychological and Behavioural Aspects of the COVID-19 Pandemic

Systematic Evidence and Takeaways

Ploutarchos Kourtidis, Henrike Sternberg,
Janina Steinert, Tim Büthe, Giuseppe A. Veltri,
Barbara Fasolo, and Matteo M. Galizzi

10.1 AIMS AND OBJECTIVES

The COVID-19 pandemic has been one of the most disruptive events of the century to date. Beyond the direct and indirect effects on people's physical and mental health, we have also experienced both rapid and gradual changes in everyday life. Since March 2020, when COVID-19 was declared a pandemic (World Health Organization, 2020e), countries around the world have introduced measures to mitigate the spread of the virus, from national lockdowns to face mask usage and social distancing. Besides such non-pharmaceutical interventions (NPIs), we saw the development of vaccines to protect people against the virus. This brought not only broad excitement to the public but, in some cases, scepticism as well. Fear about the safety of vaccines and mistrust in government were two of the most reported barriers to willingness to get vaccinated (Steinert et al., 2022a). Vaccine hesitancy (i.e., people's reluctance to receive a vaccine) predates the COVID-19 pandemic. It has been identified as one of the main threats to global health by the World Health Organization (WHO) even before the COVID-19 pandemic (World Health Organization, 2019). This is because people's reluctance to accept an available

This research has been supported by the European Union's Horizon 2020 research and innovation programme PERISCOPE: Pan European Response to the Impacts of COVID-19 and Future Pandemics and Epidemics, under grant agreement no. 101016233.

vaccine can undermine any progress achieved in preventing or mitigating a disease. Vaccine hesitancy is not the only behavioural aspect
of the pandemic. The broader unintended psychological and behavioural consequences have not yet been fully revealed nor evaluated.
In this chapter we try to distil the available systematic evidence of
the unintended consequences of the COVID-19 pandemic on human
behaviour, highlighting the contributions of behavioural science and
the lessons learned from this multi-dimensional crisis.

10.2   SYSTEMATIC EVIDENCE ON THE PSYCHOLOGICAL
AND BEHAVIOURAL ASPECTS OF THE PANDEMIC

Since the COVID-19 pandemic started as a health crisis that required
behaviour change, most of the research we discuss here is about
health-related *behaviours*. In this body of systematic research, there
is also an extensive discussion of the *psychological* mechanisms that
potentially underlie changes in people's behaviours and affect mental health. Therefore, and in order to have a broader understanding
of the multi-dimensionality of the COVID-19 health crisis, we have
identified the recent, and most relevant, systematic evidence for the
effects of the pandemic on both *physical and mental health*. The
specific behaviours and conditions discussed in this section are presented in Table 10.1.

10.3   MENTAL HEALTH CONDITIONS DURING
THE PANDEMIC

Prior to the COVID-19 pandemic, the WHO estimated that the proportion of the global population that suffers from anxiety and depression was 3.6 per cent and 4.4 per cent, respectively (World Health
Organization, 2017). Furthermore, the National Institute for Health
and Care Excellence (NICE) (2020, 2021; de Sousa et al., 2021) estimates that the prevalence of post-traumatic stress (PTS) ranges from
1 per cent to 12 per cent, while the prevalence of insomnia has a
wide range, from 5 per cent to 50 per cent, depending on the definition. In a recent report, the WHO has estimated that the COVID-19

Table 10.1 *Health-related behaviours and conditions covered in this section*

Mental health conditions	
	Depression
	Anxiety
	Post-traumatic stress
	Sleep problems
Pandemic-specific health behaviours	
	Hand-washing
	Social distancing
	Self-isolation
	Face mask-wearing
Other health-related behaviours	
	Physical activity
	Food and alcohol consumption
	Compulsive gambling
	Substance use (nicotine, opioids)
	Video gaming addiction
	Sexual behaviours
	Suicidal behaviour
	Domestic violence
	Blood donations

pandemic has increased the prevalence of depression and anxiety by 25 per cent (World Health Organization, 2022). Systematic reviews and meta-analyses conducted during the pandemic showed that these estimates have indeed sharply increased. In particular, a systematic review of nineteen studies conducted in different countries, including China, Italy, Spain, and the United States, showed that the prevalence of depression ranged from 14.6 per cent to 48.30 per cent, whereas anxiety and PTS ranged from 6.33 per cent to 50.90 per cent and from 7 per cent to 53.80 per cent, respectively (Xiong et al., 2020). In three other systematic reviews and meta-analyses that included data from 55, 107, and 206 studies, respectively, conducted mainly in China and across the globe, the pooled prevalence of depression for the general population ranged from 15.98 per cent to 28 per cent. For anxiety, the prevalence ranged from 15.50 per cent to 26.90 per cent, whereas for PTS the relevant rates ranged from 13.29 per cent to 24.10 per cent. Finally, sleep problems like insomnia ranged from 23 per cent to 27.60 per cent (Cénat et al., 2021; Nochaiwong et al., 2021; Phiri et al., 2021). A meta-review with evidence from eighteen meta-analyses of studies on the relationship between COVID-19 pandemic and mental health problems showed similar results (de Sousa et al., 2021). Another systematic review in the early phase of the pandemic showed that mental health problems increased during the first months of the pandemic, with this difference becoming insignificant over time by July 2020 (Robinson et al., 2022). Other systematic reviews that compared the prevalence of mental health problems between the general population and healthcare professionals, whose workload was heavily impacted during the pandemic, found similar rates across populations (de Sousa et al., 2021; Pappa et al., 2020; Phiri et al., 2021). However, findings from two other systematic reviews, conducted early (Jahrami et al., 2021) and later in the pandemic (Alimoradi et al., 2021), included COVID-19 patients as well, and showed that they had the highest prevalence of sleep problems, followed by healthcare professionals and the general population.

Apart from the broader effects of the COVID-19 pandemic on mental health, there is also systematic evidence about the direct relationship between a COVID-19 infection and mental health. A review of thirty-three studies, conducted mostly in Italy and China, compared the prevalence of long-term mental health problems in patients infected with COVID-19 (one to six months after the COVID-19 infection), including depression, anxiety, sleep problems, and PTS, and showed that the rates were higher than the pre-COVID-19 estimates (Bourmistrova et al., 2022). Evidence on the mental health impact of a COVID-19 infection is therefore mixed. However, there was high variability in the severity of infections among patients. Evidence from another systematic review further showed that pre-existing mental health problems were associated with increased risk of COVID-19 mortality (Fond et al., 2021). Those with severe mental health conditions were found to be particularly at risk. These findings suggest that patients with (severe) mental health disorders should have been treated as a high-risk population during the pandemic (Fond et al., 2021), and in some countries they were indeed treated as such.

Some of the determinants that contributed to a higher prevalence of mental health problems were age – younger people being at higher risk (Marconcin et al., 2022; World Health Organization, 2022; Xiong et al., 2020), gender – females being at higher risk (Loades et al., 2020; Marconcin et al., 2022; Pappa et al., 2020; Samji et al., 2022; Xiong et al., 2020), use of social media (Cénat et al., 2021; Samji et al., 2022; Xiong et al., 2020), and exposure to news about COVID-19 (Chiesa et al., 2021; Samji et al., 2022). Similar to previous disease outbreaks, the systematic evidence suggests that self and social isolation were found to be consistent predictors of mental health problems across several age groups, including children, adolescents, and young adults (Chiesa et al., 2021; Loades et al., 2020). On the other hand, physical activity was found to mitigate the negative effects of the pandemic on people's mental health regardless of age (Marconcin et al., 2022; Samji et al., 2022).

10.4 PANDEMIC-SPECIFIC HEALTH BEHAVIOURS

Given that the introduction of NPIs required a wide and immediate adoption of protective and compliance behaviours from the public, these behaviours are the most systematically examined in the literature and, understandably, also encouraged by the WHO. These 'pandemic' behaviours refer to a range of health behaviours that were per se common and simple, such as hand-washing. However, their continuous repetition, and sometimes prescribed duration (e.g., twenty seconds of hand-washing), needed to be learned for the first time or to be re-discovered through the pandemic, such as in the case of physical distancing (i.e., staying a prescribed length away from others), regular hand-washing, contact tracing, and self-isolation. A review of the literature on the systematic evidence about how these protective and compliance pandemic behaviours changed during the pandemic revealed that people adapted their behaviours in line with public health guidance, with hand-washing and avoiding crowded places the dominant behaviours at the early stages of the pandemic (Clavel et al., 2021; Usher et al., 2020). This is in line with previous systematic evidence from the H1N1 influenza pandemic (Bults et al., 2015). There are also consistent findings across three systematic reviews, namely, a positive association between knowledge about the virus and practice of health behaviours, including compliance with COVID-19 rules (Clavel et al., 2021; Kooistra & van Rooij, 2020; Rincón Uribe et al., 2021). This finding refers to the early stages of the COVID-19 pandemic, but a similar finding was also documented in previous pandemics, such as H1N1 influenza in 2009 and MERS-CoV in 2012 (Rincón Uribe et al., 2021), suggesting that people with health literacy, or knowledge about the virus (e.g., prevalence, transmission, prevention, symptomatology, risk factors), were more engaged in practising health behaviours and complying with the pandemic rules.

10.5   OTHER HEALTH-RELATED BEHAVIOURS IN THE CONTEXT OF THE PANDEMIC

Apart from the pandemic-specific behaviours described in the previous section, other behaviours that could threaten people's health have also been affected during the pandemic. In the absence of vaccines at that time, one of the very first strategies to reduce transmission of the virus was a coordinated effort to reduce people's mobility. This included advice to stay at home, work from home (as opposed to the office), the legal requirement to self-isolate in case of infection, and national or local lockdowns and curfews across different countries (Haug et al., 2020). Based on these early measures, one would intuitively expect that levels of physical activity would decrease, even though outdoor exercise was generally permitted during lockdowns. Physical activity and sedentary behaviours were indeed well examined during the pandemic. We have identified at least four systematic reviews that provide consistent evidence of a reduction in physical activity during lockdowns, including walking, cycling, and intense exercising. Likewise, sedentary behaviours such as video gaming and watching TV increased during lockdowns (López-Valenciano et al., 2021; Rivera et al., 2021; Runacres et al., 2021; Stockwell et al., 2021).

Another behaviour of interest is food and alcohol consumption. Eating and drinking habits have been heavily impacted by the pandemic, with studies reporting systematic evidence of decreased adherence to healthy diets and increased consumption of processed food, unhealthy snacks, and alcohol (Bakaloudi et al., 2021; González-Monroy et al., 2021; Khan et al., 2022). However, one review that compiled evidence from thirty-two studies across different countries reported that consumption of ordered and fast food was reduced, possibly due to mobility restrictions that allowed for home cooking (Bakaloudi et al., 2021). Furthermore, a systematic review and meta-analysis with evidence from 128 studies, conducted across 58 different countries, showed an overall equal increase and decrease of alcohol consumption, subject to a number of contextual factors and individual differences (Acuff et al., 2022). History of weight management and alcohol use problems pre-COVID-19 was associated with weight gain and increased alcohol use during the COVID-19 pandemic (Acuff et al., 2022; Khan et al., 2022). Finally, in a relatively similar vein, addictive behaviours related to smoking and substance use (e.g., opioids, nicotine) increased during the pandemic (Gelain Marin & Martins, 2020). Other addictive behaviours, such as gambling, and video gaming, also increased during the pandemic (Masaeli & Farhadi, 2021).

Along with changes in food and alcohol consumption habits, there have been changes in sexual behaviours as well. Evidence from two systematic reviews showed that there has been a decrease in sexual desire and function, including arousal and intercourse, and an overall increase in sexual self-gratification behaviours (Bazyar et al.,

2021; Masoudi et al., 2022). These findings were further confirmed by a recent narrative review with evidence from nineteen studies, conducted during the pandemic (Eleuteri et al., 2022). In addition, an upcoming, registered, systematic review is expected to shed more light on the impact of the COVID-19 pandemic on sexual behaviours (Zhang et al., 2021). Similar to other behaviours measured during the pandemic, the sexual dysfunctionalities reported in the literature have been associated with high levels of psychological distress (e.g., anxiety and depression), as well as with concerns about transmitting the virus and difficulties in reaching sexual partners. However, despite the association between psychological distress and suicidal ideation, there is no consistent evidence that suicidal rates increased during the pandemic, even among healthcare professionals who have been heavily affected by the pandemic in several ways (Eyles et al., 2021; John et al., 2021).

In addition to the health behaviours discussed, domestic violence and abusive behaviour were also affected by the COVID-19 pandemic. There is systematic evidence with data from numerous countries across the world, reporting very similar trends. The data comes from various sources, such as police records, hospital admissions, social services, helpline calls, and online surveys, and refers to physical and sexual violence, as well as to psychological abuse against partners, or other family members. The evidence largely refers to the initial stages of the pandemic, when stay-at-home guidance and lockdowns were imposed, and shows that there has been a significant increase in domestic violence incidents during and post-lockdowns (Bazyar et al., 2021; Kourti et al., 2021; Piquero et al., 2021). Analyses have highlighted the increased childcare burden, home quarantine, and financial concerns and psychological distress induced by the pandemic as key risk factors of increases in domestic violence (Ebert & Steinert, 2021). Most of the domestic violence incidents were against female partners (Kourti et al., 2021; Piquero et al., 2021). Incidentally, and in contrast to domestic violence, stay-at-home policies and lockdowns led to a significant decrease in urban crime (e.g., assaults, thefts), reducing rates by an overall 37 per cent (Nivette et al., 2021). Finally, one systematic review and meta-analysis of thirty-eight studies finds that, on average, blood donations decreased by 38 per cent during the pandemic, with some regions showing a decrease in donations up to 67 per cent (Chiem et al., 2022).

The COVID-19 pandemic and the associated policies implemented during that time have thus had an extensive impact on health-related behaviours, including mental health. The evidence discussed here was derived almost exclusively from systematic reviews that have attempted to collate the available literature to date. Besides this 'meta-review' of the systematic evidence presented here, there is a body of original systematic studies that are not captured by the literature. Nevertheless, this systematic research can broaden our understanding about the effects of the pandemic on human behaviour and part of it is briefly reported next.

10.6   SYSTEMATIC EVIDENCE ON VACCINE HESITANCY FROM A CROSS-COUNTRY ANALYSIS

As discussed, vaccine hesitancy is not a new phenomenon. It has been demonstrated in previous influenza outbreaks (e.g., H1N1) and in childhood diseases, such as measles and mumps (Dubé et al., 2015; Galarce et al., 2011; Vandermeulen et al., 2008). In the context of the COVID-19 pandemic, vaccine hesitancy has also been reported to be highly heterogeneous across Europe (Steinert et al., 2022a) and the rest of the world (Sallam, 2021), suggesting that certain countries, as well as certain populations within countries, were unusually *hesitant towards vaccination*. There have been a number of socio-demographic factors and other determinants discussed in relation to vaccine hesitancy including gender, education, fear of vaccine side effects, and mistrust in government (Lazarus et al., 2021). Another factor that has been widely discussed is misinformation about the COVID-19 disease and the developed vaccines, which is thought to have fuelled people's vaccine hesitancy and also their reluctance to comply with the pandemic rules (Pennycook et al., 2020; World

Health Organization, 2021). In response to this *infodemic* (World Health Organization, 2020a), policies around the world focused on designing effective communications strategies to (i) correct potential misconceptions about the disease, (ii) encourage compliance with the associated restrictions, and (iii) increase vaccine uptake.

Along the same lines, Steinert et al. (2022a) conducted a randomised controlled experiment across eight European countries. The experiment was part of the Periscope project (https://periscopeproject .eu/home) and funded by the European Union's Horizon 2020 Research and Innovation programme. The aim of the experiment was to (i) identify differences in COVID-19 vaccine hesitancy between countries and (ii) test the effectiveness of different communication strategies in minimising vaccine hesitancy (Steinert et al., 2022a). The experiment included only unvaccinated participants to test the effects of three different messages about COVID-19 vaccination on people's willingness to receive a COVID-19 vaccine. The first message contained information about the efficacy of COVID-19 vaccines, such as risk reduction of death and hospitalisation. The second message was about hedonistic, non-medical, benefits of vaccination, such as access to leisure activities and social events. The last message emphasised personal, non-medical, benefits of holding a vaccination certificate, such as travelling and international holiday. The experiment showed that vaccine hesitancy was highly heterogeneous across countries, ranging from 6.4 per cent of adults in Spain to 61.8 per cent of adults in Bulgaria being unwilling to get vaccinated against COVID-19. Similarly, the findings about the effectiveness of the three messages on vaccination willingness were very heterogeneous. Messages emphasising either the medical or the hedonistic benefits of vaccination significantly increased vaccination intention in Germany. Messages about the privileges from holding a vaccination certificate increased vaccination intention in both Germany and the United Kingdom, whereas no message had any significant effects in any other European country. Machine learning-based analyses of heterogeneity revealed that treatment effects were smaller or even negative in countries marked by high conspiracy beliefs and low health literacy, while they were larger in settings with higher trust in government. Overall, the high heterogeneity in vaccine hesitancy and in the responses to different messages suggests that health authorities in Europe should avoid one-size-fits-all vaccination campaigns.

10.7 SYSTEMATIC EVIDENCE ON BEHAVIOURAL SPILLOVERS

At the beginning of the pandemic and in the absence of vaccines, the main advice people had was to stay at home, wash their hands, wear a face covering, and keep social and physical distance. This was all behavioural guidance. However, policies that disrupt everyday life, by demanding an immediate change in human behaviour, are not only cognitively effortful and behaviourally costly but could also have unintended consequences, or spillover effects, on people's behaviours. For example, in the early phases of the policy response to the COVID-19 pandemic, concerns were expressed about a possible *'pandemic fatigue'*. This phenomenon was described as people's alleged tendency to become tired of complying with the rules or demotivated to follow the recommended advice during the pandemic (Petherick et al., 2021; World Health Organization, 2020c). However, the pandemic fatigue idea found no supporting evidence, at least not in the United Kingdom (Michie et al., 2020).

Another behavioural concern, expressed at the early stages of the pandemic, relates to *risk compensation* when it comes to wearing a face mask (Lazzarino et al., 2020; World Health Organization, 2020b). The hypothesis of risk compensation suggests that people tend to adjust their behaviour relative to their perceived level of risk (Brewer et al., 2007; Houston & Richardson, 2007; Peltzman, 1975). An example of this comes from research on road safety, where there was some evidence that the use of seat belts could lead to increased speeding via a reduction in perceived risk (Asch et al., 1991; Evans & Graham, 1991). In the context of the COVID-19 pandemic, potential risk compensation could manifest itself in cases of interventions designed to reduce the risk of infection or serious illness. For instance, people's engagement in one protective behaviour (e.g., wearing a face mask or regular testing) could have a negative compensatory spillover effect on other health behaviours, such as reduced physical distance or increased mobility. The hypothesis is that engagement in a protective behaviour could create a, possibly false, sense of safety, thus reducing people's perceived risk and, consequently, their engagement in other protective behaviours. The early evidence on risk compensation and face mask usage generally showed mixed results. For instance, in a hypothetical experiment, face mask usage was found to be associated with reduced physical distancing in the United Kingdom, whereas in the United States, mandates on face mask usage led to increased mobility in public places (Luckman et al., 2021; Yan et al., 2021). In contrast, direct evidence from field and incentivised experiments found that use of face masks *increased* physical distancing and other recommended health behaviours in Germany and the United Kingdom, respectively (Guenther et al., 2021; Seres et al., 2021).

Similar concerns were expressed about the then-upcoming roll-out of the first COVID-19 vaccines and the related potential unintended effects on people's behaviour (Trogen & Caplan, 2021). Such potential spillover effects of vaccination against COVID-19, and the sense of safety it might create, were systematically examined by another experiment conducted as part of the Periscope project (https://periscopeproject.eu/home). Kourtidis et al. (in press) recruited vaccinated and unvaccinated participants in the United Kingdom to test whether (i) communication strategies that target vaccine hesitancy (e.g., messages containing information about the efficacy of COVID-19 vaccines or the benefits of vaccination at individual and societal level), (ii) people's vaccination status (i.e., being/not being vaccinated against COVID-19), and, finally, (iii) vaccination willingness (i.e., being yet unvaccinated but willing to receive a COVID-19 vaccine) can affect people's engagement in other health behaviours, such as physical distancing and face mask usage. In line with previous research, Kourtidis et al. (in press) did not find any evidence for the risk compensation hypothesis, suggesting that engagement in health behaviours or exposure to messages about vaccination does not mitigate people's engagement in other health behaviours. What they found instead was that among participants, those who were vaccinated, as well as those who were unvaccinated but willing to receive a COVID-19 vaccine, were *more likely* to engage in health-related and other pro-social behaviours, such as wearing a face mask, self-isolating, and donating and volunteering to charities (Kourtidis et al., in press).

10.8   SYSTEMATIC EVIDENCE ON PEOPLE'S ASSESSMENT OF THE RISK OF CONTAGION

Behavioural and social scientists responded to the COVID-19 pandemic by conducting research that covered many aspects of both the management of the emergency and the expected effects on different aspects of our societies. For example, among the topics considered are risk compensation (Mantzari et al., 2020), social media use and anxiety (Marzouki et al., 2021), negative shocks and cognitive function (Bogliacino et al., 2021), and other aspects (Krpan et al., 2021). From a behavioural science perspective, one of the critical aspects of research in the context of the COVID-19 pandemic has been how people would assess risk. This includes several types of risks, from the risk of death due to COVID-19 to risk related to receiving the COVID-19 vaccines. However, what has not been established is how people evaluate the risk of different causes of COVID-19 infection. Could distorted risk perception lead people to behave in ways that increase their risk of infection? We assume that for the majority of people the understanding of COVID-19 risk will follow the widespread public health guidance featured on television or radio, or in newspapers, restaurants and bars, shops, and offices. A cross-country analysis of public health warning identified the following risk minimisation advice as particularly prevalent: wearing face masks; being outdoors rather than indoors; short duration of person-to-person contacts; having fewer rather than more people present; and maintaining physical distance with others.

To assess people's perception of these risks a discrete choice experiment (hereafter DCE) (Louviere et al., 2010) respondents presented with a series of binary choices between hypothetical scenarios that are made up of all the possible combinations of the characteristics of interest and asked to select the preferred scenario (Veltri et al., 2024). In the DCE the characteristics were made up from the public health guidance to reduce transmission: (i) personal protective equipment: mask versus no mask, (ii) settings: indoors versus outdoors, (iii) duration of contact: short (fifteen minutes) versus long (ninety minutes), (iv) number of people: small (two people) versus large (ten people), and (v) physical distance: short (one metre) versus long (two metres).

The findings of Veltri et al. (2024) are in line with the general idea that people reduce or 'substitute' complex multi-dimensional choices with relatively simpler ones (Kahneman, 2011; Raab & Gigerenzer, 2015). In the context of the study, participants assessed COVID-19 contagion scenarios based only on a few criteria, some of which were completely neglected (duration, distance, number of people involved). Differentiating by country, gender, and age allowed us to reveal some differences between subgroups of our sample, but it also confirmed the overall finding that some scenario attributes or choice criteria are barely used, or even completely disregarded, in the evaluation of the riskiness of a situation. This finding has two implications for public health and public policy. First, policymakers should maximise their attention to the choice criteria people actually use when evaluating the contagiousness of a COVID-19 situation, ensuring at the same time that the signals are accurately interpreted. In the DCE, presence of face masks and type of environmental settings played the biggest role. The second course of action is, instead, to focus on the attributes that people use the least. Distance, number of people, and duration of meeting played a considerably less important role in our study participants' evaluations of contagion risk. Focusing on raising awareness about the safety-related behavioural aspects that are less utilised by people could be translated in 'boosting intervention'.

10.9 SYSTEMATIC EVIDENCE ON VACCINE GLOBAL DISTRIBUTION AND PRIORITIES

The global distribution of COVID-19 vaccines remains highly unequal. At the time of writing (April 2022), less than 15 per cent of individuals in low-income countries have received at least one COVID-19 vaccine shot (https://ourworldindata.org/covid-vaccinations). Against this backdrop, Steinert et al. (2022b) conduct a DCE in six European countries to elicit citizens' preferences on the global distribution of COVID-19 vaccines. Specifically, the experimental setup allows them to evaluate whether distribution preferences are shaped by *vaccine nationalism*, that is, choosing to give the (scarce) vaccine dose to a hypothetical person from one's own country, or by *global solidarity*, that is, choosing to give the vaccine dose to a hypothetical person who lives in a low-income country with a limited healthcare capacity (Steinert et al., 2022b).

First, the study reveals pronounced public preferences for needs-based equity in vaccine distribution: across all six countries, participants consistently showed a strong preference for allocating the vaccine to the candidate with a higher mortality risk, irrespective of whether the recipient lived in the participant's own country or in the Global South. Second, French, Italian, Spanish, and Swedish participants also showed a significant preference for allocating scarce vaccines to recipients in a country of the Global South with low healthcare capacity over an otherwise identical recipient in their own country. In the Polish survey, results were inconclusive, whereas German respondents revealed a higher preference for allocating the vaccine to a recipient in their own country, all else equal.

Across all countries, female, younger, and more educated respondents were more supportive of greater global equity in COVID-19 vaccine distribution. In contrast, respondents who were themselves more vulnerable to a severe COVID-19 disease progression due to comorbidities were less willing to allocate vaccines to a person from the Global South.

10.10   BEHAVIOURAL INSIGHTS AS A RESPONSE TO THE COVID-19 PANDEMIC

Given the scale of the COVID-19 disease and its rapid spread, it is questionable whether the world could have been fully prepared to tackle the then-forthcoming crisis. In the absence of pharmaceutical interventions, like vaccines or antiviral drugs, governments around the world initially relied exclusively on NPIs, introducing measures that required enormous collective effort and behavioural change. The challenge that immediately emerged was how to communicate these measures to the public and persuade them to follow governments' guidance. This is where behavioural science could offer its insights to help mitigate the spread of the virus.

Before COVID-19, there was already evidence and applied knowledge on how behavioural insights can inform policymaking (Dolan al., 2012; Kahneman, 2011; Michie et al., 2011; Thaler & Sunstein, 2009; The Behavioural Insights Team, 2014). In the context of the COVID-19 pandemic, given the limited empirical evidence on the effects of urgent NPIs on human behaviour, there was early scientific advice, mainly from the United Kingdom and the United States, on how to apply behavioural science to public health policies (Bavel et al., 2020; Lunn et al., 2020; West et al., 2020). Particularly in the United Kingdom, there has been extensive public discussion about the involvement of behavioural science in the government's response to the pandemic (Sanders et al., 2021). The early scientific advice was mainly based on leveraging psychological and behavioural phenomena to increase public engagement and effectiveness of communication strategies, including social norms (e.g., promoting social desirability), credibility of sources to deliver public health messages (e.g., community and religious leaders), science communication to minimise exposure to misinformation (e.g., persuasion through evidence-based information), promotion of collective interest (e.g., moral decision-making), motivation and compliance (e.g., engagement in preventive behaviours), and risk communication (e.g., natural frequencies versus probabilities, perceived risk).

Beyond this early advice, there was also empirical evidence from research on communication strategies, assessing for instance the effects of ambiguous information or authoritative language in messages on compliance with COVID-19 rules (Kostopoulou & Schwartz, 2021; Krpan & Dolan, 2022). In the prospect of COVID-19 vaccine development, behavioural science helped in identifying barriers to vaccine uptake (de Figueiredo et al., 2020) and in developing communication strategies that target vaccine hesitancy (Steinert et al., 2022a). With the vaccine development and subsequent roll-out, behavioural research on vaccine hesitancy was further updated (de Figueiredo et al., 2020; Steinert et al., 2022a). The communication strategies tested during the pandemic included not only nudges to increase vaccine uptake (e.g., reminders to increase salience of available vaccines, frames to highlight safety of vaccines) but also textual and visual information about the safety, efficacy, and the associated, individual and collective, benefits of vaccination (Dai et al., 2021; Freeman et al., 2021; Palm et al., 2021; Sotis et al., 2021). There was also extensive discussion on the potential unintended adverse effects of the pandemic on mental health (Lunn et al., 2020; West et al., 2020), risk perception (Attema et al., 2021; Clavel et al., 2021; Guenther et al., 2021), and compensatory behaviours, as discussed earlier (Evans & Graham, 1991; Freeman et al., 2021; Kourtidis et al., in press).

In summary, there was a rapid response from behavioural science to help manage the COVID-19 pandemic, initially by employing theoretical models of human behaviour and applied scientific knowledge and subsequently by conducting empirical research to provide behavioural insights. The support of behavioural science during this global health crisis has therefore been significant (Ruggeri et al., 2024). The importance of behavioural insights in tackling the pandemic was formally expressed not only at the national level by the governments but also at continental and international levels by the European Centre for Disease Prevention and Control (ECDC) and the WHO, respectively.

Both institutions initiated an open call for behavioural science support at the very first stages of the pandemic (European Centre for Disease Prevention and Control, 2021; World Health Organization, 2020d). The ECDC call concluded that behavioural science research was not sufficiently involved in informing policymaking, since the management of the pandemic was dominated by medical and epidemiological experts. However, the contributions of behavioural science to designing and optimising communication strategies were recognised, while the need for its integration into wider pandemic preparedness was highlighted (European Centre for Disease Prevention and Control, 2021). The WHO call resulted in the formation of its Technical Advisory Group on Behavioural Insights and Sciences for Health, an expert group to inform health policies (World Health Organization, 2020d).

10.11 PREPAREDNESS FOR FUTURE PANDEMICS

We conclude by briefly summarising some of the lessons learned during this health crisis to help us prepare for future crises. As we discussed here, behavioural science has significantly contributed to the management of the pandemic. However, since its role in informing public health policy has been heavily debated (Sanders et al., 2021; Ruggeri et al., 2024), it would be useful for policymakers to clarify how behavioural science is utilised in decision-making through transparent and accountable processes. This could also increase trust and confidence in governments and institutions, which have been found to be associated with increased compliance and vaccine uptake (Lazarus et al., 2021; Steinert et al., 2022a; Williams et al., 2021b; Wright et al., 2021). Compliance could also be increased through consistent advice and precise communication, as opposed to confusing and ambiguous guidance, which has been found to undermine compliance during the pandemic (Kostopoulou & Schwartz, 2021; Williams et al., 2021a, b).

As discussed, widespread misinformation was an additional barrier to efforts to mitigate the spread of COVID-19. In light of this, behavioural science and policymaking could improve science communication and minimise the impact of false information, by leveraging various insights such as (i) nudging people to consider the accuracy of information and credibility of sources – for example, employing accuracy reminders (Pennycook et al., 2020), (ii) communicating risk more efficiently – for example, using natural frequencies versus probabilities (Gigerenzer, 2015), and (iii) pre-exposing people to misinformation – for example, adopting pre-emptive debunking (Bavel et al., 2020; van der Linden et al., 2020). This not only would help fight misinformation but could also increase people's health literacy, which has been associated with increased compliance with COVID-19 rules (Clavel et al., 2021; Faasse & Newby, 2020; Kooistra & van Rooij, 2020). However, when it comes to risk communication strategies, information should be communicated with caution, taking into account not only the specific formats (e.g., pictograms, natural frequencies) but also the audience they refer to (experts, laypeople), in order to be more effective (Gigerenzer, 2015). This would also include a cautious and ethical use of fear as a driver of behaviour change, the effectiveness of which has been extensively debated in the context of the COVID-19 pandemic (Ghio et al., 2021; Lunn et al., 2020; Mertens et al., 2020; Stolow et al., 2020; Swami & Gupta, 2021).

Although previous guidance on public health interventions for influenza pandemics in Europe highlighted potential indirect effects of such interventions, such guidance mainly referred to practical costs, such as food supply and monetary compensation for disrupted business and services (European Centre for Disease Prevention and Control, 2009). The indirect costs at a behavioural and psychological level were only briefly and speculatively discussed, while there were several 'unclear risks' to be uncovered. The systematic evidence presented here could, therefore, update the existing guidance to reflect the emerging evidence from the COVID-19 pandemic. Since the pandemic has had negative multi-dimensional effects on people's lives, future policy responses should be alert to the psychological consequences and behavioural spillovers of measures such as lockdowns and self-isolation on physical and mental health. In this regard, future policies could further promote alternative mental health services to which people can turn in the absence of conventional practices and social contacts. This would be of great importance, given the increased prevalence of mental health problems associated with the COVID-19 pandemic.

The continuous emergence of new coronavirus variants that evade immunity (e.g., Omicron) has shown us that optimal communication strategies do not only encourage pharmaceutical interventions but cross-promote engagement in protective behaviours that complement vaccine-induced immunity, even when vaccination rates among the population are high (Flemming, 2022). Shaping the post-COVID-19 world requires changes at various levels that would enable us to meet newly emerged needs, not only in terms of healthcare systems capacity but also in terms of working practices, social norms, and digital literacy. Behavioural science should thus continue informing the multi-disciplinary discussion about policy responses to future pandemics by systematically capturing and sharing the evidence about the direct and the spillover effects of future health crises on people's health and behaviour.

REFERENCES

Acuff, S. F., Strickland, J. C., Tucker, J. A., & Murphy, J. G. (2022). Changes in alcohol use during COVID-19 and associations with contextual and individual difference variables: A systematic review and meta-analysis. *Psychology of Addictive Behaviors, 36,* 1–19.

Alimoradi, Z. Broström, A., Tsang, H. W. H., Griffiths, M. D., Haghayegh, S., Ohayon, M. M., et al. (2021). Sleep problems during COVID-19 pandemic and its' association to psychological distress: A systematic review and meta-analysis. *EClinicalMedicine, 36,* 100916.

Asch, P., Levy, D. T., Shea, D., & Bodenhorn, H. (1991). Risk compensation and the effectiveness of safety belt use laws: A case study of New Jersey. *Policy Sciences, 24,* 181–197.

Attema, A. E., L'Haridon, O., Raude, J., & Seror, V. (2021). Beliefs and risk perceptions about COVID-19: Evidence from two successive French representative surveys during lockdown. *Frontiers in Psychology, 12,* 1–16.

Bakaloudi, D. R., Jeyakumar, D. T., Jayawardena, R., & Chourdakis, M. (2021). The impact of COVID-19 lockdown on snacking habits, fast-food and alcohol consumption: A systematic review of the evidence. *Clinical Nutrition.* https://doi.org/10.1016/j.clnu.2021.04.020

Bavel, J. J. Van, Baicker, K., Boggio, P. S., Capraro, V., Cichocka, A., Cikara, M., et al. (2020). Using social and behavioural science to support COVID-19 pandemic response. *Nature Human Behaviour*, 4, 460–471.

Bazyar, J., Chehreh, R., Sadeghifar, J., Karamelahi, Z., Ahmadimazhin, S., Vafery, Y., & Daliri, S. (2021). Effects of the COVID-19 pandemic on the intimate partner violence and sexual function: A systematic review. *Prehospital and Disaster Medicine*, 36, 593–598.

Bogliacino, F., Codagnone, C., Montealegre, F., Folkvord, F., Gómez, C., Charris, R., et al. (2021). Negative shocks predict change in cognitive function and preferences: Assessing the negative affect and stress hypothesis. *Scientific Reports*, 11(1), 3546. DOI: 10.1038/s41598-021-83089-0

Bourmistrova, N. W., Solomon, T., Braude, P., Strawbridge, R., & Carter, B. (2022). Long-term effects of COVID-19 on mental health: A systematic review. *Journal of Affective Disorders*, 299, 118–125.

Brewer, N. T., Cuite, C. L., Herrington, J. E., & Weinstein, N. D. (2007). Risk compensation and vaccination: Can getting vaccinated cause people to engage in risky behaviors? *Annals of Behavioral Medicine*, 34, 95–99.

Bults, M., Beaujean, D. J. M. A., Richardus, J. H., & Voeten, H. A. C. M. (2015). Perceptions and behavioral responses of the general public during the 2009 Influenza A (H1N1) pandemic: A systematic review. *Disaster Medicine and Public Health Preparedness*, 9, 207–219.

Cénat, J. M., Blais-Rochette, C., Kokou-Kpolou, C. K., Noorishad, P.-G., Mukunzi, J. N., McIntee, S.-E., et al. (2021). Prevalence of symptoms of depression, anxiety, insomnia, posttraumatic stress disorder, and psychological distress among populations affected by the COVID-19 pandemic: A systematic review and meta-analysis. *Psychiatry Research*, 295, 113599.

Chiem, C., Alghamdi, K., Nguyen, T., Han, J. H., Huo, H., & Jackson, D. (2022). The impact of COVID-19 on blood transfusion services: A systematic review and meta-analysis. *Transfusion Medicine and Hemotherapy*, 49, 107–118.

Chiesa, V., Antony, G., Wismar, M., & Rechel, B. (2021). COVID-19 pandemic: Health impact of staying at home, social distancing and 'lockdown' measures: A systematic review of systematic reviews. *Journal of Public Health (Bangkok)*, 43, e462–e481.

Clavel, N., Badr, J., Gautier, L., Lavoie-Tremblay, M., & Paquette, J. (2021). Risk perceptions, knowledge and behaviors of general and high-risk adult populations towards COVID-19: A systematic scoping review. *Public Health Reviews*, 42, 1–12.

Dai, H., Saccardo, S., Han, M. A., Roh, L., Raja, N., Vangala, S., et al. (2021). Behavioural nudges increase COVID-19 vaccinations. *Nature*, 597, 404–409.

de Figueiredo, A., Simas, C., Karafillakis, E., Paterson, P., & Larson, H. J. (2020). Mapping global trends in vaccine confidence and investigating barriers to vaccine uptake: A large-scale retrospective temporal modelling study. *The Lancet*, 396, 898–908.

de Sousa, G. M., de Oliveira Tavares, V. D., de Meiroz Grilo, M. L. P., Coelho, M. L. G., de Lima-Araújo, G. L., Schuch, F. B., & Galvão-Coelho, N. L. (2021). Mental health in COVID-19 pandemic: A meta-review of prevalence meta-analyses. *Frontiers in Psychology*, 12, 1–9.

Dolan, P., Hallsworth, M., Halpern, D., King, D., Metcalfe, R., Vlaev, I., et al. (2012). Influencing behaviour: The mindspace way. *Journal of Economic Psychology*, 33, 264–277.

Dubé, E., Vivion, M., & MacDonald, N. E. (2015). Vaccine hesitancy, vaccine refusal and the anti-vaccine movement: Influence, impact and implications. *Expert Review of Vaccines*, 14, 99–117.

Ebert, C., & Steinert, J. I. (2021). Prevalence and risk factors of violence against women and children during COVID-19, Germany. *Bulletin of the World Health Organization*, 99, 429–438.

Eleuteri, S., Alessi, F., Petruccelli, F., & Saladino, V. (2022). The global impact of the COVID-19 pandemic on individuals' and couples' sexuality. *Frontiers in Psychology*, 12, 1–13.

European Centre for Disease Prevention and Control. (2009). Guide to public health measures to reduce the impact of influenza pandemics in Europe: 'The ECDC Menu'. www.ecdc.europa.eu/sites/default/files/media/en/publications/Publications/0906_TER_Public_Health_Measures_for_Influenza_Pandemics.pdf

European Centre for Disease Prevention and Control. (2021). Behavioural Insights research to support the response to COVID-19: A survey of implementation in the EU/EEA. www.ecdc.europa.eu/sites/default/files/documents/Behavioural-Insights-research-to support-the-response-to-COVID-19.pdf

Evans, W. N., & Graham, J. D. (1991). Risk reduction or risk compensation? The case of mandatory safety-belt use laws. *Journal of Risk and Uncertainty*, 4, 61–73.

Eyles, E., Moran, P., Okolie, C., Dekel, D., Macleod-Hall, C., Webb, R. T., et al. (2021). Systematic review of the impact of the COVID-19 pandemic on suicidal behaviour amongst health and social care workers across the world. *Journal of Affective Disorders Reports*, 6, 100271.

Faasse, K., & Newby, J. (2020). Public perceptions of COVID-19 in Australia: Perceived risk, knowledge, health-protective behaviors, and vaccine intentions. *Frontiers in Psychology*, 11, 1–11.

Flemming, A. (2022). Omicron, the great escape artist. *Nature Reviews Immunology*, 22, 75–75.

Fond, G., Nemani, K., Etchecopar-Etchart, D., Loundou, A., Goff, D. C., Lee, S. W., et al. (2021). Association between mental health disorders and mortality among patients with COVID-19 in 7 countries: A systematic review and mate-analysis. *JAMA Psychiatry*, 78, 1208.

Freeman, D., Loe, B. S., Yu, L.-M., Freeman, J., Chadwick, A., Vaccari, C., et al. (2021). Effects of different types of written vaccination information on COVID-19 vaccine hesitancy in the UK (OCEANS-III): A single-blind, parallel-group, randomised controlled trial. *Lancet Public Health*, 6, e416–e427.

Galarce, E. M., Minsky, S., & Viswanath, K. (2011). Socioeconomic status, demographics, beliefs and A(H1N1) vaccine uptake in the United States. *Vaccine*, 29, 5284–5289.

Gelain Marin, M., & Martins, R. M. (2020). The impact of COVID-19 pandemic on addictive behaviors: An integrative review. *Estudos de Psicologia*, 25, 367–374.

Ghio, D., Lawes-Wickwar, S., Tang, M. Y., Epton, T., Howlett, N., Jenkinson, E., et al. (2021). What influences people's responses to public health messages for managing risks and preventing infectious diseases? A rapid systematic review of the evidence and recommendations, *BMJ Open*, 11, e048750.

Gigerenzer, G. (2015). *Risk Savvy: How to Make Good Decisions*. Penguin.

González-Monroy, C., Gómez-Gómez, I., Olarte-Sánchez, C. M., & Motrico, E. (2021). Eating behaviour changes during the COVID-19 pandemic: A systematic review of longitudinal studies. *International Journal of Environmental Research and Public Health*, 18, 11130.

Guenther, B., Galizzi, M. M., & Sanders, J. G. (2021). Heterogeneity in risk-taking during the COVID-19 pandemic: Evidence from the UK lockdown. *Frontiers in Psychology*, 12, 1–15.

Haug, N., Geyrhofer, L., Londei, A., Dervic, E., Desvars-Larrive, A., Loreto, V., et al. (2020). Ranking the effectiveness of worldwide COVID-19 government interventions. *Nature Human Behaviour*, 4, 1303–1312.

Houston, D. J., & Richardson, L. E. (2007). Risk compensation or risk reduction? Seatbelts, state laws, and traffic fatalities. *Social Science Quarterly*, 88, 913–936.

Jahrami, H., BaHammam, A. S., Bragazzi, N. L., Saif, Z., Faris, M., & Vitiello, M. V. (2021). Sleep problems during the COVID-19 pandemic by population: A systematic review and meta-analysis. *Journal of Clinical Sleep Medicine*, 17, 299–313.

John, A., Eyles, E., Webb, R. T., Okolie, C., Schmidt, L., Arensman, E., et al. (2021). The impact of the COVID-19 pandemic on self-harm and suicidal behaviour: Update of living systematic review. *F1000Research, 9*, 1097.

Kahneman, D. (2011). *Thinking, Fast and Slow*. Penguin.

Khan, M. A. B., Menon, P., Govender, R., Abu Samra, A. M. B., Allaham, K. K., Nauman, J., et al. (2022). Systematic review of the effects of pandemic confinements on body weight and their determinants. *British Journal of Nutrition, 127*, 298–317.

Kooistra, E. B., & van Rooij, B. (2020). Pandemic compliance: A systematic review of influences on social distancing behaviour during the first wave of the COVID-19 outbreak. *SSRN Electronic Journal*, 1–35. https://doi.org/10.2139/ssrn.3738047

Kostopoulou, O., & Schwartz, A. (2021). To unpack or not? Testing public health messaging about COVID-19. *Journal of Experimental Psychology, 27*, 751–761.

Kourti, A., Stavridou, A., Panagouli, E., Psaltopoulou, T., Spiliopoulou, C., Tsolia, M., et al. (2021). Domestic violence during the COVID-19 pandemic: A systematic review. *Trauma, Violence, & Abuse*, 1–27. https://doi.org/10.1177/15248380211038690

Kourtidis, P., Fasolo, B., & Galizzi, M. M. (in press). Encouraging vaccination against COVID-19 has no compensatory spillover effects. *Behavioural Public Policy*.

Krpan, D., & Dolan, P. (2022). You must stay at home! The impact of commands on behaviors during COVID-19. *Social Psychological and Personality Science, 13*, 333–346.

Krpan, D., Makki, F., Saleh, N., Brink, S. I., & Klauznicer, H. V. (2021). When behavioural science can make a difference in times of COVID-19. *Behavioural Public Policy, 5*, 153–179.

Lazarus, J. V., Ratzan, S. C., Palayew, A., Gostin, L. O., Larson, H. J., Rabin, K., et al. (2021). A global survey of potential acceptance of a COVID-19 vaccine. *Nature Medicine, 27*, 225–228.

Lazzarino, A. I., Steptoe, A., Hamer, M., & Michie, S. (2020). Covid-19: Important potential side effects of wearing face masks that we should bear in mind. *British Medical Journal, 369*, m2003.

Loades, M. E., Chatburn, E., Higson-Sweeney, N., Reynolds, S., Shafran, R., Brigden, A., et al. (2020). Rapid systematic review: The impact of social isolation and loneliness on the mental health of children and adolescents in the context of COVID-19. *Journal of the American Academy of Child and Adolescent Psychiatry, 59*, 1218–1239.

López-Valenciano, A., Suárez-Iglesias, D., Sanchez-Lastra, M. A., & Ayán, C. (2021). Impact of COVID-19 pandemic on university students' physical activity levels: An early systematic review. *Frontiers in Psychology*, 11, 1–10.

Louviere, J. J., Flynn, T. N., & Carson, R. T. (2010). Discrete choice experiments are not conjoint analysis. *Journal of Choice Modelling*, 3, 57–72.

Luckman, A., Zeitoun, H., Isoni, A., Loomes, G., Vlaev. I., Powdthavee, N., & Read, D. (2021). Risk compensation during COVID-19: The impact of face mask usage on social distancing. *Journal of Experimental Psychology*, 27, 722–738.

Lunn, P. D., Belton, C. A., Lavin, C., McGowan, F. P., Timmons, S., & Robertson, D. A. (2020). Using behavioral science to help fight the Coronavirus. *Journal of Behavioral Public Administration*, 3, 1–15.

Mantzari, E., Rubin, G. J., & Marteau, T. M. (2020). Is risk compensation threatening public health in the COVID19 pandemic? *British Medical Journal*, 370, m2913.

Marconcin, P., Werneck, A. O., Peralta, M., Ihle, A., Gouveia, E. R., Ferrari, G., et al. (2022). The association between physical activity and mental health during the first year of the COVID-19 pandemic: A systematic review. *BMC Public Health*, 22, 209.

Marzouki, Y., Aldossari, F. S., & Veltri, G. A. (2021). Understanding the buffering effect of social media use on anxiety during the COVID-19 pandemic lockdown. *Humanities and Social Sciences Communications*, 8, 47.

Masaeli, N., & Farhadi, H. (2021). Prevalence of internet-based addictive behaviors during COVID-19 pandemic: A systematic review. *Journal of Addictive Diseases*, 39, 468–488.

Masoudi, M., Maasoumi, R., & Bragazzi, N. L. (2022). Effects of the COVID-19 pandemic on sexual functioning and activity: A systematic review and meta-analysis. *BMC Public Health*, 22, 189.

Mertens, G., Gerritsen, L., Duijndam, S., Salemink, E., & Engelhard, I. M. (2020). Fear of the coronavirus (COVID-19): Predictors in an online study conducted in March 2020. *Journal of Anxiety Disorders*, 74, 102258.

Michie, S., van Stralen, M. M., & West, R. (2011). The behaviour change wheel: A new method for characterising and designing behaviour change interventions. *Implementation Science*, 6, 42.

Michie, S., West, R., & Harvey, N. (2020). The concept of 'fatigue' in tackling COVID-19. *British Medical Journal*, 371, m4171.

National Institute for Health and Care Excellence. (2020). Post-traumatic stress disorder: How common is it? https://cks.nice.org.uk/topics/post-traumatic-stress-disorder/background-information/prevalence

National Institute for Health and Care Excellence. (2021). Insomnia: How common is it? https://cks.nice.org.uk/topics/insomnia/background-information/prevalence

Nivette, A. E., Zahnow, R., Aguilar, R., Ahven, A., Amram, S., Ariel, B., et al. (2021). A global analysis of the impact of COVID-19 stay-at-home restrictions on crime. *Nature Human Behaviour*, 5, 868–877.

Nochaiwong, S., Ruengorn, C., Thavorn, K., Hutton, B., Awiphan, R., Phosuya, C., et al. (2021). Global prevalence of mental health issues among the general population during the coronavirus disease-2019 pandemic: A systematic review and meta-analysis. *Scientific Reports*, 11, 10173.

Palm, R., Bolsen, T., & Kingsland, J. T. (2021). The effect of frames on COVID-19 vaccine resistance. *Frontiers in Political Science*, 3, 1–11.

Pappa, S., Ntella, V., Giannakas, T., Giannakoulis, V. G., Papoutsi, E., & Katsaounou, P. (2020). Prevalence of depression, anxiety, and insomnia among healthcare workers during the COVID-19 pandemic: A systematic review and meta-analysis. *Brain, Behavior, and Immunity*, 88, 901–907.

Peltzman, S. (1975). The effects of automobile safety regulation. *Journal of Political Economy*, 83, 677–725.

Pennycook, G., McPhetres, J., Zhang, Y., Lu, J. G., & Rand, D. G. (2020). Fighting COVID-19 misinformation on social media: Experimental evidence for a scalable accuracy-nudge intervention. *Psychological Science*, 31, 770–780.

Petherick, A., Goldszmidt, R., Andrade, E., Furst, R., Hale, T., Pott, A., & Wood, A. (2021). A worldwide assessment of changes in adherence to COVID-19 protective behaviours and hypothesized pandemic fatigue. *Nature Human Behaviour*, 5, 1145–1160.

Phiri, P., Ramakrishnan, R., Rathod, S., Elliot, K., Thayanandan, T., Sandle, N., et al. (2021). An evaluation of the mental health impact of SARS-CoV-2 on patients, general public and healthcare professionals: A systematic review and meta-analysis. *EClinicalMedicine*, 34, 100806.

Piquero, A. R., Jennings, W. G., Jemison, E., Kaukinen, C., & Knaul, F. M. (2021). Domestic violence during the COVID-19 pandemic: Evidence from a systematic review and meta-analysis. *Journal of Criminal Justice*, 74, 101806.

Raab, M., & Gigerenzer, G. (2015). The power of simplicity: A fast-and-frugal heuristics approach to performance science. *Frontiers in Psychology*, 6, 1–6.

Rincón Uribe, F. A., Godinho, R. C. S., Machado, M. A. S., Oliveira, K. R. D. S. G., Neira Espejo, C. A., de Sousa, N. C. V., et al. (2021). Health knowledge, health behaviors and attitudes during pandemic emergencies: A systematic review. *PLoS One*, 16, e0256731.

Rivera, P. A., Nys, B. L., & Fiestas, F. (2021). Impact of COVID-19 induced lockdown on physical activity and sedentary behavior among university students: A systematic review. *Medwave*, 21, e8456–e8456.

Robinson, E., Sutin, A. R., Daly, M., & Jones, A. (2022). A systematic review and meta-analysis of longitudinal cohort studies comparing mental health before versus during the COVID-19 pandemic in 2020. *Journal of Affective Disorders, 296,* 567–576.

Ruggeri, K., Stock, F., Haslam, S. A., Capraro, V., Boggio, P., Ellemers, N.,…, Galizzi, M. M., Milkman, K. L., Petrovic, M., Van Bavel, J. J., & Willer, R. (2024). A synthesis of evidence for policy from behavioural science during COVID-19. *Nature, 625,* 134–147, https://doi.org/10.1038/s41586-023-06840-9

Runacres, A., Mackintosh, K. A., Knight, R. L., Sheeran, L., Thatcher, R., Shelley, J., & McNarry, M. A. (2021). Impact of the COVID-19 pandemic on sedentary time and behaviour in children and adults: A systematic review and meta-analysis. *International Journal of Environmental Research and Public Health, 18,* 11286.

Sallam, M. (2021). COVID-19 vaccine hesitancy worldwide: A concise systematic review of vaccine acceptance rates. *Vaccines, 9,* 160.

Samji, H., Wu, J., Ladak, A., Vossen, C., Stewart, E., Dove, N., et al. (2022). Review: Mental health impacts of the COVID-19 pandemic on children and youth – a systematic review. *Child and Adolescent Mental Health, 27,* 173–189.

Sanders, J. G., Tosi, A., Obradovic, S., Miligi, I., & Delaney, L. (2021). Lessons from the UK's lockdown: Discourse on behavioural science in times of COVID-19. *Frontiers in Psychology, 12,* 1–24.

Seres, G., Balleyer, A., Cerutti, N., Friedrichsen, J., & Süer, M. (2021). Face mask use and physical distancing before and after mandatory masking: No evidence on risk compensation in public waiting lines. *Journal of Economic Behavior and Organization, 192,* 765–781.

Sotis, C., Allena, M., Reyes, R., & Romano, A. (2021). COVID-19 vaccine passport and international traveling: The combined effect of two nudges on Americans' support for the pass. *International Journal of Environmental Research and Public Health,* S18, 8800.

Steinert, J. I., Sternberg, H., Prince, H., Fasolo, B., Galizzi, M. M., Büthe, T., & Veltri, G. A. (2022a). COVID-19 vaccine hesitancy in eight European countries: Prevalence, determinants, and heterogeneity. *Science Advances, 8,* 1–15.

Steinert, J. I., Sternberg, H., Veltri, G. A., & Büthe, T. (2022b). How should COVID-19 vaccines be distributed between the global north and south? A discrete choice experiment in six European countries. *medRxiv.* https://doi.org/101016233, 1–24.

Stockwell, S., Trott, M., Tully, M., Shin, J., Barnett, Y., Butler, L., et al. (2021). Changes in physical activity and sedentary behaviours from before to during the COVID-19 pandemic lockdown: A systematic review. *BMJ Open Sport & Exercise Medicine, 7,* e000960.

Stolow, J. A., Moses, L. M., Lederer, A. M., & Carter, R. (2020). How fear appeal approaches in COVID-19 health communication may be harming the global community. *Health Education & Behavior*, 47, 531–535.

Swami, M. K., & Gupta, T. (2021). Psychological impact of fear-based messages in context of COVID 19. *International Journal of Social Psychiatry*, 67, 1081–1082.

Thaler, R. H., & Sunstein, C. R. (2009). *Nudge: Improving Decisions about Health, Wealth and Happiness*. Penguin.

The Behavioural Insights Team. (2014). EAST: Four simple ways to apply behavioural insights. www.bi.team/wp-content/uploads/2015/07/BIT-Publication-EAST_FA_WEB.pdf

Trogen, B., & Caplan, A. (2021). Risk compensation and COVID-19 vaccines. *Annals of Internal Medicine*, 174, 858–859.

Usher, K., Jackson, D., Durkin, J., Gyamfi, N., & Bhullar, N. (2020). Pandemic-related behaviours and psychological outcomes; A rapid literature review to explain COVID-19 behaviours. *International Journal of Mental Health Nursing*, 29, 1018–1034.

van der Linden, S., Roozenbeek, J., & Compton, J. (2020). Inoculating against fake news about COVID-19. *Frontiers in Psychology*, 11, 1–7.

Vandermeulen, C., Roelants, M., Theeten, H., VanDamme, P., & Hoppenbrouwers, K. (2008). Vaccination coverage and sociodemographic determinants of measles–mumps–rubella vaccination in three different age groups. *European Journal of Pediatrics*, 167, 1161–1168.

Veltri, G. A., Steinert, J. I., Sternberg, H., Galizzi, M. M., Fasolo, B., Kourtidis, P., Buthe, T., & Gaskell, G. (2024). Assessing the perceived effect of non-pharmaceutical interventions on SARS-CoV-2 transmission risk: An experimental study in Europe. *Scientific Reports* (in press).

West, R., Michie, S., Rubin, G. J., & Amlôt, R. (2020). Applying principles of behaviour change to reduce SARS-CoV-2 transmission. *Nature Human Behaviour*, 4, 451–459.

Williams, S., Drury, J., Michie, S., & Stokoe, E. (2021a). Covid-19: What we have learnt from behavioural science during the pandemic so far that can help prepare us for the future. *British Medical Journal*, 375, n3028.

Williams, S. N., Armitage, C. J., Tampe, T., & Dienes, K. A. (2021b). Public perceptions of non-adherence to pandemic protection measures by self and others: A study of COVID-19 in the United Kingdom. *PLoS One*, 16, e0258781.

World Health Organization. (2017). Depression and other common mental disorders: Global health estimates. https://apps.who.int/iris/bitstream/handle/10665/254610/WHO-MSD-MER-2017.2-eng.pdf

World Health Organization. (2019). Ten threats to global health in 2019. www .who.int/news-room/spotlight/ten-threats-to-global-health-in-2019

World Health Organization. (2020a). Managing the COVID-19 infodemic: Promoting healthy behaviours and mitigating the harm from misinformation and disinformation. www.who.int/news/item/23-09-2020-managing-the-covid-19-infodemic-promoting-healthy-behaviours-and-mitigating-the-harm-from-misinformation-and-disinformation

World Health Organization. (2020b). Mask use in the context of COVID-19. https://apps.who.int/iris/handle/10665/337199

World Health Organization. (2020c). Pandemic fatigue: Reinvigorating the public to prevent COVID-19. https://apps.who.int/iris/bitstream/handle/10665/335820/WHO-EURO-2020-1160-40906-55390-eng.pdf

World Health Organization. (2020d). Technical Advisory Group on Behavioural Insights and Sciences for Health. www.who.int/initiatives/behavioural-sciences/tag-on-behavioural-insights-and-sciences-for-health

World Health Organization. (2020e). WHO director-general's opening remarks at the media briefing on COVID-19–11 March 2020. www.who.int/director-general/speeches/detail/who-director-general-s-opening-remarks-at-the-media-briefing-on-covid-19---11-march-2020

World Health Organization. (2021). Fighting misinformation in the time of COVID-19, one click at a time. www.who.int/news-room/feature-stories/detail/fighting-misinformation-in-the-time-of-covid-19-one-click-at-a-time

World Health Organization. (2022). COVID-19 pandemic triggers 25% increase in prevalence of anxiety and depression worldwide. www.who.int/news/item/02-03-2022-covid-19-pandemic-triggers-25-increase-in-prevalence-of-anxiety-and-depression-worldwide

Wright, L., Steptoe, A., & Fancourt, D. (2021). Predictors of self-reported adherence to COVID-19 guidelines. A longitudinal observational study of 51,600 UK adults. *Lancet Regional Health – Europe*, 4, 100061.

Xiong, J., Lipsitz, O., Nasri, F., Lui, L. M. W., Gill, H., Phan, L., et al. (2020). Impact of COVID-19 pandemic on mental health in the general population: A systematic review. *Journal of Affective Disorders*, 277, 55–64.

Yan, Y., Bayham, J., Richter, A., & Fenichel, E. P. (2021). Risk compensation and face mask mandates during the COVID-19 pandemic. *Scientific Reports*, 11, 3174.

Zhang, Q., Lu, H., Li, F., Li, X., Wang, T., Yang, Q., & Mi, L. (2021). The impact of COVID-19 on sexual behaviors of young women and men. *Medicine (Baltimore)*, 100, e24415.

11 Behavioural Science and the Irish COVID-19 Response

Liam Delaney and Emma Watson

11.1 COVID-19 IN IRELAND

Five months after the first case of COVID-19 in Wuhan, China, the virus reached the island of Ireland on 29 February 2020. At this point, the city of Wuhan had been in lockdown for one month, while Italy had reported close to 10,000 cases per day as Europe enmeshed in the first wave. In addition to recommendations from international bodies, the Irish government was equipped with insights from the government response of neighbouring countries, where the virus had been circulating for several weeks.

In the absence of a vaccine, non-pharmaceutical interventions were indicated by international bodies as the primary strategy to mitigate the spread of the virus (ECDC, 2020; WHO, 2020). This strategy aimed to curb the spread of infection by reducing physical contact between individuals and was rapidly adopted as the leading response by governments internationally. Van Bavel et al. (2020: 467) asserted, '[T]he unique nature and speed of this pandemic means that the two most important ways by which we can fight this disease are through determined public health-mandated measures and changing our individual and collective behaviours.' The publication of Ireland's National Action Plan in response to COVID-19 on 16 March indicated a clear understanding of the importance of individual and collective behaviour in the fight against the virus.

11.2 STRUCTURE OF COVID-19 RESPONSE AND INTEGRATION OF BEHAVIOURAL SCIENCE

The National Public Health Emergency Team (NPHET) is a long-standing structure which has been utilised over many years to provide a forum to steer strategic approaches to public health emergencies in Ireland and mobilise the necessary health service responses. The NPHET for COVID-19 was established in late January 2020 by the Department of Health, tasked with providing national direction, guidance, support and expert advice on the development and implementation of a strategy to contain COVID-19 in Ireland. Chaired by the chief medical officer, the multi-disciplinary and multi-sectoral team consisted of representatives from across the health and social care services, as well as other relevant experts from medical and science fields.

The NPHET COVID-19 Behavioural Change Subgroup first met on 18 March, establishing terms of reference and a research agenda. The subgroup included four representatives from the Department of Health, the head of the Economic and Social Research Institute's (ESRI) Behavioural Research Unit, and one of this chapter's authors (Liam Delaney). The organisational structure illustrates how behavioural science research contributed to the core emergency response. The role of behavioural science was as an evidence input alongside a wide range of other capacities, including expertise in healthcare utilisation, vulnerable groups, medical devices, and health legislation. Recommendations based on this evidence were fed directly into the communications group.

It was apparent that 'how individuals respond to advice on how best to prevent transmission will be as important as government actions, if not more important' (Anderson et al., 2020: 934). Behavioural insights relevant to the mitigation strategy were summarised in a publication by a subgroup member and colleagues from the ESRI Behavioural Research Unit (Lunn et al., 2020a). The review summarised the behavioural science literature across a range of contexts, including evidence on crises, emergencies, and risk communication. It identified seven key themes: hand-washing; face touching; entering and coping with isolation; encouraging collective action; avoiding undesirable behaviour; crisis communication; and risk perception.

The influence of behavioural science on the Irish policy response was evident during this initial period. Minutes from NPHET weekly meetings regularly refer to output from this group in influencing their understanding of public sentiment, response to restrictions, and likely well-being effects. The work carried out by the subgroup extended beyond adoption of health-protective behaviours by the public. Its interdisciplinary nature incorporated wide scoping reviews and synthesis of evidence across a range of disciplines to inform recommendations.

11.3   CONTRIBUTIONS OF BEHAVIOURAL SCIENCE IN IRELAND

11.3.1   *Risk Communication*

The pandemic presented an unprecedented event and therefore lacked directly relevant evidence at this early stage. Evidence from risk communication theory and research includes findings from previous crisis events such as natural disasters and public health emergencies. For example, the Centre for Disease Control Crisis and Emergency Risk Communication (CERC; Reynolds et al., 2002) is a key compendium for risk communication practitioners. It provides an outline of the elements of a crisis, emphasises the importance of message development and audience research, and of the development of a risk communication plan, as well as provides guidance for delivery and collaboration with media. Technical reports and publications from international bodies, such as the World Health Organization (WHO, 2017), provided additional evidence-based recommendations for policy response. All state the importance of message development, audience research, audience relations, and message delivery.

11.3.2   *Government Communication Strategy*

The Department of Health developed a COVID-19 Communication Strategy in line with WHO (2020) best practice guidelines, launching the first public health campaign in February 2020 with the aim of creating public awareness of the virus and the role of the individual in the mitigation strategy. The department commenced a communications research programme, comprising nationally representative online surveys, media and web analytics, social listening, and focus groups, to monitor public engagement with public health advice and information and to identify emerging issues. Based on an analysis of these outputs, the subgroup provided weekly recommendations on enhancing the communications strategy and further developing the research programme. The communication strategy aimed to educate and empower the public to adopt desired behaviours in compliance with public health measures, improve self-efficacy to assess risk and make informed judgements, and promote social cohesion, resilience, and a sense of collective action. The subgroup also identified public perceptions and social norms that influence adherence or understanding of public health guidance and suggested solutions to address emerging issues.

11.4 RESEARCH OUTPUTS AND IMPACTS

Prior to the first meeting, a range of research inputs had been established. Alongside the review conducted by the ESRI, behavioural science researchers at the University College Dublin (UCD) Geary Institute had undertaken an ongoing review of the literature, with a focus on emerging global evidence as well as specific issues arising such as non-linear disease transmission. Translating scientific knowledge into non-technical concepts for a wider audience is widely discussed in risk communication literature (Bennett & Calnan, 1999) and draws on processes, such as decision-making and heuristics, examined in the field of behavioural science. In addition, risk communication may be subject to misinterpretation due to, for example, complexity or misperception of probabilities or risk to self. Understanding audience beliefs and risk perception provides data that can inform a communication strategy and, as in the case of the Irish policy response, allow for messaging to be tailored on an iterative basis. The public opinion survey was designed to capture public risk perception, attitudes, and beliefs. A nationally representative sample was recruited by market research.

11.4.1   Rapid Behavioural Studies

The ESRI proposed three specific research areas on which to focus; Comprehension of Behavioural Measures Thus Far, Tests of Social Distancing Communication, and Monitoring Fatigue. The ESRI indicated the importance of identifying marginal behaviours within the population, proposing these to be measured as an outcome variable for the purposes of these studies. Given the timescale, the studies would be conducted on a learning by doing approach, where initial sampling would be small and later expand. It was agreed to conduct preliminary studies on social distancing interventions that would inform government communication on the topic the following week.

A series of rapid online behavioural studies were conducted with nationally representative samples by the Behavioural Research Unit in the ESRI, providing an understanding of the public's comprehension and adoption of measures. This provided insight into the impact of the communications strategy and behavioural interventions, as well as identifying emerging areas of concern. Additionally, these studies identified marginal populations for which communications were tailored to enhance impact. The studies aimed to address the following issues: public awareness, comprehension, and adoption of health-protective behaviours; comprehension and compliance to symptom identification and self-isolation advice; attitudes to evolving restrictive measures; risk perception; and decision-making in response to policy changes.

Lunn et al. (2020b) describe one such online experimental study testing two novel public health messages on social distancing, where messages focused on the potential to infect vulnerable people or many people. The first message was designed to exploit the 'identifiable victim' effect by highlighting the risk of transmission to vulnerable persons. The second sought to counteract intuitive underestimation of exponential transmission. Results indicated that messages that invoke thoughts of infecting vulnerable people or large numbers of people can motivate social distancing. These findings informed Department of Health and the Health Service Executive (HSE) campaigns, including the design of nationally distributed posters aimed at promoting social distancing. Similar research contributed to the design of a range of nationally distributed public health material, such as decision aids to support self-isolation (Lunn et al., 2020a). In addition to contributing to the design, tone, and content of various messages and communications, the subgroup informed the development of a number of specific tools, including a poster on hand-washing at home that was disseminated nationwide to all households (Murphy & Mooney, 2020). A follow-up survey provided self-report data measuring the impact of the poster on increasing hand-washing frequency. Similar communication tools were developed to support other public health recommendations, such as self-isolation planning and compliance.

Throughout this phase, the subgroup highlighted the risk of unintended consequences as a result of misperception of public health advice and official communications. Evidence of reduced non-COVID-19 healthcare utilisation was identified in the early stages of the pandemic. The subgroup found contributing factors to include strong messaging advising the public to 'stay at home', an increase in fear-based emotions, and increased personal risk perception amongst vulnerable groups, such as the elderly. This evidence informed both NPHET recommendations and government messaging in providing the public with a decision tree from which to evaluate which service to access if in need of medical attention.

Despite evidence indicating high levels of public trust, awareness, and compliance of public health advice, social media analysis found a perception of erosion of trust and fraying of compliance. The subgroup discussed factors that may be contributing to the emerging dissonance. It found high adherence in the majority of the population, borne out in the research, and cited evidence of a tendency to focus on visible non-compliance. Specifically, young people were increasingly targeted by media reports of low compliance. The subgroup identified a degree of divisive commentary and recommended shifting emphasis back to collective messaging, such as 'no one is safe until everyone is safe'. Additionally, attention on nursing homes and the high median age of those at risk was drawing risk perception away from the individual. The subgroup recommended the use of communication from a collective safeguarding perspective and continued emphasis on the 'why' for various measures. It advised that if risk perceptions further declined despite higher numbers of cases, an emphasis should be placed on emotional messaging.

Beyond their advisory role to NPHET and the communications strategy, members of the subgroup engaged with national discourse across various media channels. In the early stages of the first wave, predictions of 'behavioural fatigue', describing a reduction in adherence to restrictions over time, began to circulate in the media. Subgroup members engaged in the debate, presenting evidence from behavioural science to combat the spread of misinformation. At later stages, research findings on well-being impacts were described in an *Irish Times* article published in April 2020, as well as key findings from the group's research on effective messaging. The article included interpretation of the results by a subgroup member that illustrated high levels of adherence to public health measures. As case numbers began to fall in late April, the approach to easing restrictions was increasingly debated. The *Irish Times* cited evidence from studies carried out by the group on public attitudes to various scenarios in which restrictions were eased, with the lead researcher and subgroup member providing interpretation of the findings. Such engagement reflected risk communication principles of clarity, openness, and transparency, as well as demonstrating to the public the role of experts and evidence in the public health strategy. This engagement was important in maintaining public confidence, amplifying key messages, and addressing emerging concerns and misinformation.

11.5 WELL-BEING IMPACTS

A particular contribution of the group was to monitor well-being impacts. Well-being was monitored in a number of ways during this period in Ireland. A number of questions relating to anxiety, life satisfaction, and coping were included in weekly (and sometimes twice weekly) national online surveys to build a broad profile of the extent to which people were being affected by the evolving situation. A number of day reconstruction studies were conducted to examine the situational context of positive and negative affect during the initial phases (e.g., Lades et al., 2020). These were particularly useful in highlighting the potential stressors involved in rapid changes to work and childcare arrangements and the potential protective effects of access to outdoor activities. The national statistical agency also included well-being questions in online follow-ups to nationally representative studies that were conducted prior to COVID-19. These surveys largely confirmed findings arising from online quota sampling, highlighting far higher negative well-being and employment impacts during the early phases of COVID-19 that somewhat attenuated towards the summer.

Evidence indicated a significant impact of the pandemic on the well-being of young people in particular. Beyond the broad social and economic viewpoint, initial survey data found this cohort to have the lowest level of well-being and life satisfaction in the population. Similarly, a day reconstruction study found an adverse impact of the restrictions on the overall well-being of young people (Lades et al., 2020). A second day reconstruction study conducted at the end of April found young people reporting life satisfaction as 4/10, akin to living with chronic illness, compared to a typical pre-pandemic level of 8/10.

As restrictions eased in June, the subgroup identified potential challenges in getting some population cohorts to sustain compliance or to comply with a re-introduction of stringent measures. Young people were a group of particular concern due to such significant impacts on well-being (Lades et al., 2020) and/or perceived risk to their own cohort as lower than others, as well as cohorts who have more limited capability to comply because of social and other factors. Beyond advising on communications to support adherence to current guidance, the subgroup expressed that longer term consequences may also affect their capability to manage and mitigate risks and look after their overall health and well-being. Government and health strategies to address these potential consequences would be important over the medium to longer term.

11.6 INTERNATIONAL ENGAGEMENT

Beyond reviewing and synthesising emerging evidence from across the globe, subgroup members continuously engaged with international colleagues, experts, and institutions, as well as participating in and collaborating on evolving research efforts in response to the pandemic. They participated in the International COVID-19 Behavioural Insights and Policy Group established by the Organisation for Economic Co-operation and Development (OECD), presenting on the work carried out by the group and contributing to an OECD brief on the application of behavioural insights to COVID-19 (OECD, 2020). Similarly, members presented on the subgroup's work at a WHO COVID-19 response webinar series, and they continue to collaborate on various international research projects. Additionally, the work carried out by the subgroup was recognised by international colleagues who acknowledged the successful contribution of behavioural science and behavioural expertise to the national pandemic response.

11.7 SUBSEQUENT DEVELOPMENTS

As described in Lunn (2021) the development of behavioural science capacity within the emergency COVID-19 response in Ireland found its strongest expression in the initial phases of COVID-19, where information was rapidly collected and deployed in an emergency context. The changing of the Irish government in August 2021 and the general change in the COVID-19 context saw a loosening in the extent to which behavioural science was a direct input into emergency response. For example, the NPHET structure was substantially simplified, including removing the specialist groups such as the Behavioural Change Subgroup. A number of behavioural science inputs continued, including the redeployment of the Behavioural Change Subgroup as an advisory function to the Department of Health, continuous updating on information on behavioural aspects of vaccine roll-outs in a number of forums, and the development of a fortnightly Social Activity Monitoring function developed by the ESRI. Throughout the remainder of the COVID-19 period until the time of writing, behavioural science continued to be a significant, if scattered, presence in terms of providing input to government decision-making.

11.8 REFLECTIONS

The rapid development of a behavioural change group informed by a multi-disciplinary team of behavioural scientists added significant capacity to the early Irish COVID-19 response. It enabled rapid monitoring of public opinion, risk attitudes, well-being, and responses to specific interventions. Also, it provided information on potential psychological consequences of physical distancing policies and adverse behavioural spillovers such as reluctance to pursue medical appointments that informed policy in real time. The structure of the emergency response ensured that such evidence was fed into policy in a timely manner and considered alongside a range of other inputs outside the expertise of the behavioural science group such as the technical aspects of medical technology and healthcare capacity. Furthermore the group operated in a transparent manner, including regular contact with the media, publication of minutes of meetings, and publication of research findings. In that sense, the response provides a useful template for the potential embeddedness of behavioural science into public policy and emergency response in particular. As discussed in Daly and Delaney (2021) a question arises as to whether the contribution of research on adverse mental health effects is sufficiently embedded into core considerations of policy options. In the Irish case, the remit of the behavioural science group included monitoring well-being effects but, like in the United Kingdom, the main focus of the group was to examine compliance with restrictions, and the extent to which mental health impacts were factored into the terms of reference of the overall response is relatively limited. While there may be a case for focusing on compliance in the early stages of an emergency such as this, it is also very clear that as emergency response extends into months and even years, such factors arguably need to be embedded more deeply on a structural level.

REFERENCES

Anderson, R. M., Heesterbeek, H., Klinkenberg, D., & Hollingsworth, T. D. (2020). How will country-based mitigation measures influence the course of the COVID-19 epidemic? *The Lancet*, 395(10228), 931–934.

Bennett, P., & Calnan, K. (eds.) (1999). *Risk Communication and Public Health*. New York: Oxford University Press.

Daly, M., & Delaney, L. (2021). Incorporating well-being and mental health research to improve pandemic response. *LSE Public Policy Review*, 2(2), 1–8.

ECDC. (2020a). Guidelines for the implementation of non-pharmaceutical interventions against COVID-19. *European Centre for Disease Prevention and Control, Stockholm*.

Lades, L. K., Laffan, K., Daly, M., & Delaney, L. (2020). Daily emotional well-being during the COVID-19 pandemic. *British Journal of Health Psychology*, 25(4), 902–911.

Lunn, P. D. (2021). Coronavirus in Ireland: One behavioural scientist's view. *Mind & Society*, 20, 229–233.

Lunn, P. D., Belton, C. A., Lavin, C., McGowan, F. P., Timmons, S., & Robertson, D. A. (2020a). Using behavioral science to help fight the Coronavirus. *Journal of Behavioral Public Administration*, 3(1). https://doi.org/10.30636/jbpa.31.147

Lunn, P. D., Timmons, S., Belton, C. A., Barjaková, M., Julienne, H., & Lavin, C. (2020b). Motivating social distancing during the Covid-19 pandemic: An online experiment. *Social Science & Medicine*, 265, 113478.

Lunn, P. D., Timmons, S., Julienne, H., Belton, C. A., Barjaková, M., Lavin, C., & McGowan, F. P. (2021). Using decision aids to support self-isolation during the COVID-19 pandemic. *Psychology & Health*, 36(2), 195–213.

Murphy, R., & Mooney, R. (2020). A brief case study on using a behaviourally informed poster to improve hand washing in homes. Research Services and Policy Unit, Department of Health.

OECD. (2020). Regulatory policy and COVID-19: Behavioural insights for fast-paced decision making. OECD Policy Responses to Coronavirus (COVID-19). OECD Publishing, Paris. https://doi.org/10.1787/7a521805-en

Reynolds, B., Galdo, J. H., Sokler, L., & Freimuth, V. S. (2002). Crisis and emergency risk communication. www.cdc.gov/communications/emergency/cerc.htm.

Van Bavel, J. J., Baicker, K., Boggio, P. S., Capraro, V., Cichocka, A., Cikara, M., et al. (2020). Using social and behavioural science to support COVID-19 pandemic response. *Nature Human Behaviour*, 4(5), 460–471.

World Health Organization. (2017). Communicating risk in public health emergencies: A WHO guideline for emergency risk communication (ERC) policy and practice. World Health Organization.

World Health Organization. (2020). COVID-19 global risk communication and community engagement strategy, December 2020–May 2021: Interim guidance, 23 December 2020 (No. WHO/2019-nCoV/RCCE/2020.3). World Health Organization.

12 On the Use of Behavioural Science in a Pandemic

Adam Oliver

12.1 WHEREOF ONE CANNOT SPEAK, THEREOF ONE MUST BE SILENT

Scientific expertise – even social scientific expertise – is normally focused within very specific domains, and yet the relevant outcomes – health, social, and economic – of an event such as a pandemic involve considerations that extend far beyond the range of any individual's, or discipline's, area of competence. The pronouncements by a behavioural scientist who has spent most of their career studying, say, the effectiveness of smoking cessation or weight reduction interventions on whether a government ought to impose policies with such far-reaching implications as a national lockdown should thus be treated with a healthy degree of scepticism.

To use an analogy (or two), if a person experiences a problem with their car and does not possess the skills to fix it, they will seek the expertise of a motor mechanic. Similarly, if one wants to gain an understanding of infections, the best course of action would be to consult a virologist. However, this does not mean that a mechanic or a virologist necessarily have the requisite skills to manage effectively General Motors or the National Health System (NHS). The behavioural scientists advising the UK government and those solicited for their views by the media on what often appears to be an almost daily basis are principally health and social psychologists, who have tended to weight the *direct* (potential) health consequences of the pandemic far more than the health, social, economic, personal financial/livelihood, and liberty-related consequences of the *responses* to the pandemic, often showing little appreciation of the latter at all.[1] Expertise in a narrow domain does not equate to all-encompassing wisdom, and the ridicule directed at people who complain that they are tired of 'experts' may often be unwarranted.[2]

An example of a behavioural scientist overstepping the boundaries of his expertise occurred at the beginning of the pandemic, in the spring of 2020, when David Halpern, the head of the UK Behavioural Insights Team, attempted to explain a policy of herd immunity in a BBC interview.[3] It is not entirely clear why Halpern was commenting at all on herd immunity. It is possible that someone somewhere muddled up the herd effect – a behavioural science finding that people are likely to be influenced heavily by the behaviours of those around them – with herd immunity – the long-standing and normally reasonable public health notion that if a sufficient proportion of the population become infected with a virus and thus gain immunity, then the virus cannot easily transmit and the population as a whole is protected. In any case, unfortunately for Halpern, his attempt at explanation came at a time when the government was attempting to

---

[1] Similar observations can be made with respect to those seated within disciplines other than behavioural science, such as epidemiology and public health. It ought also to be acknowledged that many behavioural scientists are balanced in their assessments, but nuance doesn't 'sell'.

[2] A personal anecdote may illustrate the point, and demonstrates that the media, even if unintentionally, may be complicit in undermining expertise. In December 2021, a journalist from the BBC World Service contacted me at midnight to ask if I would be interviewed (very) early that morning to offer my view on the effect a video from December 2020 (that had just come to light), which appeared to demonstrate that a Christmas party had been held in Downing Street following a national lockdown, would have on the public's willingness to comply with COVID-19 restrictions. Placing to one side my own unwillingness to address such matters on camera at 3 a.m. in the morning, my (or anyone's else's) view on this is no more valid than that of the next person. It is a question that requires no real expertise to answer (the answer would be, more or less, a guess), and yet the journalist appeared to believe that my view would hold merit due to my 'behavioural public policy expertise'. Other behavioural scientists would no doubt have accepted his request, and their musings might have been highlighted under a banner of 'Expert says ... this (or that)'. The media presumably solicit voices in this way to give their stories legitimacy, and it is not difficult to find so-called experts – obsessed, as they frequently are, with having an impact – who will corroborate the sometimes sensationalist and often dramatic headlines that the media aim to deliver.

[3] www.bbc.co.uk/news/uk-51828000

deny that herd immunity was official policy, when it was not known that having already contracted COVID-19 gave immunity from the virus, when the virus was spreading exponentially and appeared extremely harmful, when there were no vaccines against and little medical knowledge about the virus, and when many experts, including most behavioural scientists, were calling for a more assertive response from the government.

It is likely that pursuing herd immunity in the spring of 2020 would have led to far many more unnecessary deaths and illnesses than that which occurred. Halpern, by appearing to overlook that likelihood in his comments (or at least in the way that his comments were edited), paid the price for stepping outside the parameters of his own expertise, in that he has since been absent from the public debate on the pandemic response. Inadvertently, he also undermined the credibility of behavioural science to a degree, in that many associated his comments with behavioural science thinking, when, in fact, they were nothing of the sort.

Yet, as intimated earlier, many behavioural scientists have supported and advocated broad policy responses on the basis of only partial considerations of the serious and wide-ranging consequences that the pandemic and the responses to it have had and will have. Others who call for unprecedented restrictions on individual freedoms – some of whom have gained extensive media exposure, which has no doubt fuelled them – have done this for two years and have on the whole been challenged relatively weakly for underemphasising the potential health, social, and economic consequences of their recommendations. Admittedly, their focus on the immediate health impacts of the pandemic is a powerful narrative, more powerful than the fallout from the probable consequences of the responses to the pandemic that governments and the citizenry will have to deal with for years to come, although this power imbalance may change as more people tire of being constrained.

In tackling an event with important multifarious considerations, the most appropriate person to sit in judgement in deciding the correct course of action is therefore someone who can balance the different specific single (or at least limited) consequences to which different experts tend to attach all weight, embedded, as they usually are, in their own disciplinary silos. In liberal democracies, that person, or persons, will usually be an elected official; in more authoritarian countries, an appointed autocrat. Of course, there is a form of 'expertise' in being able to exercise such balanced decision-making, and, of course, the siloed forms of expertise serve as crucial inputs in their deliberations. The experts in the various camps (and others without such expertise) may disagree with the decision-makers' overall assessments and judgements, but as long as they have considered the relevant implications – for example, health, behavioural, epidemiological, and economic – seriously that is all that can be asked of them. We may question whether the perfect model of a trusted Periclean or Lincolnian public servant, resistant to the pulling of particular interests, anymore anywhere exists, but turning to those who see only half, or less, of the full picture, perhaps principally because their self-styling may make them sound most relevant to a pandemic response (e.g., 'health psychologists', 'public health' scholars, the World 'Health' Organization), is not the answer.

The credibility of behavioural science took another hit at the start of the pandemic due to proclamations from some within the field that people might have been overreacting to the possible threat of COVID-19. In fact, there are good behavioural science-informed reasons to suggest that people might have been overreacting, just as they had overreacted to the threat of swine flu a decade ago. For example, ambiguity aversion over uncertain events might lead to a tendency to believe that the worst is likely to happen, the overweighting of small probabilities would make a person believe that an unlikely event is more likely to happen than it objectively is, the availability heuristic may cause people to place too much emphasis on what is happening elsewhere or in the recent past, and cascade effects might cause fear to spread quickly throughout a population. However, there are also good behavioural science-informed explanations that partly explain why people may underreact to a pandemic threat, including overconfidence that the threat will prove unfounded, loss aversion associated with the negative (economic, social, and indirect health) consequences of attempts to mitigate the threat, and, again, the availability heuristic working in the opposite direction to that suggested earlier if the consequences of recent pandemics proved mild (e.g., from the perspective of the United Kingdom and many other countries, swine flu once again).[4] Behavioural scientists study human behaviour, which is complex, with different phenomena driving people in different directions, and with even the same phenomena driving people in different directions depending on timing and context. When it comes to assessing the sense of threat at the beginning of a pandemic and the extent to which that threat is eventually realised, behavioural scientists simply cannot predict with any degree of accuracy whether or not people are over- or underreacting.

What we can perhaps say, on the basis of recent history, is that in the United Kingdom and many other countries the worst effects of pandemic threats are rarely realised, and yet many people, partly for the reasons outlined earlier, react initially as though the worst may well happen. Over the last twenty years alone, excluding COVID-19, there have been at least four major pandemic scares (severe acute respiratory syndrome (SARS), Middle East respiratory syndrome, swine flu, and Ebola), and all of these ended up causing either relatively localised or minor harms. Indeed, a catastrophic global pandemic has not been witnessed by anyone younger than 100 years old (and even centurions would have been too young to remember the last one). Ipso facto, there will often be an implicit overreaction to a pandemic simply because the threat usually fails to materialise, and, fingers crossed, this is also likely to be the case going forward (in fact, to possibly an even greater degree for the foreseeable future, because the availability heuristic prompted by our

---

[4] One of the reasons why several countries in South East Asia responded faster and more aggressively to the COVID-19 pandemic than many Western countries was because the memory of the 2003 SARS outbreak, from which they suffered more, was vivid.

COVID-19 experiences is likely to be in overdrive). The only times when a reaction that is usually an overreaction is not an overreaction is, of course, when the pandemic threat is realised, but this is not the consequence of superior predictive abilities. It is simply the consequence of an independent event matching the implications of particular behavioural heuristics.

12.2   WHEREOF ONE CAN SPEAK, THEREOF ONE MUST BE HUMBLE

This chapter may appear generally critical of using expertise in policy formation, but that is not the intention. One would want economists rather than laypersons with unformed views to conduct economic forecasting, and the same can be said in relation to behavioural scientists, epidemiologists, climatologists (and their relevant domains), and any other form of expertise that one can think of. Rather, I am arguing that experts of course ought to be used but that they should know their proper place, which is to inform policy, not to decide upon policy (unless they are experts in policy formation). The message to experts is to stick to what they know and acknowledge the limits and limitations of their own realms of expertise.

That said, what is the appropriate role for behavioural scientists in relation to a pandemic response? My suggestion, as per the discussion so far, is for them to leave the judgements on which interventions ought to be introduced to those appointed to balance all relevant considerations and instead focus on assessing how the introduced interventions might be made more effective with input from their knowledge of behavioural science (e.g., present bias, probability weighting, and loss aversion). There are, of course, many domains of policy – indeed, given their forte in uncovering and then applying systematic human behavioural patterns, perhaps all domains of policy – where behavioural science expertise can be usefully deployed in this way, including in relation to interventions intended to get the economy moving again (or moving at all during lockdowns), in securing volunteering behaviours to help the vulnerable, to encourage people to report and escape from domestic abuse, and so on. But perhaps the most visible ways in which behavioural scientists have thus far been involved in the pandemic response (at least in terms of their more modest scope that I am arguing for in this chapter) is in relation to interventions intended to limit the spread of, and enhance resistance to, the virus: that is, handwashing, social distancing, mask-wearing, voluntary testing (and isolating in the event of a positive result), and vaccine uptake.

For example, research managed by the University of Pennsylvania's Behavior Change for Good Initiative suggests, at least over the short term, that defaulting people into a vaccination slot significantly increases vaccine uptake.[5] Sometimes – perhaps often – behavioural interventions will not offer any incremental positive effectiveness, but that knowledge in and of itself is useful and can point to more nuanced interventions that may demonstrate an effect in slightly altered contexts or when directed at different groups. For example, Krpan et al. (2021) analysed four behavioural interventions – asking people to write a letter to a vulnerable person, to plan a meaningful activity that they could not do under certain Covid restrictions, to read a text on why social distancing is important to the economy, and to consider information that challenged misconceptions about the benefits of social distancing – and did not observe a positive 'general' effect from any of them. However, in delving into their data a little more deeply, they discovered that the 'information' intervention was effective over those people who had started practising social distancing recently (and was detrimental over those who had been practising social distancing for a while).

It is not my intention in this chapter to review the behavioural interventions that have been designed, tried, and tested (or not tested) for the purposes of improving the policy responses to the

---

[5] 'The University of Pennsylvania's Behavior Change for Good Initiative Unveils Effective Strategies to Boost Vaccination Rates', news (upenn.edu). https://news .wharton.upenn.edu/press-releases/2021/02/the-university-of-pennsylvanias-behavior-change-for-good-initiative-unveils-effective-strategies-to-boost-vaccination -rates/#:~:text=Conducted%20with%20Walmart%20and%20two,rates%20by%20 up%20to%2011%25

pandemic – it is merely to contend that this is where, in relation to a pandemic behavioural scientists can most appropriately apply themselves. Moreover, behavioural scientists will not offer a panacea. The essence of 'behavioural public policy' – the term that is now used to encapsulate the application of behavioural science to public policy design – is that context matters to the effectiveness of any intervention. Behavioural scientists are likely to be able to help only at the margins, but even at the margins many lives might be saved.

12.3 WHEREOF THERE ARE EXTERNALITIES, THEREOF WE CAN UNITE

There are strong disagreements among those working in behavioural public policy about the extent to which paternalism ought to be practised by policymakers. Some, including myself, align with the German political economist Wilhelm von Humboldt (1791–92/1993) – who greatly influenced John Stuart Mill – that so long as people are not harming others, they ought to be free from state interference to be the authors of their own lives. And yet, to date, soft forms of paternalism – that people ought to be targeted for behavioural change for their own good – have dominated the development of behavioural public policy. Anti-paternalists in behavioural public policy disapprove of that direction but accept that interventions aimed at ameliorating negative externalities (and perhaps at least sometimes at generating positive externalities) – that is, to couple freedom with security – are legitimate arms of state action. A pandemic response can unite the paternalists and anti-paternalists among us, because although there is some emphasis on protecting people for their own good, the main thrust of behaviour change initiatives in these circumstances is to encourage people to engage in actions – hand-washing, social distancing, mask-wearing, vaccine uptake – to protect people other than themselves.[6]

---

[6] It is possible, although by no means certain, that such practices can evolve into social norms that may help in future emergencies. For example, wearing face masks when one has a cold has been a long-held cultural expectation in Japan that negated any resistance to this practice during the coronavirus crisis of the like observed in some other countries.

In the liberal democracies, it is normally preferable to try to encourage the citizenry to change their behaviours voluntarily and autonomously, rather than imposing too many coercive controls, by, for example, appealing to their natural inclination towards cooperative 'give and take', a theme on which I have written fairly extensively elsewhere (e.g., Oliver, 2019), or by trying to get them to focus on a future world of normality or continued disruption, if they do/do not comply with certain recommendations in the more immediate moment. People are likely to tire of, and increasingly resist, control, which is understandable to those of us who think that freedom is not only a basic human right – that it is part of what makes us human – but that it ultimately makes for a better functioning and more cooperative society, a view that was dominant among liberals from Adam Smith and Thomas Paine to John Stuart Mill and Abraham Lincoln (see, e.g., Anderson, 2017) and was also a central postulate among the members of the Austrian School of Economics and their later disciples. Unfortunately, in circumstances where freedom can lead to even a small number of people potentially imposing serious negative externalities on others – which, we now know, can happen during an infectious disease pandemic – stricter controls over the behaviours of all citizens may become inevitable, even if those controls themselves impose large costs.[7]

I therefore suspect that most behavioural scientists accept the *legitimacy* of the micro-interventions around social distancing, mask-wearing, and the like that have been introduced to ameliorate the worst effects of the pandemic, because without these interventions people may have imposed substantial additional harms on

---

[7] So that the reader doesn't think that I am contradicting myself, I do not believe that it is the role of the behavioural scientist to *advocate* for stricter controls, given their typical focus on only a limited range of the implications of controls versus no controls – that is the role of elected politicians in liberal democracies, after (hopefully) considering all possible implications of the various courses of action. My point is that even anti-paternalistic behavioural scientists can often accept the legitimacy of hard controls on individual behaviours where negative externalities are significant if controls are not imposed.

others. To conclude, then, the use of pandemic-related behavioural science is to explore whether the systematic patterns in human behaviour that have been uncovered in this multi-disciplinary field can be employed to improve the design – that is, the effectiveness – of these interventions. This endeavour might not offer the media exposure that some behavioural scientists appear to crave, but if successful it may negate the perceived need for even harder, more coercive, controls, the long-term legitimacy of which, in the liberal democracies, is highly questionable.

REFERENCES

Anderson, E. (2017). *Private Government: How Employers Rule Our Lives (and Why We Don't Talk about It)*. Princeton and Oxford: Princeton University Press.

Krpan, D., Makki, F., Saleh, N., Brink, I., & Klauznicer, H. V. (2021). When behavioural science can make a difference in times of COVID-19. *Behavioural Public Policy*, 5(2), 153–179.

Oliver, A. (2019). *Reciprocity and the Art of Behavioural Public Policy*. Cambridge: Cambridge University Press.

von Humboldt, W. (1791–92/1993). *The Limits of State Action*. Indianapolis: The Liberty Fund.

13 Behavioural Public Health?

Experts' Biases and Responses to Pandemics

Matteo M. Galizzi

In order to reach citizens to influence and change their individual and population behaviours, public health policies must typically act through a series of 'expert' decision-makers whose behaviours and decisions are crucial to achieve the ultimate goals of public policies. These experts include, for example, health policymakers and leaders of national and regional health systems and public health organisations; managers of territorial health agencies and hospitals; managers of hospital units and public health departments; hospital doctors, general practitioners (GPs), and other health professionals with decision-making responsibilities in terms of public health.

These expert decision-makers are interesting from a behavioural economics perspective because they set or influence rules and public health messages that target the general population. Biases, mis-reactions, or distorted perceptions or decisions by these expert decision-makers are therefore particularly worrying because they potentially have deleterious cascade effects on citizens and thus on public health as a whole.

Behavioural economics has traditionally focused on the biases of the decision-makers considered less experienced or informed, such as consumers and citizens. Behavioural health economics is no exception to this rule, the literature having developed behavioural analyses

This chapter is a shorter, revised, version of the following original article published in the journal *Sistemi Intelligenti*: Matteo M. Galizzi (2022). Behavioural public health? Experts' biases and responses to pandemics. *Sistemi Intelligenti*, 34(2), 371–401. https://doi.org/10.1422/105045, www.rivisteweb.it/doi/10.1422/105045. The author is very grateful to Federica Bellei and to the publisher Società Editrice Il Mulino – Bologna for granting permission to republish a version of the original article in this book.

especially at the level of patients and citizens, to understand, influence, and change individual risky behaviours such as lack of exercise, overeating and unhealthy diets, smoking, and the absence of prevention or diagnostic tests (Galizzi & Wiesen, 2018; Jarke et al., 2022; Loewenstein et al., 2017).

Behavioural economics analyses of expert health decision-makers have been much rarer, with a few dozen behavioural studies on doctors and other healthcare professionals more generally and very few studies on health policy-makers and public health decision-makers specifically. Some notable exceptions are the works by Gigerenzer and Edwards (2003), Loewenstein (2005a, b), Gigerenzer et al. (2007), Wegwarth and Gigerenzer (2011), Bakshi et al. (2017, 2020), Crea et al. (2019), and a few others that we will discuss in greater detail in this chapter.

A possible reason behind the scarce behavioural economics literature on expert health decision-makers may be related to the assumption that these experts might be considered free from cognitive biases or distortions because they are perceived as fully rational and well-informed decision-makers who benefit from their long work experience in the field.

In this chapter we review some of the biases by health policy-makers, public health decision-makers, and other experts that have emerged during the current COVID-19 pandemic.

There is no doubt that the COVID-19 pandemic has highlighted the formidable and tireless work on the ground of thousands of doctors, nurses, and healthcare professionals. Their behaviours have literally saved, and continue to save, the lives of millions of people, and it is no wonder that they have often been considered 'heroes' by the public.

However, the COVID-19 pandemic has also documented an unprecedented series of distorted or sub-optimal decisions and behaviours by health policy-makers and expert health decision-makers in countries considered to be at the forefront of public health, such as the United Kingdom or Italy, for example. Some of these biased decisions and behaviours have had dramatic effects and deserve a critical analysis under the lens of behavioural economics.

In this chapter we list and describe some of the behavioural distortions emerged during the COVID-19 pandemic. Many of these behavioural biases have not been previously documented, or categorised as such, or may have been discussed under different names.

Here is different bias

It describes the incorrect belief that the spread of an infectious agent (e.g., a virus or bacterium) is entirely explained by the environment and its socio-cultural factors, thus neglecting the epidemiological characteristics and features of the agent itself and of the host. Statements dictated by this bias have been made by leaders of national or regional healthcare organisations. For example, on 22 September 2020, the UK prime minister justified the different responses to COVID-19 in the United Kingdom compared to Italy saying that 'this is ... a freedom-loving country'. Looking at the minutes, it turns out that the meetings of the UK government's Scientific Advisory Group for Emergencies (SAGE) were called 'SAGE meeting on Wuhan Coronavirus (COVID-19)' until the sixteenth SAGE meeting on 16 March 2020. It is only starting from the seventeenth SAGE meeting on 18 March 2020 that the term 'Wuhan' before 'Coronavirus' was dropped. A similar sort of 'exceptionalism' bias has been proposed as an explanation of the United Kingdom's resistance to follow the recommendations of the World Health Organization (WHO) or to learn from the previous experiences of other countries, such as Italy, during the COVID-19 pandemic (O'Toole, 2020; Sample, 2020a; Woodcock, 2020). For example, on 1 December 2020, the former UK chief medical officer (CMO) Dame Sally Davis explicitly told the committee hearing of the Parliament that 'British exceptionalism undermined pandemic preparedness' and that 'our infectious diseases experts ... did not really believe that another SARS would get to us, and I think it's a form of British exceptionalism' (Sample, 2020a).

Wrong guidelines, yet still sticking to the guidelines bias

It describes the attitude by experienced decision-makers and doctors who continue to adhere, passively and uncritically, to guidelines even when the guidelines are manifestly inadequate or outdated by later evidence. In the early stages of the COVID-19 epidemic, both WHO and the Italian Ministry of Health issued guidelines according to which only patients returning from Wuhan or in contact with someone exposed to the virus should be tested for COVID-19. Although cases of abnormal pneumonia were inexplicably intensifying in the province of Bergamo at least from mid-January 2020 (Cereda et al., 2021; Galizzi & Ghislandi, 2020; Imarisio et al., 2020; Nava, 2020), the practice of the Lombardy regional health system remained uncritically adhering to those guidelines at least until early March, when the situation became out of control. The so-called Italian patient 0 was identified in mid-February 2020 thanks to a doctor who deviated from the guidelines and decided to test the patient for COVID-19.

Absolute number of cases neglect bias

It describes the distorted perception of the severity of an epidemic due to the emphasis on (low) percentage frequencies rather than (high) absolute numbers. In the early stages of the outbreak several experienced decision-makers argued that the COVID-19 mortality rate was not particularly high. The United Kingdom's CMO said mortality would be 1 per cent or less (Costello, 2020; Devlin & Boseley, 2020). However, talking about, say, 2 per cent mortality generates a distorted representation of fatal cases of the epidemic when the absolute number of infected is high. Take, for example, the province of Bergamo, the most affected in the world by COVID-19, which has 1,100,000 inhabitants. If the virus infects one in three inhabitants of the province (which is in line with the contagion rate in the province calculated by the national institute for statistics (ISTAT) in July 2020), it means that about 366,667 are infected with the virus, of which 7,333 die from the virus, which is, tragically, even an underestimate of the 8,000–11,000 deaths in the province of Bergamo alone.

If the same epidemiological data for Bergamo were extrapolated in absolute numbers, deaths throughout Italy would be quantifiable as about 400,000 deaths, which is a much more salient, tangible (and chilling) figure than talking abstractly of about a 2 per cent mortality.

Baseline neglect bias

It describes the attitude by health decision-makers to report the absolute number of infections ('positive cases') in a day without reporting the number of tests conducted. Since the beginning of the pandemic, in fact, decision-makers from regional and national health systems, such as in Italy and the United Kingdom, have continuously discussed the data on cases found positive to the swab tests, presenting them in absolute terms: for example, '1,281 cases today'. In order to be interpretable in a meaningful way and in order to draw correct inference on the evolution over time and on the comparability across different countries, the data on positive cases needs to be complemented at least by the ratio between the tests found positive and the total number of tests conducted. This is especially true when the comparability over time or across countries involves settings at either different phases of the pandemic or with different testing capacity. For example, right at the beginning of the first wave in Italy there was only one laboratory in northern Italy – the Policlinico San Matteo hospital in Pavia – that had the technical expertise and capability of conducting the tests for COVID-19. At the peak of the crisis the hospitals in Bergamo were so rapidly overwhelmed by the incoming flows of patients in critical conditions that few diagnostic tests were actually conducted, mainly prioritising the ones to test healthcare professionals, to uncover potential new hotspots (e.g., nursing homes), and to discharge patients after effective treatment.

Bottleneck resources neglect bias

It describes the underestimation of the crucial role of the bottlenecks in the healthcare systems. The provinces of Brescia, Pavia, and Bergamo in the Lombardy region – some of the provinces most affected by COVID-19 in Italy – had some of the highest numbers of hospital beds per inhabitant in Italy, in Europe, and even in world (e.g., 4.45 beds per thousand inhabitants in Brescia). The sudden swept of the first wave of the pandemic, however, showed that the real scarce resource and the key bottleneck in the local health system was not the total number of hospital beds but the number of beds in the intensive care unit (ICU) and sub-intensive care unit. In Bergamo, the Papa Giovanni XXIII hospital alone – one of the most modern and technologically advanced hospitals in the country – had an ICU of eighty beds, the largest in all Europe. Even so many beds were not enough to contain the overwhelming impact of the first wave of the pandemic: on 28 March 2020, COVID-19 patients in critical conditions occupied 498 of the 779 beds available in the entire hospital almost two-thirds of the total. It was precisely this inescapable bottleneck that forced local health decision-makers to make dramatic choices at that time, including deciding to whom, among the many COVID-19 patients in critical conditions, those life-saving resources should be dedicated to.

Silver bullet bias

It describes the distorted belief that to respond to an epidemic such as COVID-19 it is sufficient to implement a single policy measure, whatever it is, that is considered 'the' right thing to do. It is a distorted belief because there is no evidence that a single policy measure would really solve a pandemic. As the WHO Director-General said on 6 April 2020 in his opening remarks at the media briefing on COVID-19, 'There is no black or white answer, and no silver bullet' (WHO, 2020a, b).

Realistically, in order to beat COVID-19 we need a strategy combining different interventions and approaches, a 'combination prevention' that uses at the same time different preventive measures of reduction of transmissions through not only frequent and accurate cleaning of the hands but also physical distancing, use of masks, respiratory etiquette (e.g., cough or sneeze into own elbow), surface and object cleaning, and reduction of permanence in closed and poorly ventilated public spaces; rapid and capillary tests; detailed and timely contact tracing systems; self-isolation, quarantines, and support measures for isolating and self-isolating people; school and workplace closures; travel restrictions and border closures; avoiding crowding; and other combined measures to implement physical distancing (Association of Directors of Public Health, 2020; WHO, 2019).

Wash-your-hands bias

It describes the distorted belief that, in order to respond to an epidemic such as COVID-19, it is enough to convince citizens to do something pro-active, such as to wash their hands more often or for longer (Hutton, 2020). For example, on 3 March 2020 the UK prime minister Boris Johnson said in his first televised press conference flanked by the UK CMO Professor Chris Whitty and the UK government chief scientific adviser (GCSA) Sir Patrick Vallance: 'I was at a hospital the other night where I think there were actually a few coronavirus patients and I shook hands with everybody. ... We should all basically just go about our normal daily lives. The best thing you can do is to wash your hands with soap and hot water while singing Happy Birthday twice.' Two days after, on 5 March, there was the first official report of somebody dying in a hospital having tested positive for COVID-19 caught in the United Kingdom. This perception is distorted not only because it focuses exclusively on a single vehicle of infection, the one through contaminated objects (fomite transmission), and neglects the other vehicles of infection, that is, the ones through droplets transmission or through airborne transmission, much more insidious and widespread (Association of Directors of Public Health, 2020; Sample, 2020b), but also because it exploits the, seemingly reassuring but substantially wrong, idea that in order to effectively fight the pandemic it is enough to engage in some simple, familiar, pro-active behaviour. From this perspective, the bias is a special case of the *silver bullet* bias, emphasising a familiar pro-active behaviour. The emphasis on a simple, familiar, pro-active behaviour runs the risks of tapping into the 'illusion of control' tendency and of over-simplifying the real threats for a pandemic. For example, the idea to also cover one's face was not considered by the UK health policy-makers. Covering the face is a simple behaviour too. It is actually easier to enforce and directly and publicly verify than washing the hands. Covering the face, however, is a less familiar behaviour than washing the hands. It may also appear more defensive, passive, perhaps even submissive, than washing the hands, seemingly accepting the fact that the epidemic is overwhelming and predominant (see the *double standard* bias discussed later). From this perspective, this distorted perception is in line with other similar biases in health and healthcare, such as the 'therapeutic illusion', that is, the tendency to over-prescribe healthcare treatments or to believe that it is always worth actively fighting a terminal disease with new cycles of therapies, instead of improving the quality of life in the last moments with, for example, palliative care (Casarett, 2016; Dolan, 2019).

Bergamo is running bias

It is a sub-case of the previous bias, which refers to the distorted attitude of emphasising the vitality of doing, of activism, to show how the economic and productive system does not give up in the face of an epidemic. This unfortunate slogan of Confindustria Bergamo (the local Confederation of Business Industry), initially endorsed also by the mayor of Bergamo, contributed to strengthen the resistances by the local entrepreneurs to the idea of setting up a so-called 'red zone' (a full lockdown) in Val Seriana, despite the discovery of a COVID-19 outbreak that had already infected an entire local hospital (in Alzano Lombardo) (Galizzi & Ghislandi, 2020; Imarisio et al., 2020; Nava, 2020).

Follow the expert bias

It describes a distorted, or opportunistic, attitude of health decision-makers by which they claim to just follow the advice of independent experts, when this is not actually, or consistently, the case. It nests a series of diverse cases that all share the same, false, presumption that health policies are directly informed by independent experts. These cases are instances where either (i) experts are directly employed or line-managed by the decision-makers or (ii) experts have vested interests or conflicts of interest or are supported and funded by companies and lobbies with vested interests or conflicts of interest; or finally (iii) health decision-makers follow the advice of independent experts, but only selectively or intermittently, as based, opportunistically, on the specific content of the scientific advice.

For the first case – **experts directly employed or line-managed by the decision-makers** – a typical example came from the Lombardy region in Italy during the first wave of the COVID-19 pandemic. On 12 March 2020, the Lombardy region established two 'experts' units (a 'crisis unit' and a 'task force') to manage the pandemic emergency. Every single one of the 170 (!) experts in those units were directly appointed and line-managed by the region itself. It was only by 7 April 2020 (therefore after the lockdown decided by the national government) that the Lombardy region established a 'scientific committee'. While this consisted of twenty-six independent members, all of which had clear medical and public health expertise, it is still unclear how this scientific committee interacted with the crisis unit and task force in informing the decisions of the Lombardy regional policy-makers (Bosa et al., 2021, 2022).

An archetypical example of the second case of the bias – namely, **experts with vested interests or supported and financed by companies and lobbie**s – is instead the group of 'experts' behind the so-called Great Barrington Declaration (https://gbdeclaration.org). Pompously presented by three academics from major universities (Harvard, Oxford, and Stanford) and symbolically reconvened physically together in a wooden-panelled room, the declaration aimed to convince health decision-makers to let COVID-19 take its course in order to 'naturally' reach 'herd immunity', without the need of implementing further restrictions or containment measures (see also the *I am not an expert but...* bias). The declaration was welcomed by Scott Atlas, the White House science adviser under the Trump administration – a colleague at Stanford University of one of the three authors – and by the health and human services secretary of the US administration (Mandavilli & Stolberg, 2020). However, it quickly became known that various economic lobbies opposed to restrictive policies and new lockdowns had a central role in the declaration (Greenhalgh et al., 2020; Mandavilli & Stolberg, 2020). On 2 November 2020 the UK CMO said the idea behind the Great Barrington Declaration was 'dangerously flawed and operationally impractical', while the UK GCSA added that the government's SAGE had reviewed the proposal and found 'fatal flaws in the argument' (Sample & Syal, 2020).

Arguably the most typical example of the last case – **health decision-makers following the advice of independent experts, but only selectively or intermittently** – is illustrated by the relationship of the UK government with the experts. The United Kingdom was indeed a pioneer in the use of science advice in crises and in government. It was the first country in the world to create in 1855 the post of the CMO, as the 'nation's doctor' acting as the interface between the government and the medical professionals and being responsible for advising on epidemics and disease prevention. The United Kingdom was also the second country (after the United States in 1957) to appoint in 1964 a GCSA, as the prime minister's top adviser on scientific issues. During a public health emergency, the GCSA and the CMO co-chair SAGE. During the COVID-19 pandemic SAGE worked tirelessly to provide timely evidence to the UK government. Despite the fact that SAGE was not designed for a semi-permanent role (the key is the 'E' for emergencies) and that many of its members worked pro bono, by the end of 2020 it had met seventy times (during the H1N1 epidemics in 2009 it met about twenty times, and less than five times for the Ebola and Zika epidemics); it had produced more than 360 working papers; and it often worked over a twenty-four-hour shift pattern at very short notice. It is reckoned that, overall, SAGE provided high-quality advice across a large range of areas and under massive strain (Sasse et al., 2020). It is also fair to acknowledge that it was a good call by the CMO and the GCSA to also involve the specialist committees of experts on modelling (Scientific Pandemic Influenza Group on Modelling, SPI-M), on emerging infectious diseases (New and Emerging Respiratory Virus Threats Advisory Group, NERVTAG), and on social and behavioural interventions (Scientific Pandemic Influenza Group on Behaviors, SPI-B) – originally established to advise the Department of Health – and to bring them together under SAGE (Sasse et al., 2020). The key issue, however, is that during the COVID-19 pandemic the UK government chose sometimes to listen to its scientific experts, while sometimes clearly not to. At the very beginning of the crisis in the United Kingdom, for example, the government argued it was just 'following the science' when it delayed the first national lockdown while waiting for scientists to provide certainty. It was acting as if it was waiting for scientists to make judgements and decisions that only politicians could make, or – according to Professor Graham Medley, chair of the SPI-M sub-committee – as if it was 'passing the buck' to scientists (Conn et al., 2020). This alleged 'following the science' position, however, was often undermined by the ambiguous and contradictory statements by the government. For example, on 27 March 2020 the UK prime minister failed to timely and appropriately react to the scandal of his chief of staff Dominic Cummings' trip from London to Durham and then to Barnard Castle in the north-east of England during a national lockdown. This likely caused an erosion of public trust in the government's recommendations and in the science behind them. When restrictions were lifted in May, moreover, the government failed to bring different streams of experts' advice together to form a coherent strategy. For example, scientific experts were not consulted or were ignored about policies implemented during the summer, such as the 'travel corridors' (i.e., passengers allowed to travel for holidays to specific countries without isolating); the 'eat out to help out' scheme (i.e., customers receiving government-subsidised half-priced meals for eating out in restaurants), which is now reckoned to have spread the infections (Fetzer, 2022); or the return of students to universities (Conn et al., 2020). After the summer, on 21 September 2020, SAGE recommended, to 'be considered for immediate introduction', a two-week 'circuit breaker' to curb a rise in cases that was becoming 'exponential'. At the end of September such a recommendation was rejected by the UK prime minister, and so it was several other times by ministers in early October. It later emerged that these decisions not to endorse the SAGE recommendation were influenced by a meeting involving the prime minister himself, the chancellor of the exchequer, and the three proponents of the earlier-discussed 'herd immunity' approach (see also the *I am not an expert but...* bias), including one of the three main signatories of the Great Barrington Declaration and the Swedish epidemiologist who was behind the COVID-19 approach in Sweden (Insight, 2020; McNally, 2020). It was argued that it was wrong to present the prime minister such a 'fringe view' while he was weighing a crucial decision and that the delay in imposing further restrictions resulted in an estimated 1.3 million extra COVID-19 infections (McNally, 2020). In sum, while at the start of the crisis the UK government seemed to hide *behind* the science, at the end of 2020 it seemed to hide *from* the science, until there was no other option.

I am not an expert but... bias

It describes the distorted attitude of 'experts' to voice, express, or support judgements related to areas of scientific expertise that are outside of, or not aligned with, the areas of their own scientific expertise. The most emblematic instance of such a distorted attitude is arguably the one around the claims about 'herd immunity' expressed in the United Kingdom in the early phase of the COVID-19 pandemic. In early March 2020 **herd immunity** came to be seen as the UK government's strategy, despite the fact that it was, and still continues to be, a highly unorthodox and controversial strategy in the scientific debate (Arrowsmith et al., 2020; Meyerowitz-Katz, 2020; Stewart & Busby, 2020). This was likely due to confusing communication by policy-makers and scientific advisers about the government's overall strategy and the science behind it. In an interview on 10 March 2020, for example, the chief executive officer of the Behavioural Insights Team, a SAGE member, appeared to suggest that one way to deal with the pandemic was to 'cocoon' the vulnerable and for the rest of the population to naturally reach herd immunity:

> There's going to be a point, assuming the epidemic flows and grows, as we think it probably will do, where you'll want to cocoon, you'll want to protect those at-risk groups so that they basically don't catch the disease, and by the time they come out of their cocooning, herd immunity's been achieved in the rest of the population. (Conn et al., 2020; Easton, 2020)

The day after, the UK prime minister added, 'I must level with the British public: many more families are going to lose loved ones before their time' (Conn et al., 2020). That same day, on 11 March 2020, the WHO formally declared COVID-19 a pandemic and criticised the 'alarming levels of inaction' by some countries. Then on 13 March 2020, the UK GCSA explained on the radio the government's strategy:

> Our aim is to try and reduce the peak, not suppress it completely. Also, because the vast majority of people get a mild illness, to build up some kind of herd immunity, so more people are immune to this disease, and we reduce the transmission. At the same time, we protect those who are most vulnerable to it. Those are the key things we need to do. (Conn et al., 2020; Stewart & Busby, 2020)

On 14 March 2020, an open letter was signed by more than 500 key scientists in the United Kingdom criticising the government's position and stating that 'going for "herd immunity" at this point does not seem a viable option, as this will put NHS at an even stronger level of stress, risking many more lives than necessary' (Arrowsmith et al., 2020). Such a confusing communication was heavily criticised by leading experts on strategy and national security: 'it appeared that the government was preparing to let the disease rip through the community as part of a cold-blooded experiment in disease management' (Freedman, 2020). By looking at the minutes of the SAGE meetings it appears that the concept of 'cocooning' was in fact repeatedly discussed in the thirteenth, fourteenth, and fifteenth SAGE meetings on 5, 10, and 13 March, respectively (UK Government, 2020a, b, c). The same minutes state that the prime minister's chief of staff Dominic Cummings was also present when the 'cocooning' idea was first discussed by SAGE during its thirteenth meeting on 5 March 2020. Also his aide and prime minister's special adviser Ben Warner was there. Among the behavioural science members of SPI-B only Dr David Halpern and Professor Brooke Rogers (by phone) attended that meeting (UK Government, 2020a).

There is evidence that... bias

It describes the distorted attitude of citing studies in support of an idea in a way that is detached from a systematic consideration of the context of the study and of the complex and more general empirical evidence. It is clearly always possible to find some study directly or indirectly supporting whatever argument one wants to make. This attitude to a partial reporting of the evidence, however, conflicts with the very spirit of the scientific method that would suggest that one should review systematically and transparently *all* the studies conducted on a hypothesis and evaluate the overall scientific evidence both in support of the hypothesis and against it (Maynard & Munafo', 2018; Miguel et al., 2014; Munafo' et al., 2017; Simonsohn et al., 2014a, b). It is similar to another bias, the tendency to select a sub-set of variables in a study so that the report of the results is effectively incomplete (*outcome reporting bias*: Gigerenzer and Gray, 2011). The most striking example of this bias was the justification provided by the UK government in support of its decision to delay the lockdown in the first wave of COVID-19. The justification used in that occasion was based on the argument that closing too soon would tire citizens by generating 'behavioral fatigue' (Devlin, 2020). The minutes of the fifteenth SAGE meeting on 13 March 2020 stated that 'there is some evidence that people find quarantining harder to comply with the longer it goes on. The evidence is not strong but the effect is intuitive' (UK Government, 2020c). That meeting was attended by Ben Warner, and also by Dr David Halpern, Professor Brooke Rogers, and Dr James Rubin – the only three behavioural science members of SPI-B (UK Government, 2020c). There is no further mention of this idea or of 'behavioural fatigue' in the minutes of any other SAGE meetings, before or after that meeting. In March 2020 the Minister of Health and Social Care Matt Hancock publicly endorsed the behavioural fatigue idea in an interview: 'The evidence of past epidemics and past crises of this nature shows that people do tire of these sorts of social distancing measures, so if [we] start them too early, they lose their effect and actually it is worse. The social science and the behavioural science are a very important part of the scientific advice that we rely on' (Conn et al., 2020). Similar remarks were made also by the CMO, Professor Chris Whitty, who said the idea was based on both 'common sense' and 'behavioural science' (Conn et al., 2020). It is unclear to which evidence they were referring to. Neither by then nor today has a systematic review of the literature ever provided evidence in support of behavioural fatigue in the context of a pandemic or an epidemic such as COVID-19 (Abbasi, 2020; Chater, 2020). Most of the studies on what is informally labelled as **behavioural fatigue** come from laboratory studies with students in very different contexts, such as the studies on ego depletion that have been replicated only partially (Hagger et al., 2016). These studies, moreover, have nothing to do with lockdown or epidemics and are of variable scientific quality as evidenced by the fact that they have not been systematically replicated. The only noteworthy exception was a single study on the pandemic in Hong Kong in 2009 (Cowling et al., 2010). The justification was so weak that the entire UK behavioural science community rallied behind an open letter to disavow the scientific basis of the government's justification and to demand more evidence and transparency in support of its decision (Hahn et al., 2020). The open letter was signed by more than 650 behavioural scientists within hours. The executive editor of the *British Medical Journal* published an editorial on 6 August 2020 titled 'Behavioural fatigue: A flawed idea central to a flawed pandemic response' (Abbasi, 2020). The embarrassment of the UK government's 'experts' following the behavioural fatigue claim was second only to the embarrassment from another, equally unfounded, claim, namely the justification for not introducing restrictions based on 'herd immunity' (see the *I am not an expert but...* bias).

Double standard bias

It describes the use of double standard in assessing scientific evidence. A particularly worrying example of this bias refers, again, to the scientific experts advising the UK policy-makers. On the one hand, as discussed earlier, SAGE actively delayed the introduction of the first lockdown in the United Kingdom by giving credit to the 'behavioural fatigue' idea that was, at the very best, a mere hypothesis, a pure speculation with virtually no support in terms of evidence. On the other hand, however, the same SAGE delayed the recommendations to use face coverings and to ban mass gatherings based on the argument that there was not enough evidence to do so. In other words, while in the latter case SAGE set up a too high bar on the evidence, in the former it set a too low bar on the evidence, thus effectively using two different standards for assessing scientific evidence. The case of SAGE's advice against **banning large gatherings** is emblematic. The minutes of the thirteenth SAGE meeting on 5 March 2020 state: 'SAGE agreed there is no evidence to suggest that banning very large gatherings would reduce transmission. Preventing all social interaction in public spaces, including restaurants and bars, would have an effect, but would be very difficult to implement' (UK Government, 2020a). It is difficult to see the logic here: if banning all social interactions in public spaces, including restaurants and bars, would have an effect on reducing transmission, why would not the effect be the same for large gatherings too, where the risk of transmission should be even higher due to more people involved? Also, banning large gatherings is arguably easier to implement than banning all social interactions in public spaces. The supporting evidence could have been little, weak, or mixed by then, but the precautionary principle should have suggested to recommend banning mass gatherings. The same argument was reiterated in the next SAGE meeting on 10 March 2020, whose minutes state: 'SAGE noted that public gatherings pose a relatively low but not zero public risk. People are more likely to be infected by people they know, not strangers.' The latter sentence, incidentally, is another example of the *here is different* bias. In the week of 13 March 2020 the following mass gatherings were therefore allowed to take place, among others: the Cheltenham Festival of horseracing (10–13 March, between 60,000 and 68,500 attendants in each of the four days: Wood & Carroll, 2020); the Liverpool versus Atletico Madrid Champions League match (11 March, about 54,000 attendants: Conn, 2020); and the Stereophonics concert in Cardiff (14–15 March, about 15,000 attendants over the two days: McEvoy, 2020). An estimated number of 340 league and cup football matches took place in England in March 2020, with a combined attendance of 1.625 million people (Olczak et al., 2020). Causal inference on the links between these and other mass gatherings and COVID-19 cases and deaths is not straightforward of course. However, some estimates find evidence that the football matches in England in March 2020 were consistent with more COVID-19 cases and deaths, even controlling for measurable characteristics of local areas: on average, a football match was consistent with around six additional COVID-19 cases per 100,000 people, and two additional COVID-19 deaths per 100,000 people (Olczak et al., 2020). By that time, football matches such as the Atalanta–Valencia Champions League final match in Milan on 19 February 2020 were already identified as likely super-spreading events one month earlier in northern Italy (Galizzi and Ghislandi, 2020; Giuffrida, 2020). There is a striking asymmetry in the use of evidence for decision-making here because, as seen earlier, the decision to delay the first lockdown was made on arguably even less, even weaker, and even more mixed evidence about the possible risks related to 'behavioural fatigue'. Why were thus different conclusions drawn in the case for banning mass gatherings? As already seen, on 13 March 2020 SAGE stated that 'the evidence' on the 'behavioural fatigue' 'is not strong but the effect is intuitive'. Even if the evidence was not strong in the case of banning mass gatherings either, why did not SAGE find their effects 'intuitive' in their case as well? It seems indeed quite intuitive and common sense to expect that transmission would be reduced by avoiding mass gatherings. Despite using two different standards in assessing the available evidence, the decisions of delaying the first lockdown and of allowing mass gatherings likely had a common effect: the likely increase in spreading the virus. Professor Neil Ferguson, an epidemiological modeller member of SAGE, said Members of Parliament that 'had we introduced lockdown a week earlier we'd have reduced the final death toll by at least half' (Ferguson, 2020; Sasse et al., 2020).

This time is different bias

It describes the distorted perception that the current epidemic is completely unprecedented and different from all the previous epidemics. Many expert decision-makers immediately declared that the COVID-19 epidemic could only take everyone unprepared because nothing like that had ever been seen before, since no one, realistically, could remember the Spanish flu a hundred years ago. It is certainly true that every epidemic is unique and peculiar in its own way, and history never repeats itself in exactly the same way. However, governments and international institutions could, and probably should also have learned some lessons by looking at previous experiences, during the Zika virus epidemic in 2015–2016; the Ebola virus outbreak in 2014–2016 in West Africa; the Middle East respiratory syndrome (MERS) virus outbreak in 2015; the H1N1 virus pandemic, or 'swine flu', in 2009–2010; the SARS (severe acute respiratory syndrome) epidemic in 2002; the HIV pandemic in 1976; the H3N2 pandemic, or 'Hong Kong flu', in 1969–1970; the H2N2 virus pandemic, or 'Asian flu', in 1957–1958; and the H1N1 pandemic, or 'Spanish flu', in 1918–1919. One thing they certainly should have learned was how to improve emergency management, for example by preparing health systems and resources to face an epidemic (see the next *planning and coordination hot–cold gap/projection* bias).

Planning and coordination hot–cold gap/projection bias

It describes the distorted attitude where in the moments immediately following an epidemic – and in the wake of the strong emotions evoked by the epidemic itself (*hot*) – the health policy-makers state their objectives to invest more resources and to plan better coordination to face the next epidemic, but such intentions then remain a dead letter with the passage of time and the waning of attention on the past epidemic (*cold*) – until it is rekindled, too late, when the next epidemic starts. This bias is somewhat the equivalent at the level of health policy-makers of the *hot–cold empathy gap*, and the related *projection* bias, in medical decision-making (Loewenstein, 2005a, b). The history of the Global Health Security Agenda (GHSA: https://ghsagenda.org/) is emblematic. The GHSA was activated on the proposal of US president Obama in 2014 in the wake of the Ebola epidemic. The original mission of the GHSA was to expand the range of action of a previous, then dormient, initiative, the Global Health Security Initiative, founded in 2001 by the G7 following the terrorist attacks on the World Trade Center in New York in order to thwart attacks with bacteriological weapons, and since then only functioning on paper. The GHSA was supported by sixty-nine countries and international organisations, including the WHO. Italy got the first mandate for the leadership of its steering group for the five years 2014–2019. The main mission of the GHSA was precisely to coordinate common standards for disease surveillance, diagnostic tests, and the management of emergencies, including those from epidemics of animal origin – such as the coronavirus. In practice, the GHSA should have concretely implemented the international regulations approved by the WHO in 2005 in the wake of the aforementioned SARS epidemic of 2002, but that remained a dead letter since then. Another example concerns the so-called pandemic preparedness plans. In 2009 and 2013 the WHO called on all countries to update and strengthen their pandemic preparedness plans. Nonetheless, in 2017 the European Center for Disease Prevention and Control (ECDC) revealed that Italy's pandemic plan was last updated before 2009. The pandemic plan of the Lombardy region highlighted important gaps even after the H1N1 epidemic of 2010 (Tedeschi, 2020). It is no coincidence that the Italian prime minister stated on 10 June 2020 that 'there was no manual to follow in the crisis, only decisions to be made day by day' (Cuzzocrea, 2020).

There will be a vaccine soon bias

It is a sub-case of both the *silver bullet* bias and the *this time is different* bias, which describe the distorted perception that the present epidemic will be automatically and entirely resolved by a vaccine. Vaccines have clearly worked by massively reducing the infections and deaths by COVID-19, saving estimated 20 million lives globally (Watson et al., 2022). It is a distorted perception because, historically, epidemics have been defeated by coordinated attacks of multiple joint measures, rather than solely and exclusively by a vaccine. For example, if it is true that the H1N1 epidemic was eradicated thanks to the vaccine, it is also true that even before the distribution of the vaccine it was largely controlled by means of antiviral treatments (zanamivir and oseltamivir, or Tamiflu). The MERS and SARS outbreaks were defeated entirely with tracking and isolation measures, while, to date, there are no vaccines against Zika, Ebola, and HIV viruses, for example.

REFERENCES

Abbasi, K. (2020). Behavioural fatigue: A flawed idea central to a flawed pandemic response. *British Medical Journal*, 370, m3093. www.bmj.com/content/370/bmj.m3093

Arrowsmith D., Beck, C., Benning, M., Bianconi, G., Griffin, J., Huang, W., et al. (2020). Public request to take stronger measures of social distancing across the UK with immediate effect, 14 March 2020. https://webspace.maths.qmul .ac.uk/v.nicosia/UK_scientists_statement_on_coronaviru s_measures.pdf.

Association of Directors of Public Health. (2020). Protecting our communities: Pulling together to achieve sustainable suppression of SARS-CoV-2 and limit adverse impacts. Guidance for Directors of Public Health, 11 October.

Bakshi, N., Katoch, D., Sinha, C., Ross, D., Quarmyne, M., Loewenstein, G., & Lakshmanan, K. (2020). Assessment of patient and caregiver attitudes and approaches to decision-making regarding bone marrow transplant for sickle cell disease: A qualitative study. *JAMA Network Open*, 3(5), e206742.

Bakshi, N., Sinha, C. B., Ross, D., Khemani, K., Loewenstein, G., & Krishnamurti, L. (2017). Proponent or collaborative: Physician perspectives and approaches to disease modifying therapies in sickle cell disease. *PLoS ONE*, 12(7), e0178413.

Bosa, I., Castelli, A., Castelli, M., Ciani, O., Compagni, A., Galizzi, M. M., et al. (2021). Corona-regionalism? Differences in regional responses to COVID-19. *Health Policy*, 125(9), 1179–1187.

Bosa, I., Castelli, A., Castelli, M., Ciani, O., Compagni, A., Galizzi, M. M., et al. (2022). Response to Covid-19: Was Italy (un)prepared? *Health Economics, Policy and Law*, 17(1), 1–13.

Casarett, D. (2016). The science of choosing wisely: Overcoming the therapeutic illusion. *The New England Journal of Medicine*, 374, 1203–1205.

Cereda, D., Manica, M., Tirani, M., Rovida, F., Demicheli, V., Ajelli, M., et al. (2021). The early phase of the COVID-19 epidemic in Lombardy, Italy. *Epidemics*, 37, 100528. https://doi.org/10.1016/j.epidem.2021.100528

Chater, N. (2020). People won't get 'tired' of social distancing: The government is wrong to suggest otherwise. *The Guardian*, 16 March. www.theguardian .com/commentisfree/2020/mar/16/social-distancing-coronavirus-stay-home-government

Conn, D. (2020). It was wrong to play against Atletico, says Liverpool's public health director. *The Guardian*, 2 April.

Conn, D., Lawrence, F., Lewis, P., Carrell, S., Pegg, D., Davies, H., & Evans, R. (2020). Revealed: The inside story of the UK's Covid-19 crisis. *The Guardian*, 29 April.

Costello, A. (2020). The UK's Covid-19 strategy dangerously leaves too many questions unanswered. *The Guardian*, 15 March. www.theguardian.com/ commentisfree/2020/mar/15/uk-covid-19-strategy-questions-unanswered-coronavirus-outbreak

Cowling, B. J., Ng, D. M. W, Ip, D. K. M., Liao, Q., Lam, W. W. T., Wu, J. T., et al. (2010). Community psychological and behavioural response through the first wave of the 2009 influenza A (H1N1) pandemic in Hong Kong. *The Journal of Infectious Diseases*, 202(6), 867–876.

Crea, G., Galizzi, M. M., Linnosmaa, I., & Miraldo, M. (2019). Physician altruism and moral hazard: (No) evidence from Finnish prescriptions data. *Journal of Health Economics*, 65, 153–169.

Cuzzocrea, A. (2020). 'Non avevemo il manuale'. Il premier difende le scelte ma teme l'avviso di garanzia. *Repubblica*, 10 June. https://rep.repubblica.it/pwa/generale/2020/06/10/news/ora_il_premier_teme_l_avvis o_ma_difende_tutte_le_scelte_non_avevamo_il_manuale_-258902228/

Devlin, H. (2020). Behavioural scientists form new front in battle against coronavirus. *The Guardian*, 13 March. www.theguardian.com/world/2020/mar/13/behavioural-scientists-form-new-front-in-battle-against-coronavirus

Devlin, H., & Boseley, S. (2020). Coronavirus: The essential guide. What do we know? How should we react? *The Guardian*, 7 March, 12–13.

Dolan, P. (2019). *Happy Ever After*. Penguin.

Easton, M. (2020). Coronavirus: Care home residents should be 'cocooned'. BBC News, 11 March.

Ferguson, N. (2020). Oral evidence to the House of Commons Science and Technology Committee inquiry into UK science, research and technology capability and influence in global disease outbreaks (HC 136). The Stationary Office, Q869.

Fetzer, T. (2022). Subsidizing the spread of COVID-19: Evidence from the UK's Eat-Out-to- Help-Out scheme. *The Economic Journal*, 132(643), 1200–1217.

Freedman, L. (2020). Strategy for a pandemic: The UK and COVID-19. *Survival*, 62(3), 25–76.

Galizzi, M. M., & Ghislandi, S. (2020). Bergamo's response to the coronavirus pandemic. *Cambridge Core blog*. www.cambridge.org/core/blog/2020/04/18/bergamos-response-to-the-coronavirus-pandemic/

Galizzi, M. M., & Wiesen, D. (2018) Behavioural experiments in health. In J. Hamilton, A. Dixit, S. Edwards, and K. Judd (eds.), *Oxford Research Encyclopedia of Economics and Finance*. Oxford, UK: Oxford University Press.

Gigerenzer, G., & Edwards, A. (2003). Simple tools for understanding risks: From innumeracy to insight. *British Medical Journal*, 327, 741–744.

Gigerenzer, G., Gaissmaier, W., Kurz-Milcke, E., Schwartz, L. M., & Woloshin, S. (2007). Helping doctors and patients make sense of health statistics. *Psychological Science in the Public Interest*, 8, 53–96.

Gigerenzer, G., & Gray, J. A. M. (2011). *Better Doctors, Better Patients, Better Decisions: Envisioning Health Care 2020*. Cambridge, MA: MIT Press.

Giuffrida, A. (2020). Bergamo mayor says football match escalated infections in Italian province. *The Guardian*, 24 March.

Greenhalgh, T., McKee, M., & Kelly-Irving, M. (2020). The pursuit of herd immunity is a folly: So who's funding this bad science? *The Guardian*, 18 October. www.theguardian.com/commentisfree/2020/oct/18/covid-herd-immunity-funding-bad-science-anti-lockdown?CMP=Share_iOSApp_Other

Hagger, M. S., Chatzisarantis, N. L. D., Alberts, H., Anggono, C. O., Batailler, C., Birt, A. R., Brand, R., Brandt, M. J., Brewer, G., Bruyneel, S., Calvillo, D. P., Campbell, W. K., Cannon, P. R., Carlucci, M., Carruth, N. P., Cheung, T., Crowell, A., De Ridder, D. T. D., Dewitte, S., ... Zwienenberg, M. (2016). A Multilab Preregistered Replication of the Ego-Depletion Effect. *Perspectives on Psychological Science*, 11(4), 546–573. https://doi.org/10.1177/1745691616652873

Hahn, U., Chater, N., Lagnado, D., Osman, M., & Raihani, N. (2020). Why a group of behavioural scientists penned an open letter to the UK government questioning its coronavirus response. *Behavioural Scientist*, 16 March. https://behaviouralscientist.org/why-a-group-of-behavioural-scientists-penned-an-open-letter-to-the-uk-government-questioning-its-coronavirus-response-covid-19-social-distancing/

Houston, D. J., & Richardson, L. E. (2007). Risk compensation or risk reduction? Seatbelts, state laws, and traffic fatalities. *Social Science Quarterly*, 88(4), 913–936. https://doi.org/10.1111/j.1540-6237.2007.00510.x

Hutton, R. (2020). Keep calm and wash your hands: Britain's strategy to beat virus. *Bloomberg*, 11 March. www.bloomberg.com/news/articles/2020-03-11/keep-calm-and-wash-your-hands-britain-s-strategy-to-beat-virus

Imarisio, M., Ravizza, S., & Sarzanini, F. (2020) Come nasce un'epidemia: la strage di Bergamo, il focolaio più micidiale d'Europa. *Rizzoli Editore*.

Insight. (2020). 48 hours in September when ministers and scientists split over Covid lockdown. *The Sunday Times*, 13 December.

Jarke, H., Ruggeri, K., Graeber, J., Tünte, M. R., Ojinaga-Alfageme, O., Verra, S., et al. (2022). Health Behavior & Decision-Making in Healthcare. In K. Ruggeri (ed.), *Psychology & Behavioural Economics: Applications for Public Policy* (pp. 53–81). Routledge.

Lecconews. (2020). Componenti del comitato tecnico scientifico di regione Lombardia. www.lecconews.news/wp/wp-content/uploads/2020/04/all-decreto-cts.pdf.pdf

Levym, D. T., & Miller, T. (2000). Review: Risk compensation literature – The theory and evidence. *Journal of Crash Prevention and Injury Control*, 2(1). https://doi.org/10.1080/10286580008902554

Liebst, L. S., Ejbye-Ernst, P., de Bruin, M., Thomas, J., & Lindegaard, M. R. (2022). No evidence that mask-wearing in public places elicits risk compensation behavior during the COVID-19 pandemic. *Scientific Reports*, 12(1), 1511.

Loewenstein, G. (2005a). Hot-cold empathy gaps and medical decision-making. *Health Psychology*, 24(4), S49–S56.

Loewenstein, G. (2005b). Projection bias in medical decision-making. *Medical Decision Making*, 25, 96–105.

Loewenstein, G., Schwartz, J., Ericson, K., Kessler, J. B., Bhargava, S., Hagmann, D., et al. (2017). Behavioural insights for health care policy. *Behavioural Science and Policy*, 3(1), 53–66.

Lourenço, S. M., Greenberg, J. O., Littlefield, M., Bates, D. W., & Narayanan, V. G. (2018). The performance effect of feedback in a context of negative incentives: Evidence from a field experiment. *Management Accounting Research*, 40, 1–14.

Lunn, P., Belton, C., Lavin, C., McGowan, F., Timmons, S., & Robertson, D. (2020). Using behavioural science to help fight the coronavirus. *Journal of Behavioral Public Administration*, 3(1), 1–15. https://doi.org/10.30636/jbpa.31.147

MacLellan, K., & Piper, E. (2020). Johnson warns Britons: More loved ones are going to die from coronavirus. Reuters News, 11 March.

Makhanova, A., Miller, S. L., & Maner, J. K. (2015). Germs and the out-group: Chronic and situational disease concerns affect intergroup categorization. *Evolutionary Behavioural Sciences*, 9, 8–19.

Mandavilli, A., & Stolberg, S. G. (2020). A viral theory cited by health officials draws fire from scientists. *New York Times*, 19 October. www.nytimes.com/2020/10/19/health/coronavirus-great-barrington.html

Marcus, J. L., Glidden, D. V., Mayer, K. H., Liu, A. Y., Buchbinder, S. P., Amico, K. R., et al. (2013). No evidence of sexual risk compensation in the iPrEx trial of daily oral HIV preexposure prophylaxis. *PLOS One*, 8(12), e81997.

Marsh, S. (2020). Doctors raise alarm over 'dire' situation in NHS as Covid cases rise. *The Guardian*, 29 December.

Maynard, O., & Munafo', M. R. (2018). Nudging transparent behavioural science and policy. *Behavioural Public Policy*, 2(2), 198–206.

McEvoy, S. (2020). Intensive care consultant says it was 'downright insane' to allow two sell-out Stereophonics concerts to go ahead in front of 15,000 fans in Cardiff less than 10 days before lockdown. Daily Mail Online, 22 April.

McNally, A. (2020). Backers of 'herd immunity' shouldn't have been allowed near Boris Johnson. *The Guardian*, 14 December.

Meyerowitz-Katz, G. (2020). Herd immunity is a fatal strategy we should avoid at all costs. *The Guardian*, 17 April.

Miguel, E., Camerer, C., Casey, K., Cohen, J., Esterling, K. M., Gerber, A., et al. (2014). Promoting transparency in social science research. *Science*, 343(6166), 30–31.

Munafo', M. R., Nosek, B. A., Bishop, D. V. M., Button, K. S., Chambers, C. D., du Sert, N. P., et al. (2017). A manifesto for reproducible science. *Nature Human Behaviour*, 1(0021). https://doi.org/10.1038/s41562-016-0021

Nava F. (2020). *Il focolaio*. Editori Laterza.

Olczak, M., Reade, J. J., & Yeo, M. (2020). Mass outdoor events and the spread of an airborne virus: English football and Covid-19. CEPR Press. COVID Economics 47, 4 September.

O'Toole, F. (2020). Coronavirus has exposed the myth of British exceptionalism. *The Guardian*, 20 April. www.theguardian.com/commentisfree/2020/apr/11/coronavirus-exposed-myth-british-exceptionalism

Sample, I. (2020a). British exceptionalism undermined pandemic preparedness, MPs told. *The Guardian*, 2 December.

Sample, I. (2020b). Surfaces may be less of infection risk than previously thought. *The Guardian*, 5 October, 14–15. www.theguardian.com/politics/2020/dec/02/british-exceptionalism-undermined-pandemic-preparedness-mps-told

Sample, I., & Syal, R. (2020). Chris Whitty Decries Great Barrington Declaration plan to let Covid run wild. *The Guardian*, 3 November. www.theguardian.com/world/2020/nov/03/chris-whitty-decries-great-barrington-plan-to-let-covid-run-wild

Sasse, T., Haddon, C., & Nice, A. (2020). Science advice in a crisis. Institute for Government. 18 December.

Simonsohn, U., Nelson, L. D., & Simmons, J. P. (2014a). P-curve and effect size: Correcting for publication bias using only significant results. *Perspectives on Psychological Science*, 9(6), 666–681.

Simonsohn, U., Nelson, L. D., & Simmons, J. P. (2014b). P-curve: A key to the file drawer. *Journal of Experimental Psychology: General*, 143(2), 534–547.

Stewart, H., & Busby, M. (2020). Coronavirus: Science chief defends UK plan from criticism. *The Guardian*, 13 March. www.theguardian.com/world/2020/mar/13/coronavirus-science-chief-defends-uk-measures-criticism-herd-immunity

Tedeschi, M. (2020). *Il grande flagello: Covid-19 a Bergamo e Brescia*. Scholé Editrice Morcelliana.

UK Government. (2020a). SAGE 13 minutes: Coronavirus (COVID-19) response, 5 March. www.gov.uk

UK Government. (2020b). SAGE 14 minutes: Coronavirus (COVID-19) response, 10 March. www.gov.uk

UK Government. (2020c). SAGE 15 minutes: Coronavirus (COVID-19) response, 13 March. www.gov.uk

Watson, O. J., Barnsley, G., Toor, J., Hogan, A. B., Winskill, P., & Ghani, A. C. (2022). Global impact of the first year of COVID-19 vaccination: A mathematical modelling study. Lancet Infectious Diseases, 23 June. https://doi .org/10.1016/S1473-3099(22)00320-6

Wegwarth, O., & Gigerenzer, G. (2011). Statistical illiteracy in doctors. In G. Gigerenzer and J. A. M. Gray (eds.), *Better Doctors, Better Patients, Better Decisions: Envisioning Health Care 2020* (pp. 137–152). Cambridge, MA: MIT Press.

WHO. (2019). Non-pharmaceutical public health measures for mitigating the risk and impact of epidemic and pandemic influenza. Global influenza programme, October.

WHO. (2020a). Rolling updates on coronavirus disease (COVID-19). 28 February. www.who.int/emergencies/diseases/novel-coronavirus-2019/events-as-they-happen

WHO. (2020b). WHO Director General's opening remarks at the media briefing on COVID- 19. 6 April.

Wood, G., & Carroll, R. (2020). Cheltenham faces criticism after racegoers suffer Covid-19 symptoms. *The Guardian*, 2 April.

Woodcock, A. (2020). Coronavirus: Boris Johnson suggests high coronavirus infection rates are due to UK's 'love of freedom'. *The Independent*, 22 September.

PART II Health Behaviours and Policies during Covid-19

Edited by Joan Costa-Font

14 The Effect of COVID-19 on Health and Health Behaviours

Evidence from Spain

Lydia Prieto and Judit Vall Castelló

14.1 INTRODUCTION

The COVID-19 pandemic has had social and economic impacts of an unprecedented magnitude, changing individuals' health behaviours. This chapter examines the effect of COVID-19 on health status and health behaviours during the pandemic in Spain vis-à-vis the situation before the onset of the virus. Our aim is to provide evidence on the most affected health outcomes to contribute to the policy debate on the design of the most effective policies to overcome the negative impacts of the pandemic. We chose to focus on analysing the effect of COVID-19 in Spain, one of the earliest and most hardly hit countries by the COVID-19 pandemic.[1] At the time of writing this chapter, since the first confirmed case detected on 20 January 2020, almost 9.4 million confirmed cases have been reported in Spain, resulting in over 92,376 deaths.[2] Furthemore, we focus on mental health and health behaviours.

---

[1] Although the Spanish healthcare system is considered one of the best among its neighbours, the fast increase in the number of cases in the first COVID-19 wave challenged the system by putting strong pressure on public hospitals, which were already in a weakened situation due to the reduction in beds and shortage of professionals after a decade of austerity. The congestion of the primary and public hospital care prompted the Spanish government to enact a series of restrictive measures in order to prevent the healthcare system from collapsing. From 14 March to 21 June 2020, the government restricted people's movement (except for essential workers), shut down social and cultural activities, closed the entire school system, and imposed a restrictive lockdown on the Spanish population.

[2] Pàgina recompte casos Covid (WHO), https://covid19.who.int/region/euro/country/es

14.1.1 Mental Health Effects

The effect of COVID-19 on physical health has been extensively documented, but less attention has been put on mental health. Although psycho-emotional harmony is an essential foundation for one's welfare, psychopathologies have received little attention due to social stigma. Fortunately, more and more importance is being given every day thanks to some efforts to highlight the number of people suffering from it. According to the first studies on the psychological effects of lockdown (Wang et al., 2020), there are two factors that exert a strong impact on physical and psychological well-being: the loss of habits and routines and psychosocial stress. To avoid infections, Spain had one of the strictest lockdowns and social distancing measures. This was followed by an increase in anxiety levels about many of the elements associated with COVID-19 (Valiente et al., 2021). Therefore, we can expect an important disruption in health behaviours and mental health among the Spanish population.

14.1.2 Effects on Health Behaviours

Since the pandemic's emergence, there have been significant repercussions on physical, psychological, and behavioral health, according to the literature currently available in a number of high-income countries. The social and cultural peculiarities of the Spanish example, however, might result in some disparate effects. Recent studies have indicated that post-traumatic stress disorder (PTSD), anxiety, and depressive symptoms are all becoming more common (Balluerka et al., 2020; González-Sanguino et al., 2020) and distress (Valiente et al., 2021). Balluerka et al. (2020) show specific anxiety and fear triggers related to the pandemic: a large increase in uncertainty, fear of suffering a severe illness, and fear of losing loved ones.[3] However, despite the potentially high rates of depression and anxiety cases, according to Valiente et al.

---

[3] The feeling of loneliness was the strongest predictor of depression, anxiety, and PTSD (González-Sanguino et al., 2020) together with increased substance use (Valiente et al., 2021). The strongest predictor of distress was, by far, high levels of anxiety about the COVID–19 pandemic (Valiente et al., 2021).

(2021), an analysis of subjective well-being and life satisfaction levels of the Spanish population shows that daily emotional experiences were characterised as being more positive than negative experiences.

The disruption of habits caused by the outbreak of the pandemic and the establishment of new and unhealthy habits can also lead to physical problems (Balluerka et al., 2020), besides the mental effects. Indeed, health behaviours reveal several significant changes in the consumption of potentially addictive substances (like tobacco, cannabis, and alcohol) during lockdown. Along with an increase in the use of video games, television, and social media, there was a significant reduction in physical activity (Balluerka, et al., 2020). Similarly, the pandemic gave rise to an increase in the consumption of high-caloric foods (Balluerka et al., 2020).

14.1.3 Gender Effects

There have been some important heterogeneous effects of the COVID outbreak among genders. For instance, being women were mire likely to exhibit depressive symptoms, anxiety, and PTSD (Ausín et al., 2021; González-Sanguino et al., 2020). The over-stimulation of COVID-19 information is found to be a strong predictor of high levels of anxiety for women (González-Sanguino et al., 2020). Similarly, feelings of loneliness were more common among women (Ausín et al., 2021). Furthermore, the symptomatology for depression, anxiety, and PTSD increased significantly more for women than for men (Ausín et al., 2021). The most plausible explanation that has been put forward to rationalise some of these differential gender impacts is the increase in the care burden at home, which has been mostly assumed by women, as well as the observed increase in domestic violence.

In terms of labour market impacts, it is important to note that the Spanish society was still recovering from the 2008 crisis, which had hit the country very intensively with severe employment losses.[4]

---

[4] More specifically, the unemployment rate reached 27 per cent in the first trimester of 2013 and there was constant closing of businesses during the eighteen months after the beginning of the crisis in Spain; Índice de cifras de negocios empresariales (INE),

Although milder, the COVID-19 crisis also had a large impact on the Spanish economy. In the second quarter of 2020, the unemployment rate in Spain was 16.7 per cent compared to the mean in the European Union of 6.7 per cent (Eurostat, 2023). Macroeconomic indicators can predict changes in the mental health status of the population through the significant correlation of psychological conditions with socio-economic characteristics (Codagnone et al., 2020). Household income, change in earnings, unemployment, household size, and so on, which depend on the economic context, can be predictors of depressive symptoms, anxiety, and PTSD (Codagnone et al., 2020).

This is important because the level of stress generated during the COVID-19 crisis has been proven to be highly correlated with economic vulnerability and exposure to a negative economic shock (Codagnone et al., 2020). Explained in another way, having a positive personal economic situation protected the population in terms of depression, anxiety, and PTSD (González-Sanguino et al., 2020), and gross annual income seems to be the strongest predictor of well-being in pandemic (Valiente et al., 2021). Higher income was related to better health in pandemic, controlling for other factors. Economic threats act as vulnerability factors that affect health and well-being.

In this chapter, we provide evidence and examine the changes in health status and health behaviour in the Spanish context during the current pandemic. We draw on the European Health Survey, which was implemented in Spain during 2019–2020, to identify the changes in health outcomes before and after the pandemic. The health survey consists of a number of questions on health status and health behaviours. More specifically, we focus on self-perceived health status and depressive symptomatology, use of medical resources, tobacco consumption, use of drugs, and consumption of certain foods.

We then look at gender differences in each of the outcomes to see if there are any psychological differences between the two

www.ine.es/dyngs/INEbase/es/operacion.htm?c=Estadistica_C&cid=1254736176958 &menu=ultiDatos&idp=1254735576550

groups. Our ultimate goal is to identify who is more vulnerable and at a higher risk of experiencing mental distress when confronted with this type of extreme event. Overall, our findings indicate that women and younger people are suffering from more severe psychological pathologies than before the COVID-19 outbreak (González-Sanguino et al., 2020; Valiente et al., 2021). The need to study the impact on the most vulnerable groups is critical in order to target high-prevalence subgroups and define more appropriate therapeutic support.

In this chapter we document that *the first months of the pandemic had an important impact on mental health and health behaviours*. Furthermore, we show that the effects of the pandemic were very much gender specific. Finally, we find that the pandemic in Spain led to important changes in the use of medical resources, use of drugs, and daily consumption patterns.

The remainder of the chapter is organised as follows. In Section 14.2, we describe the data used, in Section 14.3 we go through the data and examine the differences between the pre-pandemic and pandemic periods, and in Section 14.4 we provide our conclusion.

14.2 SURVEY EVIDENCE

In this study, we are using two sources of data. First, we exploit the EHIS implemented in Spain in 2019–2020 in order to measure the impact of the outbreak of the pandemic on health and health behaviours of the Spanish population. This survey is run by the Spanish National Statistics Institute (INE) and coordinated by Eurostat. The population scope of the survey is people aged fifteen and over and living in a family dwelling, and the sample size is 22,072 personal interviews distributed in 2,500 census sections. Because of the outbreak of the pandemic, we can compare two periods of the survey: a pre-pandemic period from 15 July 2019 until 14 March 2020 and a pandemic period from 15 March 2020 until 24 July 2020. It is important to note that although the data collection method changed from 17 March 2020 the sample distribution stayed homogeneous through the period in order to ensure the representativeness of the sample in all the periods.

This health survey enables us to analyse different aspects of population health and we focus on the following ones: health status (reported self-assessed health status including mental health) and the use of medical resources and health determinants or habits.

The second data source that we use is the Spanish National Health Survey 2017, which provides the same information as the EHIS 2020 and is also run by the INE. This additional dataset allows us to have another data reference point for the situation in the pre-pandemic period.

14.3   EFFECTS ON HEALTH STATUS

We begin by analysing the results on the health status outcome. More specifically, we focus on a self-assessment measure that captures the individual perceived health status in the last twelve months.

Figure 14.1 shows the evolution in the percentage of people that report having a good health status in the last twelve months.[5] In Figure 14.1 we first notice that both men and women report healthier status during the pandemic: 78.3 per cent of people reported having good health during the pandemic as opposed to 74.3 per cent right before the outbreak of the pandemic. Also, we can see that men have better self-perceived health than women in all periods. We find that 7.5 per cent (7.5 per cent in 2019 and 7.4 per cent in 2020) more men report a good self-assessed health status both before and during the pandemic. Furthermore, this gap does not change as a result of the outbreak of the pandemic.

The pandemic has proven to affect mental health in many ways. In Figures 14.2, 14.3, and 14.4 we can observe the percentage

---

[5] To construct the good self-assessed health variable, we have combined the categories 'very good' and 'good' self-perceived health status reported by individuals for the question 'In the last twelve months, would you say that your state of health has been very good, good, fair, poor, very poor?' in the EHIS 2020. On the other hand, the other categories we find in the survey are 'fair', 'bad', and 'very bad', which we consider as bad self-assessed health status.

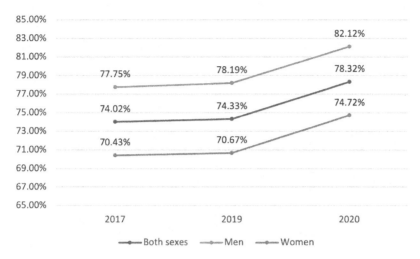

FIGURE 14.1 Percentage of people reporting good self-assessed health status in the last twelve months
Note: The year 2019 contains the observations collected in the pre-pandemic period, and the year 2020 contains observations collected in the pandemic period. To construct the good self-assessed health variable, we have combined the categories 'very good' and 'good' self-perceived health status reported by individuals. On the other hand, the other categories we find in the survey are 'fair', 'bad', and 'very bad', which we consider as bad self-assessed health status.
Sources: The EHIS in Spain 2020 made by the INE and coordinated by Eurostat and the Spanish National Health Survey 2017 made by the INE.

of people who agreed to having some type of depressive symptoms according to the Spanish Personal Health Questionnaire Depression Scale (PHQ-8).[6] From what we can see, women are more likely to report some type of depressive symptom. The more substantial changes for both genders between the pre-pandemic and pandemic period are a decrease of 5 per cent for the category 'Feeling of tiredness', an increase of 3.35 per cent for 'Little interest or joy in doing things', and an increase of 2.8 per cent for 'Feeling down or depressed'.

---

[6] PHQ-8 is an eight-item questionnaire based on the DSMIV (Diagnostic and Statistical Manual of Mental Disorders) criteria for depression, designed to monitor the prevalence of active depressive symptoms and the severity of depressive symptomatology in the population. This is an adaptation of the PHQ-9 scale. The reference period is the last two weeks.

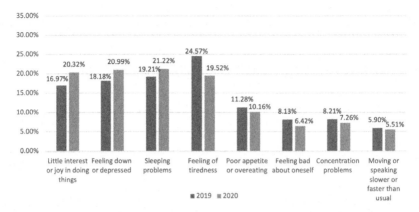

FIGURE 14.2 Percentage of people who agreed to having any type of
depressive symptomatology
Note: The year 2019 contains the observations collected in the pre-
pandemic period, and the year 2020 contains observations collected in
the pandemic period. The categories of the depressive symptomatology
correspond to the Spanish Personal Health Questionnaire Depression
Scale (PHQ-8).
Source: The EHIS in Spain 2020 made by the INE and coordinated by
Eurostat.

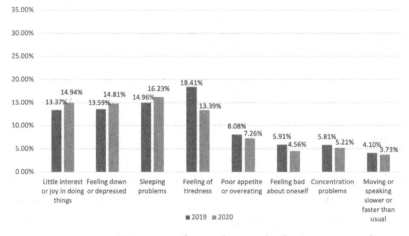

FIGURE 14.3 Percentage of men who agreed to having any type of
depressive symptomatology
Note: The year 2019 contains the observations collected in the pre-
pandemic period, and the year 2020 contains observations collected in
the pandemic period. The categories of the depressive symptomatology
correspond to the Spanish Personal Health Questionnaire Depression
Scale (PHQ-8).
Source: The EHIS in Spain 2020 made by the INE and coordinated by
Eurostat.

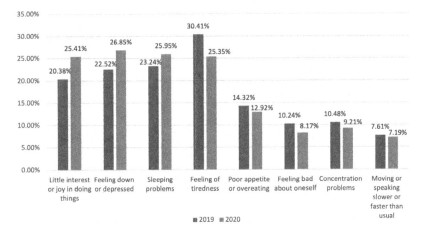

FIGURE 14.4 Percentage of women who agreed to having any type of depressive symptomatology

Note: The year 2019 contains the observations collected in the pre-pandemic period, and the year 2020 contains observations collected in the pandemic period. The categories of the depressive symptomatology correspond to the Spanish Personal Health Questionnaire Depression Scale (PHQ-8).

Source: The EHIS in Spain 2020 was made by the INE and coordinated by Eurostat.

In Figures 14.3 and 14.4 we analyse the results by adding the gender dimension. In the case of men, we find that the major change between periods is a 5 per cent drop in the category 'Feeling of tiredness', followed by a 1.6 per cent increase in the category 'Little interest or joy in doing things' and a 1.35 per cent drop in reporting 'Feeling bad about oneself'. For women, we find a 5 per cent decrease in the category 'Feeling of tiredness', followed by an increase by 5 per cent of 'Little interest or joy in doing things' and a 4.3 per cent increase of 'Feeling down or depressed'.

14.4 BEHAVIOURAL EFFECTS

14.4.1 Healthcare Behaviours

We use visits to the doctor as our main outcome to represent the use of health resources in order to analyse changes in healthcare behaviours. Figure 14.5 shows the percentage of people who visited the family

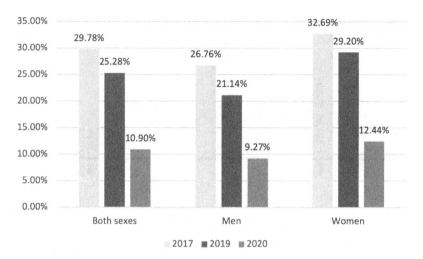

FIGURE 14.5 Percentage of people that visited the family doctor in the last four weeks before the interview
Note: The year 2019 contains the observations collected in the pre-pandemic period, and the year 2020 contains observations collected in the pandemic period.
Sources: The EHIS in Spain 2020 made by the INE and coordinated by Eurostat and the Spanish National Health Survey 2017 made by the INE.

doctor in the four weeks preceding the interview. We discover a much larger drop in visits between the pre-pandemic and pandemic periods than between 2017 and 2019. The percentage decreases from 25 per cent to 10 per cent. In the case of women, the difference between periods is greater. Visits drop by 16.8 per cent for them, a 5 per cent greater drop than for men. A similar pattern is found for specialist care.[7] Indeed, in Figure 14.6 we plot the change in the percentage of people that reported visits to a specialist doctor in the last four weeks

[7] It is important to note that the survey asks for face-to-face consultations, home visits, and telephone consultations. For the outcome 'visits to a specialist doctor' we refer to the question 'When was the last time you consulted a specialist doctor for yourself?' in the EHIS 2020 and we consider people who reported visits to the doctor in the last four weeks. On the other hand, we do not consider people who chose any of the other possible answers: 'between four and twelve weeks', 'twelve weeks or more', 'never'.

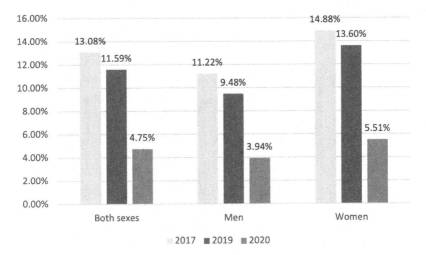

FIGURE 14.6 Percentage of people that visited a specialist doctor in the last four weeks before the interview
Note: The year 2019 contains the observations collected in the pre-pandemic period, and the year 2020 contains observations collected in the pandemic period.
Sources: The EHIS in Spain 2020 made by the INE and coordinated by Eurostat and the Spanish National Health Survey 2017 made by the INE.

before the interview. The percentage changed from 11.6 per cent to 4.75 per cent. The drop in the number of people visiting a specialist doctor in the last four weeks was different by gender. The percentage decreased by 8 per cent for women and by 5.5 per cent for men.

14.4.2 Use of Medication

When examining the behaviour for the consumption of medication between periods, we use the variable that captures drug consumption and we differentiate between prescribed and unprescribed drugs.[8] Figure 14.7 shows the percentage of people that consumed prescribed drugs. While 52.7 per cent of people reported consuming

---

[8] We use the positive answers to the following question of the survey to plot the consumption of prescribed drugs: 'During the last two weeks, have you taken any medication prescribed by a doctor?' For the consumption of unprescribed drugs, we have

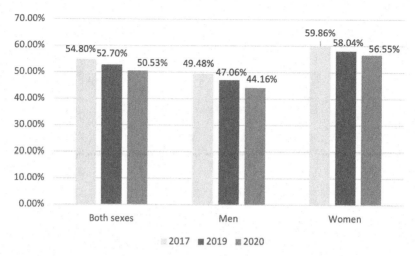

FIGURE 14.7 Percentage of people that consumed prescribed drugs
Note: The year 2019 contains the observations collected in the
pre-pandemic period, and the year 2020 contains observations
collected in the pandemic period.
Sources: The EHIS in Spain 2020 made by the INE and coordinated
by Eurostat and the Spanish National Health Survey 2017 made by
the INE.

prescribed drugs before the pandemic, the consumption reported was
50.5 per cent during the pandemic. We observe a higher consumption
of prescribed drugs for women in all periods. The drop in the percentage of prescribed drug consumption is 3 per cent for men and a half of
it for women, 1.5 per cent.

Figure 14.8 shows the percentage of people that consumed
unprescribed drugs. While 15.6 per cent of people reported consuming unprescribed drugs before the pandemic, the consumption was
12.8 per cent during the pandemic. We observe a higher consumption
of unprescribed drugs for women in all periods. The drop in the percentage of unprescribed drug consumption is 3.7 per cent for men and
a half of it for women, 1.8 per cent.

considered the positive answers to the following question of the EHIS 2020 survey:
'During the last two weeks have you taken any medication, including herbal medicines or vitamins that were not prescribed by a doctor?'

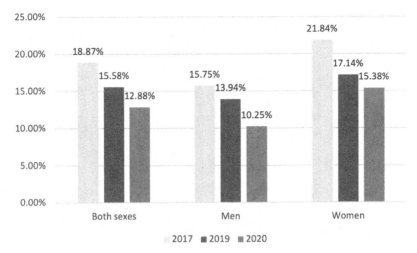

FIGURE 14.8 Percentage of people that consumed unprescribed drugs
Note: The year 2019 contains the observations collected in the
pre-pandemic period, and the year 2020 contains observations
collected in the pandemic period.
Sources: The EHIS in Spain 2020 made by the INE and coordinated
by Eurostat and the Spanish National Health Survey 2017 made by
the INE.

14.4.3   Tobacco Consumption

Figure 14.9 shows the percentage of the population consuming
tobacco,[9] daily and occasionally, before and during the pandemic.
The percentage of smokers remains similar in both periods with a
mild reduction during the pandemic. The decrease goes from 22.5 per
cent to 21.4 per cent. From what we can see in Figure 14.9, a higher
percentage of men are smoking in all periods. Both men and women
diminish the number of daily and occasional consumers by around
1 per cent.

[9] To construct the percentage of people consuming tobacco, we have combined the
categories 'daily smoker' and 'occasional smoker' in the EHIS 2020 question 'Can
you tell me if you smoke? Do not consider e-cigarettes or other similar electronic
devices.' On the other hand, we consider the categories 'do not smoke usually now
but I used to' and 'I do not smoke usually now or never' as people who do not consume tobacco.

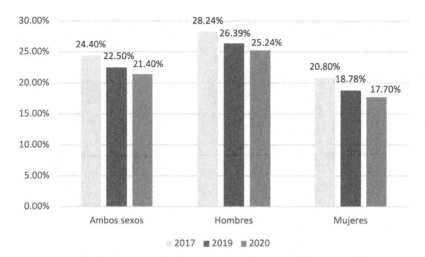

FIGURE 14.9 Percentage of people consuming tobacco
Note: The year 2019 contains the observations collected in the
pre-pandemic period, and the year 2020 contains observations
collected in the pandemic period. To construct the percentage of
people consuming tobacco, we have combined the categories 'daily
smoker' and 'occasional smoker' in reported tobacco consumption
by individuals. On the other hand, we consider the category 'not a
smoker' as people who do not consume tobacco.
Sources: The EHIS in Spain 2020 made by the INE and coordinated by
Eurostat and the Spanish National Health Survey 2017 made by the INE.

14.4.4   Food Consumption

To analyse any change in the consumption pattern of certain food products, we use twelve categories of food products grouped by most, mid,
and least consumed products on a daily basis.[10] In Figures 14.10–14.12

[10] We use the question 'How often do you eat the following foods' in EHIS 2020 and
the answer 'every day' to plot the daily consumption of the twelve categories of food
products of the survey: 'fresh fruit (excluding juices)', 'meat', 'egg', 'fish', 'pasta, rice,
potatoes', 'bread, cereals', 'vegetables, salads, and greens', 'legumes', 'sausages and
cold meats', 'dairy products', 'sweets', 'sugared soft drinks', 'fast food', 'snacks or
savoury finger foods', and 'natural fruit or vegetable juice'. We build the groups for
Figures 14.10–14.12 based on the percentage of people consuming the products on a
daily basis, dividing the whole into the most consumed in Figure 14.10 ('fresh fruit
(excluding juices)', 'bread, cereals', 'vegetables, salads, and greens', 'dairy products',
and 'sweets'), the mid consumed products in Figure 14.11 ('meat', 'pasta, rice, potatoes', 'sausages and cold meats', 'sugared soft drinks', and 'natural fruit or vegetable
juice'), and the least consumed food products in Figure 14.12 ('egg', 'fish', 'legumes',
'fast food', and 'snacks or savoury finger foods').

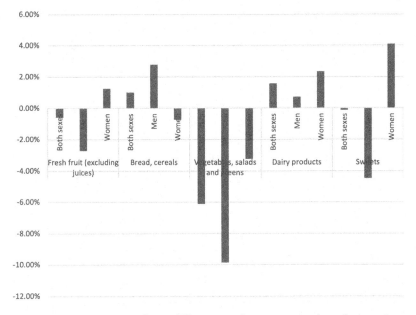

FIGURE 14.10 Relative difference in the percentage of people reporting daily consumption of certain foods before and after the pandemic for the most daily consumed foods
Note: The year 2019 contains the observations collected in the pre-pandemic period, and the year 2020 contains observations collected in the pandemic period.
Source: The EHIS in Spain 2020 was made by the INE and coordinated by Eurostat.

we can see the relative change in the percentage of the population consuming this set of products on a daily basis. Although in absolute terms we find larger percentage changes in meat (decrease of 3.3 per cent), vegetables (decrease of 2.9 per cent), and sugared soft drinks (decrease of 2.6 per cent), if we look at Figures 14.10–14.12, we find the biggest relative changes with respect to prior daily consumption in legumes (55.5 per cent less), fish (50 per cent less), and egg (44.1 per cent less). These drops in daily consumption belong to the group of the least daily consumed products and are bigger in the case of men in all situations.[11] In addition to the least consumed food

---

[11] For legumes, it is 64 per cent men vs 42.4 per cent women, for fish, it is 72.2 per cent men vs 22.7 per cent women, and for egg, it is 50.4 per cent men vs 35.3 per cent women.

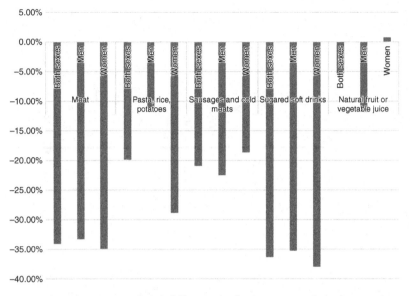

FIGURE 14.11 Relative difference in the percentage of people reporting
daily consumption of certain foods before and after the pandemic for
the mid daily consumed foods
Note: The year 2019 contains the observations collected in the pre-
pandemic period, and the year 2020 contains observations collected in
the pandemic period.
Sources: The EHIS in Spain 2020 was made by the INE and coordinated
by Eurostat.

products, the mid consumed food products decrease in the percentage of daily consumers in all cases, of which the bigger drops are in
soft drinks (36.4 per cent), meat (34 per cent), and sausages and cold
meat (21 per cent).

Concerning the most consumed food products, vegetables, salads, and greens is the group that experienced the biggest drop in daily
consumption, by 6 per cent, and the reduction is larger among men (10
per cent). Overall, all daily consumption decreased except for those
products that remained the same or increased relatively until 1.5 per
cent. The food products that experienced a minor change in daily
consumption are sweets (0.1 per cent less), fresh fruit (0.6 per cent
less), and bread and cereals (1 per cent more).

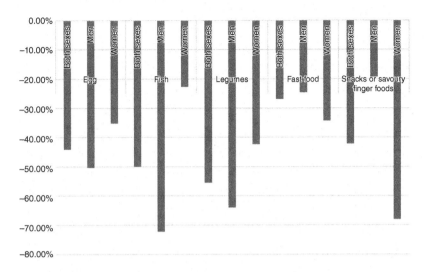

FIGURE 14.12 Relative difference in the percentage of people reporting daily consumption of certain foods before and after the pandemic for the least daily consumed foods
Note: The year 2019 contains the observations collected in the pre-pandemic period, and the year 2020 contains observations collected in the pandemic period.
Source: The EHIS in Spain 2020 was made by the INE and coordinated by Eurostat.

Although there hasn't been much of a shift in daily consumption of sweets, fruit, bread, and cereals, we can still identify a gender difference. For example, daily consumption of sweets decreased by 4.5 per cent for men while it increased by 4.1 per cent for women. If we take into account the gender dimension, the sharpest differences in the change in daily consumption after the COVID-19 outbreak were for fish, where we find a 50-percentual-point reduction in daily consumption among men, and snacks or savoury finger foods, where we find a 49-percentual-point reduction in consumption among women. For the most daily consumed food products, the bigger changes are in sweets and vegetables, salads, and greens, whose consumption decreased by 8.6 per cent and 6.6 per cent, respectively, for men.

14.5   CONCLUSION

This chapter documents significant changes in health status and health behaviour due to the COVID-19 outbreak, which expands on other more specific behavioural interventions discussed in Chapter 10. In terms of changes in health status, we document an improved physical health and mental well-being during the first months of the pandemic, irrespective of gender. Even though women exhibit lower self-perceived well-being across the board, *the gender well-being gap did not widen during the pandemic*, which is consistent with the finding of Valiente et al. (2021).

Both the pandemic and the lockdown gave rise to new habits. With regard to healthcare use, we show that *doctor visits decreased prior to the virus's disruption*. In general, we see a greater decrease in visits to the family doctor, consistent with some level of congestion in the health system, which was focused instead on COVID-19 mitigation. Nonetheless, women do reveal a greater drop in visits to family and specialist doctors. Similarly, medicine consumption reveals some reduction compared to the pre-pandemic period, especially among men.

Finally, this chapter documents that the pandemic and the lockdown *also disrupted a number of health-related behaviours*. This includes the consumption of potentially addictive substances and food consumption (Balluerka et al., 2020). We find a slight reduction in smoking by a decline of daily and occasional smokers.[12] Similarly, we find evidence of a reduction in daily consumption of all food products except for sweets, fresh fruit, and bread and cereals. Salads and greens is the group that experienced the biggest drop in daily consumption. By gender, we find that men consume lesser snacks and savoury finger foods and fish, as well as sweets and vegetables, salads, and greens, the consumption of which decreased by approximately 7 per cent.

---

[12] We cannot observe an increase in the percentage of smokers, but the potential smokers that become non-smokers every year did not quit.

REFERENCES

Ausín, B., González-Sanguino, C., Castellanos, M. Á., & Muñoz, M. (2021). Gender-related differences in the psychological impact of confinement as a consequence of COVID-19 in Spain. *Journal of Gender Studies*, 30(1), 29–38.

Balluerka, N., Gómez, J., Hidalgo, M. D., Gorostiaga, A., Espada, J. P., Padilla, J. L., & Santed, M. Á. (2020). *LAS CONSECUENCIAS PSICOLÓGICAS DE LA COVID-19 Y EL CONFINAMIENTO*. Bilbao: Universidad del País Vasco.

Codagnone, C., Bogliacino, F., Gómez, C., Charris, R., Montealegre, F., Liva, G., et al. (2020). Assessing concerns for the economic consequence of the COVID-19 response and mental health problems associated with economic vulnerability and negative economic shock in Italy, Spain and the United Kingdom. *PLOS ONE*, 15(10), 1–16.

Euroostat (2023). Statistical Office of the European Union. https://ec.europa.eu/eurostat

González-Sanguino, C., Ausín, B., Castellanos, M. Á., Saiz, J., López-Gómez, A., Ugidos, C., & Muñoz, M. (2020). Mental health consequences during the initial stage of the 2020 Coronavirus pandemic (COVID-19) in Spain. *Brain, Behavior, and Immunity*, 87, 172–176.

Valiente, C., Contreras, A., Peinado, V., Trucharte, A., Martínez, A. P., & Vázquez, C. (2021). Psychological adjustment in Spain during the COVID-19 Pandemic: Positive and negative mental health outcomes in the general population. *The Spanish Journal of Psychology*, 24, 1–13.

Wang, C., Pan, R., Wan, X., Tan, Y., Xu, L., Ho, C. S., & Ho, R. C. (2020). Immediate psychological responses and associated factors during the initial stage of the 2019 Coronavirus disease (COVID-19) epidemic among the general population in China. *Journal of Environmental Research and Public Health*, 17(5), 17–29.

15 Mental Health and Health Behaviours among Vulnerable Populations during the COVID-19 Pandemic in the United States

Daniel Banko-Ferran, Rania Gihleb, and Osea Giuntella

15.1 INTRODUCTION

According to the 2020 US Census Household Pulse Survey, four in ten adults in the United States reported symptoms of anxiety and depression disorders during COVID-19, a four-fold increase with respect to pre-pandemic levels (see Zablotsky et al., 2023). Polls and previous studies (Panchal et al., 2020) suggest that the pandemic increased difficulty in sleeping and eating, as well as alcohol consumption and substance use, and worsened chronic conditions. The necessary public health measures adopted to contain the spread of the virus increased isolation and economic uncertainty. The disruptions of routines impacted individuals' time allocation across activities, and their inability to interact with others posed significant implications for their well-being (Giuntella et al., 2021; Proto & Zhang, 2021).

In this chapter, we review the evidence on the effects of the COVID-19 pandemic on health behaviours and explore observational data on mental health, anxiety medications, and time use. We focus on the most vulnerable populations: young adults, parents and children, essential workers, and minorities. First, we explore the heterogeneity in the impact of COVID-19 on mental health and then examine more closely the impact on time use with a specific focus on health behaviours (exercise, sleeping, eating habits) and personal care.

15.2 COVID-19 AND MENTAL HEALTH

15.2.1 Heterogeneity by Age: Young Adults a Vulnerable Population

While even before the pandemic young adults were one of the most vulnerable populations for mental health problems, the closure of campuses and the economic uncertainty during the pandemic further accentuated pressure and anxiety in this demographic group. More than half of individuals aged eighteen to twenty-four reported symptoms of anxiety and/or depression during the pandemic. Young adults were more likely than the rest of the adult population to report substance use and suicidal thoughts. The closure of campuses and the transition to remote learning and remote work had significantly larger effects on young adults. According to the 2020 Household Pulse Survey 56.2 per cent of individuals aged eighteen to twenty-four reported symptoms of depression, while this number was less than 40 per cent among adults aged fifty to sixty-four and lower than 30 per cent among elderly individuals (over sixty-five years old). Survey data suggests that a fourth of young adults reported starting or increasing substance use during the pandemic and 26 per cent reported serious thoughts of suicide (Czeisler et al., 2020). The numbers were significantly lower (13 per cent and 11 per cent) among all adults.

Giuntella et al. (2021) documented large disruptions to physical activity, sleep, time use, and mental health among young adults at the onset of the pandemic in spring 2020. Using a longitudinal dataset linking biometric and survey data before and during the COVID-19 pandemic, they showed that average steps declined by more than 50 per cent and risk of reporting depression symptoms increased by 90 per cent with respect to pre-pandemic levels. Barbieri et al. (2021) explored the trends one year later. Despite the vaccine roll-out and the ease of social distancing measures, there was a persistent impact of the pandemic on both physical activity and mental health. Steps were still 35 per cent lower than at the peak of the pandemic. And approximately half of the participants reported depression symptoms, a 36 per cent increase compared to the pandemic.

We examine the heterogeneity in the impact of COVID-19 on the mental health of individuals in different age groups. We used data from the National Health Interview Survey, which in both 2019 and 2020 had questions on diagnosed depression and anxiety. Figure 15.1 documents how young adults (aged eighteen to twenty-four) suffered the highest increase in the use of medication for depression symptoms (+25 per cent). While we observe an increase in all other groups, the changes are less dramatic among older cohorts. This group also experienced a larger increase in diagnosed anxiety (+16 per cent, Figure 15.2) and in the likelihood of taking medicine for anxious feelings (+23 per cent, Figure 15.3).

Our findings are therefore consistent with previous evidence highlighting the high costs that COVID-19 and the corresponding public health interventions had on young adults. Interestingly,

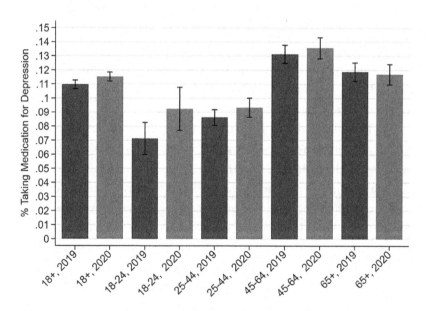

FIGURE 15.1 Use of medication for depression symptoms among adults (18+) and young adults (18–24) before (in 2019) and during (in 2020) the first COVID-19 wave
Source: National Health Interview Survey 2019–2020.

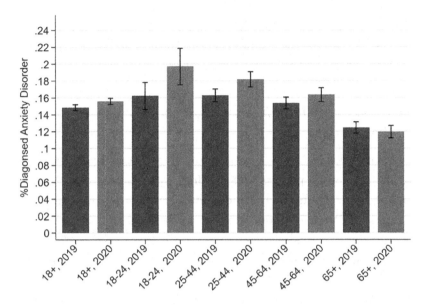

FIGURE 15.2 Diagnosed anxiety among adults (18+) and young adults (18–24) before (in 2019) and during (in 2020) the first COVID-19 wave
Source: National Health Interview Survey 2019–2020.

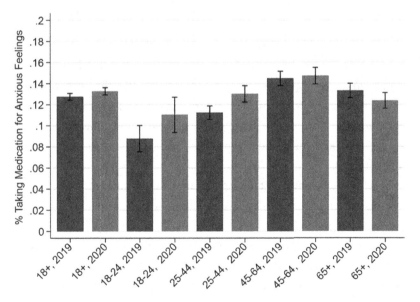

FIGURE 15.3 Proportion of people taking medicines for anxious feelings among adults (18+) and young adults (18–24) before (in 2019) and during (in 2020) the first COVID-19 wave
Source: National Health Interview Survey 2019–2020.

despite their higher risk of contracting COVID-19, when examining changes in medications for depression and anxiety we do not observe much of an effect among those over sixty-five (if anything, there is a decline).

15.2.2   Parents and Children: The Pandemic Burden on Women

As many schools closed across the country to contain the spread of the pandemic, parents and children experienced large disruptions to their habits and routines. Several studies documented how parents and their children experienced worsening mental health (Calear et al., 2022; Makridis et al., 2022; Stark et al., 2020) and how these effects were particularly severe for mothers' mental health (Thapa et al., 2020).

Women were significantly more likely than men to report symptoms of anxiety and depression. Household responsibilities and burnout contributed to higher quit rates and a marked decline in working hours in this population. Figure 15.4 documents the increase in the share of women reporting the use of medication for depression in 2020. Although even before the pandemic women were twice as likely as men to report taking any medication for depression, the gap increased in 2020, with the share of women using medication for depression increasing from 14 per cent to 15.5 per cent, while there was little change among men. The differences are less marked for anxiety when looking at the entire population (Figure 15.5).

However, when restricting the analysis to individuals in child-rearing age (eighteen to forty-five), there is a clear gap arising between men and women in 2020 (see Figure 15.6). These results are consistent with evidence from the Kaiser Family Foundation Health Tracking Pools documenting that mothers were more likely than fathers to report negative mental health impacts (49 per cent vs 40 per cent). Time spent on secondary childcare increased by more than an hour a day with parents juggling multiple tasks.

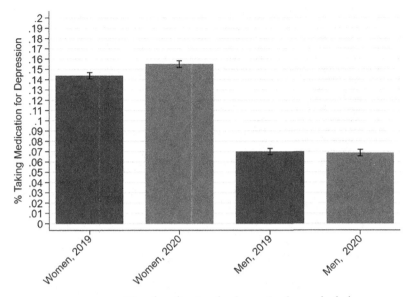

FIGURE 15.4 Use of medication for depression by gender before (in 2019) and during (in 2020) the first COVID-19 wave
Source: National Health Interview Survey 2019–2020.

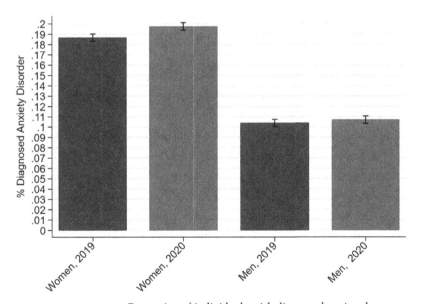

FIGURE 15.5 Proportion of individuals with diagnosed anxiety by gender before (in 2019) and during (in 2020) the first COVID-19 wave
Source: National Health Interview Survey 2019–2020.

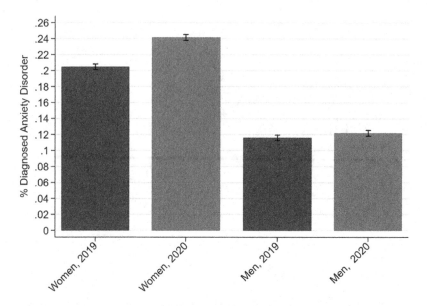

FIGURE 15.6 Proportion of individuals with diagnosed anxiety by gender among individuals of child-rearing age (18–45) before (in 2019) and during (in 2020) the first COVID-19 wave
Source: National Health Interview Survey 2019–2020.

15.2.3 Minorities

The impact of the pandemic on mental health was more pronounced among minorities. Black and Hispanic adults were significantly more likely to report symptoms of anxiety and/or depressive disorders. These groups were more exposed to COVID-19, experienced more cases and deaths, and were more exposed to the financial impact of the COVID-19 recession. Furthermore, Black parents suffered the impact of school and day-care closures more as they struggled to find care for their children. These effects were more pronounced among minorities without social ties, trust, and identity in the community (see Chapter 18).

Despite comprising only 13 per cent of the population, African Americans represented 21.8 per cent of cases in the United States in June 2020 according to the Centers for Disease Control and Prevention. In the United States, COVID-19 killed African Americans, Native Americans, and Latin Americans at higher rates than other races (Tai et al., 2021).

This is partly attributed to higher health risks before the pandemic as well as decreased ability to work from home: only 20 per cent of African Americans could work from home compared to 30 per cent for whites in March 2020, according to the Bureau of Labor Statistics.

A Eurofound survey entitled 'Living, working and COVID-19' found that racial/ethnic minorities were over-represented in non-teleworking jobs. As a result, racial/ethnic minorities reported more job insecurity, lower overall health, and lower mental well-being during the crisis. In Canada, the United States, and the United Kingdom, racial/ethnic minorities were particularly vulnerable to volatile labour market conditions. These challenges were exacerbated by lack of social networks and discrimination (less data was available in other Organisation for Economic Co-operation and Development countries).

Notably, when it comes to gender and minority groups, the pandemic impacted the mental health of minority men but not white men, while women of all ethnic and racial groups experienced lower mental health. Black and Asian men (and women of all ethnicities) experienced higher average increases in mental distress than white British men in the UK Household Longitudinal study, even after controlling for demographic and socio-economic characteristics (Proto & Quintana-Domeque, 2021). This suggests that the differential impact by ethnicity might be driven by the higher risk of infection, unemployment, income loss, and financial insecurity that minority individuals experienced, which may have impacted minority men more than white men. Individuals belonging to minorities were also more likely to be younger and live in larger households. Despite being healthier and having lower COVID morbidity rates, younger people's mental health deteriorated more due to loss of social activity (Banks & Xu, 2020). Thus, the inequalities in mental health between minority and white populations worldwide increased during the pandemic.

Interestingly, when examining National Health Interview Survey data on medication for mental health and anxiety, we find no evidence of significant differences between 2019 and 2020 among African Americans and Hispanics (Figure 15.7). However, both groups

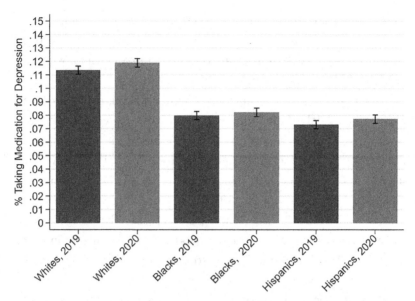

FIGURE 15.7 Use of medication for depression symptoms by ethnicity
before (in 2019) and during (in 2020) the first COVID-19 wave
Source: National Health Interview Survey 2019–2020.

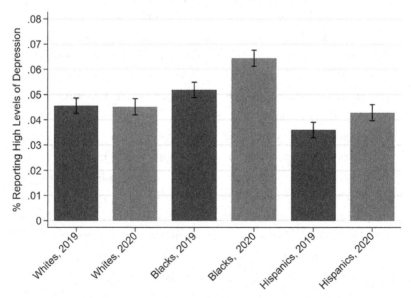

FIGURE 15.8 Proportion of higher levels of depression by ethnicity
before (in 2019) and during (in 2020) the first COVID-19 wave
Source: National Health Interview Survey 2019–2020.

were more likely to report high levels of depression during the pandemic (Figure 15.8). These findings suggest that minorities may have also had worse access to mental health services during the pandemic or may have faced significant stigma.

15.2.4 Essential Workers

Workers deemed 'essential' and who worked outside of the home during the pandemic suffered the largest impact to their mental health among all groups. During the pandemic, essential workers reported higher rates of anxiety or depressive disorder (42 per cent vs 30 per cent), substance abuse (25 per cent vs 11 per cent), and suicidal thoughts (22 per cent vs 8 per cent), according to a Kaiser Family Foundation report. About one third of US workers were deemed essential. Essential workers were more likely to be Black, have lower household income, and not hold a college degree; they often were healthcare workers or made up the indispensable non-healthcare workforce such as first responders, transport workers, retail workers, and hospitality staff. Correlations between the pandemic and higher levels of stress, anxiety, and depression among essential workers have been documented in Chapters 14 and 16 in this book.

Healthcare workers were hit particularly hard early in the pandemic. Figure 15.9 suggests that they were more likely to be diagnosed with and treated for a mental health condition. Their mental health decreased significantly more than for workers in non-health fields, leading to greater rates of depression and suicide. Healthcare workers were more likely to suffer from moral injury or the psychological distress resulting from the inability to help COVID-19 patients due to inadequate staff and resources. They had to care for colleagues who were ill, putting more work on themselves while offering comfort to dying patients who were isolated from loved ones and consoling patients' family members remotely. One need not look further for evidence of this disparate toll than the tragic case of Dr Lorna M. Breen, who died by suicide in April 2020 during the initial phase of the pandemic.

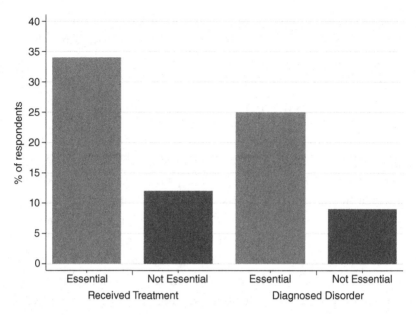

FIGURE 15.9 Diagnosis and treatment of mental disorders: differences between essential and non-essential workers
Source: APA Stress in America Survey (March 2021).

Healthcare workers working on the front lines of the pandemic experienced higher rates of mental health issues, anxiety, depression, and insomnia and were more likely to abuse alcohol when compared to non-frontline-line health workers.

Healthcare workers expressed the greatest concern for contracting COVID-19 and spreading it to loved one, but it was not just the health concerns related to the virus that contributed to the mental deterioration of these workers: financial stress also increased during this time due to larger exposure to pay cuts. Essential workers reported having more difficulty paying bills and were more likely to be 'very worried' or 'somewhat worried' about affording food (24 per cent vs 12 per cent) during the pandemic. They also reported more job insecurity according to data from a Eurofound survey (12 per cent vs 7 per cent). The physical activity of healthcare workers also decreased substantially during the pandemic.

Most healthcare workers reported a reduction in the frequency and duration of their physical exercise.

Parental status amplified the effect of COVID-19 on essential workers. Essential workers with children were affected by school closures, leading to trade-offs between decreased labour force participation and responsibility for childcare at home.

Many studies documented these effects on essential workers occurring worldwide (see, for instance, Quintana et al., 2021). Spain had one of the largest rates of COVID-19 infection among healthcare workers, resulting in higher reported symptoms of acute stress, anxiety, and depression. Healthcare workers in the United Kingdom during the first year of the pandemic also reported spikes in poor mental health.

15.3 COVID-19 AND TIME USE

The pandemic disrupted our routines and radically affected our daily use of time. We explored data from the American Time Use Survey to examine the heterogenous effects of COVID-19 on time use. We focus in particular on time spent on activities that have direct effects on our health (i.e., sleeping, exercising, and eating or preparing food). An important caveat to this analysis is that the Labor Department interrupted the survey data collection in mid-March 2020 because of the pandemic and did not resume it until mid-May. Thus, the data does not include the period where severe lockdowns took place. For this reason, some of the effects may not be directly comparable to previous studies that documented changes in time use at the peak of the first COVID-19 wave.

Interestingly, and consistent with previous evidence (Giuntella et al., 2021), we show that, if anything, sleep duration increased during the pandemic, with a decline in the share of individuals reporting to sleep less than seven hours across all age groups (see Figure 15.10). We also find no evidence of significant heterogeneity in the way the pandemic affected sleep across race and ethnicity (results available upon request).

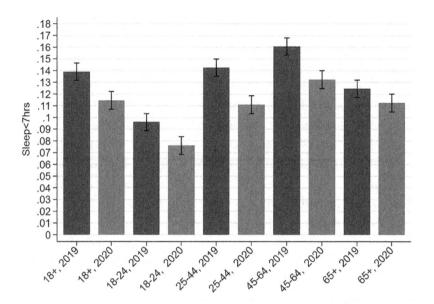

FIGURE 15.10 Share of individuals sleeping less than 7 hours among adults (18+) and young adults (18–24) before (in 2019) and during (in 2020) the first COVID-19 wave
Source: Data drawn from the 2019–2020 American Time Use Survey.

The increase in sleep likely reflects the reduction in schedule constraints associated with remote work and the lack of night entertainment and social events because of the COVID-19 restrictions. On average individuals slept nine minutes longer during the pandemic compared to 2019. As displayed in Figure 15.11, when exploring time spent working out, we found that individuals were generally more likely to engage in at least twenty minutes of physical activity.

Although this result is at odds with Giuntella et al. (2021), who found a substantial decline in physical activity during term among college students, it is consistent with what was found in other studies (i.e., Ding et al., 2020; Yamada et al., 2020) that document an increase in exercise during COVID-19 when examining the general population.[1] We also find an increase in screen time across all age

[1] See also www.nytimes.com/2020/10/07/well/move/pandemic-exercise-habits-study.html

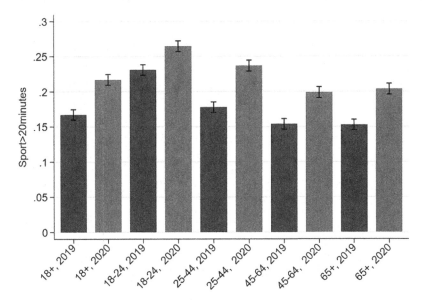

FIGURE 15.11 Share of individuals engaging in at least 20 minutes of physical activity before (in 2019) and during (in 2020) the first COVID-19 wave
Source: Data drawn from the 2019–2020 American Time Use Survey.

groups (Figure 15.12). Among the eighteen- to twenty-four-year-olds, we observe a 15 per cent increase in time spent communicating on the Internet, using their phones, or watching TV, to approximately twenty-five minutes in 2020. We observe instead a decline in time spent grooming (Figure 15.13).

The evidence on how COVID-19 impacted weight-related lifestyle is mixed. A study on a population of UK adults (Robinson et al., 2021) shows that during April–May of the 2020 COVID-19 social lockdown they experienced barriers to weight management and negative changes to eating habits (with 56 per cent reporting snacking more frequently). Similarly, Park et al. (2022) showed evidence that changes in eating habits were common during the pandemic with adults consuming more unhealthy snacks and drinking more sugar-sweetened beverages. At the same time, Di Renzo et al. (2020) used survey data from Italy and found evidence of higher adherence to a

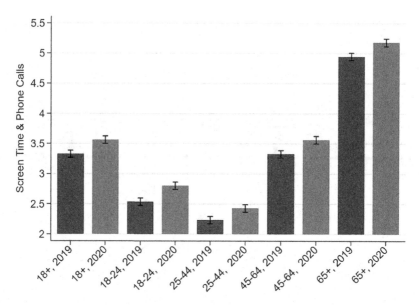

FIGURE 15.12 Screen time across age groups before (in 2019) and during (in 2020) the first COVID-19 wave
Source: Data drawn from the 2019–2020 American Time Use Survey.

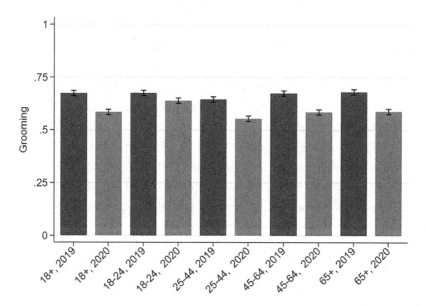

FIGURE 15.13 Time spent grooming across age groups before (in 2019) and during (in 2020) the first COVID-19 wave
Source: Data drawn from the 2019–2020 American Time Use Survey.

Mediterranean diet among young adults. These results suggest that the effects of the pandemic may have been context-specific and depend on both the healthiness of local diets and the strictness of lockdown and remote work policies, which may have increased time spent cooking and preparing food.

An American Psychological Association survey of US adults in 2021 found that 61 per cent of them experienced undesired changes in their weight. Longitudinal data on 269 participants in a study conducted by the University of California, San Francisco (Lin et al., 2021), found an average weight gain of 0.6 pounds every ten days after governments issued shelter-in-place orders in the first wave of the COVID-19 pandemic (19 March to 6 April 2020). A 2021 Gallup poll suggests that 36 per cent of Americans gained weight during the pandemic. However, when using data from Cosmos, a Health Insurance Portability and Accountability Act limited data set of more than

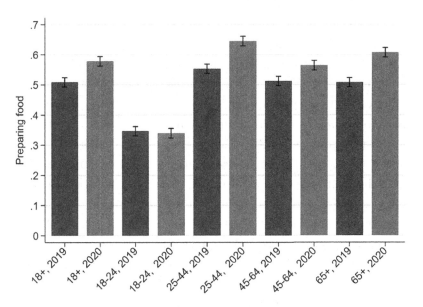

FIGURE 15.14 Time spent on food preparation across age groups before (in 2019) and during (in 2020) the first COVID-19 wave
Source: Data drawn from the 2019–2020 American Time Use Survey.

nineteen million patient records stored by Epic System, the Epic Research team found little evidence of a change in the weight gain trend compared to previous years. While 39 per cent of people in the sample gained weight, 35 per cent of people lost weight. This is also potentially consistent with the idea that the pandemic may have had different effects on people with different personalities and pre-pandemic habits (see Giuntella et al., 2021; Proto & Zhang, 2021).

As displayed in Figure 15.14, time-use data for the United States reveal that individuals spent significantly more time cooking, although the average effect is less than ten minutes per day, and if anything, it declined among the eighteen- to twenty-four-year-olds. Generally, individuals spent more time eating, although again among young adults if anything there was a decline in the time spent eating, which may also be consistent with increased snacking as found in other studies.

15.4   CONCLUSIONS

In this chapter, we documented how vulnerable populations were more exposed to the negative impact of COVID-19 and the necessary public health measures implemented to mitigate its spread. There is growing concern that the mental impact of COVID-19, as seen for other disasters, may outlast its physical impact. Our evidence suggests that it will be crucial to support and facilitate access to mental health services even as the number of cases and deaths associated with COVID-19 declines. It also highlights the need for intervention aimed at reaching communities that may have worse access to or face more barriers to mental care services. At the same time, we found mixed evidence when analysing the effect of the COVID-19 pandemic on time use and health behaviours. If anything, sleep duration increased during the pandemic, while there is no clear evidence of an effect of the pandemic on healthy eating and weight gain, and the current evidence on the impact of COVID-19 on physical activity is also mixed and heterogeneous across different samples of the population.

REFERENCES

Banks, J., & Xu, X. (2020). The mental health effects of the first two months of lockdown during the COVID-19 pandemic in the UK. *Fiscal Studies*, 41(3), 685–708.

Barbieri, P. N., Giuntella, O., Saccardo, S., & Sadoff, S. (2021). Lifestyle and mental health 1 year into COVID-19. *Scientific Reports*, 11(1), 1–6.

Calear, A. L., McCallum, S., Morse, A. R., Banfield, M., Gulliver, A., Cherbuin, N., et al. (2022). Psychosocial impacts of home-schooling on parents and caregivers during the COVID-19 pandemic. *BMC Public Health*, 22(1), 1–8.

Czeisler, M. É., Lane, R. I., Petrosky, E., Wiley, J. F., Christensen, A., Njai, R., et al. (2020). Mental health, substance use, and suicidal ideation during the COVID-19 pandemic – United States, June 24–30, 2020. *Morbidity and Mortality Weekly Report*, 69(32), 1049–1057.

Ding, D., Del Pozo Cruz, B., Green, M. A., & Bauman, A. E. (2020). Is the COVID-19 lockdown nudging people to be more active: A big data analysis. *British Journal of Sports Medicine*, 54(20), 1183–1184.

Di Renzo, L., Gualtieri, P., Pivari, F., Soldati, L., Attinà, A., Cinelli, G., et al. (2020). Eating habits and lifestyle changes during COVID-19 lockdown: An Italian survey. *Journal of Translational Medicine*, 18(1), 1–15.

Giuntella, O., Hyde, K., Saccardo, S., & Sadoff, S. (2021). Lifestyle and mental health disruptions during COVID-19. *Proceedings of the National Academy of Sciences*, 118(9), e2016632118.

Lin, A. L., Vittinghoff, E., Olgin, J. E., Pletcher, M. J., & Marcus, G. M. (2021). Body weight changes during pandemic-related shelter-in-place in a longitudinal cohort study. *JAMA Network Open*, 4(3), e212536–e212536.

Makridis, C., Piano, C., & DeAngelis, C. (2022). The effects of school closures on homeschooling and mental health: Evidence from the Covid-19 pandemic. *Social Science Research Network*. https://ssrn.com/abstract=4001953 or https://dx.doi.org/10.2139/ssrn.4001953

Park, S., Lee, S. H., Yaroch, A. L., & Blanck, H. M. (2022). Reported changes in eating habits related to less healthy foods and beverages during the COVID-19 pandemic among US adults. *Nutrients*, 14(3), 526.

Proto, E., & Zhang, A. (2021). COVID-19 and mental health of individuals with different personalities. *Proceedings of the National Academy of Sciences*, 118(37), e2109282118.

Quintana-Domeque, C., Lee, I., Zhang, A., Proto, E., Battisti, M., & Ho, A. (2021). Anxiety and depression among medical doctors in Catalonia, Italy, and the UK during the COVID-19 pandemic. *PloS One*, 16(11), e0259213.

Robinson, E., Boyland, E., Chisholm, A., Harrold, J., Maloney, N. G., Marty, L., et al. (2021). Obesity, eating behavior and physical activity during COVID-19 lockdown: A study of UK adults. *Appetite*, 156, 104853.

Stark, A. M., White, A. E., Rotter, N. S., & Basu, A. (2020). Shifting from survival to supporting resilience in children and families in the COVID-19 pandemic: Lessons for informing US mental health priorities. *Psychological Trauma: Theory, Research, Practice, and Policy*, 12(S1), S133–S135.

Tai, D. B. G., Shah, A., Doubeni, C. A., Sia, I. G., & Wieland, M. L. (2021). The disproportionate impact of COVID-19 on racial and ethnic minorities in the United States. *Clinical infectious diseases*, 72(4), 703–706.

Thapa, S. B., Mainali, A., Schwank, S. E., & Acharya, G. (2020). Maternal mental health in the time of the COVID-19 pandemic. *Acta Obstetricia et Gynecologica Scandinavica*, 99(7), 817–818.

Yamada, M., Kimura, Y., Ishiyama, D., Otobe, Y., Suzuki, M., Koyama, S., et al. (2020). Recovery of physical activity among older Japanese adults since the first wave of the COVID-19 pandemic. *The Journal of Nutrition, Health & Aging*, 24(9), 1036–1037.

Zablotsky, B., Lessem, S. E., Gindi, R. M., Maitland, A. K., Dahlhamer, J. M., & Blumberg, S. J. (2023). Overview of the 2019 national health interview survey questionnaire redesign. *American Journal of Public Health*, 113(4), 408–415.

16 Mental Health Interventions during the COVID-19 Pandemic

The 'Welcomed Lockdown' Hypothesis

Joan Costa-Font and Cristina Vilaplana-Prieto

16.1 INTRODUCTION

Pandemics can exert important detrimental effects on individuals' mental well-being, as the risk of contagion can trigger anxiety concerns and depressive symptoms. However, these effects are only partly the direct result of the risk of exposure to COVID-19 and are also because of the stringency of policy interventions. Indeed, COVID-19 has uniquely disrupted the well-being of individuals. First, unlike previous epidemics, it spread at an unprecedentedly rapid pace, especially in European countries, which had barely a few weeks to react. Individuals could not learn from previous pandemics as they were localised overseas, mostly in East Asian countries. Second, policy measures that have been put in place to fight COVID-19 have been heterogeneous across European countries which makes it an ideal setting to undertake empirical analysis of the effect of different policy stringency measures on well-being. Furthermore, individuals might exhibit information overload, as during the period of the COVID-19 pandemic infection numbers were recorded and communicated on a daily basis to the general population, especially when outbreaks occurred.

Previous studies have documented the detrimental mental health effects of COVID-19 and policy restrictions. Banks and Xu (2020) document a reduction of mental well-being among those who had a mental disorder prior to COVID-19, while other studies have explored the effects of lockdown, finding a rise in mental distress compared to pre-pandemic levels (Sibley et al., 2020). However, most studies are country-specific and do not explore the different effect of risk exposure combined with policy restrictions, which is what we discuss in this chapter. We attempt to add to this discussion.

This chapter discusses the 'welcomed lockdown' hypothesis (Costa-Font et al., 2022), namely the extent to which there is a level of risk where mobility restrictions are not a hindrance to well-being. That is, we examine the well-being effects of mobility restrictions resulting from COVID-19, controlling for risk exposure (proxied by COVID-19 fatality rate). We suggest that in an environment of high mortality lockdowns no longer lead to a reduction in well-being, consistent with the 'welcome lockdown' hypothesis.

16.2   RELATED LITERATURE

16.2.1   Previous Pandemics

Evidence from several pandemics and epidemics across the world suggests clear evidence of impacts on mental health, which in some cases are long-lasting. Maunder (2009) documents the effects of lockdown for severe acute respiratory syndrome, Pfefferbaum et al. (2012) for H1N1 flu, and Choi et al. (2016) for Middle East respiratory syndrome. Some evidence implies that lockdown gives rise to feelings of boredom, frustration, and isolation from the rest of the world (Blendon et al., 2004).[1]

16.2.2   Lockdown Due to Covid-19 Outbreak

The evidence discussed in previous chapter suggesting mental health effects of COVID-19 is widely heterogenous. Brooks et al. (2020) concluded that most of the studies reviewed reported negative psychological effects, such as post-traumatic stress, confusion, and anger. Using Google Trends data for Europe and the United States, Brodeur et al. (2020) found a substantial increase in search intensity for boredom, loneliness, worry, and sadness, although searches for stress, suicide, and divorce had decreased. Adams-Prassl et al. (2020) compared US

---

[1] Such effects result in part from difficulties in obtaining supplies, problems in receiving medical treatment, or other reasons not related to the health emergency (Wilken et al., 2017).

states that had established strict confinement with those that had not, finding a slight worsening of mental health indicators in the former.

In the United Kingdom, Pierce et al. (2020) observed that mental distress increased after one month of lockdown. In New Zealand, Sibley et al. (2020) explored the immediate effects of confinement by comparing samples of participants assessed before and during the first eighteen days of lockdown, finding that people in the pandemic lockdown group reported higher rates of mental distress compared to people in the pre-pandemic group before lockdown.

Nonetheless, some studies document no worsening of mental health. Bu et al. (2020) reported no change in levels of loneliness during the strictest confinement in the United Kingdom. Similarly, Luchetti et al. (2020) observed no significant changes in the average loneliness across three mental health assessments that took place from January to April. Finally, Foa et al. (2020) found that the negative effects associated with the outbreak of the pandemic were concentrated in the period before lockdown. Once confinement took effect, feelings of sadness, stress, and fear declined, whereas happiness, optimism, and contentment increased. Fancourt et al. (2020) reported a decrease in anxiety and depression levels over the first twenty weeks after the introduction of the confinement in England. Their data suggests that the highest levels of depression and anxiety occur in the early stages of lockdown but decrease fairly rapidly as individuals adapt to the circumstances.

16.3 DATA AND MEASUREMENT

As in Costa-Font et al. (2022) we exploit data from a survey launched online through the website https://COVID19-survey.org/ (Fetzer et al., 2020). The questionnaire was translated into sixty-nine languages. The first call of the online survey was published via social media on 20 March 2020, through the accounts of people connected to traditional media (journalists, TV presenters) along with social media influencers, international and national non-governmental organisations, and university networks. In the period between 20 March and 6 April, 103,153 questionnaires were collected from 178 countries.

We focus on 22 European countries,[2] which results in a final sample containing 48,434 observations, because at the time of the survey, the pandemic was hitting the European continent harder than the Americas (250,516 confirmed cases in Europe vs 60,834 in America; 11,986 deaths in Europe vs 813 in America; WHO, 2020). Moreover, the countries had reasonably similar healthcare systems, at least when compared with the rest of the world. To control for differences in age, gender, education, and income between survey respondents and the general population in each country, we use weights in the descriptive statistics and estimations.

We examine the effect of lockdowns on a commonly employed Depression Index obtained from eight questions of the Patient Health Questionnaire (PHQ-9) that were included in the survey questionnaire, with the exception of suicidal idea, which was not asked.[3] The Depression Index is calculated by adding the eight items and rescaling to values between 0 and 100 (average interitem covariance: 283.55; alpha Cronbach: 0.8776). Similarly, we examine evidence from an Anxiety Index computed from the answers to following four questions: 'nervous when I think in current circumstances', 'worried about my health', 'worried about the health of my family', and 'stressed about leaving my house'. Each item is answered with a scale taking values between 0 and 5. The Anxiety Index is calculated by adding the four items and rescaling the total to lie between 0 and 100 (average interitem covariance: 219.80; Cronbach alpha: 0.8421). The depression scale has been validated by Kroenke et al. (2001), and the anxiety scale has been validated by Kapoor et al. (2021).

---

[2] Austria, Belgium, Bulgaria, Czech Republic, Denmark, Finland, France, Germany, Greece, Hungary, Ireland, Italy, Netherlands, Norway, Portugal, Romania, Slovakia, Spain, Sweden, Switzerland, Ukraine, United Kingdom.

[3] Information is available for the remaining eight items: 'little interest or pleasure in doing things', 'feeling down or hopeless', 'trouble falling asleep or staying asleep or sleeping too much', 'feeling tired or having little energy', 'poor appetite or overeating', 'feeling bad about oneself (or that you are a failure or have let yourself or your family down)', 'trouble concentrating on things, such as reading the newspaper or watching television', and 'moving or speaking so slowly that other people could have noticed or so fidgety or restless that you have been moving a lot more than usual'.

In terms of lockdown measures, we define a binary variable that takes the value 1 if, for the day on which the interviewee answered the survey, lockdown is in force in their country of residence and the value 0 otherwise (see Table 16.1). Additionally, we use the Pandemic

Table 16.1 *Descriptive statistics by country*

	N	Anxiety Index	PHQ-8 Depression Index	Day lockdown became effective
Austria	1,074	60.06	41.22	16 March
Belgium	569	59.44	41.71	18 March
Bulgaria	329	60.18	45.03	13 March
Czech Republic	267	56.41	41.85	16 March
Denmark	506	56.96	39.79	13 March
Finland	635	55.17	37.93	16 March
France	2,721	60.69	42.06	17 March
Germany	10,097	59.33	41.93	17 March
Greece	328	60.18	43.98	23 March
Hungary	239	62.22	44.54	28 March
Ireland	711	61.13	41.50	27 March
Italy	1,849	61.18	44.68	9 March
Netherlands	1,423	55.78	39.43	16 March
Norway	302	59.42	38.78	12 March
Portugal	550	65.92	43.18	19 March
Romania	801	64.16	40.90	25 March
Slovakia	609	58.63	41.12	16 March
Spain	2,270	62.87	40.73	14 March
Sweden	5,853	53.52	38.87	No lockdown
Switzerland	4,188	60.53	40.57	17 March
Ukraine	1,452	57.07	42.62	17 March
United Kingdom	11,252	61.78	42.16	24 March
Total	48,434	59.55	41.42	

Note: Information from lockdown dates obtained from https:// auravision.ai/COVID19-lockdown-tracker/. Individual sample weights have been used to correct for differences in income, education, age, and gender structure between the general population of the country and the corresponding sample.

Severity Index. This is a binary variable that takes the value 1 if the case fatality rate (ratio between deaths and confirmed cases in percentage) is higher than 2 per cent. The Pandemic Severity Index classifies epidemics into five categories, with category 5 being the worst (Department of Health and Human Services, 2007). The variable 'Pandemic Category 5' indicates if COVID-19 has reached the 'worst-case' scenario pandemic for each day and country. Figure 16.1 shows the combination between lockdown and the Pandemic Severity Index for each country and date. Finally, the survey provides information on socio-demographic characteristics,[4] though unfortunately, the survey does not collect information on household composition nor on marital status and occupation.

16.3.1 Empirical Strategy

Next, we estimate two event study specifications. First, to test the adaptation to lockdown we propose the following model:

$$Y_{ict} = \sum_{j=-7}^{j=7} \gamma_{0k} D_{kc} L_{ct} + \gamma_1 P_{ct} + \sum_{j=-7}^{j=7} \gamma_{2k} D_{kc} L_{ct} P_{ct} + \gamma_3 X_{ict} + C_c + T_t + \epsilon_{ict}$$

$$(16.1)$$

where Y_{ict} refers to the mental health of the individual i living in country c who has answered the online survey on date t. Our dependent variable (Y_{ict}) refers to either the PHQ-8 Depression Index or the Anxiety Index. L_{ct} is a dummy variable taking the value 1 if a lockdown order has come into force for country c and day t, and 0 otherwise, and D_{kc} are dummy variables for the seven days before or after the lockdown became effective.

P_{ct} is a dummy variable taking the value 1 if the pandemic has reached category 5 according to the Pandemic Severity Index (i.e., the case fatality rate, which is the ratio between deaths and confirmed cases, is above 2 per cent) for country c and day t, and 0 otherwise.

---

[4] These includes age, gender, marital status, number of years of education, number of household members, number of comorbidities (cardiovascular diseases, diabetes, hepatitis B, chronic obstructive pulmonary disease, chronic kidney diseases, and cancer), and monthly household income before taxes.

	March												April					
	20	21	22	23	24	25	26	27	28	29	30	31	1	2	3	4	5	6
Austria																		
Belgium																		
Bulgaria																		
Czech Republic																		
Denmark																		
Finland																		
France																		
Germany																		
Greece																		
Hungary																		
Ireland																		
Italy																		
Netherlands																		
Norway																		
Portugal																		
Romania																		
Slovakia																		
Spain																		
Sweden																		
Switzerland																		
Ukraine																		
United Kingdom																		

Colour	Meaning
White	No lockdown and fatality rate lower than 2 per cent.
Light grey	Lockdown has become effective and fatality rate lower than 2 per cent.
Medium grey	No lockdown, but fatality rate higher or equal than 2 per cent.
Black	Lockdown has become effective and fatality rate higher or equal than 2 per cent.

FIGURE 16.1 Combination of lockdown measures and fatality rate by date and country

Note: Information from lockdown dates obtained from https:// auravision.ai/COVID19-lockdown-tracker/. The case fatality rate is the percentage of deceased with respect to confirmed cases. Category 5 corresponds to the highest level of the Pandemic Severity Index. Information of confirmed cases and deceased per 1,000,000 inhabitants obtained from https://ourworldindata.org/coronavirus-data-explorer

To control for differences in composition, X_{ict} refers to socio-demographic characteristics (age, gender, marital status, years of education, number of household members, income, number of comorbidities). Finally, C_c and T_t denote country fixed effects and day fixed effects. Robust standard errors clustered at the day levels are obtained. The eighth day before lockdown came into force is the reference period. The sum of the estimated coefficients $\gamma_{0k} + \gamma_{2k}P_{ct}$ should be interpreted as the effect of being in the jth day before or after lockdown was effective as compared to eight days before it.

The second event study model is used to test the effect of increasing fatality rate; we propose the following:

$$Y_{ict} = \sum_{j=-7}^{j=7} \delta_{0k}D_{kc}P + \delta_1 L_{ct} + \sum_{j=-7}^{j=7} \delta_{2k}D_{kc}L_{ct}P_{ct} + \delta_3 X_{ict} + C_c + T_t + \zeta_{ict}$$

$$(16.2)$$

where D_{kc} are dummy variables for the seven days before or after the category 5 pandemic level is reached, and the other terms have the same interpretation as in the previous model. The eighth day before lockdown came into force is the reference period. The estimated coefficients $\delta_{0k} + \delta_{2k}P_{ct}$ should be interpreted as the effect of being in the jth day before or after the day in which the fatality rate exceeded 2 per cent as compared to eight days before it.

16.4   RESULTS

We estimate an event study specification including a number of controls,[5] day fixed effects and country fixed effects, and robust standard errors including weights and clustered standard errors at the day level. Figure 16.2 and Table 16.2 report the results for the event study considering the adaptation to lockdown.

On the day the lockdown becomes effective, there is an increase in the levels of depression and anxiety of 1.638 and 5.953

---

[5] Controls include male, other gender, age and its square, married, years of education and number of household members, having any comorbidity and number of comorbidities, and household income quartile.

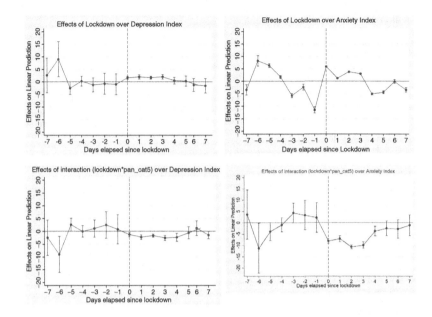

FIGURE 16.2 Event study results: effect of the days before/after lockdown and interaction between days before/after lockdown and pandemic of category 5 over Depression Index and Anxiety Index
Note: Dark dashed line is used to signal the day when lockdown became effective.

points, respectively, which represents an increase by 3.95 per cent and 9.99 per cent with respect to the mean value, respectively. However, the effect of the interaction with category 5 pandemic is negative in both cases. The resulting net effect is positive, although very small, for depression (+0.89 per cent) and negative for anxiety (–3.78 per cent). These results imply that the immediate effect of lockdown over anxiety levels is negative if it occurs in a context of high mortality.

Figure 16.3 and Table 16.2 show the results of the event study considering the moment in which the pandemic reaches category 5. The immediate effect is an increase in the level of depression (0.893 points) and anxiety (8.220 points), which represents an increase of 2.16 per cent and 13.80 per cent with respect to the average value,

Table 16.2 *Event study results*

	Effect of the interaction between days before/after lockdown became effective and pandemic category 5		Effect of the interaction between days before/after pandemic reached category 5 and lockdown	
	Depression Index	Anxiety Index	Depression Index	Anxiety Index
Day−7	−2.481	3.696	−2.575	−2.459
	(3.553)	(5.591)	(3.572)	(3.603)
Day−6	−8.927***	−11.261**	−9.025**	−9.104**
	(3.623)	(5.692)	(3.644)	(3.675)
Day−5	2.902	−3.899	2.523	2.626**
	(1.292)	(2.014)	(1.278)	(1.298)
Day−4	−0.037	−0.906	−0.256	−0.040
	(1.161)	(1.552)	(0.985)	(1.167)
Day−3	1.072	4.343	1.227	1.075
	(1.693)	(2.235)	(1.420)	(1.704)
Day−2	2.500	3.329	0.738	2.523
	(2.657)	(3.321)	(2.112)	(2.685)
Day−1	0.780	2.236	0.981	0.781
	(2.918)	(3.351)	(2.132)	(2.952)
Day lockdown became effective	−1.269***	−8.208***	−1.622***	−1.599***
	(0.410)	(0.590)	(0.331)	(0.351)

	(1)	(2)	(3)
Day +1	-2.260***	-7.000***	-2.239***
	(0.450)	(0.690)	(0.451)
Day +2	-1.659***	-10.583***	-1.643***
	(0.300)	(0.460)	(0.300)
Day +3	-2.581***	-9.747***	-2.567***
	(0.480)	(0.741)	(0.481)
Day +4	-2.349	-3.708***	-2.350
	(0.791)	(1.081)	(0.793)
Day +5	-0.567	-1.971	-0.690
	(1.201)	(1.633)	(1.217)
Day +6	1.209	-2.595	1.209
	(1.462)	(2.064)	(1.471)
Day +7	-1.468	-4.194***	1.159
	(0.731)	(1.121)	(1.552)

Note: All models include the following explanatory variables: man, other gender (omitted: women), age and its square, number of years of education and its square, married (omitted: single), specific-country quartile income (omitted: lowest quartile), number of household members (omitted: living alone), number of comorbidities, country fixed effects, and day fixed effects. Individual sample weights have been used to correct for differences in income, education, age, and gender structure between the general population of the country and the corresponding sample. Robust standard errors.

*** , ** , and * denote statistical significance at the 1%, 5%, and 10% level.

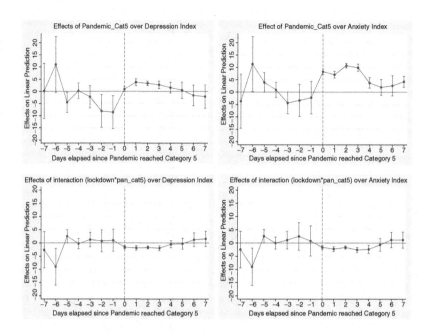

FIGURE 16.3 Event study results: effect of the days before/after pandemic reached category 5 and interaction between days before/after pandemic of category 5 and lockdown over Depression Index and Anxiety Index
Note: Dark line is used to signal the day when pandemic reached category 5 according to the Pandemic Severity Index.

respectively. The effect of interaction with lockdown is negative in both cases, resulting in a reduction in the level of depression (–1.76 per cent with respect to the mean value) and an increase in the level of anxiety (11.12 per cent with respect to the mean value). Consequently, although increasing mortality rate shoots anxiety levels above those of depression, lockdown succeeds in reducing the increase in anxiety by almost 20 per cent ((–1.599/8.220)*100).

The reason for this decrease in anxiety levels can be found at the core of health security theories (Gilbert, 2007). Living in an environment with a high mortality risk leads to a re-processing or re-interpretation of lockdown in terms of threat defence that, from a neurophysiological point of view, takes place in the frontal cortex (Baumeister et al., 2001). In this context, complex thinking declines in favour of safety-prioritised decision-making. For this reason, lockdown may no longer be interpreted as a hindrance to individual freedom and the feeling of being safe at home is prioritised.

Our results are in line with those of Michie et al. (2011, 2020), who found that a better understanding of government recommendations encourages better compliance with them. We go a step further and also find that understanding the severity of the situation reduces anxiety levels by internalising that staying at home is not an arbitrary imposition (or restriction of individual freedoms) but a protective measure for health.

16.5 DISCUSSION

Using data from March to April 2020 that identifies the effect of exposure to COVID-19 and lockdown stringency across a number of European countries, we have examined the so-called 'welcomed lockdown' hypothesis (Costa-Font et al., 2022), namely the extent to which there is a specific level of risk exposure whereby the effect of mobility restrictions improves or do not influence mental health. This chapter has argued whilst a 'preventive' lockdown in a low/ moderate mortality environment increases symptoms of depression and anxiety, in a high mortality environment (such as those in many countries during the first wave) it mitigates such negative effects on mental health, and particularly on anxiety.

All efforts to overcome interpersonal isolation play an important role in times of high stress and strain. There is evidence that having a telephone support line, staffed by psychiatric nurses, set up specifically for people in quarantine could be effective in providing them with a social network (Kwon and Lee, 2020; Liu et al., 2020). Finally, the media also plays a central role in disseminating daily information about the pandemic (Gao et al., 2020), and hence behavioural interventions can rely on its influence in preference formation.

REFERENCES

Adams-Prassl, A., Teodora Boneva, T., Golin, M., & Christopher Rauh, C. (2020). The impact of the coronavirus lockdown on mental health: Evidence from the US. Working Papers 2020–030, Human Capital and Economic Opportunity Working Group.

Banks, J., & Xu, X. (2020). The mental health effects of the first two months of lockdown and social distancing during the Covid-19 pandemic in the UK. *Fiscal Studies*, 41(3), 685–708.

Baumeister, R., Bratslavsky, E., Finkenauer, C., & Vohs, K. (2001). Bad is stronger than good. *Review of General Psychology*, 5, 323–370.

Blendon, R., Benson, J., DesRoches, C., Raleigh, E., & Taylor-Clark, K. (2004). The public's response to severe acute respiratory syndrome in Toronto and the United States. *Clinical Infectious Diseases*, 38, 925–931.

Brodeur, A., Clark, A. E., Fleche, S., & Powdthavee, N. (2020). Assessing the impact of the coronavirus lockdown on unhappiness, loneliness, and boredom using Google Trends. *arXiv:2004.12129*.

Brooks, S. K., Webster, R., Smith, L., Woodland, L., Wessely, S., Greenberg, N., & Rubin, J. (2020). The psychological impact of quarantine and how to reduce it: Rapid review of the evidence. *The Lancet*, 395, 912–920.

Bu, F., Steptoe, A., & Fancourt, D. (2020). Loneliness during a strict lockdown: Trajectories and predictors during the COVID-19 pandemic in 38,217 United Kingdom adults. *Social Science and Medicine*, 265, 113521.

Choi, W. S., Kang, C. I., Kim, Y., Choi, J. P., Joh, J. S., Shin, H. S., et al. (2016). Clinical presentation and outcomes of Middle East respiratory syndrome in the Republic of Korea. *Infection & Chemotherapy*, 48(2), 118–126.

Costa-Font, J., Knapp, M., & Vilaplana-Prieto, C. (2022). The 'welcomed lockdown' hypothesis? Mental wellbeing and mobility restrictions. *The European Journal of Health Economics*, 24(5), 679–699.

Department of Health & Human Services. (2007). Interim pre-pandemic planning guidance: community strategy for pandemic influenza mitigation in the United States: Early, targeted, layered use of nonpharmaceutical interventions (full text of the initial report outlining PSI), Centers for Disease Control, USA.

Fancourt, D., Steptoe, A., & Bu, F. (2020). Trajectories of depression and anxiety during enforced isolation due to Covid-19: Longitudinal analysis of 36,520 adults in the UK with and without diagnosed mental illness. *medRxiv*. https://doi.org/10.1101/2020.06.03.20120923

Fetzer, T., Witte, M., Hensel, L., Jachimowicz, J. M., Haushofer, J., Ivchenko, A., et al. (2020). Global behaviors and perceptions in the COVID-19 pandemic. PsyArXiv Preprints. https://doi.org/10.31234/osf.io/3kfmh

Foa, R., Gilbert, S., & Fabian, M. (2020). COVID-19 and subjective well-being: Separating the effects of lockdowns from the pandemic. Bennett Institute for Public Policy, Cambridge, UK.

Gao, J., Zheng, P., Jia, Y., Chen, H., Mao, Y., Chen, S., et al. (2020). Mental health problems and social media exposure during Covid-19 outbreak. *PLoS ONE*, 15(4), 1–10.

Gilbert, P. (2007). Evolved minds and compassion in the therapeutic relationship. In P. Gilbert, & R. Leahy (eds.), *The Therapeutic Relationship in the Cognitive Behavioural Psychotherapies* (pp. 106–142). London: Routledge.

Kapoor, H., Ticku, A., Tagat, A., & Karandikar, S. (2021). Innovation in isolation? COVID-19 lockdown stringency and culture-innovation relationships. *Frontiers in Psychology*, 12, 593359.

Kroenke, K., Spitzer, R., & Williams, J. (2001). The PHQ-9: Validity of a brief depression severity measure. *Journal of General Internal Medicine*, 16(9), 606–613.

Kwon, C., & Lee, B. (2020). Characteristics of individuals receiving telemedicine mental health services using mindfulness: Cases in South Korea during the COVID-19 pandemic. *Asian Journal of Psychiatry*, 54, 102374.

Liu, S., Yang, L., Zhang, C., Xiang, Y., Liu, Z., Hu, S., & Zhang, B. (2020). Online mental health services in China during the COVID-19 outbreak. *Lancet Psychiatry*, 7(4), e17–e18.

Luchetti, M., Lee, J., Aschwanden, D., Sesker, A., Strickhouser, J., Terracciano, A., & Sutin, A. (2020). The trajectory of loneliness in response to Covid-19. *American Psychologist*, 75(7), 897–908.

Maunder, R. (2009). Was SARS a mental health catastrophe? *General Hospital Psychiatry*, 31(4), 316–317.

Michie, S., van Stralen, M., & West, R. (2011). The behaviour change wheel: A new method for characterising and designing behaviour change interventions. *Implementation Science*, 6, 42.

Michie, S., West, R., Amlôt, R., & Rubin, J. (2020). Slowing down the COVID-19 outbreak: Changing behaviour by understanding it. *The BMJ Publishing Opinion*. https://blogs.bmj.com/bmj/2020/03/11/slowing-down-the-COVID-19-outbreak-changing-behaviour-by-understanding-it/

Pfefferbaum, B., Schonfeld, D., Flynn, B., Norwood, A., Dodgen, D., Kaul, R., & Ruzek, J. (2012). The H1N1 crisis: A case study of the integration of mental and behavioral health in public health crises. *Disaster Medicine and Public Health Preparedness*, 6(1), 67–71.

Pierce, M., Hope, H., Ford, T., Hatch, S., Hotopf, M., & John, A. (2020). Mental health before and during the COVID-19 pandemic: A longitudinal probability sample survey of the UK population. *Lancet Psychiatry, 7*(10), 883–892. https://doi.org/10.1016/S2215-0366(20)30308-4

Sibley, C., Greaves, L., Satherley, N., Wilson, M., Overall, N., Lee, C., et al. (2020). Effects of the Covid-19 pandemic and nationwide lockdown on trust, attitudes towards government, and well-being. *American Psychologist, 75*(5), 618–630.

WHO. (2020). Coronavirus disease 2019 (COVID-19): Situation Report – 65. 25 March. www.who.int/docs/default-source/coronaviruse/situation-reports/20200325-sitrep-65-covid-19.pdf

17 Wrinkles in a Pandemic?

COVID-19 and Behaviours towards Older Age Individuals

Joan Costa-Font

17.1 INTRODUCTION

As people age, they have some physical capacity losses that some health investments can help to partially offset (Costa-Font & Vilaplana, 2021). However, broader of health place limitations on such health interventions that promote healthy ageing, such as access to nutritious foods and attitudes towards old age individuals, all of which have been altered during the COVID-19 pandemic. The COVID-19 pandemic has had a specifically magnifying impact on elderly people's access to health care, and in some countries, among those in congested nursing homes that would not have rooms for self-isolation, and particularly in accessing hospital care as older people were denied access emergency health care, sometimes with fatal consequences. More generally, the pandemic has brought about either implicitly or explicitly, the question of `rationing by age, and age discrimination to practice'. It is not anymore a topic for bio-ethics debates, but an actual policy included in hospital protocols and political decisions.

Without a thought, one of the side effects of the COVID-19 pandemic has been that it has exposed the pervasive ageism that older age individuals are exposed to in western society. That is, the low regard for older population, compared to other countries at the other end of the globe. Ageism HAS Impacted public choices too in both public and private late reactions to risk exposure in many Western societies can be linked to ageism, compared to least ageist Eastern societies. In this chapter I argue that attitudes explain a core part of such effects, and I present a brief discussion about the potential; behavioral interventions can address some of such effects.

325

Below I describe how the COVID-19 pandemic has influenced decision making regarding old age individuals, and age-based decision making. We identify some cognitive biases that more widely impact on older age populations, and more specifically we will focus on the role of specific narratives regarding older age which might have steered ageism in the pandemic, and finally look at some of the effects of ageism on the access to adult care by older age individuals. older age populations? Did the pandemic or its associated mobility restrictions give rise to specific narratives regarding older age individuals? Was ageism made worse in the pandemic? Were there any specific behavioural effects on long-term care to older age individuals?

Section 17.2 focuses on the presence of age-specific effects, while Section 17.3 is on ageing and behaviour. Section 17.4 discusses old age narratives and ageing. Section 17.5 looks at how care decisions were influenced by the pandemic, and Section 17.6 ends the chapter with a discussion that puts forward a set of policy implications and suggestions.

17.2 AGE-SPECIFIC EFFECTS OF THE COVID-19 PANDEMIC

Older age population have been more heavily impacted by the covid-19 pandemic, not just because age reduced individuals' immunity and hence their life and integrity has been more at risk. Ho et al. (2020) find that people over 65 face a 13 folder higher risk of death compared to under 65, and this is due to a combination of factors including an attenuated immune response, likelihood of pre-existing conditions, poorer lung function, muscle weakness, and higher blood pressure among other explanations.

D'cruz and Banerjee (2020) identify several social factors influencing the wellbeing of the older population in a pandemic. These include their health security, loneliness and isolation, societal ageism and sexism, alongside dependency, stigma, abuse, and health care access restrictions. The evidence of a specific effect of the pandemic on older population is still been developed, but evidence so far has established that older patient prior to COVID-19 were more likely than younger counterparts to have their treatment withheld or delayed (Inouye, 2021). Similarly, age made a different to the effectiveness of vaccines as clinical trials for COVID-19 vaccine had an age off, which was potentially concerning as COVID-19 symptoms vary alongside individual's age. However, in addition the effect on health, the pandemic modified behavioural and social determinants of physical and cognitive ageing by limiting the individual's capacity to engage in investments that delay ageing. This is because during the pandemic the priority of health systems has directed towards averting the expansion of COVID-19 instead. COVID-19 deaths increase exponentially among old aged people. Indeed, they are estimated at 4.6% among individuals aged 60–70 years, yet such number increases to 13.6% among individuals aged 70 to 80 years, and 21% among those 80 years and over (Costa-font et al., 2021).

From public authorities, chronological age has been presented as the main risk of contagion although it is inaccurate and misleading. Although frailty may have exacerbated the individual's risks exposure, we know that age does not give rise to worse metal health. Indeed, according to Isaacowitz and Smith (2003), age has no predictive value for positive or negative affect in older adults. However, it is certainly true that lockdowns have inevitably depressed social interactions, which impact more heavily individuals who rely more than other age groups on the role of social influences, such as day care centres and social clubs that are so dear to the wellbeing of older populations.

Another effect of the pandemic on older age has been that of adding barriers for older age people to the access to foods (shopping) either due to limited mobility or fear to venture out to shop. One explanation for such effects is the so-called 'motivated blindness' hypothesis (James et al., 2020), namely that individuals care about their own interests (securing toilet paper or certain types of foods that are on limited supply such as pasta), without considering the wider social consequences (e.g. whether the ultimate information causing those shortages turns out to be true). Access to foods, often have not paid attention to mobility restrictions, and older people have not been prioritised to reduce the burden of shopping cues.

Finally, another effect on older people is the effect of the pandemic on individuals in need of care or support, who may have gone with unmet needs to avoid the risk of contagion and may have relied more on informal care from 'trusted' family members instead (Bergman and Meiener, 2021). Evidence in Europe reveals large disruptions in family contact, and specifically between children and their parents (Brugiavin et al., 2022), which affects older age individuals more severely than other age groups.

17.3   AGEING AND INEQUALITY DURING THE PANDEMIC

Ageing can reflect itself as a `self-fulfilling prophecy' where social expectation of what people of each age should do in different circumstances end up being reproduced across generations. These phenomena might stand behind ageist social attitudes based on past stereotypes, even though evidence from today might not necessarily be in line with such worldviews. The pandemic has affected people's health, and specifically evidence suggests that it has led individual to adjust their individuals' perceived longevity (Celidoni et al., 2022). Fear of contagion explains that individuals who expect to live longer become more likely to engage in protective activities (Celidoni et al., 2022). However, as pandemic protective measures disproportionately benefit older individuals with a higher risk of death, and entail a sacrifice by younger cohorts, they have engendered unique behavioral reactions towards older age individuals. Such reactions include stereotyping, prejudice, or discrimination (WHO, 2018) and can affect others or oneself (Levy et al., 2011).

The rise of a heavy technology-based society where zoom calls, and WhatsApp's become the normal way of communication has made it harder for older age individuals to adjust to the new demands during the pandemic even though the digital divide has been progressively closing and more generally for the rise in ageism in society. Whilst younger people might be ready to work from home this would have not been convenient for older people and might have led to *early retirement of older population which would have faced barriers to cope employed under the new circumstanced* (Marcus, 2021). However, such decision have increased their financial vulnerability as they spend their emergency savings, and reduce their retirement plan contributions, and retirement accounts (Marcus, 2021). Consistently, personal bankruptcies are increasing more quickly for older adults than any other age group in the US (Li and White 2020). Finally, the pandemic has exerted affected the behaviours of younger retirees. Indeed, Bertoni et al. (2021) fund that individuals who retired earlier responded to the pandemic by limiting their mobility more, and by adopting stricter preventive behaviours.

17.4   AGEISM AND OLD AGE RISK NARRATIVES

Age is a salient characteristic individuals used to identify themselves and might give rise to 'ageism', which can be institutional (a result of regulations), interpersonal (interactions with others), or even self-directed (stigma or mental barriers around what older age individuals should do) and is estimated that affects about 50 per cent of the global population (WHO, 2021). Jimenez–Sotomayor et al. (2020) document that 25% of tweets about the pandemic and older people had ageist content. The WHO estimates that half of world's population is ageist against older people today and more than one in three people aged 65 years or older reported being a target of ageism in Europe, widespread in institutions, laws and policies across the world (WHO, 2021). Ng et al. (2015) documents evidence of an increase in the negativity of age stereotypes in the last centuries. More generally, social norms, which influence age "appropriate behaviour". In the first wave of the pandemic, older people were often blamed in the media for lockdowns and severe policy restrictions. This specifically explains the rise of intergenerational tensions.

COVID-19 brought some trade-offs, namely closing down economic activity and restricting people's freedoms. However, the social value or status of older individuals vis-à-vis other age groups in society is often overlooked in many policy responses. Their social value differs across societies. Whilst many Asian countries report more positive perceptions towards older people, in many Western societies older people pretend to be younger to avoid the effects of ageism. Ageism is defined by the European Social Survey (2012) as the stereotyping of, and discrimination against, someone based on their age, which is often the result of social norms that praise people's youth and equalises peoples value to their contribution in the labour market. Hence, older age is typically associated with lower value.

Ageism can take different forms, and it comes in the form of exposure to ageist messages, experiencing internalised ageist beliefs, and having ageist interactions with other people. The impact of ageist attitudes includes tangible reductions in the quality of life for older people, resulting in old people being discriminated against in the sectors of recruitment, entertainment, and healthcare, among others. Ageing can explain early retirement decisions that we documented earlier, as older people are stereotyped as being less technologically proficient (age-related digital divide).

Ageist attitudes are manifested in the underfunding and in the neglect of services primarily used by old people such as health and social care. Over 40 per cent of British society believe that a thirty-year-old's treatment should be prioritised over that of a seventy-year-old with the same condition, with less than 5 per cent believing the elder person should be prioritised (International Social Survey Program, 2011). These prevalent views in society will have at least indirect impacts on prioritising healthcare for the young, harming the quality of healthcare old people are able to receive. The social media has frequently reported discriminatory attitudes towards the elderly in these past few months (e.g., 'They're on their way out anyway').

17.5   TRUSTED CARE DECISIONS

Across Organisation for Economic Co-operation and Development countries, older people and their care workers have been disproportionately affected by the COVID-19 pandemic. With 93 per cent of COVID-19 deaths being among those older than sixty, the pandemic has put the spotlight on the long-term care (LTC) sector (OECD, 2021). Furthermore, the pandemic was made worse by the high density in LTC facilities: the multiple-occupancy rooms facilitated the spread of infection and hindered the implementation of isolation measures of suspected or infected cases. Indeed, higher adult care staffing rates were strongly associated with lower death rates in nursing homes as of May 2020 (Costa-Font et al., 2021). However, among people in the community there has been a higher reliance on informal care, which is explained by the fact that informal care is generally highly trusted. In addition to trust, such decisions can be explained by how people perceive the risks of contagion.

In understanding care decisions, individuals rely on their perceived risk. According to Slovic et al. (1980), dimensions such as familiarity, dread, and exposure (i.e., the number of people exposed) play an important role in people's risk perception. Informal care is a more familiar type of care even when it entails a cost to informal caregivers. In the absence of affordable formal care, older individuals are informally cared for by family members (or go with unmet needs). Reliance on informal care explains the early expansion of the pandemic in countries with stronger family ties such as Italy, Spain, China, and Korea. Consequently, in some European countries, people took their loved ones out of nursing homes.

Quarantines have a greater impact on the old age individuals, who are more likely to live alone and in need of care. In addition to COVID-19 itself, lockdowns have had a significant impact on caregiving. To reduce the risk of contagion, caregivers in many countries have been forced to live with elderly people in need. However, when older people are less disabled, they are more likely to be left alone, with unmet needs, or with the assistance of professional caregivers when they are available. However, many of these professionals were not regarded as key workers and were unable to provide daily support in many cases. According to Ling et al. (2019), people mostly engage in protective behaviour when they believe that non-engagement poses a threat to themselves (high threat appraisal) or when they believe that their behaviour can reduce the threat (high coping appraisal). In the case of COVID-19, the former may apply to older age individuals, especially to those that are personally affected and/or belong to the high-risk group, and the latter to individuals who have confidence in the effectiveness of governmental and/or their own coping strategies.

17.6 POLICY IMPLICATIONS

Today we are envisaging the transformation of modern societies into 'longevity societies', where not only is greater focus placed on the older age but more attention is also paid to the improvement of those conditions and actions earlier in life that improve well-being at older age (Scott, 2021). In such longevity societies, COVID-19 has been a tipping point to denounce the ageing stereotypes and stigma against older population that permeates daily decision making in a long list of dimensions, from individual level decision on beauty standards where grey hair and wrinkles are hidden to collective decision making where the wellbeing of older age population is perceived second order to that of younger individuals. Policy interventions are needed to modify those attitudes thereby correcting age-based stereotypes and subsequently to improve the well-being of individuals as they age. Age cut off should not be any more barrier to employment access to health care or social care. To date, ageism is still a major barrier to the wellbeing of a longevity society because it restricts and constrains the options that are available as people age. Intervention such as nudges where older age individuals are used to normalize a stronger participation older age individuals in economic and social life are important. The latter might help broaden the diversity agenda beyond gender and sexuality into age-specific interventions.

REFERENCES

Bergmann, M., & Wagner, M. (2021). The impact of COVID-19 on informal caregiving and care receiving across Europe during the first phase of the pandemic. *Frontiers in Public Health*, 9, 673874.

Bertoni, M., Celidoni, M., Dal Bianco, C., & Weber, G. (2021). How did European retirees respond to the COVID-19 pandemic? *Economics Letters*, 203, 109853.

Brugiavini, A., Di Novi, C., & Orso, C. E. (2022). Visiting parents in times of COVID-19: The impact of parent-adult child contacts on the psychological health of the elderly. *Economics & Human Biology*, 46, 101152.

Celidoni, M., Costa-Font, J., & Salmasi, L. (2022). Too Healthy to Fall Sick? Longevity Expectations and Protective Health Behaviours during the First Wave of COVID-19. *Journal of Economic Behavior & Organization*, 202, 733–745.

Costa-Font, J., Jiménez Martin, S., & Viola, A. (2021). Fatal underfunding? Explaining COVID-19 mortality in Spanish nursing homes. *Journal of Aging and Health*, 33(7–8), 607–617.

Costa-Font, J., Knapp, M., & Vilaplana-Prieto, C. (2022). The 'welcomed lockdown' hypothesis? Mental wellbeing and mobility restrictions. *The European Journal of Health Economics*, 24(5), 679–699.

Costa-Font, J., & Vilaplana-Prieto, C. (2020). 'More than one red herring'? Heterogeneous effects of ageing on health care utilisation. *Health Economics*, 29, 8–29.

European Social Survey. (2012). Experiences and Expressions of Ageism: Topline Results (UK) from Round 4 of the European Social Survey. www.europeansocialsurvey.org/docs/findings/ESS4_gb_toplines_experiences_and_expressions_of_ageism.pdf

Ho, F. K., Petermann-Rocha, F., Gray, S. R., Jani, B. D., Katikireddi, S. V., Niedzwiedz, C. L., et al. (2020). Is older age associated with COVID-19 mortality in the absence of other risk factors? General population cohort study of 470,034 participants. *PLoS One*, 15(11), e0241824.

Inouye, S. K. (2021). Creating an anti-ageist healthcare system to improve care for our current and future selves. *Nature Aging*, 1(2), 150–152.

International Social Survey Program (2011). https://issp.org/

Isaacowitz, D. M., & Smith, J. (2003). Positive and negative affect in very old age. *The Journals of Gerontology. Series B, Psychological Sciences and Social Sciences*, 58, 143–152.

Jimenez-Sotomayor, M. R., Gomez-Moreno, C., & Soto-Perez-de-Celis, E. (2020). Coronavirus, ageism, and Twitter: An evaluation of tweets about older adults and COVID-19. *Journal of the American Geriatrics Society*, 68(8), 1661–1665.

Jmaes, H. S., & Segovia, M. S. (2020) Behavioral Eethics and the Iincidence of Ffoodborne Iillness Ooutbreaks. *Journal of Agricultural and Environmental Ethics*, 33, 531–548. https://doi.org/10.1007/s10806-020-09837-w.

Li, W., & White, J. (2020). Financial distress among the elderly: Bankruptcy reform and the financial crisis. In O. Mitchell and A. Lusardi (eds.), *Remaking Retirement: Debt in an Aging Economy* (pp. 89–105). Oxford: Oxford Academic.

Ling, M., Kothe, E. J., & Mullan, B. A. (2019). Predicting intention to receive a seasonal influenza vaccination using protection motivation theory. *Social Science & Medicine, 233,* 87–92. https://doi.org/10.1016/j.socscimed.2019.06.002

Marcus, J. (2021). In one year, pandemic forced millions of workers to retire early. AARP, 10 March.

Ng, R., Allore, H. G., Trentalange, M., Monin, J. K., & Levy, B. R. (2015). Increasing negativity of age stereotypes across 200 years: Evidence from a database of 400 million words. *PLoS One, 10,* e0117086.

OECD (2021) Health at Glance. www.oecd-ilibrary.org/sites/4c4694a2-en/index .html?itemId=/content/component/4c4694a2-en

Rhodes, M., & Baron, A. (2019). The development of social categorization. *Annual Review of Developmental Psychology, 1,* 359–386.

Scott, A. (2021). The longevity society. *The Lancet Healthy Longevity, 2,* e820–827.

Slovic, P., Fischhoff, B., & Lichtenstein, S. (1980). Facts and fears: Understanding perceived risk. In R. C. Schwing and W. A. Albers (eds.), *Societal Risk Assessment: How Safe Is Safe Enough?* (pp. 181–216). Boston, MA: Springer.

WHO. (2021). Global Report on Ageism. World Health Organization. www.who .int/teams/social-determinants-of-health/demographic-change-and-healthy-ageing/combatting-ageism/global-report-on-ageism

18 Can Behavioural Insights Explain Ethnic Minority Vaccination Gaps?

Daniele Sudsataya, Miqdad Asaria, Joan Costa-Font, and Faical Achaiki

18.1 INTRODUCTION

Pandemics such as COVID-19 are over only when we achieve herd immunity through the vaccination of a large share of the population. Therefore, one the most serious threats to the success of immunisation programmes is when some share of the population becomes vaccine hesitant. Vaccine hesitancy can delay herd immunity, which in turn encompasses more infections and deaths. In this context, an important feature of many multi-cultural societies, such as the United Kingdom and the Unites States, is the fact that the bulk of vaccine hesitancy concentrates in some ethnic minorities.

A clear gap in vaccination rates has been highlighted between various ethnic groups: this is problematic, however, as studies have shown that COVID-19 has had a disproportionate impact on racial/ ethnic minority groups. For example, the United States Centers for Disease Control and Prevention (CDC) 'reported that 21.8% of COVID-19 cases in the United States were African Americans and 33.8% were LatinX, despite the fact that these groups comprise only 13% and 18% of the US population, respectively' (Tai et al., 2020). Moreover, in New York City, 'age-adjusted confirmed COVID-19 deaths were 220 and 236 per 100,000 for African American and LatinX patients, respectively. This is double compared to 110 and 102 per 100,000 for whites and Asians, respectively' (Tai et al., 2020). Similar trends have been observed in other countries. With this data in mind, it becomes clear that allowing vaccine hesitancy to thrive within ethnic minority groups, whose members are already disproportionately affected by the pandemic, can lead to dramatic health outcomes. However, so far, we know little about what its main behavioural drivers are.

This chapter attempts to provide an assessment of the state of the art, explaining the presence of an ethnic minority vector driving vaccine hesitancy, as well as a list of potential behavioural policy interventions to curb such inequality. It specifically focuses on the behavioural insights that can explain the uneven access to vaccine across ethnic groups. This includes incentives and constraints that have been reported during the COVID-19 pandemic. This chapter discusses what kind of incentives work and when do certain incentives backfire. It then provides a series of policy recommendations.

There are several historical and socio-economic reasons widely discussed in the current literature that can explain such ethic minority vector. Different countries have employed various incentivisation strategies, ranging from the financial to the behavioural, to prompt unvaccinated members of the population to get vaccinated. But often these incentives are implemented in a standardised country-wide manner, without taking into account the cultural and regional factors that might deter the effectiveness of these incentives within local community groups (Mena Lora et al., 2021). Incentives that prove successful in increasing vaccine uptake in, for example, high-income white individuals may not be received in the same way by lower-income Latinx communities. This may be due to a multitude of underlying socio-cultural and behavioural reasons, such as safety/efficacy concerns, general governmental mistrust (historical or from contemporary unethical studies), fake media/news proliferation, and accessibility and affordability barriers (Carson et al., 2021). Policymakers must take into consideration all of these barriers and individual/community perceptions to successfully create and implement vaccine roll-out strategies that members of ethnic minority groups will be receptive to; hence, behavioural incentives could play a role in helping policymakers to tailor their interventions to the unique contexts of ethnic minorities.

18.2 BEHAVIOURAL INSIGHTS IN MINORITY GROUPS' ACCESS TO VACCINES

To understand why ethnic minority groups showcase vaccine hesitancy and lower vaccination rates, this chapter will first present some of the most influential barriers to vaccine access faced by these populations, drawing from behavioural insights to highlight the potential presence and influence of cognitive biases in augmenting the impact of these barriers. This will then inform our discussion on the effectiveness of various vaccination incentives, when can they be used, and in what contexts.

Barriers to vaccination can range from practical and logistical limitations, such as travel time and technological inaccessibility, informational limitations due to language differences and poor or inaccurate provision of vaccine news or research, to structural limitations, typically linked to racism, poverty, and household income/wage gap issues prevalent in ethnic minority groups (Watkinson et al., 2022). Cultural barriers are also prevalent, as the opinions on vaccination can vary within individuals, families, and communities according to the general views of the culture and environment in which these people are situated (Bogart et al., 2021). Many of these barriers are intrinsically linked to the underlying socio-economic determinants of health disproportionately impacting minority populations; here, behavioural concepts can help shed light on how these factors influence the decision-making process of members of these ethnic groups when choosing to receive or decline a vaccine, as well as aid in the development of policies to comprehensively address them (AuYoung et al., 2022).

18.2.1 Practical and Logistical Barriers

It is well documented that members of ethnic minority groups face many disadvantages within healthcare due to a myriad of socio-economic determinants, such as low income, lack of time due to long working hours, and long distances between low-income neighbourhoods and health centres offering quality care (Burger et al., 2021). This phenomenon is formally described as the 'inverse care law', which states that socially disadvantaged people in greater need of care receive less healthcare, of lower quality, particularly in low- and middle-income countries (Cookson et al., 2021). However, this law can be viewed differently in high-income countries, where it is often the case that socially disadvantaged people receive a higher volume of care, but what they receive is of poor quality and not adequate enough to meet the additional needs born of the socio-economic conditions of these individuals (Cookson et al., 2021). In both cases, it appears that minority ethnic groups' access to healthcare is impacted by factors unique to the context within these communities; as such barriers are typically not faced by higher-income populations, a tailored approach may be required to properly address them.

One notable practical barrier to vaccination that became prevalent during the COVID-19 pandemic is the need to book, and subsequently travel to, mass vaccination centre appointments. Ethnic minorities that live in segregated residential neighbourhoods encountered long travel journey times to keep their appointment at centralised vaccination sites. Pairing this with the fact that many members of ethnic minorities work very long hours doing arduous and energy-consuming jobs to make ends meet, it becomes clear how individuals in this context may be unable to take time off work or may be hesitant to receiving a vaccination that will add more pressure to their packed schedules, as well as potentially worsen their immediate health due to the vaccine's side effects (Watkinson et al., 2022).

The cost of travel can also be considered a strong barrier to vaccination. For individuals without immediate access to a car, traveling long distances to vaccination centres requires the use of public transportation, which can represent a financial burden as well as a further reduction in their free time. This can be even worse in communities that live outside central metropolitan areas, as they will have to pay more for longer distance transport (such as trains) or may be unable to find convenient transportation due to lack of investment in transportation infrastructure in their neighbourhoods (Fuller et al., 2021).

Ethnic minorities may also be disproportionately affected by technological limitations. The requirement of booking an appointment online, as well as having to show the appointment confirmation to enter the vaccination hub, can represent an additional barrier for individuals without technological access. The lack of a mobile phone, not having strong Wi-Fi connection/broadband Internet, or having outdated and poorly working technology can create difficulties in securing a vaccination appointment, finding directions to the hub, and finally accessing the vaccination centre. These factors combined can lead to logistical barriers that may discourage ethnic minorities from receiving a vaccine or completing a two-dose regimen, especially for individuals that are already unsure or hesitant about getting vaccinated (Watkinson et al., 2022).

From a behavioural perspective, the need to travel to more affluent city centres to receive the COVID-19 vaccine may lead to negative attitudes towards the vaccination campaigns: disadvantaged communities may feel that they are facing additional hardship when compared to higher-income populations that live in close proximity to vaccination hubs and do not have to expend as much time or resources to complete this process. From a top-down perspective, individuals may also find it unfair that no vaccination centres are being established in their local communities, potentially propagating the notion that governments and policymakers are not treating ethnic minorities with the same urgency as more affluent groups: 'why do we have to go to them; why can't they come to us?' (Jesuthasan et al., 2021).

This could be addressed in a way like how influenza vaccines are readily available for walk-in appointments in local community pharmacies, in general practitioner (GP) offices, or through hospital drop-in services.

18.2.2   *Informational Barriers*

Barriers to vaccination can also arise in the construction and communication of vaccine information. For example, within minority groups in the Bronx, United States, the most common causes for hesitancy were concerns about the side effects of the vaccine – fear that the vaccine is unsafe – and concerns over the quick approval of the vaccine; also, younger and less-educated members of these groups expressed that they did not believe that the vaccine was necessary to end the pandemic (D' Aza et al., 2021). These are all reasons that may be rooted in how scientific information is communicated, as well as being potentially manipulated by political agendas.

Moreover, as ethnic minorities may have recently moved to a country or only speak their native language in their families and communities, the language in which vaccine-related information is communicated can become a barrier to vaccine uptake. Individuals whose mother tongue is not English or who have lower levels of literacy may have difficulty understanding and interpreting vaccine research or may not understand English-only websites, patient portals, or reminder messages, leading to a higher rate of missed vaccine appointments and more generally increased hesitancy due to the hassle and the seemingly uncompromising nature of governments (AuYoung et al., 2022).

Behaviour plays an important role in this scenario: as scientific communication needs to be transparent and trustworthy to be fully accepted by hesitant individuals, news and reports need to be tailored to ethnic minority groups to render them accessible and easily understandable. Translating vaccine-related communication into other languages commonly used by minority groups can also be helpful, as well as using trusted and respected community and religious leaders to convey information. It is also important to avoid obvious media framing and ensure information is not manipulated by local groups or politicians trying to create a negative narrative (Allen et al., 2021).

18.3   STRUCTURAL AND CULTURAL BARRIERS

Finally, many barriers to vaccination may arise due to structural issues linked to racism, as well as cultural climates unique to ethnic minority groups. Firstly, many vaccine-hesitant individuals claim mistrust in their government as a primary reason for their vaccination refusal. This general distrust can be attributed to a myriad of reasons, with history playing a prevalent role in influencing behaviour. Communities who have been victims of racism in the past/present may view vaccination campaigns as further attempts to segregate or exercise control over their freedom. An example is the Tuskegee Study of Untreated Syphilis in the Negro Male, which 'passively monitored hundreds of adult black men with syphilis despite the availability of effective treatment, and led to increases in medical mistrust and mortality and decreases in both outpatient and inpatient physician interactions for older black men' (Alsan & Wanamaker, 2018). As history plays a role in the construction of a community's identity, the behaviour of the members of this group may be altered because of their past experiences and as a result cause people to be more apprehensive towards communications about vaccines coming from individuals with roles of power.

Structurally, lower-income minorities usually find themselves living in segregated communities in city outskirts, not well connected to transportation hubs and with only poor medical infrastructure available in close proximity to their neighbourhoods. Mistrust may also arise in countries that receive vaccines produced abroad.

Finally, the design architecture used by governments to collect ethnicity data can represent a barrier to individuals when filling out forms required to book vaccine appointments. The use of labels that attempt to be all encompassing may alienate ethnic minorities and mixed-race individuals (e.g., labels that poorly define patient ethnicity such as British or British mixed; see Martins et al., 2022); including race in medical data collection may make people raise questions as to why they are being asked this information, exacerbating social divisions and allowing mistrust and hesitancy to increase.

Cognitive biases such as the bandwagon effect or the anchoring effect may arise within an individual's immediate circle, creating additional cultural barriers to vaccination. The opinions of one's family, friends, or group members regarding vaccination can increase hesitancy in individuals who do not want to be 'the odd one out' in their community, as well as create a medium in which fake or manipulated scientific communications can freely propagate. Behavioural insights are particularly useful here to identify how hesitant attitudes are constructed and circulated within ethnic minority groups (Watkinson et al., 2022).

18.4   PUBLIC HEALTH MESSAGING AND COMMUNITY LEADERS

18.4.1   *Misinformation*

The UK government has repeatedly emphasised individuals' responsibility to be vaccinated rather than addressing the sources of this hesitancy and mistrust, as well as policy flaws that have contributed to an increase in COVID-19 cases. This contributes to the narrative that vaccine hesitancy is the result of ignorance, rather than other complex factors such as institutionalised racism and a lack of trust in public health and pharmaceutical companies. Public health messaging produces results by eliciting either negative or positive emotions. To avoid instilling fear and worry, it is critical to disseminate accurate information about COVID-19 vaccinations in a positive manner. When public health messaging strategies are designed in a positive manner, open and favourable attitudes are more likely to be achieved (Fuller et al., 2021).

18.4.2   *The Novelty of COVID-19 Is Important*

The novel nature of many COVID-19 vaccines, such as the mRNA-based vaccines, is cause for concern for many people. Due to differences in education levels, income, and the proliferation of word-of-mouth information within communities, public health messaging and information campaigns should provide minority groups with tailored news. 'Information campaigns that are designed to reach ethnic minority communities are essential to improve the public's understanding of and provide reassurance around the safety and efficacy of mRNA and other COVID-19 vaccines' (Fuller et al., 2021).

18.4.3 Trust

In the United States, many African Americans voiced distrust in vaccines due to 'distrust in government and the medical establishment at large based on historical mistreatment of Black communities in clinical trials' (Kerrigan et al., 2022). Others echoed the sentiment by stating the 'importance of ensuring members of their community were aware of the involvement of Black scientists in the development and approval of the COVID-19 vaccines to garner more trust and acceptance' (Kerrigan et al., 2022). Information passed through trusted channels such as community leaders, or through religious leaders in a highly religious community, can ease some of the fear and distrust, while reinforcing sentiments of solidarity and community strength.

18.4.4 Cognitive Biases

Because public health messaging and information provision can occur in a top-down manner as well as within communities between equals, policymakers need to be careful to avoid intertwining personal beliefs or misconceptions about groups in their communications. But, at the same time, messaging needs to be clear and direct to combat the possibility of anchoring bias, availability heuristics, and bandwagon effects that can all occur through fake news and word-of-mouth within communities (Ala et al., 2021).

18.5 EDUCATIONAL INTERVENTIONS AND NUDGES/REMINDERS

Drawing from strategies used by policymakers to incentivise human papillomavirus (HPV) vaccines in minority populations, similar incentives can be implemented to try and increase COVID-19 vaccine uptake today. For HPV,

> A review on patient reminder and recall systems to improve
> immunization rates concluded that reminders were associated
> with an increase of 0.6–18% for adolescent immunization....
> In this review, specific to the HPV vaccination series in
> minority adolescents, studies with a reminder component
> were associated with an increase of 0–19% in vaccine
> initiation and an increase of 3.7–37.4% in series completion.
> (Lott et al., 2020)

Moreover, 'Interventions that aimed to increase contact between patients and providers ... may have been more effective than those aimed at providing educational information or addressing vaccine-related attitudes, without any regard for the actual medical appointment or provision of HPV vaccine' (Lott et al., 2020).

In terms of education, one study found that sharing

> [p]ublic health information to highlight that vaccine hesitancy
> may result in further disease outbreaks and disproportionate
> mortality from a preventable disease with use of vaccine in
> the BAME community will bolster confidence needed for mass
> immunisation. Proven significance and efficacy of effective large-
> scale vaccination programmes leading to eradication of dreaded
> diseases like Smallpox and Polio should reinforce faith
> in validated vaccines. (Iyengar et al., 2022)

Ensuring that vaccination occurs in a familiar or comfortable environment can also help, as well as promoting the proliferation of educational information designed by and communicated through trusted community members, as reported:

> Community education by healthcare workers and BAME
> healthcare professionals represent a trusted source of health
> information for minority ethnic groups. Local campaigns
> and involvement by these professionals will help build
> confidence in communities. Training of healthcare staff for
> mass communication, easy access to vaccine sites at local sites,

decentralised administration of vaccines in presence of local trusted family physicians can also help to escalate coverage. (Iyengar et al., 2022)

According to a study on nudges for COVID-19 vaccines (not exclusively for ethnic minorities though),

Because our sample consists of predominantly elderly and white participants, we confirmed (Fig. 4) that the effects of follow-through reminders and ownership language largely held for racial and ethnic minorities as defined in Fig. 4 ($n = 29,784$) and participants under 65 years old ($n = 9,279$). Notably, the average effects of follow-through reminders on both appointments and vaccinations were comparable across white ($n = 49,909$), Hispanic ($n = 10,624$), Black ($n = 5,109$) and Asian ($n = 7,553$) participants. (Dai et al., 2021)

18.6 CONCLUSION

Vaccine hesitancy is more prevalent among certain minority ethnic groups. This has to do with cultural and historical legacies, which can be addressed by new narratives, but in addition to that the health systems in multi-cultural countries need to improve the trust of their users and tailor their vaccination campaigns using some of the behavioural insights discussed in this chapter.

REFERENCES

Ala, A., Edge, C., Zumla, A., & Shafi, S. (2021). Specific COVID-19 messaging targeting ethnic minority communities. *EClinicalMedicine*, 35, 100862. https://doi.org/10.1016/j.eclinm.2021.100862

Allen, J. D., Abuelezam, N. N., Rose, R., & Fontenot, H. B. (2021). Factors associated with the intention to obtain a COVID-19 vaccine among a racially/ethnically diverse sample of women in the USA. *Translational Behavioral Medicine*, 11, 785–792. https://doi.org/10.1093/tbm/ibab014

Alsan, M., & Wanamaker, M. (2018). Tuskegee and the health of Black men. *The Quarterly Journal of Economics*, 133, 407–455. https://doi.org/10.1093/qje/qjx029

AuYoung, M., Rodriguez Espinosa, P., Chen, W., Juturu, P., Young, M.-E. D. T., Casillas, A., et al. (2022). Addressing racial/ethnic inequities in vaccine hesitancy and uptake: Lessons learned from the California alliance against COVID-19. *Journal of Behavioral Medicine*, 46(1–2), 153–166. https://doi.org/10.1007/s10865-022-00284-8

Bogart, L. M., Dong, L., Gandhi, P., Ryan, S., Smith, T. L., Klein, D. J., et al. (2021). *What Contributes to COVID-19 Vaccine Hesitancy in Black Communities, and How Can It Be Addressed?* RAND Corporation.

Burger, A. E., Reither, E. N., Mamelund, S.-E., & Lim, S. (2021). Black-white disparities in 2009 H1N1 vaccination among adults in the United States: A cautionary tale for the COVID-19 pandemic. *Vaccine*, 39, 943–951. https://doi.org/10.1016/j.vaccine.2020.12.069

Carson, S. L., Casillas, A., Castellon-Lopez, Y., Mansfield, L. N., Morris, D., Barron, J., et al. (2021). COVID-19 vaccine decision-making factors in racial and ethnic minority communities in Los Angeles, California. *JAMA Network Open*, 4, e2127582. https://doi.org/10.1001/jamanetworkopen.2021.27582

Cookson, R., Doran, T., Asaria, M., Gupta, I., & Mujica, F. P. (2021). The inverse care law re-examined: A global perspective. *The Lancet*, 397, 828–838. https://doi.org/10.1016/S0140-6736(21)00243-9

D'Aza, D. G., Shariff, M. A., Santibanez, I. D., Horowitz, R., Asad, H., Mensah, D., et al. (2021). 590. Persisting COVID-19 vaccination hesitancy in the South Bronx. *Open Forum Infectious Diseases*, 8, S397–S398. https://doi.org/10.1093/ofid/ofab466.788

Dai, H., Saccardo, S., Han, M. A., Roh, L., Raja, N., Vangala, S., et al. (2021). Behavioural nudges increase COVID-19 vaccinations. *Nature*, 597, 404–409. https://doi.org/10.1038/s41586-021-03843-2

Enhancing public trust in COVID-19 vaccination: The role of governments. (n.d.). OECD. www.oecd.org/coronavirus/policy-responses/enhancing-public-trust-in-covid-19-vaccination-the-role-of-governments-eae0ec5a/

Fuller, H., Dubbala, K., Obiri, D., Mallare, M., Advani, S., De Souza, S., et al. (2021). Addressing vaccine hesitancy to reduce racial and ethnic disparities in COVID-19 vaccination uptake across the UK and US. *Frontiers in Public Health*, 9, 789753.

Iyengar, K. P., Vaishya, R., Jain, V. K., & Ish, P. (2022). BAME community hesitancy in the UK for COVID-19 vaccine: Suggested solutions. *Postgraduate Medical Journal*, 98, e134–e135. https://doi.org/10.1136/postgradmedj-2021-139957

Jesuthasan, J., Powell, R. A., Burmester, V., & Nicholls, D. (2021). 'We weren't checked in on, nobody spoke to us': An exploratory qualitative analysis of two focus groups on the concerns of ethnic minority NHS staff during COVID-19. *BMJ Open*, 11, e053396. https://doi.org/10.1136/bmjopen-2021-053396

Kerrigan, D., Mantsios, A., Karver, T. S., Davis, W., Taggart, T., Calabrese, S. K., et al. (2022). Context and considerations for the development of community-informed health communication messaging to support equitable uptake of COVID-19 vaccines among communities of color in Washington, DC. *Journal of Racial and Ethnic Health Disparities*, 10, 395–409. https://doi.org/10.1007/s40615-022-01231-8

Lott, B. E., Okusanya, B. O., Anderson, E. J., Kram, N. A., Rodriguez, M., Thomson, C. A., et al. (2020). Interventions to increase uptake of Human Papillomavirus (HPV) vaccination in minority populations: A systematic review. *Preventive Medicine Reports*, 19, 101163. https://doi.org/10.1016/j.pmedr.2020.101163

Martins, T., Abel, G., Ukoumunne, O. C., Mounce, L. T. A., Price, S., Lyratzopoulos, G., et al. (2022). Ethnic inequalities in routes to diagnosis of cancer: A population-based UK cohort study. *British Journal of Cancer*, 127(5), 863–871. https://doi.org/10.1038/s41416-022-01847-x

Mena Lora, A. J., Echeverria, S. L., Li, E., Morales, M., Esquiliano, R., Schultz, G., et al. (2021). 566. Impact of a culturally sensitive multilingual community outreach model on COVID-19 vaccinations at an urban safety-net community hospital. *Open Forum Infectious Diseases*, 8, S385. https://doi.org/10.1093/ofid/ofab466.764

Robinson, E., Jones, A., Lesser, I., & Daly, M. (2021). International estimates of intended uptake and refusal of COVID-19 vaccines: A rapid systematic review and meta-analysis of large nationally representative samples. *Vaccine*, 39, 2024–2034. https://doi.org/10.1016/j.vaccine.2021.02.005

Tai, D. B. G., Shah, A., Doubeni, C. A., Sia, I. G., & Wieland, M. L. (2020). The disproportionate impact of COVID-19 on racial and ethnic minorities in the United States. *Clinical Infectious Diseases*, 72(4), 703–706. https://doi.org/10.1093/cid/ciaa815

Watkinson, R. E., Williams, R., Gillibrand, S., Sanders, C., & Sutton, M. (2022). Ethnic inequalities in COVID-19 vaccine uptake and comparison to seasonal influenza vaccine uptake in Greater Manchester, UK: A cohort study. *PLOS Medicine*, 19, e1003932. https://doi.org/10.1371/journal.pmed.1003932

19 How Can We Optimise Healthcare Delivery in the Wake of the COVID-19 Pandemic?

The Rise of Digital Health Solutions in England

Georgina Connolly and Divya Srivastava

19.1 INTRODUCTION

The COVID-19 pandemic resulted in a rapid proliferation and integration of health technologies into health systems across the world (Lieneck et al., 2020; OECD, European Union, 2020). In England, for example, most general practices switched to a 'total triage' system by June 2020, supported by 99 per cent of practices adopting or maintaining a remote consultation platform (Appointments in General Practice, 2021; Dyson, 2020a; NHS England, 2020a, b). Between December 2019 and December 2020, the number of people using NHS App saw a nine-fold increase, and between June and November 2020, there was close to a three-fold increase in visits to NHS 111 online compared with the previous year (NHS Digital, 2020a). At a time when COVID-19 is threatening the sustainability of the National Health Service (NHS), due to healthcare professional (HCP) fatigue, struggling hospital infrastructure, and a growing backlog of procedures (Dyson, 2020b; GOV.UK, 2022a), digital health presents an opportunity to alleviate some of these challenges through supporting clinical decision-making and improving monitoring, enhancing access and care coordination, and increasing patient health literacy and self-management (Barbabella et al., 2017; Fisk et al., 2020). Digital health, however, is not a magic bullet, and any ongoing advances must be met with robust evaluation, regulation, and reporting (Hutchings, 2020). Healthcare use and expenditure could increase significantly with the increased availability and use of digital health technologies, and therefore it is important to understand whether these expected increases result in high value and necessary care for all.

In this chapter, first we examine the effect of the COVID-19 pandemic on the use of digital healthcare. That is, we study the effect of the pandemic shock and subsequent COVID-19 policies on the rise of digital health solutions and technologies with a focus on healthcare settings. Second, we examine how behavioural economics theories help to critically evaluate the uptake and understand key changes in delivery and healthcare utilisation. Third, we develop behaviourally feasible policy proposals that could contribute to increased uptake of digital health solutions and technologies within the NHS, for providers and patients going forward.

Using England as a case study, descriptive mixed methods analysis (Schoonenboom & Johnson, 2017) was applied to explore three key questions. First, what were the barriers to the uptake of digital health solutions before the COVID-19 pandemic? Second, how did COVID-19 influence the use of digital health solutions in England? Finally, how might the adoption of digital health solutions be optimised and sustained moving forward?

Database searches were conducted on Medline, PubMed, and Embase using search terms centred around digital health barriers (and facilitators) and the impact of COVID-19 on the use of digital health in England. Additionally, data from NHS Digital, NHS England, the Office of National Statistics (ONS), and Health Foundation was scrutinised, along with government COVID-19 policies and guidance. Relevant behavioural economics theories were then identified and used to analyse this information from a healthcare provider and patient perspective. Most of the literature referenced was drawn from studies in England; however, there is also some reference to the United Kingdom as a whole. The majority of existing contributions referenced were published during the COVID-19 pandemic (2019–2022), though studies exploring barriers to the uptake of digital health pre-pandemic range from 2008 onwards.

19.2 BARRIERS TO THE UPTAKE OF DIGITAL HEALTH SOLUTIONS PRE-COVID-19

The need to embed technological innovation in healthcare delivery in the United Kingdom has increasingly been identified as a government and NHS priority. In 2018 Jeremy Hunt noted the need for the NHS to become 'massively more teched up' (Lintern, 2018), soon after NHSX was founded in 2019, with the prerogative to embed digital health in the NHS (Department of Health and Social Care, 2019). Similarly, the 2019 NHS long-term plan outlined the need for 'digitally enabled care to go mainstream across the NHS'. Despite this, analysis by Monitor Deloitte suggested that the UK mHealth market (for health-related apps and wearable devices) accounted for a relatively low proportion of the global market in 2019 (Monitor Deloitte, 2019). Whilst the United Kingdom has been hailed as an early adopter of information and communications technology (ICT) in primary care (Currie & Seddon, 2014; OECD, 2018) and has seen successes in technology-enabled healthcare in remote areas of Scotland (where eHealth was adopted out of necessity), as well as in specific localised hubs, such as Airedale NHS Foundation Trust (Freed et al., 2018; NHS Providers, 2015; Rooney et al., 2019), it lagged behind in its adoption of digital health systems and interoperability (Peterson et al., 2016). Moreover, evidence suggests that patient uptake of digital health pre-pandemic was low in England when compared with similar high-income countries (Rodgers et al., 2019).

We argue that behavioural theory offers important explanations for the observed barriers in the uptake of health technologies by healthcare providers and patients in England, with respect to status quo bias, bounded learning, hassle costs, and financial incentives (see Box 19.1). These four theories provide a more nuanced understanding of the interplay between policies and behavioural processes. This is fundamental to addressing ongoing challenges associated with the implementation, uptake, and maintenance of digital health solutions and technologies for decision-makers, providers, and patients.

BOX 19.1 **Key definitions**

- **Availability heuristic**: describes the undue weight individuals put on salient information (Jahn & Henning, 2007). Evidence suggests that people have difficulty evaluating probabilities, so they often perceive risks according to their saliency as opposed to the real risk (Schneider & Shiffrin, 1977).
- **Bounded learning**: acknowledges that the process of learning and synthesising new information can be time consuming and create a cognitive burden, meaning individuals often take shortcuts to reach an adequate as opposed to an optimal decision; this might be by following existing processes or adopting the opinion of a group they trust (Gobet & Lane, 2012).
- **Digital health solutions and digital health technologies**: terms that can be used interchangeably and describe apps, programmes, and software used in the health and care system (NICE, 2018). Examples include electronic health records (EHRs), health information systems, remote monitoring and consultation services (e.g., virtual care, telehealth, telemedicine, telecare), tools for self-management, and health data analytics (Barbabella et al., 2017).
- **Financial incentives**: describe how payments can motivate certain behaviours across organisations or within individuals (Vlaev et al., 2019). Evidence suggests that monetary incentives can work effectively, but they need to be integrated with wider incentives (e.g., social incentives, supportive policy, and nudges) (Vlaev et al., 2019).
- **Hassle costs**: describe individual tendencies to avoid tasks that involve hassle (Gobet & Lane, 2012).
- **Loss aversion**: is summarised by the expression 'losses loom larger than gains' and describes how individuals are far more concerned with the pain of losing than the pleasure of gaining (Kahneman et al., 1991). This implies that losing £100 will invoke greater dissatisfaction than the level of satisfaction accrued through gaining £100.

- **Nudge**: refers to 'any aspect of the choice architecture that alters people's behaviour in a predictable way without forbidding any options or significantly changing their economic incentives' (Sunstein & Thaler, 2008).
- **Social norms**: describe informal rules that govern behaviour in groups and societies, such as the values, beliefs, attitudes, and/ or behaviours shared by a group of people (Finnemore & Sikkink, 1998). There are three stages involved in the lifecycle of a norm: (1) norm emergence – which is driven by norm entrepreneurs (such as role models) who persuade others to adopt a new norm; (2) norm cascades – where the new norm is accepted by many individuals (norm compliers); (3) norm internalisation – where a norm becomes wholly established in a social group and 'taken for granted' (Finnemore & Sikkink, 1998).
- **Status quo bias**: a type of cognitive bias that refers to individuals' preferences for situations or things to stay the same (Kahneman et al., 1991).
- **Tipping point**: a sociological term that describes the point in time when a group rapidly and dramatically changes their behaviour to adopt a new belief or form of practice (Schelling, 1971). Tipping points are often-termed 'natural' nudges, since they act as non-orchestrated changes to a person's environment that may influence their decision-making (Schelling, 1971).

19.3 BARRIERS FOR HEALTHCARE PROVIDERS

19.3.1 *Status Quo Bias, Bounded Learning, Hassle Costs, and Financial Incentives*

Interestingly, at a macro-scale, the NHS is broadly supportive of digital health uptake, particularly since technological innovation often drives efficiency and productivity in a system under severe financial pressure (Asthana et al., 2019). National policy reflects this notion (NHS, 2019), yet complexities within the NHS relating to fragmentation, financing, and regulation historically impeded its uptake at a local level, reinforcing non-adoption by providers, due to status quo bias, bounded learning, and hassle costs.

For example, the National Programme for IT was launched in 2002 and later dismantled in 2011 after a series of failings (Greenhalgh & Keen, 2013; Justinia, 2017). Following this, local health providers were encouraged to develop their preferred health technologies, but in many cases commissioners lacked the confidence to procure new digital systems and technologies (in the absence of national guidance), opting to stick to the 'status quo' and avoid the hassle associated with adopting new technologies (Asthana et al., 2019; Robertson et al., 2010; Takian, 2012). These failings precipitated high levels of fragmentation within digital health systems in England, further increasing the burden and hassle costs associated with technology adoption for providers. Despite some progress, underlying challenges relating to inadequate infrastructure, underinvestment, unclear regulatory guidance, and HCP resistance still exist (GOV.UK, 2020; Hutchings, 2020; National Audit Office, 2020).

Lack of clarity and alignment in clinical evidence requirements from the National Institute for Health Care Excellence (NICE) and NHS Digital also contributed to healthcare provider status quo bias, bounded learning, and hassle costs (Greenhalgh et al., 2017; Lancet, 2018; Lehoux et al., 2017; Lennon et al., 2017; The Health Foundation, 2018). The NHS Digital's 'Digital Assessment Questionnaire' contains several hundred questions, a hassle cost that can prevent small and medium-sized enterprises entering the digital health market and/or lead to the introduction of health technologies without appropriate evaluation mechanisms in place (Greenhalgh et al., 2017; Lancet, 2018; Lehoux et al., 2017; Lennon et al., 2017; The Health Foundation, 2018).

The challenges in coordinating regulation and governance in providing necessary information to developers have hindered quick roll-out of digital health solutions and technologies. The State of Nation Survey conducted in 2019 highlighted the lack of poor communication and guidance; most developers reported that they were unaware of the commercial arrangement they had in place to gain access to necessary data; one-third were not developing in line with the Code of Conduct for Data-Driven Health and Care Technology; and two-thirds of artificial intelligence developers reported that their product would not be ready for deployment at scale in one year (NHSX, 2019).

In addition to the barriers associated with national policy and regulation, much of the literature points towards an underlying 'cultural resistance' (Rodgers et al., 2019; Oderanti & Li, 2018; Almathami et al., 2020; MacNeill et al., 2014). In a health system characterised by reorganisation and reform, qualitative studies provide a voice to change-fatigued NHS staff concerned about new technologies that bring with them 'hidden work' and administrative burden (bounded learning and hassle costs) (MacNeill et al., 2014). Patient safety, patient rapport, and the potential for misdiagnosis have also been cited as key reasons to 'stick to the status quo' (Almathami et al., 2020; Cowan et al., 2019; Dinesen et al., 2016; Kayyali et al., 2017; Khoshrounejad et al., 2021), as well as uncertainty around how technological developments will change the roles of clinical staff contributing to their scepticism (Asthana et al., 2019; Taylor et al., 2015). Physicians 'didn't have any particular reason to use [eHealth]. They didn't see a clinical need.' Also, adoption of health technologies 'involves major changes in workflows and professional interactions ... you could just bring the patient in and look at them – as you were taught' (Digital Health CRC, 2020).

The important role of financial incentives in the uptake of technology can be demonstrated by comparing the United Kingdom to other high-income countries in Europe and the United States, where digital health has been adopted at a far greater speed by providers, in part due to insurance claims incentivising the development of electronic health records and other health technologies (Asthana et al., 2019; New et al., 2018). Interestingly, in UK general practice, where payments are linked to a quality and outcomes framework, most general practice systems were virtually entirely digitised before the COVID-19 pandemic (New et al., 2018). Lack of clear business models and reimbursement mechanisms is cited as a key barrier to health technology innovation in the NHS within the literature, particularly in secondary and social care (Asthana et al., 2019; Oderanti & Li, 2018). In addition to this, financial pressures are differentially distributed across the NHS, due to NHS IT strategy historically prioritising investment in smaller and more digitally advanced providers (Asthana et al., 2019). This has resulted in the differential distribution in funds across England, further heightening digital division between older populations in rural areas and their metropolitan counterparts (Rodgers et al., 2019; Asthana & Gibson, 2020). The Department of Health and Social Care has since tried to address this through supplying funding to less digitally mature areas, yet further analysis is required to evaluate whether these attempts have proved effective (Asthana et al., 2019).

19.4 BARRIERS FOR PATIENTS

19.4.1 Status Quo Bias, Bounded Learning, and Hassle Costs

Status quo bias, bounded learning, and hassle costs also played an important role in the non-adoption of health technologies by patients before the COVID-19 pandemic. Internet speed and access, lack of digital devices, and poor audio or video quality are some of the key logistical barriers outlined by patients pre-pandemic (Almathami et al., 2020; Kayyali et al., 2017; Khoshrounejad et al., 2021; MacNeill et al., 2014; Oderanti & Li, 2018; Sanders et al., 2012). Additionally, usability issues relating to the intuitive design of health technologies, accessibility, and training for patient groups can create additional barriers for hard-to-reach communities and vulnerable patient groups (Almathami et al., 2020; Kayyali et al., 2017; Khoshrounejad et al., 2021; MacNeill et al., 2014; May et al., 2011; Oderanti & Li, 2018; Sanders et al., 2012). These hassle and learning factors, along with concerns relating to privacy and security, all contributed to an underlying cultural resistance and propensity towards the status quo for many patient groups (Almathami et al., 2020; Dinesen et al., 2016; Oderanti & Li, 2018; Rodgers et al., 2019; Sanders et al., 2012).

19.5 HOW DID COVID-19 INFLUENCE THE USE OF DIGITAL HEALTH IN ENGLAND?

19.5.1 COVID-19 as a Tipping Point

COVID-19 was a tipping point for the rapid adoption of digital health in England, enforcing the short-term minimisation or removal of many of the payor, provider, and patient-level barriers that existed pre-pandemic. Behaviourally, this is important, as it facilitated rapid innovation and adoption of health technologies within the NHS, potentially paving the way for improved access, enhanced patient literacy, and supported clinician decision-making.

The tipping point affected COVID-19 policies and the way in which providers adapted during the pandemic. Right before the United Kingdom went into lockdown (23 March 2020), on 17 March 2020, NHS England and Improvement issued a note to health trusts, health service commissioners, providers including general practice services to support the provision of remote consultations (telephone-based, digital, and video-based) with increased use of email and text messages while face-to-face appointments should take place only when necessary (Fisk et al., 2020). Before the pandemic, remote consultations were not widespread, but this policy decision required providers to undergo a rapid transformation towards implementing remote consultations.

Providers were forced to respond quickly. The number of remote consultations increased once the first lockdown came into effect (Figure 19.1). This tipping point went some way to mitigate barriers in the uptake of digital health technologies. These system-level changes facilitated addressing the status quo bias (New et al., 2018), offsetting bounded learning and hassle costs, supported with financial incentives. Providers reported positive experiences around the use of digital health technologies (Hutchings, 2020).

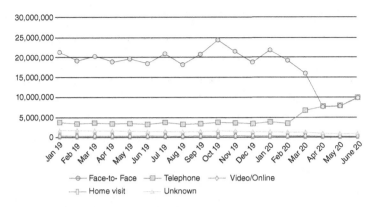

FIGURE 19.1 Appointments in general practice, January 2019–June 2020, by mode of appointment
Note: These numbers are the reported numbers of appointments, which is not the same as the estimated number of appointments for England. They may not include all data for all appointments, as multiple telephone calls could be counted under a single appointment slot, and practices using online or video appointments may not yet be reporting them in the same way as their other appointments.
Source: NHS Digital (2020b).

19.6 INFLUENCING PATIENT BEHAVIOURS

19.6.1 Availability Heuristic and Risk Saliency

The COVID-19 pandemic caused the emergence of numerous social norms, such as wearing masks in shops and on public transport, washing hands regularly, and maintaining social distance. However, for many, these norms were not internalised, due to factors such as high vaccination uptake, changing public policy (e.g., as of January 2022, masks are no longer mandated in public indoor spaces), and the associated changes in risk perception (GOV.UK, 2022b; Herbec et al., 2022; Stierand et al., 2021).

For patients, behavioural responses were mixed, reflecting the interplay of factors between policies and individual response. The policy decisions required everyone to change the way in which they seek healthcare, and this facilitated putting less weight on availability heuristic, risk saliency, and nudges towards loss aversion.

The patient response led to an increased uptake not only in remote consultations (Figure 19.1) but also increasingly in seeking information through online and digital means. A time-series analysis compared web-based internet searches for digital health products before the first lockdown (January 2019 to 23 March 2020) and then afterwards (24 March 2020 to 31 December 2020). Searches increased close to 350 per cent from 2,446 digital health products per month prior to COVID-19 lockdown measures being introduced to 8,996 per month in the period following the first COVID-19 lockdown in the United Kingdom. The greatest increases occurred in the first two months following lockdown particularly for the following conditions: musculoskeletal conditions, allergy, and healthy lifestyle-related digital health products (Leigh et al., 2021).

But the increased use of digital health technology uptake did not happen across the board for all patients. Before the pandemic, a recurrent fact was relatively lower levels of patient digital literacy and patient activation among certain groups: namely among hard-to-reach communities (ethnic minorities and lower-income/low-education groups) and vulnerable patient groups (older patients or those with long-term conditions (The Nuffield Trust, 2019; Salisbury et al., 2020)). For example, one national survey of 2,040 respondents reported that older people and those of low educational attainment were less comfortable with digital information and preferred non-digital sources to digital sources of information (Sounderajah et al., 2021). COVID-19 policies may have made things worse for these groups, exacerbating inequalities in healthcare access and utilisation, thereby widening digital disparities (Fisher & Magin, 2021; Hutchings, 2020; The Health Foundation, 2020). For these hard-to-reach groups of patients, it is plausible that among other reasons they continue to place undue weight on availability heuristic, risk saliency, and loss aversion, deterring their uptake of digital health technology. Further evidence in understanding the behavioural mechanisms to improve uptake among such population subgroups is needed.

19.7 HOW MIGHT THE ADOPTION OF DIGITAL HEALTH BE OPTIMISED AND SUSTAINED MOVING FORWARD?

19.7.1 *Motivating Healthcare Providers*

A range of supportive policies are necessary to address status quo bias, bounded learning, hassle costs, and the lack of financial incentivisation at the system level and for providers (see Box 19.2) (Oderanti & Li, 2018; The King's Fund, 2018). Learnings from user-centred approaches of provider involvement and feedback must be routinely embedded, to ensure user-friendly and accessible design of products and services, which do not incur additional learning and hassle costs (Greenhalgh et al., 2017; Taylor et al., 2015). Such approaches are effective in increasing health technology uptake in various healthcare settings (Almathami et al., 2020; Fisk et al., 2020; Foster & Sethares, 2014).

BOX 19.2 **Motivating healthcare providers**

System-level approaches to mitigate status quo bias, bounded learning, and hassle costs and to improve financial incentives:

- system-wide leadership and local leadership of trained digital health champions
- partnerships
- sustainable financing models
- simplification of regulatory requirements
- embed HCP feedback to inform service delivery, design, and implementation

Supportive policies for HCPs to mitigate status quo bias, bounded learning, and hassle costs:

- supportive workplace policies for online and in-person training
- inclusion of digital health competencies in continuous professional development for HCPs
- Inclusion of digital health competencies in education curricula

19.7.2 *Motivating Patients: Availability Heuristic, Status Quo Bias, Bounded Learning, and Hassle Costs and Shifting Social Norms*

Recent research on patient experience using remote consultations during the pandemic has highlighted several issues between demand management and patient choice – leading to both large- and small-scale ethical dilemmas for managers, support staff, and clinicians. Researchers argue that these dilemmas must be managed and informed by evidence around practical challenges, drawing on guiding principles applied with contextual judgement (Greenhalgh et al., 2021).

These dilemmas underline the need for effective behavioural public policies to normalise and internalise the use of digital health technologies as a social norm across society (see Box 19.3). This can be done by utilising availability heuristics, nudging (Thaler and Sunstein's principles of nudging) and addressing barriers associated with status quo bias, bounded learning, and hassle costs by delivering usable and accessible digital health products (Foster & Sethares, 2014).

BOX 19.3 **Motivating patients**

System-level approaches to mitigate availability heuristic, status quo bias, bounded learning, and hassle costs and support shifting social norms:

- Promote the use of digital health technologies via information campaigns.
- De-bunk privacy and security concerns via information campaigns.
- Embed patient feedback to inform service delivery, design, and implementation.
- Conduct user research during the development of digital health technologies.

Supportive policies for patients to mitigate availability heuristic, status quo bias, bounded learning, and hassle costs and support shifting social norms:

- a digital offer that considers when 'digital first' is appropriate
- digital skills training within communities to address digital disparities
- flexible offer of digital health solutions that include, for example, interpretation services for consultations to facilitate greater reach

19.8   CONCLUDING THOUGHTS

COVID-19 has been a tipping point for drastic changes in the English health system. This literature review has focused on the rapid proliferation and adoption of digital health solutions within the NHS. Status quo bias, bounded learning, hassle costs, and (lack of) financial incentives were all key barriers to the adoption of digital health pre-pandemic, underpinned by poor infrastructure, lack of investment, regulatory 'red tape', and HCP and patient resistance. COVID-19 saw the temporary removal of many of these barriers, allowing innovations to happen at speed within the NHS. Additionally, patient behaviour was guided towards digital health solutions and services due to their increased availability and the risk saliency of COVID-19.

Questions remain on whether these digital health solutions are good value for money. Many of the decisions that were taken during the pandemic were made with a short-term view; for example, some remote consultation providers offered services for free or prioritised 'off-the-shelf' products that did not necessarily meet their specific needs (Dyson, 2020a; Hutchings, 2020). Similarly, regulatory 'red tape' was torn away to prioritise remote care delivery, hence services have been adopted without the same scrutiny or requirements for clinical evidence (Commonwealth Fund, 2020).

Decision-makers should work towards a cohesive technology infrastructure, investment, clear regulation, improved usability and digital training to sustain the adoption of digital health technologies moving forward. Additionally, behavioural analysis from the perspective of patients highlights the importance of user-informed design, digital skills sessions, health technology promotion, and a digital offer that is flexible to motivate shifting societal norms.

Sustaining new models of care moving forward will be a fundamental challenge for decision-makers. Ongoing advancement must be underpinned by embedding systematic robust research and evidence generation to inform policy design and implementation. Evidence that draws on behavioural lens to understand the pandemic is growing, and this is an opportunity for researchers to engage with and inform the decision-making process.

REFERENCES

Almathami, H. K. Y., Win, K. T., & Vlahu-Gjorgievska, E. (2020). Barriers and facilitators that influence telemedicine-based, real-time, online consultation at patients' homes: Systematic literature review. *Journal of Medical Internet Research*, 22(2), e16407.

Asthana, S., & Gibson, A. (2020). The National Health Service (NHS) in 'crisis': The role played by a shift from horizontal to vertical principles of equity. *Health Economics, Policy and Law*, 15(1), 1–17.

Asthana, S., Jones, R., & Sheaff, R. (2019). Why does the NHS struggle to adopt eHealth innovations? A review of macro, meso and micro factors. *BMC Health Services Research*, 19(1), 984.

Barbabella, F., Melchiorre, M., Quattrini, S., Papa, R., & Lamura, G. (2017). *How can eHealth Improve Care for People with Multimorbidity in Europe?* WHO Regional Office for Europe.

Commonwealth Fund. (2020). Telemedicine: What should the post-pandemic regulatory and payment landscape look like? www.commonwealthfund.org/publications/issue-briefs/2020/aug/telemedicine-post-pandemic-regulation

Cowan, K. E., McKean, A. J., Gentry, M. T., & Hilty, D. M. (2019). Barriers to use of telepsychiatry: Clinicians as gatekeepers. *Mayo Clinic Proceedings*, 94(12), 2510–2523.

Currie, W. L., & Seddon, J. J. M. (2014). A cross-national analysis of EHealth in the European Union: Some policy and research directions. *Information & Management*, 51(6), 783–797.

Department of Health and Social Care. (2019). NHSX: New joint organisation for digital, data and technology. GOV.UK. www.gov.uk/government/news/nhsx-new-joint-organisation-for-digital-data-and-technology

Digital Health CRC. (2020). COVID-19 and digital technology: The roles, relevance and risks of using telehealth in a crisis. www.digitalhealthcrc.com/telehealth-webinar/

Dinesen, B., Nonnecke, B., Lindeman, D., Toft, E., Kidholm, K., Jethwani, K., et al. (2016). Personalized telehealth in the future: A global research agenda. *Journal of Medical Internet Research*, 18(3), e5257.

Dyson, M. (2020a). COVID-19: Video consultations and homeworking. The British Medical Association. www.bma.org.uk/advice-and-support/covid-19/adapting-to-covid/covid-19-video-consultations-and-homeworking

Dyson, M. (2020b). Pressure points in the NHS. The British Medical Association. www.bma.org.uk/advice-and-support/nhs-delivery-and-workforce/pressures/pressure-points-in-the-nhs

Finnemore, M., & Sikkink, K. (1998). International norm dynamics and political change. *International Organization*, 52(4), 887–917.

Fisher, K., & Magin, P. (2021). The telehealth divide: Health inequity during the COVID-19 pandemic. *Family Practice*, 39(3), 547–549.

Fisk, M., Livingstone, A., & Pit, S. W. (2020). Telehealth in the context of COVID-19: Changing perspectives in Australia, the United Kingdom, and the United States. *Journal of Medical Internet Research*, 22(6), e19264.

Foster, M. V., & Sethares, K. A. (2014). Facilitators and barriers to the adoption of telehealth in older adults: an integrative review. *CIN: Computers, Informatics, Nursing*, 32(11), 523–533.

Freed, J., Lowe, C., Flodgren, G., Binks, R., Doughty, K., & Kolsi, J. (2018). Telemedicine: Is it really worth it? A perspective from evidence and experience. *Journal of Innovation in Health Informatics*, 25(1), 14–18.

Gobet, F., & Lane, P. (2012). Bounded rationality and learning. In N. M. Seel (ed.), *Encyclopedia of the Sciences of Learning* (pp. 482–484). Springer.

GOV.UK. (2020). The future of healthcare. www.gov.uk/government/speeches/the-future-of-healthcare

GOV.UK. (2022a). Build back better: Our plan for health and social care. www.gov.uk/government/publications/build-back-better-our-plan-for-health-and-social-care/build-back-better-our-plan-for-health-and-social-care

GOV.UK. (2022b). Coronavirus (COVID-19): Guidance and support. www.gov.uk/coronavirus

Greenhalgh, T., & Keen, J. (2013). England's national programme for IT. *British Medical Journal*, 346, f4130.

Greenhalgh, T., Rosen, R., Shaw, S. E., Byng, R., Faulkner, S., Finlay, T., et al. (2021). Planning and evaluating remote consultation services: A new conceptual framework incorporating complexity and practical ethics. *Front Digit Health* [online]. www.frontiersin.org/article/10.3389/fdgth.2021.726095

Greenhalgh, T., Wherton, J., Papoutsi, C., Lynch, J., Hughes, G., A'Court, C., et al. (2017). Beyond adoption: A new framework for theorizing and evaluating no adoption, abandonment, and challenges to the scale-up, spread, and sustainability of health and care technologies. *Journal of Medical Internet Research*, 19(11), e8775.

Herbec, A., Brown, J., Jackson, S. E., Kale, D., Zatoński, M., Garnett, C., et al. (2022). Perceived risk factors for severe Covid-19 symptoms and their association with health behaviours: Findings from the HEBECO study. *Acta Psychologica*, 222, 103458.

Hutchings, R. (2020). The impact of Covid-19 on the use of digital technology in the NHS. Briefing, Nuffield Trust.

Jahn, G., & Henning, M. (2007). An introduction to applied cognitive psychology. A. Esgate and D. Groome with K. Baker, D. Heathcote, R. Kemp, M. Maguire, & C. Reed (Eds.), Psychology Press, Hove, UK and New York, 2005. No. of pages 327. ISBN 1-84169-318-9, ISBN 1-84169-317-0. Applied cognitive psychology: a textbook. D. J. Herrmann, C. Y. Yoder, M. Gruneberg, and D. G. Payne (Eds.). Lawrence Erlbaum Associates, Mahwah, NJ, 2006. No. of pages 304. ISBN 0-8058-3373-0, ISBN 0-8058-3372-2. *Applied Cognitive Psychology*, 21(4), 551–553.

Justinia, T. (2017). The UK's National Programme for IT: Why was it dismantled? *Health Services Management Research*, 30(1), 2–9.

Kahneman, D., Knetsch, J. L., & Thaler, R. H. (1991). Anomalies: The endowment effect, loss aversion, and status quo bias. *Journal of Economic Perspectives*, 5(1), 193–206.

Kayyali, R., Hesso, I., Mahdi, A., Hamzat, O., Adu, A., & Nabhani Gebara, S. (2017). Telehealth: Misconceptions and experiences of healthcare professionals in England. *International Journal of Pharmacy Practice*, 25(3), 203–209.

Khoshrounejad, F., Hamednia, M., Mehrjerd, A., Pichaghsaz, S., Jamalirad, H., Sargolzaei, M., et al. (2021). Telehealth-based services during the COVID-19 pandemic: A systematic review of features and challenges. *Frontiers in Public Health* [online]. www.frontiersin.org/article/10.3389/fpubh.2021.711762

Lancet, T. (2018). Is digital medicine different? *The Lancet*, 392(10142), 95.

Lehoux, P., Miller, F. A., Daudelin, G., & Denis, J.-L. (2017). Why learning how to chase butterflies matters: A response to recent commentaries. *International Journal of Health Policy and Management*, 7(3), 286–287.

Leigh, S., Daly, R., Stevens, S., Lapajne, L., Clayton, C., Andrews, T., et al. (2021). Web-based internet searches for digital health products in the United Kingdom before and during the COVID-19 pandemic: A time-series analysis using app libraries from the Organisation for the Review of Care and Health Applications (ORCHA). *BMJ Open*, 11(10), e053891.

Lennon, M. R., Bouamrane, M.-M., Devlin, A. M., O'Connor, S., O'Donnell, C., Chetty, U., et al. (2017). Readiness for delivering digital health at scale: Lessons from a longitudinal qualitative evaluation of a national digital health innovation program in the United Kingdom. *Journal of Medical Internet Research*, 19(2), e42.

Lieneck, C., Garvey, J., Collins, C., Graham, D., Loving, C., & Pearson, R. (2020). Rapid telehealth implementation during the COVID-19 global pandemic: A rapid review. *Healthcare (Basel, Switzerland)*, 8(4), 517.

Lintern, S. (2018). Exclusive: Hunt seeks 'full health and social care integration' under new 10 year plan. *Health Service Journal* [online]. www.hsj.co.uk/policy-andregulation/exclusive-hunt-seeks-full-health-and-social-care-integration-undernew-10-year-plan/7022319.article

MacNeill, V., Sanders, C., Fitzpatrick, R., Hendy, J., Barlow, J., Knapp, M., et al. (2014). Experiences of front-line health professionals in the delivery of telehealth: A qualitative study. *British Journal of General Practice*, 64(624), e401–e407.

May, C. R., Finch, T. L., Cornford, J., Exley, C., Gately, C., Kirk, S., et al. (2011). Integrating telecare for chronic disease management in the community: What needs to be done? *BMC Health Services Research*, 11(1), 131.

Monitor Deloitte. (2019). Connected health. Deloitte United Kingdom. www2.deloitte.com/uk/en/pages/life-sciences-and-healthcare/articles/connected-health.html

National Audit Office. (2020). Digital transformation in the NHS: National Audit Office (NAO) Report. www.nao.org.uk/report/the-use-of-digital-technology-in-the-nhs/

New, J. P., Leather, D., Bakerly, N. D., McCrae, J., & Gibson, J. M. (2018). Putting patients in control of data from electronic health records. *British Medical Journal*, 360, j5554.

NHS. (2019). The NHS long term plan. www.longtermplan.nhs.uk/publication/nhs-long-term-plan/

NHS Digital. (2020a). Coronavirus pandemic prompts a surge in the number of people using NHS tech in 2020. https://digital.nhs.uk/news/2020/surge-in-people-using-nhs-tech-2020

NHS Digital. (2020b). Appointments in General Practice, June 2020; Information from NHS England, licenced under the current version of the Open Government Licence. https://digital.nhs.uk/data-and-information/publications/statistical/appointments-in-general-practice/june-2020#:~:text=21.3%20million%20

appointments%20are%20estimated%20to%20have%20happened%20in%20
June%202020.&text=57%25%20of%20appointments%20in%20June

NHS Digital. (2021). Appointments in general practice, October. https://digital.nhs
.uk/data-and-information/publications/statistical/appointments-in-general-
practice/october-2021

NHS England. (2020a). Millions of patients benefiting from remote consultations as family doctors respond to COVID-19. 28 May. www.england.nhs
.uk/2020/05/millions-of-patients-benefitingfrom-remote-consultations-as-
family-doctors-respond-to-covid-19

NHS England. (2020b). Next steps on general practice response to Covid 19. Letter
to GPs and their commissioners. 19 March. www.england.nhs.uk/coronavirus/
wp-content/uploads/sites/52/2020/03/preparednessletter-primary-care-
19-march-2020.pdf

NHS Providers. (2015). Telemedicine at Airedale NHS Foundation Trust: Better
care in the community for elderly patients. www.airedaledigitalcare.nhs.uk/
seecmsfile/?id=33

NHSX. (2019). *Artificial Intelligence: How to Get It Right. Putting Policy into
Practice for Safe Data-Driven Innovation in Health and Care*. NHSX.

NICE. (2018). Evidence standards framework for digital health technologies.
www.nice.org.uk/about/what-we-do/our-programmes/evidence-standards-
framework-for-digital-health-technologies

Oderanti, F. O., & Li, F. (2018). Commercialization of eHealth innovations in the
market of the UK healthcare sector: A framework for a sustainable business
model. *Psychology & Marketing*, 35(2), 120–137.

OECD, European Union. (2018). Health at a glance: Europe 2018: State of health
in the EU cycle. www.oecd-ilibrary.org/social-issues-migration-health/health-
at-a-glance-europe-2018_health_glance_eur-2018-en

OECD, European Union. (2020). Health at a glance: Europe 2020: State of health
in the EU cycle. www.oecd-ilibrary.org/social-issues-migration-health/health-
at-a-glance-europe-2020_82129230-en

Peterson, C. B., Hamilton, C., & Hasvold, P. (2016). *From Innovation to Implementation:
eHealth in the WHO European Region*. WHO Regional Office for Europe.

Robertson, A., Cresswell, K., Takian, A., Petrakaki, D., Crowe, S., Cornford, T.,
et al. (2010). Implementation and adoption of nationwide electronic health
records in secondary care in England: Qualitative analysis of interim results
from a prospective national evaluation. *British Medical Journal*, 341, c4564.

Rodgers, M., Raine, G., Thomas, S., Harden, M., & Eastwood, A. (2019). Informing
NHS policy in 'digital-first primary care': A rapid evidence synthesis. Health

Services and Delivery Research. NIHR Journals Library, Southampton, UK. www.ncbi.nlm.nih.gov/books/NBK551744/

Rooney, L., Rimpiläinen, S., Morrison, C., & Nielsen, S. L. (2019). *Review of Emerging Trends in Digital Health and Care: A Report by the Digital Health and Care Institute*. Digital Health and Care Institute, Glasgow. https://doi .org/10.17868/67860

Salisbury, C., Quigley, A., Hex, N., & Aznar, C. (2020). Private video consultation services and the future of primary care. *Journal of Medical Internet Research*, 22(10), e19415.

Sanders, C., Rogers, A., Bowen, R., Bower, P., Hirani, S., Cartwright, M., et al. (2012). Exploring barriers to participation and adoption of telehealth and telecare within the whole system demonstrator trial: A qualitative study. *BMC Health Services Research*, 12(1), 220.

Schelling, T. C. (1971). Dynamic models of segregation. *Journal of Mathematical Sociology*, 1(2), 143–186.

Schneider, W., & Shiffrin, R. M. (1977). Controlled and automatic human information processing: I. Detection, search, and attention. *Psychological Review*, 84(1), 1–66.

Schoonenboom, J., & Johnson, R. B. (2017). How to construct a mixed methods research design. *KZfSS Kölner Zeitschrift für Soziologie und Sozialpsychologie*, 69(2), 107–131.

Sounderajah, V., Clarke, J., Yalamanchili, S., Acharya, A., Markar, S. R., Ashrafian, H., et al. (2021). A national survey assessing public readiness for digital health strategies against COVID-19 within the United Kingdom. *Scientific Reports*, 11(1), 5958.

Stierand, J., Luebber, F., Krach, S., Paulus, F. M., & Rademacher, L. (2021). Perceived risk of infection linked to changes in comfort in social situations from before to during the COVID-19 pandemic. *Frontiers in Psychiatry* [online]. www .frontiersin.org/article/10.3389/fpsyt.2021.678072

Sunstein, C., & Thaler, R. H. (2008). *Nudge: Improving Decisions about Health, Wealth, and Happiness*. New Haven: Yale University Press.

Takian, A., Petrakaki, D., Cornford, T., Sheikh, A., & Barber, N. (2012). Building a house on shifting sand: Methodological considerations when evaluating the implementation and adoption of national electronic health record systems. *BMC Health Services Research*, 12(1), 105.

Taylor, J., Coates, E., Brewster, L., Mountain, G., Wessels, B., & Hawley, M. S. (2015). Examining the use of telehealth in community nursing: Identifying the factors affecting frontline staff acceptance and telehealth adoption. *Journal of Advanced Nursing*, 71(2), 326–337.

The Health Foundation. (2018). Against the odds: Successfully scaling innovation in the NHS. www.health.org.uk/publications/against-the-odds-successfully-scaling-innovation-in-the-nhs

The Health Foundation. (2020). Public perceptions of health and social care in light of COVID-19. November. www.health.org.uk/publications/public-perceptions-of-health-and-social-care-in-light-of-covid-19-november-2020

The King's Fund. (2018). Digital change in health and social care. www.kingsfund.org.uk/publications/digital-change-health-social-care

The Nuffield Trust. (2019). Will a digital NHS reap the rewards policy-makers are aiming for? www.nuffieldtrust.org.uk/news-item/will-a-digital-nhs-reap-the-rewards-policy-makers-are-aiming-for

Vlaev, I., King, D., Darzi, A., & Dolan, P. (2019). Changing health behaviors using financial incentives: A review from behavioral economics. *BMC Public Health*, 19(1), 1059.

20 Biases in Vaccine Authorisation

Erring on the Side of Rare Events in SARS-CoV-2 Vaccines

Joan Costa-Font, Miqdad Asaria,
and Elias Mossialos

20.1 INTRODUCTION

Decisions regarding the authorisation of new vaccines against
SARS-CoV-2 have been highly heterogeneous across countries, resulting in significant regulatory misalignment regarding the vaccines approved for use in different countries (Avorn & Kesselheim,
2020; European Medicines Agency, 2021). This book chapter argues
that such misalignment reflects an appeal to a version of the 'precautionary principle', which we define as 'erring on the side of rare
events' (ESRE) (Costa-Font et al., 2021). ESRE is a form of extreme
implementation of the precautionary principle that arises when
misinformed public opinion places disproportionate attention on
small and rare risks in making risk–benefit assessments. It is a
specific behavioural bias that emerges under the presence of information ambiguity, namely probabilities of rare events that are not
precisely known, which reflects an extreme fixation on rare though
salient and highly publicised events. Ambiguity aversion reflects a
preference for known uncertainty, which gives rise to pessimistic
risk judgements and promotes inaction. This is especially the case
in the health domain when decisions are portrayed in a loss frame.
For instance, rare side events are presented as losses associated with
vaccination (Attema et al., 2018). For instance, perceived ambiguity around cancer prevention and screening programmes has been
found to reduce the uptake of these interventions (Han et al., 2007).

Similarly, ambiguity aversion in a sample of physicians influences their therapeutic decisions with regard to stroke prevention (Raptis et al., 2017).

More generally, these studies suggest that conflicting information discourages individuals to undertake beneficial interventions such as vaccination, and instead their behaviour is guided by ESRE. This inaction may have resulted in avoidable hospitalisations and deaths due to COVID-19 as well as extended periods of economic and social restrictions, the costs of which are likely to largely outweigh vaccine side effects. In the remainder of this chapter, we describe the predictable nature of the ESRE phenomenon and discuss how ESRE emerges from the interplay between the mainstream media, social media, policymakers, and the public, impacting decision-making both at the individual and at the government level, which explains why some governments ignore the basic principles of risk–benefit decision-making. We argue that ESRE refers to a predictable decision-making bias in the presence of ambiguity and a potential health loss frame. Salient and conflicting risk information has been further fuelled by intense media coverage. In this way, an excessive focus on rare side effects has opened the door to vaccine misinformation, encouraged vaccine hesitancy, and reduced the potential benefits of the COVID-19 vaccination programme worldwide.

Media (including social media) reporting has amplified ESRE, which has contributed to the exaggeration of the risks of rare vaccine side effects. Government decisions regarding SARS-CoV-2 vaccines have responded to the ESRE criterion. Decisions made about vaccines in some countries have had far-reaching consequences for vaccine hesitancy globally. Section 20.2 discusses some cognitive biases that affect decision-making under risk. Section 20.3 discusses the role of the media, especially the effect of social media. Section 20.4 provides a discussion of public reactions to ESRE, and Section 20.5 provides some conclusions and policy implications.

20.2 COGNITIVE BIASES WHEN THINKING
ABOUT RISK IN DECISION-MAKING

Vaccine decision-making typically takes place in the presence of large scientific uncertainty (heterogeneous and conflicting information) with respect to the distribution of a future risk, which can induce societies to become fixated on the irreversibility of its effects, and hence take up a 'better safe than sorry approach' to new technologies (Gollier et al., 2000) or what some call the 'precautionary principle' (PP). The PP has been used before to justify a ban on genetically modified crops in Europe. However, the European Commission expects some proportionality between risk decision-making and levels of protection in applying such principles (EC, 2002). As a result, even though European regulators have judged many genetically modified crops as safe, some countries have refused to authorise them, hence deviating from rational risk policy principles. Part of the explanation for this behaviour can be found in understanding the ambiguity aversion that health regulators and individuals face in considering substantial but rare risks that they know little about. That is, the presence of large scientific uncertainty gives rise to cognitive, emotional, and behavioural responses that heighten the perceived risks of a course of action, as well as more generally pessimistic appraisals of risk-reducing actions such as vaccination, including fear and anxiety of its side effects, or avoidance of decision-making more generally (Golman et al., 2021). Indeed, aversion to ambiguity about a given prospect is driven by an implicit comparison with a less ambiguous prospect, which might be the risk of other vaccines not subject to rare side effects or the perceived control of the prospect of outright non-vaccination.

That said, the use of the PP has little benefit in decision-making as withholding a vaccine (or a drug) from the market can gives rise to loss of lives (Sunstein, 2003), especially in the middle of a pandemic. Individual decision-making under risk is subject to several cognitive biases, including the tendency to overestimate small and underestimate large base rate (Lichtenstein et al., 1978). People tend be very loss averse – that is, they anchor their risk evaluations on a status quo of no vaccine side effects and are willing to forego large and expected benefits to avoid the risks of unexpected losses such as vaccine-related blood clots. This means that individual decision-making system-atically deviates from risk–benefit estimates. Similarly, given the scientific uncertainly with regard to vaccination, regulators reveal ambiguity aversion (Fox & Tversky, 1995) by preferring to restricting the approval of vaccines to a small and limited choice set. Other rel-evant biases include framing effects resulting from excessive media coverage of rare events and media amplification. Media amplification portrays vaccination in a 'loss frame' (as we discuss in Section 20.3), which influences the decision on 'how to report' and 'what is/what is not news', which, in turn, gives rise to 'reporting biases' and 'selection biases', respectively. Reporting biases can influence the 'slant' of sto-ries and hence impact on attitudes when the public has very limited prior knowledge to form their own independent views (Vilella-Vila & Costa-Font, 2008). Finally, the decisions of regulators might instead reflect expert overconfidence, which leads to ignoring accurate risk information, as well as a deviation from risk–benefit assessments. Risk–benefit analysis is a type of cost–benefit analysis to help assess the trade-off between the benefits and risks of drugs and vaccines, reaching a balance between vaccine efficacy and vaccine safety. It is the standard approach used to guide decision-makers on how best to manage the risks associated with new health technologies. The ratio of risk to benefit is the most basic information that a regulator relies on when deciding whether a new technology is safe and acceptable for the target population. Such analyses often also include the preferences of patients and the wider population, and more generally public percep-tions of risk, either directly or through the involvement of patient or public representatives in decision-making processes.

The WHO establishes that risk–benefit assessment should:

1. address the population at risk (not the individual at risk),
2. take into account contextual issues (economics, availability of alterna-tive vaccines, socio-political and cultural factors),

3. be prompted by a newly identified risk but must remain holistic, and

4. run in parallel to active enquiry, cooperation, and exchange of information.

20.3 THE ROLE OF TRADITIONAL AND SOCIAL MEDIA

Unlike mainstream media, social media is not produced by journalists trained in science communication. On the contrary, information disseminated through social media is often misleading, inaccurate, or even false. In November 2020, 26 per cent of respondents to a nationally representative survey in the United Kingdom reported that they had seen or heard COVID-19 anti-vaccine messages on social media, 14 per cent believed that the role of coronavirus vaccination programmes was simply to track and control the population, and 15 per cent believed that the vaccination programmes were solely designed to profit pharmaceutical companies (Duffy, 2020). In response to such findings various social media outlets have announced efforts to tackle false information regarding COVID-19 vaccination. Despite such efforts, an Ofcom survey in the United Kingdom in March 2021 found that 28 per cent of respondents had come across information about COVID-19 that could be considered false or misleading (Ofcom, 2021). Loomba et al. (2021) conducted a randomised controlled trial in the United Kingdom and the United States to quantify how exposure to online misinformation around COVID-19 vaccines impacted intentions to vaccinate. They found that misinformation induced a decline in intention to take the COVID-19 vaccine of 6.2 percentage points in the United Kingdom and 6.4 percentage points in the United States.

With the rise of social media and its use to propagate 'fake news' and conspiracy theory, mainstream media has increasingly resorted to sensational 'clickbait' headlines and a focus on dramatic negative stories to compete for readers attention. As a result, risk communication has fallen prey to the 'rush to panic', even on matters that have significant knock-on effects for population health. This is exemplified by the recent front-page headline in the Italian newspaper *La Repubblica*: 'AstraZeneca, Fear across Europe' (Adnkronos, 2021; Nieman Reports, 2021; Symons, 2021). Following the media coverage around the

AstraZeneca (AZ) vaccine's side effects it was estimated that approximately 15–20 per cent of people in European countries would refuse to accept the vaccine (Adnkronos, 2021). A recent YouGov poll reports that 55 per cent of Germans and 61 per cent of French people now see the AZ vaccine as unsafe (YouGov, 2021). In the United States, only 38 per cent consider the AZ vaccine safe, while 27 per cent believe it to be unsafe and a further 35 per cent are unsure.

20.4   PUBLIC REACTION TO ESRE DECISION-MAKING

A poll conducted in March 2021 reports that most of the population did not perceive the AZ vaccine to be safe in five out of the six European countries polled, the exception being Great Britain (see Figure 20.1). In some countries such as France, this may reflect their higher levels of hesitancy towards vaccines in general; however, in other countries such

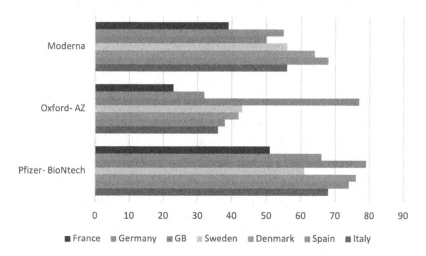

FIGURE 20.1 International perceptions of vaccine safety
Note: Percentage of the country sample to the question 'From your knowledge of "Pfizer Biotech/Oxford AZ/Modera" coronavirus vaccine … How safe, unsafe, do you think the "Pfizer Biotech/Oxford AZ/Modera" is?' Responses 'very unsafe' and 'somewhat unsafe' have been grouped together, and 'very safe' and 'somewhat safe' have been grouped together. Sample refers to 1,673 British, 2,021 German, 1,022 French, 1,016 Italian, 1,050 Spanish, 1,004 Danish, and 1,017 Swedish adults. Carried out by YouGov during 15–18 March 2021.

as Germany, Sweden, Spain, and Italy the majority of the population considered Pfizer BioNTech and Moderna vaccines to be safe whilst considering the AZ vaccine unsafe. This is despite regulators such as the European Medicines Agency reaffirming their decisions regarding the safety of the AZ vaccine. Accordingly, governments around the world have decided to bow to public pressure to restrict the use of the AZ vaccine, recognising that, as with any new health technology, public support is a key condition for the successful adoption of vaccines.

20.5 CONCLUSIONS AND POLICY IMPLICATIONS

Governments guided by ESRE in their decision-making have typically done so in high-income countries where COVID transmission rates are currently low, the most vulnerable members of the population are already vaccinated, stocks of alternative and typically more expensive vaccines have been procured, and the complex cold chain infrastructure is in place to deliver these alternative vaccines. ESRE epitomises the importance of accounting for ambiguity in health communication and suggests that trusted information sources should have been the primary actors in disseminating information regarding rare events associated with the vaccines. In the absence of reliable communication, theories of ambiguity aversion predict the development of ESRE, which fuels vaccine hesitancy.

Misinformation publicised through social media has been found to linger with fake news regarding vaccines that is proving very hard to correct, with efforts to do so having been shown to backfire (Pluviano et al., 2017). Regulating misinformation from social media and the exaggeration of risks from the mainstream media and balancing a respect for public opinion are important priorities if we are to keep ESRE from negatively affecting health policymaking.

REFERENCES

Adnkronos. (2021). AstraZeneca, Sileri: 'In Italy 15–20% will say no to this vaccine'. 11 April. www.adnkronos.com/astrazeneca-sileri-in-italia-15-20-dira-no-a-questo-vaccino_1k0wvRABWH6qU4bK0xq0B9#

Avorn, J., & Kesselheim, A. (2020). Regulatory decision-making on COVID-19 vaccines during a public health emergency. *JAMA*, 324(13), 1284–1285.

Costa-Font, J., Asaria, M., & Mossialos, E. (2021). Erring on the side of rare events? A behavioural explanation for COVID-19 vaccine regulatory misalignment. *Journal of Global Health*, 11, 03080.

Duffy, B. (2020). Coronavirus: Vaccine misinformation and the role of social media. 14 December, London Kings College. www.kcl.ac.uk/policy-institute/assets/coronavirus-vaccine-misinformation.pdf

EC (European Commission). (2002). Communication from the Commission on the Precautionary Principle. COM (2000) 1 final. European Commission, Brussels. https://publications.europa.eu/en/publication-detail/-/publication/21676661-a79f-4153-b984-aeb28f07c80a/language-en

European Medicines Agency. (2021). COVID-19 vaccine AstraZeneca: Benefits still outweigh the risks despite possible link to rare blood clots with low blood platelets. www.ema.europa.eu/en/news/covid-19-vaccine-astrazeneca-benefits-still-outweigh-risks-despite-possible-link-rare-blood-clots

Fox, R., & Tversky, A. (1995). Ambiguity aversion and comparative ignorance. *The Quarterly Journal of Economics*, 110(3), 585–603.

Gollier, C., Jullien, B., & Treich, N. (2000). Scientific progress and irreversibility: An economic interpretation of the 'Precautionary Principle'. *Journal of Public Economics*, 75(2), 229–253.

Golman, R., Gurney, N., & Loewenstein, G. (2021). Information gaps for risk and ambiguity. *Psychological Review*, 128(1), 86–103.

Han, P. K., Moser, R. P., & Klein, W. M. (2007). Perceived ambiguity about cancer prevention recommendations: Associations with cancer-related perceptions and behaviours in a US population survey. *Health Expectations*, 10(4), 321–336.

Lichtenstein, S., Slovic, P., Fischhoff, B., Layman, M., & Combs, B. (1978). Judged frequency of lethal events. *Journal of Experimental Psychology: Human Learning and Memory*, 4, 551–578.

Loomba, S., de Figueiredo, A., Piatek, S. J., de Graaf, K., & Larson, H. J. (2021). Measuring the impact of COVID-19 vaccine misinformation on vaccination intent in the UK and USA. *Nature Human Behaviour*, 5(3), 337–348.

Nieman Reports. (2021). What newsrooms can learn about trust from coverage of the AstraZeneca vaccine. https://niemanreports.org/articles/what-newsrooms-can-learn-about-trust-from-coverage-of-the-astrazeneca-vaccine/

Ofcom. (2021). Covid-19 news and information: Consumption and attitudes. www.ofcom.org.uk/research-and-data/tv-radio-and-on-demand/news-media/coronavirus-news-consumption-attitudes-behaviour

Pluviano, S., Watt, C., & Della Sala, S. (2017). Misinformation lingers in memory: Failure of three pro-vaccination strategies. *PloS One*, 12(7), e0181640.

Raptis, S, Chen, J. N., Saposnik, F., Pelyavskyy, R., Liuni, A., & Saposnik, G. (2017). Aversion to ambiguity and willingness to take risks affect therapeutic decisions in managing atrial fibrillation for stroke prevention: results of a pilot study in family physicians. *Patient Preference and Adherence*, 11, 1533–1539.

Sunstein, C. R. (2003). Beyond the precautionary principle. *University of Pennsylvania Law Review*, 151(3), 1003–1058.

Symons, X. (2021). COVID-19 vaccine confidence and the ethics of media reporting. ABC: Religion and Ethics. www.abc.net.au/religion/vaccine-confidence-and-the-ethics-of-media-reporting/13317478

Thaler, R. H., Tversky, A., Kahneman, D., & Schwartz, A. (1997). The effect of myopia and loss aversion on risk taking: An experimental test. *The Quarterly Journal of Economics*, 112(2), 647–666.

Vilella-Vila, M., & Costa-Font, J. (2008). Press media reporting effects on risk perceptions and attitudes towards genetically modified (GM) food. *The Journal of Socio-Economics*, 37(5), 2095–3106.

YouGov. (2021). Europeans now see AstraZeneca vaccine as unsafe, following blood clots scare. https://yougov.co.uk/topics/international/articles-reports/2021/03/22/europeans-now-see-astrazeneca-vaccine-unsafe-follo

21 Trust and the COVID-19 Pandemic

Caroline Rudisill and Sayward Harrison

21.1 INTRODUCTION

Trust is a key component of decision-making and is interconnected with notions of reliability, dependability, and confidence in individuals and institutions. It also has an important role in the development and implementation of successful public policy as the public must rely on others (e.g., elected officials, political appointees, government employees) to design and implement policies in the public's best interest. Trust is particularly important in health-related contexts because of inherent information asymmetry between laypeople and professionals (e.g., scientists, clinicians) in public health and medicine. When considering decisions regarding individual and societal health, laypeople must often rely on others to distil complicated medical and epidemiological information and to assess the risks and benefits associated with particular health actions (or inactions). Specifically, within healthcare settings, individuals often know little about the aetiology, diagnosis, treatment, and prognosis of medical conditions and must rely on actors within the healthcare system, including trusted healthcare providers, to provide accurate information and advice.

In the case of the COVID-19 pandemic, individuals sift through rapidly evolving information and recommendations conveyed from multiple sources, including political leaders, healthcare providers, and experts from public health and medicine. Recommendations from local, national, and global organisations have – at times – been in conflict, particularly early in the pandemic when scientific understanding of the virus and its transmission was in nascent stages.

Changing recommendations on issues such as masks has been a key source of mistrust among laypeople – and this highlights an interesting aspect of trust and infectious disease. The inherent nature of a pandemic means scientific evidence and subsequent clinical recommendations and best practices shift rapidly; laypeople are living in a situation where scientific research unfolds in front of them and this presents a new decision-making context and environment where trust can easily be shaken.

In winter and spring of 2020, there was asymmetry about what the SARS-CoV-2 virus was and the risks it posed. While scientific experts and public health leaders were rapidly working to understand the virus and develop action plans, individuals had no personal experience with the virus until cases emerged in their own social networks. While information asymmetry may have diminished as basic understanding of the SARS-CoV-2 virus has advanced, the emergence of new variants and subsequent changes to recommended mitigation strategies have created renewed confusion and uncertainty for many individuals.

The context of the pandemic, including the urgent nature of the threat and rapidly changing knowledge about the virus, creates a principal–agent relationship whereby key actors (e.g., public health scientists, healthcare providers) act as agents on behalf of the public (i.e., principals). This principal–agent relationship is made stronger by the degree to which informational asymmetry exists. During the COVID-19 pandemic, laypersons have relied on their healthcare providers, public health professionals, the scientific community, and government officials to be decision-makers on their behalf in an environment of great uncertainty. The principal–agent relationship raises questions of whether the agent is acting to maximise their own utility or that of the principal or both jointly. Inducing demand for services or actions could be perceived as utility maximising for the principal but not the agent. For instance, the pandemic stoked fears among some groups that government officials would use the public health emergency as a guide to grab power and enact government restrictions over citizens. Concerns were also raised by individuals about whether healthcare providers and broader healthcare systems stood to profit from the prevention and treatment modalities that they were endorsing.

Good governance and use of clear and effective health communication may counteract such concerns. While known strategies that benefit public health (and thus both the principal and the agent) may be recommended (e.g., vaccination), perceptions could exist about motivations, the scientific process, and the strength of evidence. Trust is a key element in such a context. If the recommendations provided are clear, able to be accomplished (i.e., feasible), and from a trusted actor, then questions of whose utility is being maximised are less prominent. For instance, across a large body of literature, receiving a strong vaccination recommendation from a trusted healthcare provider is strongly associated with an individual's decision to vaccinate themselves or their child (Nagata et al., 2013; Radisic et al., 2017; Smith et al., 2017) against an infectious disease.

The definition of trust varies across broader socio-cultural contexts, communities, and individuals, and a universal definition of trust is lacking. For instance, a recent review of the literature identified forty-five separate measures that have been utilised in research to quantify trust in healthcare systems, with measures of trust most often focusing on constructs of honesty, communication, competence, and confidence in care (Ozawa & Sripad, 2013). The review also highlighted current gaps in trust-related research, including a lack of trust-focused measures that have been validated for non-Western samples.

Beyond variations in measures of trust, greater understanding is needed in how trust varies across individual characteristics, such as the personality or developmental context. Some people are inherently more likely to trust the words and advice of others; for instance, trust has been linked to agreeableness (Mooradian et al., 2006) – one of the 'Big Five' personality traits that have been extensively studied by developmental psychologists. The ability to rely on the advice and opinions of others is also related to one's approach to risky behaviours (risk-seeking vs risk-avoiding) (Hurley, 2006). Inherent risk-takers would be more likely to trust quickly while those who are more inclined to be cautious need to feel more control before trusting a situation or person. One's culture and personal experiences are also important for shaping trust. Baumrind's seminal work examined the critical role of parenting style in shaping many aspects of children's developmental trajectory, with authoritative parenting (i.e., high responsiveness, developmentally appropriate demands/ expectations, trust between caregiver and child) linked to positive socialisation (Baumrind, 1967, 1971, 1991). Attachment theory also established the critical nature of attachment figures – particularly that of caregiver–child during infancy – in shaping individuals' later-life expectations about others (i.e., with secure early attachments fostering positive and trusting expectations about the self and others in the future) (Bowlby, 1988). More recent research suggests that intra-family processes, including value messages (i.e., about fairness) and discussions about whether people are generally fair and trustworthy, also influence individual beliefs about whether to trust in others (Wray-Lake & Flanagan, 2012).

Trust is a key individual-level factor relating to the acceptance and uptake of health-related advice. Others include perceived risk of action and inaction, barriers ranging from lack of transportation to costs of services to service availability and opportunity costs associated with behaviour (e.g., time, money, effort). Individual-level factors such as self-efficacy sit within contexts of social norms, historical experience, and structure and access to healthcare and the public health system.

Importantly, trust in government, the media, and healthcare systems have shaped individual behavioural responses to a previous pandemic (i.e., H1N1 virus) (Prati et al., 2011; Rubin et al., 2009; Rudisill, 2013; van der Weerd et al., 2011) and appear to play a similar role for COVID-19. Trust in the government as an information source has been found to be related to COVID-19 vaccine acceptance in a nineteen-country survey (n = 13,426) in June 2020 (Lazarus et al., 2021). Further, it is also positively related to cooperation with an employer's vaccine recommendation (Lazarus et al., 2021). Another survey in the United States (n = 3,000) in March 2020 found a positive association between trust in government and COVID-19 vaccination intentions (Thunström et al., 2021).

Evidence about the relationship between trust and perceptions of COVID-19 risk is less clear, and there is limited research on this issue. An online survey examining trust in governmental response and trust in scientists, medical doctors, and nurses conducted in March and April 2020 in ten countries (n = 6,991) found that trust in government was negatively related to risk perceptions for the total sample. However, this result was only maintained at the individual country level for two sample countries (i.e., Spain and South Korea). Trust in scientists, medical doctors, and nurses was positively related to risk perceptions about COVID-19 in the total sample. Again, results varied by country, with only the United States and South Korea showing a positive relationship between trust in medical doctors and nurses and risk perceptions; no individual country demonstrated a relationship between trust in scientists and risk perception (Dryhurst et al., 2020).

Given the important role of trust in shaping individual perceptions and behaviours, this construct has unique importance during a global pandemic, which is, by nature, a time of great uncertainty. Trust also has unique salience because widespread and rapid uptake of mitigation behaviours may be needed to reduce the morbidity and mortality of highly infectious new viruses. Thus, this chapter will examine the role of trust in decision-making during ambiguous situations with COVID-19 as the key context of discussion. We will utilise a recent multi-country study examining trust in a variety of key pandemic-related stakeholders (e.g., government and public health institutions) as a means of exploring variation in trust and potential implications for risk perceptions and key health behaviours.

21.2   THE ROLE OF TRUST IN DECISION-MAKING DURING TIMES OF UNCERTAINTY

In contexts of risk, we evaluate information and attach credibility to that information when making decisions. This is amplified in situations of uncertainty. Trust generally acts as a mechanism (heuristic) to reduce complexity in decision-making (Siegrist, 2021). If one trusts an institution or a person, then they can circumvent the cognitively costly process of deeming whether information provided from that entity is accurate and relevant to them. Mistrust will reduce credibility in messaging, making it less effective. The informational asymmetry inherent in healthcare decision-making is magnified in situations of uncertainty like the COVID-19 global pandemic, especially at the beginning of the pandemic when there was limited knowledge about the novel SARS-CoV-2 virus.

Responses to epidemiological risks vary depending on the values individuals and societies hold, as well as institutional norms and practices (Brown, 2020; Szmukler, 2003). Critically important is whether individuals trust key institutional stakeholders who are leading public health responses and key scientific tasks such as vaccine development, testing, and distribution. Trust in healthcare systems and medical experts also likely plays an important role in the adoption of various recommended mitigation measures during a viral outbreak; individuals' beliefs about whether various institutions can be trusted to 'do the right thing' or 'protect them' are important if associated with key behaviours recommended by those institutions (e.g., social distancing and vaccination) (Gerhold, 2020).

During the COVID-19 pandemic, the World Health Organization (WHO) has repeatedly invoked the importance of trust to encourage the uptake of COVID-19 vaccines using perspectives from behavioural science. For instance, in a report from an October 2020 meeting of the WHO Technical Advisory Group (see Figure 21.1) (World Health Organization, 2020), principles of behavioural science were highlighted as critical to encourage COVID-19 vaccine uptake. This includes engaging with trusted members of the community who the public can associate with (i.e., through 'shared identity and values') to promote vaccine uptake. Second, the WHO purports that people must have trust in the vaccine itself and its related safety profile. Finally, issues with mistrust were deemed critical for vulnerable populations who may require targeted efforts from trusted healthcare

FIGURE 21.1 Acceptance and uptake of safe and effective vaccines against COVID-19 (WHO)
Note: Circles added by chapter authors.
Source: Behavioural considerations for acceptance and uptake of COVID-19 vaccines, WHO technical advisory group on behavioural insights and sciences for health, meeting report, 15 December 2020, available at: www.who.int/publications/i/item/9789240016927

workers, friends, and neighbours to be reached with key vaccination messages and services.

The WHO thus prioritised trust building even in very early stages of the pandemic, before people had the chance to have entrenched opinions, feelings, and thoughts about the COVID-19 vaccine (Brewer, 2007). It also focused on the handling of adverse events as part of reinforcing or maintaining trust, recognising that poor handling of messaging could result in the eroding of future vaccine acceptance (World Health Organization, 2020). Good communication with the incorporation of uncertainty and risk–benefit profile also supports trust. This framework set forth by experts convened by the WHO places trust as a central construct in efforts to encourage COVID-19 vaccination globally, but this framework could also be a basis for communicating other important pandemic-related behaviours such as social distancing, following quarantine/isolation recommendations, engaging in COVID-19 testing, and adhering to masking recommendations.

21.3 THE PUBLIC'S TRUST IN HANDLING OF THE PANDEMIC

21.3.1 Results from Our Rapid Response Online Survey in July 2020 about Trust

The rapid pace of change in policy and public health guidance during the early months and years of the COVID-19 pandemic (e.g., changes to mitigation recommendations, travel policy, vaccination requirements) created a high level of uncertainty and even bewilderment for many. This is particularly the case for laypeople who are unlikely to be familiar with scientific methodologies and processes (i.e., vaccine development, manufacturing, and testing practices) from which public policy and clinical recommendations are ideally derived. This uncertainty was compounded by widespread upheaval caused by the global pandemic (e.g., economic impacts, supply chain disruption, school and work closures), as well as by the suffering experienced by millions who have lost loved ones, become disabled, and/or experienced ongoing illness because of the SARS-CoV-2 virus.

To understand public perceptions of the COVID-19 pandemic – including the role of trust in institutions in predicting key pandemic-related behaviours, we surveyed adults from four countries highly impacted by COVID-19 over 10–14 July 2020. We recruited individuals to participate in the web-based survey using the Ipsos MORI online global omnibus panels that use quota sampling to derive nationally representative samples. In total, 4,313 adults completed the survey, including residents of Italy (n = 1,051), Spain (n = 1,079), the United Kingdom (UK) (n = 1,098), and the United States (n = 1,085). These countries were selected because they each had experienced high morbidity and mortality, as well as concentrated outbreaks, during the initial 2020 wave of the pandemic; by the time of the survey, the initial wave was receding in all four countries. Their responses to COVID-19 have been heterogenous (Brown, 2020), ranging from early national stay-at-home orders (i.e., Italy) to never enacting stay-at-home orders (e.g., some US states). Each had unique experiences with other recent pandemics (e.g., severe acute respiratory syndrome, avian flu, H1N1) and range in healthcare system structure (e.g., single payer national health service, hybrid public/private funding), as well as COVID-19 policy authority (e.g., national, regional, state, local).

All participants were recruited through the Ipsos MORI national online panel, were aged eighteen years or older, and were provided with the survey in their country's official language. We asked respondents about their COVID-19-related experiences, risk perceptions, behaviours, financial impacts, and vaccination intentions regarding a potential COVID-19 vaccine. We elicited respondents' trust in five key institutional stakeholders, namely the national government, the local government, the healthcare system, the European Union, and the WHO (Table 21.1). All these stakeholders play a key role in either communicating about and/or regulating and implementing COVID-19-related policy.

Table 21.1 Trust in handling of the COVID-19 pandemic

	Italy (n = 1,051)			Spain (n = 1,079)			United Kingdom (n = 1,098)			United States (n = 1,085)		
	Trust	Don't trust	Don't know	Trust	Don't trust	Don't know	Trust	Don't trust	Don't know	Trust	Don't trust	Don't know
National government	510 (48.6)	501 (47.6)	40 (3.8)	438 (40.6)	605 (56.1)	36 (3.3)	518 (47.2)	516 (47.0)	63 (5.8)	356 (32.8)	692 (63.8)	38 (3.5)
Local government	505 (48.0)	506 (48.1)	40 (3.8)	443 (41.0)	589 (54.6)	48 (4.4)	585 (53.3)	407 (37.1)	106 (9.6)	661 (60.9)	379 (34.9)	46 (4.2)
Healthcare system	748 (71.2)	273 (26.0)	30 (2.9)	859 (79.6)	191 (17.7)	29 (2.7)	909 (82.8)	139 (12.6)	50 (4.6)	687 (63.3)	352 (32.4)	46 (4.3)
European Union	413 (39.3)	593 (56.4)	45 (4.3)	456 (42.2)	574 (53.2)	50 (4.6)	467 (42.5)	480 (43.7)	151 (13.8)	454 (41.8)	316 (29.1)	316 (29.1)
World Health Organization	526 (50.1)	478 (45.4)	47 (4.5)	532 (49.3)	510 (47.3)	37 (3.5)	690 (62.8)	309 (28.2)	99 (9.0)	616 (56.8)	380 (35.0)	90 (8.3)

Note: Number (percentage), number is rounded to the nearest integer.

Uses weighted sample with sampling weights provided by IPSOS MORI to ensure that the study population is representative of the target population (age: eighteen to sixty-five for Spain, eighteen to seventy for Italy, and eighteen to seventy-five for the United Kingdom and the United States). Weights were based on age within gender, region, and working status. UK data was also weighted by social grade, and for the United States, household income.

Question: To what extent do you trust or not trust the way the following ('your national government officials', 'your local government officials', 'the healthcare system in your country', 'The European Union', 'World Health Organization (WHO)') are dealing with the COVID-19 pandemic? Answer choices are 'trust a great deal', 'trust a fair amount', 'do not trust very much', 'do not trust at all', and 'don't know'.

Trust = 'trust a great deal' and 'trust a fair amount'.

Don't trust = 'do not trust very much' and 'do not trust at all'.

The following question assessing institutional trust was presented to participants:

To what extent do you trust or not trust the way the following are dealing with the COVID-19 pandemic?

COLUMNS
Trust a great deal
Trust a fair amount
Do not trust very much
Do not trust at all
Don't Know
ROWS
Your national government officials
Your local government officials
The healthcare system in your country
The European Union
World Health Organization (WHO)

The total sample had a mean age of 45.0 years. Participants were 50.6 per cent female and 49.3 per cent male and 85.5 per cent urban and 14.5 per cent rural. There were an average of 2.9 people in respondents' households, and 31.9 per cent of respondents had children in the household. A total of 61.1 per cent of the sample was working full- or part-time at the time of the survey.

Across all four countries, respondents were most likely to say they trusted their country's healthcare system either a great deal or a fair amount (ranging from 63.3 per cent in the United States to 82.8 per cent in the United Kingdom). Importantly, respondents in the United Kingdom and the United States also reported relatively high levels of trust in the WHO and local governments. Among US respondents, local governments ranked second in trust (60.9 per cent), while for UK respondents, local governments (53.3 per cent) ranked third, behind the WHO (62.8 per cent). Local governments did not have as high levels of trust in Spain (41.0 per cent) and Italy (48.0 per cent).

Conversely, respondents from Italy (47.6 per cent), Spain (56.1 per cent), the United Kingdom (47.0 per cent), and the United States (63.8 per cent) reported that they did not trust the national government (i.e., not very much or not at all). Most respondents from Italy (56.4 per cent) and Spain (53.2 per cent) reported lacking trust in the European Union.

Trust in individuals and stakeholder organisations, particularly governments, plays a key role in predicting whether individuals follow public health guidance (Rubin et al., 2009), including vaccination recommendations. While trust in healthcare systems was high across respondents from the four countries highly impacted by the COVID-19 pandemic, low levels of trust in national governments in all countries surveyed at the end of the first wave of the pandemic presents a cause for concern and may have had important effects on engagement in recommended mitigation policies such as vaccination and mask-wearing during later stages of the pandemic. Mistrust may reduce the credibility of government-led risk communication, making it less effective. Trusted entities are more likely to successfully deliver the messages of public health and health policy planners.

21.3.2 Conveying Uncertainty to the Public

Science is not a study of certainty but instead focuses on investigating uncertainties and understanding errors in findings and the possibility for new evidence to emerge that refutes previously accepted beliefs. The phenomenon of having laypeople watch science 'play out' in front of their eyes is one that needs close study, as changes in understanding of the virus and its transmission and shifts in recommended mitigation strategies have been met with mistrust, scepticism, hostility, and even violence from some segments of the population.

The scientific process and thus recommendations to the public about preventive behaviours during COVID-19 have evolved from high levels of uncertainty at the start of the pandemic to a much richer understanding of the virus and its means of transmission, prevention, and treatment today. Initial advice that masks do not substantially curb the spread of COVID-19 enough to recommend universal masking shifted to many jurisdictions adopting mask mandates. Initial recommendations for surface cleaning were later displaced by mitigation approaches designed to curb spread via droplets and aerosols. Communicating the likelihood of future changes in recommended policy may be helpful in building trust in messaging. Evidence also suggests that communicating uncertainty to the public does not greatly diminish trust and does not increase mistrust in the entity conveying the uncertainty or in the message itself (van der Bles, 2020).

21.4 THE PUBLIC'S TRUST IN INFORMATION SOURCES

Information that is relevant, timely, and comprehensible enables individuals to make decisions about health risks for themselves and incorporate public health advice into everyday behaviour (World Health Organization, 2017). Information sources about COVID-19 are many and constitute a range of experience and knowledge of different types (from scientists and experts to friends and family). In general, who individuals trust for health information varies depending on health literacy levels – individuals with low health literacy tend to rely on social media, the television, and celebrity websites and are less likely to trust the advice of specialist doctors and dentists (Chen et al., 2018).

21.4.1 Role of Science, Experts, and Government

It does not help encourage the public's trust in scientists when it appears that government is debating the public-facing role of scientists in a public health emergency. This is not a partisan issue. The WHO was repeatedly attacked in political spheres by some US politicians, leading to Trump administration's plans to withdraw from the WHO, which were reversed by the Biden administration. Our international survey took place less than one week after the Trump administration announced the withdrawal. The WHO was still the third highest trusted group in the United States, after healthcare systems and local governments, and the United States had the second highest percentage of respondents trusting in the WHO (56.8 per cent), after the United Kingdom (62.8 per cent). Therefore, these attacks did not seem to undermine trust in the WHO as one might expect – at least in the early weeks following continued public discussion of the WHO's handling of the pandemic.

21.4.2   Local Voices to Build Trust

National level political and scientific leaders are important for conveying reliable information, but local actors can reinforce and convey these messages as trusted entities in local contexts, which is more likely to lead to behavioural change and cooperation (Bavel et al., 2020). Such local leaders include civic and religious figures. A survey of underserved and vulnerable populations (n = 8,759) in the United States found that trust in health information was greatest when coming from doctors, then government followed by family, friends, charities, and religious groups. Those not fluent in English trusted religious organisations more than those fluent in English, while those fluent in English were more likely to trust doctors (Wheldon et al., 2020). Overall, doctors have consistently been reported to be the most trusted source of information in multiple studies over time (e.g., see data from 2005 to 2015 across five waves of the Health Information National Trends Survey) (Jackson et al., 2019).

21.4.3   Social Trust: What Will Others Do and Social Norms

The role of peers also matters, particularly with young people. They are more likely to rely on social media as a trusted source for information regarding COVID-19 than older people (Fridman, 2020). A study of US college students (n = 647) found that thinking more peers would get vaccinated was positively associated with intentions to vaccinate against COVID-19 and flu (Graupensperger, 2021a). There is evidence of peer effects in the COVID-19 context where young adults who perceived that their peers had lower adherence to COVID-19 guidelines (e.g., masks) also had lower adherence themselves (Graupensperger, 2021b).

21.5 THE ROLE OF TRUST IN VACCINATION UPTAKE

Given the uncertainty regarding the SARS-CoV-2 vaccine (e.g., dozens of vaccines have been under development, with fast-tracked timeline), individuals may rely on heuristic shortcuts – such as whether they trust an institution – to reduce complexity in vaccination decision-making. For instance, some evidence from the United States suggests that acceptance of COVID-19 vaccines under initial Emergency Use Authorizations (EUAs) is lower when compared to vaccines that have received full approval from the US Food and Drug Administration (FDA); yet the urgent nature of a deadly new virus necessitates the existence of the EUA process that adheres to the rigor of traditional standards for vaccine development and clinical trials yet fast-tracks the process during public health emergencies (Kreps et al., 2020). Public health support (CDC or WHO) as opposed to support from a politician for the COVID-19 vaccine (President Trump) was also found to be related to higher acceptability amongst a sample of 1,971 US residents (Kreps et al., 2020). Moreover, trust in vaccine development, approval, and delivery is necessary for public support of the vaccine (Opel et al., 2020). Leaders and other high-profile citizens such as medical experts receiving their vaccines publicly can increase public trust because of the visual image of their behaviour (Vergara et al., 2021).

21.5.1 Vaccine Development and Information and Reporting about Side Effects

Concerns about the COVID-19 vaccine range widely and include worries about the fast pace of development, possible side effects, and lack of belief in its efficacy or necessity. These stem from many sources, including rumour and conspiracy theories (Islam et al., 2021), which emerge in micro (e.g., household, peer circles) to macro (e.g., social media) contexts. Understanding such concerns is important as beliefs and attitudes about vaccination are directly linked with vaccination refusal. Ensuring high levels of trust in the vaccine development, testing, and surveillance systems is critical to achieve widespread vaccination and, thus, to ensure both individual and public health protection from a variety of infectious diseases. Mistrust in the benefits of COVID-19 vaccination (alongside lower levels of concerns about COVID-19) was found to be the greatest predictor of COVID-19 vaccine hesitancy in four US states (California, New York, Texas, and Florida) and English-speaking Canada (n = 7,678) (Gerretsen et al., 2021). Trusted stakeholders disseminating information about the benefits and safety profile of the COVID-19 vaccine can assist in overcoming these concerns, particularly in lower socio-economic status communities and minority populations (Ayers et al., 2021).

21.5.2   Using Financial Incentives to Encourage Uptake

Financial incentives have, thus far, largely been unsuccessful in efforts to increase COVID-19 vaccination uptake (Chang et al., 2021; Dave et al., 2021; Walkey et al., 2021); however, a programme focused on incentivising those who take individuals to get the vaccine has shown some success (Wong et al., 2022), and an experiment in Sweden showed a positive effect of incentives on vaccination (Campos-Mercade et al., 2021). This differs from evidence on the effectiveness of financial incentives for flu (Bronchetti et al., 2015; Yue et al., 2020), Hepatis B (Topp et al., 2013; Weaver et al., 2014), and HPV vaccinations (Mantzari et al., 2015). In the context of the polarised COVID-19 pandemic, financial incentives may reinforce the notion that people are being pushed to do something they do not want to do by the government or their employer and may perceive payment as an attempt to convince them to do something in the government's or employer's interest. Even more, some question whether the use of financial incentives is coercive or exploitative – particularly for individuals made vulnerable by their low socio-economic status. If not coercive, financial incentives may certainly shift decision-making processes around vaccination and the ways that individuals value this health behaviour (Savulescu et al., 2021). However, context is an important consideration for incentive-based interventions. A recent systematic review found moderate to large impacts of non-financial incentives on reducing vaccination hesitancy in low-income communities (Jarrett et al., 2015). Thus other types of incentives may need to be considered beyond traditional financial incentives. Social incentives are one such alternative, such as requiring vaccination from patrons if they wish to eat indoors at a restaurant (Volpp & Cannuscio, 2021).

Text reminders (a nudge) have been successful at encouraging COVID-19 vaccination appointments and uptakes in the general population (Dai et al., 2021), and targeted reminder messages using behavioural science-underpinned design among healthcare workers increased COVID-19 vaccine registration (Santos et al., 2021). Similar other systems-based interventions including the use of reminder–recall systems and educational interventions about vaccines or vaccination that are embedded within existing trusted healthcare systems show efficacy in reducing mistrust and hesitancy (Jarrett et al., 2015).

21.6   POLICYMAKERS' TRUST IN THE PUBLIC

Promoting shared identity, collective self-efficacy, and hope has been shown to encourage cooperation. At the opposite end of the spectrum, threatening and punitive policies that make individuals feel like they are not trusted may lead to a vicious cycle of them being less likely to follow advice, resulting in the potential for greater societal division and discord (Bavel et al., 2020).

Trust is important for predicting not only behavioural response but also the feasibility of policy approaches. Assuming that people cannot be trusted to do as they are told and designing policies as such (highly regulated and punitive) runs the risk of further deteriorating adherence by both parties (Brown, 2020). That is, it is important to convey to the public that those who are setting forth advice recognise that people are likely to follow this advice also encourages cooperation (Bavel et al., 2020). This is likely dependent on the country context, as some countries have successfully secured high vaccination rates through mandates with little resistance (e.g., Portugal). Other European countries (e.g., Austria) have seen significant internal disagreement about vaccination mandates but still have vaccination rates higher than the United States, where vaccination mandates are much more limited.

21.7 THE WAY FORWARD

Trust is not static. Trust in institutions can be strengthened or weakened through action and inaction, and, during a global pandemic, trust plays a central role in decisions to adopt a wide variety of health behaviours that impact not only individual health but public health as well. The nature of trust and in whom one trusts may change over time. The rapidly shifting nature of the COVID-19 pandemic has created a unique opportunity to better understand how trust informs decision-making and engagement in recommended public health behaviours and strategies, including COVID-19 precautions (Algan et al., 2021). Identifying ways to build trust in our medical and public health professionals, as well as in the broader scientific community, is important not only to continue to make progress in quelling the current pandemic but also to be better prepared for future public health emergencies. The COVID-19 pandemic presents an opportunity to engage the public in science in a way that impacts their daily lives. If done well, this could have positive outcomes for the appreciation of scientific efforts and encouragement of future scientists and public health professionals. Whatever trust has been lost or gained during the pandemic can also shift in the opposite direction. Thus, the importance of conveying accurate and clear information from trusted actors and addressing misinformation must remain at the forefront of efforts to end the current pandemic and prevent future ones.

REFERENCES

Algan, Y., Cohen, D., Davoine, E., Foucault, M., & Stantcheva, S. (2021). Trust in scientists in times of pandemic: Panel evidence from 12 countries. *Proceedings of the National Academy of Sciences*, 118(40), e2108576118.

Ayers, C. K., Kondo, K. K., Williams, B. E., Kansagara, D., Advani, S. M., Smith, M., et al. (2021). Disparities in H1N1 vaccination rates: A systematic review and evidence synthesis to inform COVID-19 vaccination efforts. *Journal of General Internal Medicine*, 36(6), 1734–1745.

Baumrind, D. (1967). Child care practices anteceding three patterns of preschool behavior. *Genetic Psychology Monographs*, 75(1), 43–88.

Baumrind, D. (1971). Current patterns of parental authority. *Developmental Psychology*, 4(1, Pt. 2), 1–103.

Baumrind, D. (1991). The influence of parenting style on adolescent competence and substance use. *The Journal of Early Adolescence*, 11(1), 56–95.

Bavel, J. J. V., Baicker, K., Boggio, P. S., Capraro, V., Cichocka, A., Cikara, M., et al. (2020). Using social and behavioural science to support COVID-19 pandemic response. *Nature Human Behaviour*, 4(5), 460–471.

Bowlby, J. (1988). *A Secure Base: Clinical Applications of Attachment Theory*. London: Routledge.

Brewer, N. T., Chapman, G. B., Gibbons, F. X., Gerrard, M., McCaul, K. D., & Weinstein, N. D. (2007). Meta-analysis of the relationship between risk perception and health behavior: The example of vaccination. *Health Psychology*, 26(2), 136–145.

Bronchetti, E. T., Huffman, D. B., & Magenheim, E. (2015). Attention, intentions, and follow-through in preventive health behavior: Field experimental evidence on flu vaccination. *Journal of Economic Behavior & Organization*, 116, 270–291.

Brown, P. (2020). Studying COVID-19 in light of critical approaches to risk and uncertainty: Research pathways, conceptual tools, and some magic from Mary Douglas. *Health, Risk & Society*, 22(1), 1–14.

Campos-Mercade, P., Meier Armando, N., Schneider Florian, H., Meier, S., Pope, D., & Wengström, E. (2021). Monetary incentives increase COVID-19 vaccinations. *Science*, 374(6569), 879–882.

Chang, T., Jacobson, M., Shah, M., Pramanik, R., & Shah, S. B. (2021). *Financial incentives and other nudges do not increase COVID-19 vaccinations among the vaccine hesitant*. Working Paper 29403, National Bureau of Economic Research.

Chen, X., Hay, J. L., Waters, E. A., Kiviniemi, M. T., Biddle, C., Schofield, E., et al. (2018). Health literacy and use and trust in health information. *Journal of Health Communication*, 23(8), 724–734.

Dai, H., Saccardo, S., Han, M. A., Roh, L., Raja, N., Vangala, S., et al. (2021). Behavioural nudges increase COVID-19 vaccinations. *Nature*, 597(7876), 404–409.

Dave, D., Friedson, A. I., Hansen, B., & Sabia, J. J. (2021). Association between statewide COVID-19 lottery announcements and vaccinations. *JAMA Health Forum*, 2(10), e213117–e213117.

Dryhurst, S., Schneider, C. R., Kerr, J., Freeman, A. L. J., Recchia, G., van der Bles, A. M., et al. (2020). Risk perceptions of COVID-19 around the world. *Journal of Risk Research*, 23(7–8), 994–1006.

Fridman, I., Lucas, N., Henke, D., & Zigler, C. K. (2020). Association between public knowledge about COVID-19, trust in information sources, and adherence to social distancing: Cross-sectional survey. *JMIR Public Health and Surveillance*, 6(3), e22060.

Gerhold, L. (2020). COVID-19: Risk perception and coping strategies. 25 March. https://osf.io/preprints/psyarxiv/xmpk4

Gerretsen, P., Kim, J., Caravaggio, F., Quilty, L., Sanches, M., Wells, S., et al. (2021). Individual determinants of COVID-19 vaccine hesitancy. *PLoS One*, 16(11), e0258462.

Graupensperger, S., Abdallah, D. A., & Lee, C. M. (2021a). Social norms and vaccine uptake: College students' COVID vaccination intentions, attitudes, and estimated peer norms and comparisons with influenza vaccine. *Vaccine*, 39(15), 2060–2067.

Graupensperger, S., Lee, C. M., & Larimer, M. E. (2021b). Young adults underestimate how well peers adhere to COVID-19 preventive behavioral guidelines. *The Journal of Primary Prevention*, 42(3), 309–318.

Hurley, R. F. (2006). The decision to trust. *Harvard Business Review*, 84(9), 55–62.

Islam, M. S., Kamal, A. M., Kabir, A., Southern, D. L., Khan, S. H., Hasan, S. M. M., et al. (2021). COVID-19 vaccine rumors and conspiracy theories: The need for cognitive inoculation against misinformation to improve vaccine adherence. *PLoS One*, 16(5), e0251605.

Jackson, D. N., Peterson, E. B., Blake, K. D., Coa, K., & Chou, W. S. (2019). Americans' trust in health information sources: Trends and sociodemographic predictors. *American Journal of Health Promotion*, 33(8), 1187–1193.

Jarrett, C., Wilson, R., O'Leary, M., Eckersberger, E., Larson, H. J. (2015). Strategies for addressing vaccine hesitancy: A systematic review. *Vaccine*, 33(34), 4180–4190.

Kreps, S., Prasad, S., Brownstein, J. S., Hswen, Y., Garibaldi, B. T., Zhang, B., & Kriner, D. L. (2020). Factors associated with US adults' likelihood of accepting COVID-19 vaccination. *JAMA Network Open*, 3(10), e2025594–e2025594.

Lazarus, J. V., Ratzan, S. C., Palayew, A., Gostin, L. O., Larson, H. J., Rabin, K., et al. (2021). A global survey of potential acceptance of a COVID-19 vaccine. *Nature Medicine*, 27(2), 225–228.

Mantzari, E., Vogt, F., & Marteau, T. M. (2015). Financial incentives for increasing uptake of HPV vaccinations: A randomized controlled trial. *Health Psychology*, 34(2), 160–171.

Mooradian, T., Renzl, B., & Matzler, K. (2006). Who trusts? Personality, trust and knowledge sharing. *Management Learning*, 37(4), 523–540.

Nagata, J. M., Hernández-Ramos, I., Kurup, A. S., Albrecht, D., Vivas-Torrealba, C., & Franco-Paredes, C. (2013). Social determinants of health and seasonal influenza vaccination in adults ≥65 years: A systematic review of qualitative and quantitative data. *BMC Public Health*, 13, 388.

Netburn, D. (2021). A timeline of the CDC's advice on face masks. *Los Angeles Times*, 27 July.

Opel, D. J., Salmon, D. A., & Marcuse, E. K. (2020). Building trust to achieve confidence in COVID-19 vaccines. *JAMA Network Open*, 3(10), e2025672.

Ozawa, S., & Sripad, P. (2013). How do you measure trust in the health system? A systematic review of the literature. *Social Science & Medicine*, 91, 10–14.

Prati, G., Pietrantoni, L., & Zani, B. (2011). Compliance with recommendations for pandemic influenza H1N1 2009: The role of trust and personal beliefs. *Health Education Research*, 26(5), 761–769.

Radisic, G., Chapman, J., Flight, I., & Wilson, C. (2017). Factors associated with parents' attitudes to the HPV vaccination of their adolescent sons: A systematic review. *Preventive Medicine*, 95, 26–37.

Rubin, G. J., Amlôt, R., Page, L., & Wessely, S. (2009). Public perceptions, anxiety, and behaviour change in relation to the swine flu outbreak: Cross sectional telephone survey. *British Medical Journal*, 339, b2651.

Rudisill, C. (2013). How do we handle new health risks? Risk perception, optimism, and behaviors regarding the H1N1 virus. *Journal of Risk Research*, 16(8), 959–980.

Santos, H. C., Goren, A., Chabris, C. F., & Meyer, M. N. (2021). Effect of targeted behavioral science messages on COVID-19 vaccination registration among employees of a large health system: A randomized trial. *JAMA Network Open*, 4(7), e2118702–e2118702.

Savulescu, J., Pugh, J., & Wilkinson, D. (2021). Balancing incentives and disincentives for vaccination in a pandemic. *Nature Medicine*, 27(9), 1500–1503.

Siegrist, M. (2021). Trust and risk perception: A critical review of the literature. *Risk Analysis*, 41(3), 480–490

Smith, L. E., Amlôt, R., Weinman, J., Yiend, J., & Rubin, G. J. (2017). A systematic review of factors affecting vaccine uptake in young children. *Vaccine*, 35(45), 6059–6069.

Szmukler, G. (2003). Risk assessment: 'Numbers' and 'values'. *Psychiatric Bulletin*, 27(6), 205–207.

Thunström, L., Ashworth, M., Finnoff, D., & Newbold, S. C. (2021). Hesitancy toward a COVID-19 vaccine. *Ecohealth*, 18(1), 44–60.

Topp, L., Day, C. A., Wand, H., Deacon, R. M., van Beek, I., Haber, P. S., et al. (2013). A randomised controlled trial of financial incentives to increase hepatitis B vaccination completion among people who inject drugs in Australia. *Preventive Medicine*, 57(4), 297–303.

van der Bles, A. M., van der Linden, S., Freeman, A. L. J., & Spiegelhalter, D. J. (2020). The effects of communicating uncertainty on public trust in facts and numbers. *Proceedings of the National Academy of Sciences of the United States of America*, 117(14), 7672–7683.

van der Weerd, W., Timmermans, D. R., Beaujean, D. J., Oudhoff, J., & van Steenbergen, J. E. (2011). Monitoring the level of government trust, risk perception and intention of the general public to adopt protective measures during the influenza A (H1N1) pandemic in The Netherlands. *BMC Public Health*, 11, 575.

Vergara, R. J. D., Sarmiento, P. J. D., & Lagman, J. D. N. (2021). Building public trust: A response to COVID-19 vaccine hesitancy predicament. *Journal of Public Health (Oxford)*, 43(2), e291–e292.

Volpp, K. G., & Cannuscio, C. C. (2021). Incentives for immunity: Strategies for increasing COVID-19 vaccine uptake. *New England Journal of Medicine*, 385(1), e1.

Walkey, A. J., Law, A., & Bosch, N. A. (2021). Lottery-based incentive in Ohio and COVID-19 vaccination rates. *JAMA*, 326(8), 766–767.

Weaver, T., Metrebian, N., Hellier, J., Pilling, S., Charles, V., Little, N., et al. (2014). Use of contingency management incentives to improve completion of hepatitis B vaccination in people undergoing treatment for heroin dependence: A cluster randomised trial. *The Lancet*, 384(9938), 153–163.

Wheldon, C. W., Carroll, K. T., & Moser, R. P. (2020). Trust in health information sources among underserved and vulnerable populations in the U.S. *Journal of Health Care for the Poor and Underserved*, 31(3), 1471–1487.

Wong, C. A., Pilkington, W., Doherty, I. A., Zhu, Z., Gawande, H., Kumar, D., & Brewer, N. T. (2022). Guaranteed financial incentives for COVID-19 vaccination: A pilot program in North Carolina. *JAMA Internal Medicine*, 182(1), 78–80.

World Health Organization (2017). *Communicating Risk in Public Health Emergencies: A WHO Guideline for Emergency Risk Communication (ERC) Policy and Practice*. Geneva: World Health Organization.

World Health Organization (2020). *Behavioural Considerations for Acceptance and Uptake of COVID-19 Vaccines: WHO Technical Advisory Group on*

Behavioural Insights and Sciences for Health, Meeting Report, 15 October. Geneva: World Health Organization.

Wray-Lake, L., & Flanagan, C. A. (2012). Parenting practices and the development of adolescents' social trust. *Journal of Adolescence, 35*(3), 549–560.

Yue, M., Wang, Y., Low, C. K., Yoong, J. S., & Cook, A. R. (2020). Optimal design of population-level financial incentives of influenza vaccination for the elderly. *Value Health, 23*(2), 200–208.

22 How Do Individuals Perceive the Risk of COVID-19 Compared to Food Poisoning and Influenza?

Natasha Aldulaimi, Joan Costa-Font, and Luca Salmasi

22.1 INTRODUCTION

The high transmissibility of the coronavirus pandemic (SARS-CoV-2), has influenced the way individuals perceive the effect of COVID-19 on their their welfare and safety also conceptualized as risks perceptions. Risk perceptions influence the individual adherence to preventative measures such as social distancing, wearing a face covering, and self-isolation that are essential in maintaining population safety (Lang et al., 2021). Generally speaking, risk perceptions refer to the subjective judgment of the magnitude and severity of a risk. However, how are risk perceptions formed? How do such risk perceptions compare to other similar risks? An understanding of the factors that influence risk perception and how such perceptions of risk affect individual choices is necessary to predict the success of campaigns and public health interventions (de Zwart et al., 2009).

There has been considerable research into the influences of risk perception on many health-related behaviours, such as the perceived risk of smoking to health. Such research denouements that demographic characteristics such as age and gender influence the risk perception of smoking (Lundborg & Andersson, 2008; Viscusi, 1991). This risk perception of lung cancer has been shown to influence behaviour, such as whether someone smokes and, if so, the extent to which they attempt to quit (Jacobson et al., 2014). There are many similarities between the strategies used by governments to influence risk perceptions regarding COVID-19 and smoking, including the reliance on public information campaigns. However, unlike smoking, COVID-19 is likely to cause immediate costs to the individual, whereas the consequences of smoking are expected to be severe in the future. The risk of smoking to one's self is brought on by the individual's own behaviour choices, whereas the chance of illness from COVID-19 is greatly impacted by the behaviour of others. Similarly, risks and consequences of smoking are generally well known to society and have been researched by experts over many years, whereas COVID-19 is a new infection, and hence the risk are highly unknown which gives rise 'erring on the side of rare events' ESRE as documented in this by by Chapter 18. Due to these differences, risk perceptions of smoking, cannot be blindly assumed to be relevant when estimating public COVID-19 risk perception and behaviour. Does the same apply to the perceived risk of the Flu, or food poisoning?

This chapter explores the different explanations underpinning how individuals perceive risks of COVID-19 and other similar risks in a pandemic in different countries. Previous studies on risk perceptions during pandemics have found that people who perceive themselves to be more vulnerable or susceptible to the threat engage more in protective behaviour (e.g., study by Brug et al. (2004)). The chapter will consider some theoretical explanations for risk perception formation in behavioral science, and report some descriptive evidence from a recent survey.

22.2   BACKGROUND

22.2.1   Risk Perception Formation

Subjective judgements of risk determine how people view and react to hazards. A rational model of risk perception would involve individuals weighing up the likelihood of an action's benefits and consequences to determine the probability of an adverse outcome. However, members of the public are not rational thinkers. To lay individuals, a risk is defined as the 'probability of something bad happening'. This incorporates subjectivity into risk perception, which can be influenced by many factors (Brown, 2014). There are many factors that influence risks perceptions including voluntariness, controllability, familiarity, equity, benefits, understanding, uncertainty, dread, reversibility, personal stake, ethical nature, origin, and catastrophic potential of the risk, as well as trust in institutions. Risks that are voluntary, equitable, natural in origin, highly controllable, beneficial, and presented by trustworthy sources are likely to be of lower concern than those with no benefits and where individuals feel there is inequity, involuntariness, and lack of control (Paek & Hove, 2017).

To explain COVID-19 risk perception, and important framework is the mental noise model. The mental noise model relates to how people perceive a risk under stress. The psychological consequences of being in a stressful situation creates 'mental noise', which reduces a person's ability to comprehend information rationally. This has great influence on how a risk is perceived and understood. Factors that cause a high level of mental noise include a lack of controllability, voluntariness, familiarity, dread, and uncertainty (Paek & Hove, 2017). Another theoretical framework is the trust determination model, which suggests that trust is essential for risk communication and we can rely on the risk information that we receive only when trust has been developed. Key influencers of the development of trust are communication, caring, and honesty (Paek & Hove, 2017).

Finally, the negative dominance model states that in highly concerning situations, negative information has a higher processing weight than positive information. This asymmetric relationship means that people tend to give negative outcomes greater value than positive outcomes when processing information in situations of fear, dread, and anxiety (Paek & Hove, 2017). Other influences include the use of heuristics to simplify evaluations of risk.

22.2.2 Socio-demographic Effects on Risk Perception

A number of studies have examined individual difference sin risk perceptions. In general, women have been found to have greater risk perceptions than men, although this has not been proven across all risks or populations. This variation in findings has been explained by differences in cultural, social, and gender equality across the world. Cultural and social values have a great impact on an individual's feeling of control, equity, and trust, which, in turn, have been shown to influence risk perception (Hitchcock, 2001).

Research regarding the effects of age on risk perception is varied, with some studies suggesting older people are more risk-averse than younger people, while others show no difference or the opposite effect. This variation may be due to the nature of the risk. Past research has suggested that older adults exhibit greater risk perceptions when they refer to behaviours of health and ethical subjects, whereas younger adults have greater risk perceptions towards behaviours associated with social domains (Bonem, 2015). However, the influence of age on health-specific risk perception varies across studies, with one cross-sectional study suggesting evidence of no significant differences in medical risk perceptions across age groups (Field & Schreer, 2000).

Overall, there is an understanding that education levels influence risk perceptions. Past literature has suggested that those with higher levels of education have lower risk perceptions than those with lower levels of education (Savage, 1993; Sund et al., 2017). However, specific to medical risk-taking, it has been suggested that those with higher levels of education may reveal a greater risk perceptions than those with lower education levels. For example, Rimal and Juon (2010) suggested that younger and better educated women reported greater levels of stress and perceived risk towards breast cancer than those who were older and less educated (Rimal & Juan, 2010). This suggests that the effect of education on risk perception is dependent on the type of risk.

22.2.3   Effect of Risk Perception on Behaviour

An individual's perceived susceptibility to a threat is a key influencer of behaviour choices (Ferrer & Klein, 2015). This section will enunciate a number of psychological theories that offer insights on how risk perception affects behaviour. The Bayesian learning model suggests that individuals process and combine new information with previous understandings of their absolute risk and required behaviour to form their posterior risk belief and make their behaviour choices (Heino et al., 2018).

Similarly, the health belief model (HBM) states that an individual's actions are based on their belief of a threat and their judgement of the effectiveness of their actions in reducing a threat (Brown, 2014). The four original constructs of the HBM are the perceived susceptibility to obtain the risk, the perceived severity of the risk, the perceived benefits of acting, and the perceived obstacles in acting (Brown, 2014).

Relatedly, the protection motivation theory (PMT) involves weighing the threat of a risk against the ability to effectively act. This model involves a threat appraisal and a coping appraisal. The threat appraisal evaluates the factors that influence the probability of making a maladaptive response, for example smoking or not wearing a seat belt. The coping appraisal relates to the efficacy of a preventative action, as well as an individual's ability to complete the action. This theory is very similar to the HBM, but the two theories differ due to their origins and research methodology. The PMT was developed to explain the effects of fear-arousing communications on attitude change (Prentice-Dunn & Rogers, 1986).

However, to explain the reaction to COVID-19 risks more specifically, other approaches are relevant. The extended parallel processing model states that when an individual's perceived threat and action efficacy are high, individuals engage in protective behaviours. However, if efficacy is low, the desire to partake is determined by fear of the risk (Popova, 2012).

Another important theory is the theory of reasoned action which states that behaviour intentions are influenced by two factors: attitudes (whether individuals believe the behaviour will result in positive or negative outcomes) and subjective norms (beliefs on whether other individuals will approve or disprove of the behaviour). Accordingly, an individual's actions are therefore influenced by what they believe are the consequences of their behaviour (Nguyen, 2018).

Finally, a framework closer to rational choice is the subjective expected utility theory, which is an approach to decision-making under risk that allows for subjective evaluation of variables under consideration and the probabilities associated with them, to maximise subjective expected utility (Shanteau & Pinegot, 2009). These theoretical frameworks can help explain different dimensions of how an individual's perception of COVID-19 influenced their choice of behaviour and confirm that the effects of risk perceptions on behaviour may vary across individuals.

22.2.4   Evidence on Risk Perception to COVID-19

Previous research has explored variations in COVID-19 risk perceptions across countries in Europe, the United States, the Middle East, and Ethiopia. A study conducted in France involved surveying participants on two occasions at different times during a national lockdown. Participants were asked their opinions on the infection fatality ratio, personal risk of catching the disease, risk as perceived by others, and expected prevalence ratio. The results of this study showed that participants generally over-estimated the risk of COVID-19, and COVID-19 risk perception was significantly greater than influenza risk perception. Women and those of younger age also had higher risk perceptions of COVID-19 than men and older age groups (Attema et al., 2021).

Similarly, a study carried out in the United Kingdom concluded that risk perception was associated with protective behaviours. Being male, having no direct experience with COVID-19, being more politically right-wing or conservative, having more individualistic worldviews, having higher trust in government, and having a sense of higher collective efficacy were associated with lower risk perceptions than being female, having direct experience with COVID-19, having greater pro-social tendencies, having greater trust in science and medical professionals, and having higher personal efficacy (Schneider, 2021).

A study using data from the United States found that those living in areas with high death rates had significantly higher COVID-19 risk perceptions than those living in areas with low death rates, and this in turn corresponded to the amount of time individuals spent staying at home. This suggests that COVID-19 risk perception varies between individuals and may influence behaviour (Elharake et al., 2021). A further survey in the United States studied the effects of age on COVID-19 risk perception and mental health during the pandemic. Those of older age perceived a higher risk from dying of COVID-19 but lower risk of catching the virus than younger individuals. This showed that the effects of age on risk perceptions vary across measurements (de Bruin, 2020). Similarly, Bundorf (2021) show that individuals dramatically reduced activity outside of their home during the pandemic, and adherence to protective behaviour was significantly influenced by risk perceptions. Risk perception was influenced by demographics such as gender (males had lower perception of their likelihood of catching the disease than females), ethnicity (Hispanic and non-Hispanic Black Americans reported greater risk perceptions than white Americans), and education (those with higher education believed they were less likely to have a severe disease course than those without higher education). Interestingly, age did not influence risk perception (Bundorf, 2021).

In a different part of the word, a survey carried out in the Middle East explored the risk perceptions of COVID-19 across three countries – Saudi Arabia, Jordan, and Egypt. Participants' perception of the seriousness of the pandemic and their susceptibility and anxiety towards COVID-19 were highest in respondents from Saudi Arabia and lowest in those from Jordan. Interestingly, such differences are attributed to the low cases and deaths reported in Jordan, as well as the fact that Saudi Arabia has had previous infectious disease outbreaks (such as severe acute respiratory syndrome and Ebola), which may have acted as reference points to individuals completing the survey (Shahin & Hussein, 2020). The varying effects of age on COVID-19 risk perception are highlighted by a study carried out in Ethiopia. The perceived threat of COVID-19 significantly decreased with age, but the perceived vulnerability was not associated with age (Birhanu et al., 2021).

An international study analysed COVID-19 risk perceptions and protective behaviours in ten countries from America, Asia, and

Europe. Results found that participants from the United Kingdom reported the highest levels of concern regarding COVID-19. High risk perception was associated with being male, having 'pro-social' tendencies, and having previous exposure to the virus. Trust in science and medical practitioners correlated with high risk perceptions, whereas trust in the government correlated with low risk perceptions. Risk perception positively correlated with the adoption of preventative health behaviours across all countries (Dryhurst et al., 2020).

22.3   EVIDENCE FROM THE COVID-19 PANDEMIC

In this chapter we provide some evidence of a four country survey covering four countries – Italy, Spain, the United Kingdom, and the United States – to explore the variation in absolute and relative risk perception of COVID-19 and how risk perception influences participant behaviour. A survey was developed at the beginning of the pandemic and contained questions on participants' demographics, including age, gender, and education, as well as psychological and social factors such as physical and mental health and trust in institutions. Individuals were asked to rate their mental health on a scale from very poor to very good. Example questions regarding participant trust in institutions such as national government, local government, the healthcare service, trust in the EU and trust in the World Health Organization (WHO). Possible answers included 'trust very much', 'trust a fair amount', 'do not trust very much', 'do not trust at all', and 'do not know'. Respondents were also asked whether they believed they had been previously infected with COVID-19. They were then asked to rate how they viewed the risk of infection of three diseases – COVID-19, influenza, and food poisoning – to both them and to an average resident within their nation on a scale from 0 to 100: What would you say the risk is of you personally becoming infected with the following types of illness in the next twelve months? COVID-19, influenza, food poisoning. What would you say is the risk of an average resident becoming infected with the following types of illness in the next twelve months? COVID-19, influenza,

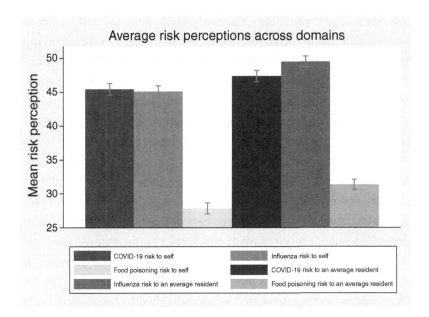

FIGURE 22.1   Average absolute risk perceptions to self and an average resident

food poisoning. Participants were also asked about their adherence to COVID-19 protective behaviours, such as wearing face coverings when out and avoiding restaurants.

We compare the mean perceived subjective risk of COVID-19, influenza, and food poisoning, to self and to an average resident. The relative risks of COVID-19 to self and to an average resident are determined by comparing the reported risk of COVID-19 infection with the reported risk of influenza and food poisoning infection. There were 4,313 respondents to the survey. The mean age of the respondents was 44.1 years (standard deviation 14.4), ranging from 18 to 75; 1,628 (37.75 per cent) respondents reported being female whilst 1,587 (36.80 per cent) were male.

Respondents rated their perception of risk of becoming infected with COVID-19, influenza, and food poisoning on a scale from 0 to 100. They were then asked to rate the risk of an average resident in their country being infected with each disease. Figure 22.1 shows the average absolute risk perception scores across each domain. Overall, evidence suggests that the perceived risk of COVID-19 infection is similar to the risk of influenza infection, and infection with COVID-19 or influenza is more likely than infection with food poisoning. Furthermore, confidence intervals suggest that participants believe that they themselves (risk to self) are less likely to become infected with each disease than an average resident of their country (risk to an average resident).

The relative risk of COVID-19 was estimated for each respondent by determining the difference between their COVID-19 risk perceptions and their influenza and food poisoning risk perceptions. We estimate the overall mean relative risk perceptions of COVID-19 to self and an average resident when compared to influenza and food poisoning. Importantly, we find that there is little difference between an individual's COVID-19 risk perception and influenza risk perception. This evidence is suggestive that when individual lack knowledge of a risk they use evidence of the closest possible risk.

On average, participants from Italy and the United Kingdom reported lower perceptions of COVID-19 infection risk to themselves and to an average resident in their country than those from Spain and the United States. This correlates to the trends in national case rate at the time of survey; the number of cases recorded per 100,000 from the lowest to the highest was in Italy, then the United Kingdom, then Spain, and finally the United States. Such results may suggest that although regional proximity to risk does not influence risk perception, proximity to risk on a national level may significantly influence perceived COVID-19 risk to self and an average resident. The relative risk of COVID-19 to self and an average resident, compared to influenza and food poisoning, followed a similar trend, as participants from the United Kingdom and Italy recorded lower mean relative risk perceptions than those from Spain and the United States. Country death rate, however, does not seem to influence risk perception as the United States reported a dramatically lower death rate per 100,000 than Italy, Spain, and the United Kingdom at the time of the survey. This suggests that respondents distinguished between risk of infection and risk of death.

In general, women reported a greater absolute risk perception than men across domains. Similarly, those younger than fifty-five reported greater absolute risk perceptions than those fifty-five and older. This finding was statistically significant for each domain apart from COVID-19 infection risk to self. Not surprisingly, those aged from fifty-five to seventy-five reported the greatest relative risk of COVID-19 infection to self, compared to influenza. In contrast, those aged from eighteen to twenty-four reported the highest relative COVID-19 risk of infection compared to influenza for an average resident. Relative risk by age group suggests that the relative risk of COVID-19 infection compared to food poisoning increases with age; however, the test results suggest that this is significant when assessing relative risk to self but not relative risk to an average resident.

Greater absolute risk perceptions are typically recorded by those with higher education than by people without higher education. This is important as the differences in absolute risk perceptions between education groups is only statistically significant with respect to COVID-19 infection (to self and an average resident). Individuals with higher education also had a greater relative COVID-19 risk perception than those without higher education. This suggest that COVID-19 was a different risk to that individuals were knowledgeable about, as they had no experience. However, higher education individuals might have been at an advantage in forming risk perception of COVID-19 of the risks, insofar education might have influenced trust with the information sources. The significance of education follows from several theoretical frameworks described including the Bayesian updating framework (educated people provide higher credibility to scientific sources) as well as the theory of reason action. Parallel Processing models which indicated that both perceived efficacy due to knowledge, and trust exert an influence in the formation of risk perceptions.

22.4   RISK OPTIMISM

In addition to understanding how people form their beliefs, an important feature to examine is how individual beliefs towards oneself differ

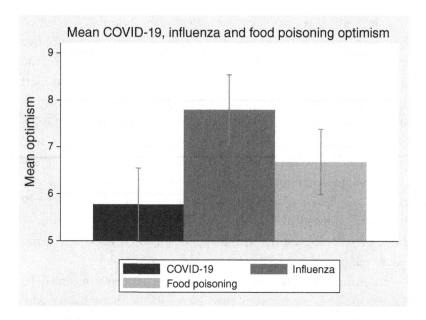

FIGURE 22.2 Mean optimism levels for COVID-19, influenza, and food poisoning

from those of others. Consistently, we estimate a' as the gap in reported perceived risk of infection to an average resident and risk of infection to themselves for each disease. Figure 22.2 shows the average COVID-19, influenza, and food poisoning optimism levels across participants.

The test results suggest that individuals are significantly more-optimistic towards influenza than COVID-19, but there is no significant difference between COVID-19 optimism and food poisoning optimism. This result is not entirely surprising, as COVID-19 is a risk that, like poisoning, depends largely on others behavior. Hence, unlike previous research optimism does not seem to explain risk perception formation (Costa-Font et al., 2009).

22.5   DISCUSSION

Our estimates suggest that the mean risk perception of COVID-19 to self and an average resident is similar to the risk perception of influenza and significantly greater than the risk perception of food poisoning. Our results contrast with a previous study conducted in France, which concluded that the risk perception of COVID-19 was significantly greater than the risk perception of influenza (Attema et al., 2021). This may be due to variations in risk perception measures as the French survey compared COVID-19 and influenza risk perceptions based on the perceived infection fatality, whilst this study compares risk of infection. The similarity between COVID-19 and influenza risk perceptions may be explained by the comparability of the diseases: they are both contagious respiratory diseases, which lead to similar symptoms. There are some factors, based on the risk perception model, that may suggest that public risk perception of COVID-19 should be greater than influenza. This include the lower understanding and greater uncertainty with COVID-19 compared to influenza as it is a new disease. Furthermore, due to the highlighted catastrophic potential, there is also greater public dread, consistent with the mental noise model.

The differences in the risk perception of food poisoning compared to COVID-19 and influenza can be explained by the risk perception model. Food poisoning exerts little catastrophic potential in well-developed countries, compared to coronavirus and influenza, which can both cause high mortality rates. Influenza and COVID-19 are highly infectious and whether someone catches the disease is greatly related to the behaviour of other people (e.g., those with the virus). However, food poisoning is due to undercooked food, and therefore, individuals gain reassurance by the controllability and 'voluntary' nature of becoming unwell.

Results from this study conclude that females report greater absolute risk perceptions than males across all domains. This suggests that females may have an all-round greater risk perception than males, and this difference in risk perception is not specific to COVID-19. This is expected, as previous research has shown that females report greater risk perceptions than males across a variety of risks, both health and non-health related.

Respondents who have completed a form of higher education, either fully or in part, recorded a significantly greater absolute and relative risk of COVID-19 to self and an average resident than those with no form of higher education. The differences in risk perception by education level contrast with what we expect from previous COVID-19 research, which has suggested that education either has no influence on risk perception or that those with lower education levels have higher risk perceptions. This may be due to differences in how the risk is measured. It is interesting that the differences in risk perception by education level are significant only regarding risk perceptions of COVID-19. This may be explained by how those with different levels of education perceive unfamiliar and uncertain situations. Generally, those who are better educated tend to have greater knowledge on the risks of most conditions than those who are uneducated. The lack of knowledge regarding COVID-19, due to the unfamiliarity and uncertainty of the pandemic, may worry educated individuals more than those who are uneducated because they are used to being in control and clearly understanding risks.

At the time of the completion of the survey, most governments, the European Union, and the WHO were highlighting the high risk of COVID-19. According to the trust determination model, trust in these institutions should be associated with an increase in risk perception. This association can be observed between risk perception and trust in the European Union and the WHO but not between risk perception and trust in the national government. This may be because those who trust their government believe that their government's policies reduce the risk of infection to themselves and an average resident in their country.

The risk perception model suggests that perceived risk is influenced by the hazard magnitude multiplied by the probability of mortality or morbidity. This would suggest that risk perception is influenced by either COVID-19 deaths (mortality and morbidity) or COVID-19 cases (magnitude). Although results suggest no correlation between either at a regional level, we can observe that, on average, respondents from countries with higher COVID-19 case rates reported greater risk perceptions than respondents from countries with lower COVID-19 case rates. This may suggest that proximity to risk influences risk perception on a national level rather than a regional level and may be due to how quickly people view the virus to spread across areas within a nation. It may reflect that individuals received their information from national sources rather than from friends or nearby contacts. The television and radio were perhaps perceived as more important than direct discussions, potentially due to reduced social contact resulting in more reliance on the national news than personal conversations.

The mental noise model proposes that those under stressful situations are less able to comprehend information rationally to form appropriate risk perceptions. The results from this study show that respondents who had poor mental health (poor or very poor mental health) reported greater absolute risk perceptions across domains than those who had good (good or very good) mental health. Interestingly, those with poor mental health also had greater mean relative risk perceptions of COVID-19 than those with good mental health. This may be due to the overwhelming and unprecedented awareness of risk regarding COVID-19 and the reduced ability of those more stressed to rationally compare this information with the risk of other diseases.

Those who were previously infected with COVID-19 reported greater absolute risk perceptions than those who were not across all domains except for the risk of influenza to an average resident. This general increase in risk perception in those previously infected with COVID-19 is an example of anchoring, where individuals who have been infected with COVID-19 believe that the chance of infection from other diseases is therefore high. The availability heuristic suggests that those who had been infected with COVID-19 would have a greater relative risk of the virus than those without previous infection, as they are able to specifically recall the experience. This is the case for the relative risk of COVID-19 to self and an average resident when compared to influenza. However, opposite results were observed when comparing COVID-19 with food poisoning. This may be due to food poisoning being viewed as a completely 'separate' disease with no similarities to COVID-19. Although absolute risk perceptions across diseases were influenced by previous COVID-19 infection, the relative risk of COVID-19 compared to food poisoning was high in both groups, and so previous COVID-19 infection did not influence results. These results suggest that individuals can distinguish between different types of risks in forming their perceptions.

Interestingly, optimism was significantly greater for influenza than COVID-19. This may be due to the widely publicised high prevalence of COVID-19, perhaps making individuals more aware of their personal vulnerability to catching the infection.

22.6   POLICY IMPLICATIONS

Most individuals do not process risk information in probability terms and hence understanding the formation of relative risk information might be useful to then identify how such perceptions influence healthy behaviours (Viscusi & Hakes, 2003). Results from this study suggest that men and individuals with less education exhibit lower risk perceptions of COVID-19, compared to their counterparts, and could therefore be targeted by public health campaigns to increase compliance with protective behaviours. Targeting these population groups can also influence influenza risk perception, which may potentially increase COVID-19 protective behaviour adherence. Carefully designed behavioral interventions such as reminders and information nudges should target male and low education individuals, for example, information campaigns featuring well-respected male role models aired on sports channels. There is scope for education and information nudges perhaps located in popular male locations. The same principles could be used to target less-educated and non-working individuals. Policymakers may also choose to target older populations as, even though the association between age and COVID-19 risk perception is less clear, older age groups were, overall, less compliant to protective behaviours than younger age groups.

In contrast to expectations, regional proximity to risk does not significantly influence risk perception. This is the result of the risk being globalised unlike other epidemics where risks were more local-ised (Rudisill et al., 2012). However, I observe that mean risk per-ception by country follows a similar trend to the national case rate. The virus may therefore be perceived as a 'national' risk rather than a 'regional' risk, perhaps due to how quickly it can spread or due to mes-saging and regulations highlighting the 'national' threat of the virus. This may be advantageous to policymakers who aim to use country-wide restrictions. However, if regional restrictions are preferred, policymakers may need to alter messaging and data publications to emphasise the COVID-19 risk at a regional level. This may be through direct public communication with local healthcare workers and com-munity leaders or targeted local campaigns at places of employment.

REFERENCES

Attema, A. E., L'haridon, O., Raude, J., Seror, V., & Coconel Group. (2021). Beliefs and risk perceptions about COVID-19: Evidence from two successive French representative surveys during lockdown. *Frontiers in Psychology*, 12, 619145.

Birhanu, Z., Ambelu, A., Fufa, D., Mecha, M., Zeynudin, A., Abafita, J., et al. (2021). Risk perceptions and attitudinal responses to COVID-19 pandemic: An online survey in Ethiopia. *BMC Public Health*, 21(1), 981.

Bonem, E. M. (2015). Age differences in risk: Perceptions, intentions and domains. *Journal of Behavioural Decision Making*, 28(4), 317–330.

Brown, V. J. (2014). Risk perception: It's personal. *Environmental Health Perspectives*, 122(10), A276–A279.

Brug, J., Aro, A. R., Oenema, A., de Zwart, O., Richardus, J. H., & Bishop, G. D. (2004). SARS risk perception, knowledge, precautions, and information sources, the Netherlands. *Emerging Infectious Diseases*, 10(8), 1486–1489. https://doi.org/10.3201/eid1008.040283

Bundorf, M. K. (2021). Risk perceptions and protective behaviours: Evidence from COVID-19 pandemic. Working Paper 28741. National Bureau of Economic Research. www.nber.org/papers/w28741.

Costa-Font, J., Mossialos, E., & Rudisill, C. (2009). Optimism and the perceptions of new risks. *Journal of risk research*, 12(1), 27–41.

De Bruin, W. B. (2020). Age differences in COVID-19 risk perceptions and mental health: Evidence from a national U.S. survey conducted in March 2020. *The Journals of Gerontology*, 76(2), e24–e29.

De Zwart, O., Veldhuijzen, I. K., Elam, G., Aro, A. R., Abraham, T., Bishop, G. D., et al. (2009). Perceived threat, risk perception, and efficacy beliefs related to

SARS and other (emerging) infectious diseases: Results of an international survey. *International Journal of Behavioural Medicine*, 16, 30–40.

Dryhurst, S., Schneider, C. R., Kerr, J., Freeman, A. L. J., Recchia, G., van der Bles, A. M., et al. (2020). Risk perceptions of COVID-19 around the world. *Journal of Risk Research*, 23(7–8), 994–1006.

Elharake, J. A., Shafiq, M., McFadden, S. M., Malik, A. A., & Omer, S. B. (2021). The association of COVID-19 risk perception, county death rates, and voluntary health behaviors among U.S. adult population. *The Journal of Infectious Diseases*, 225(4), 593–597. https://academic.oup.com/jid/advance-article/doi/10.1093/infdis/jiab131/6167840

Ferrer, R., & Klein, W. M (2015). Risk perceptions and health behavior. *Current Opinion in Psychiatry*, 1(5), 85–89.

Field, J. V., & Schreer, G. E. (2000). Age differences in personal risk perceptions: A note on an exploratory descriptive study. *RISK: Health, Safety & Environment*, 11(4), 287–295.

Heino, M., Vuorre, M., & Hankonen, N. (2018). Bayesian evaluation of behavior change interventions: A brief introduction and a practical example. *Health Psychology and Behavioural Medicine*, 6(1), 49–78.

Hitchcock, J. L. (2001). Gender differences in risk perception: Broadening the contexts. *RISK: Health, Safety & Environment*, 12(3), 179.

Jacobson, J. D., Catley, D., Lee, H. S., Harrar, S. W., & Harris, K. J. (2014). Health risk perceptions predict smoking-related outcomes in Greek college students. *Psychology of Addictive Behaviours*, 28(3), 743–751.

Lang, R., Benham, J. L., Atabati, O., Hollis, A., Tombe, T., Shaffer, B., et al. (2021). Attitudes, behaviours and barriers to public health measures for COVID-19: A survey to inform public health messaging. *BMC Public Health*, 21(1), 1–15.

Lundborg, P., & Andersson, H. (2008). Gender, risk perceptions and smoking behaviour. *Journal of Health Economics*, 27(5), 1299–1311.

Paek, H.-J., & Hove, T. (2017). Risk perceptions and risk characteristics. Oxford Research Encyclopedias. https://oxfordre.com/communication/view/10.1093/acrefore/9780190228613.001.0001/acrefore-9780190228613-e-283

Popova, L. (2012). The extended parallel process model: Illuminating the gaps in research. *Health Education & Behavior*, 39(4), 455–473.

Prentice-Dunn, S., & Rogers, R. W. (1986). Protection motivation theory and preventive health: Beyond the health belief model. *Health Education Research*, 1(3), 153–161.

Rimal, R. V., & Juon, H. S. (2010). Use of the risk perception attitude framework for promoting breast cancer prevention. *Journal of Applied Social Psychology*, 40(2), 287–310.

Rudisill, C., Costa-Font, J., & Mossialos, E. (2012). Behavioral adjustment to avian flu in Europe during spring 2006: the roles of knowledge and proximity to risk. *Social Science & Medicine*, 75(8), 1362–1371.

Savage, I. (1993). Demographic influences on risk perceptions. *Risk Analysis*, 13(4), 413–420.

Schneider, C. R., Dryhurst, S., Kerr, J., Freeman, A. L. J., Recchia, G., Spiegelhalter, D., & van der Linden, S. (2021). COVID-19 risk perception: A longitudinal analysis of its predictors and associations with health protective behaviours in the United Kingdom. *Journal of Risk Research*, 24(3–4), 294–313.

Shahin, M. A. H., & Hussien, R. M. (2020). Risk perception regarding the COVID-19 outbreak among the general population: A comparative Middle East survey. *Middle East Current Psychiatry*, 27(71), 1–19.

Shanteau, J., & Pingenot, A. (2009). Subjective expected utility theory. In M. W. Kattan (ed.), *Encyclopedia of Medical Decision Making*, 1st ed. SAGE Publishers.

Sund, B., Svensson, M., & Anderssond, H. (2017). Demographic determinants of incident experience and risk perception: do high-risk groups accurately perceive themselves as high-risk?. *Journal of Risk Research*, 20, 99–117.

Viscusi, W. K. (1991). Age variations in risk perceptions and smoking decisions. *The Review of Economics and Statistics*, 73(4), 577–588.

Viscusi, W. K., & Hakes, J. (2003). Risk ratings that do not measure probabilities. *Journal of Risk Research*, 6(1), 23–43.

Index

action efficacy, 405
adaptation, 4, 12, 43, 46–54, 139, 277, 314
addictive behaviours, 197
addictive substances, 273
adult care, 326
advance care planning, 5, 16, 93
advance decision to refuse treatment, 103
adverse events, 119
age-based decision making, 326
age discrimination, 325
ageism, 325
alcohol consumption, 290
ambiguity aversion, 235
anchoring, 19
antibiotic prescriptions, 105
anxiety, 6–7, 17, 45, 93, 97, 155, 192, 194,
        198, 203, 227, 272–274, 290–292,
        294, 296–297, 299–301, 309,
        311–312, 316–317, 320–321, 371,
        403, 407
Anxiety Index, 314
anxious feelings, 292
attentional spotlight, 45
attitudes, xxiii, 1–2, 4, 12, 16–17, 30, 61,
        93, 120, 127, 129, 133, 136, 138,
        148–150, 156–159, 161, 171–172,
        224, 226, 229, 325, 328, 330, 332,
        339, 342, 344, 352, 372, 393, 405
Australia, 128

BAME, 94
bandwagoning effects, 23
banning large gatherings, 257
barriers for physicians, 94
baseline neglect bias, 246
behaviour change, 192
behavioural consequences, 192
behavioural economics, 53, 106, 242–243
behavioural fatigue, 256
behavioural guidance, 201
behavioural insights, 207
behavioural intervention, 11, 100

behavioural public policy, 239
behavioural science, 149, 155
Behavioural Research Unit, 224
beliefs, 172
benefits of vaccination, 149
biodiversity, 137
Black parents, 296
bodily hypervigilance, 17
Bomb Risk Elicitation Task, 62
boosting intervention, 204
boredom, 310
bottleneck resources neglect bias, 246
bravery narrative, 95

Canada, 297
cancer, 97
carbon emissions, 48
carbon gases, 44
care burden, 273
Centre for Disease Control Crisis and
        Emergency Risk Communication, 222
certainty effect, 14
chief medical officer, 251
childhood diseases, 199
children, 172
choice criteria, 204
chronic condition, 101
climate, 42
        change, 42, 46
clinician behaviour, 100
clinician performance, 105
clinicians, 96
closure of campuses, 291
cognitive biases, 17
communications strategies, 200
compensatory behaviour, 15
compensatory spillover effect, 202
concordance of messengers, 21
conjunction fallacy, 18
consumption decisions, 154
contagion, 42
contextual cues, 21